ORGANISATIONAL DIAGNOSIS

ENDORSEMENTS

"Using **real-life, global case studies**, this book provides an integrated and holistic approach to organisational diagnosis."

Dr Anna-Rosa le Roux, Head Organisational Effectiveness, Woolworths Financial Services

"*Organisational Diagnosis* is a must-have reference for every diagnosis survey consultant!

This holistic, practical guide is based on sound, scientific principles that will help you easily identify which measurements are best-aligned with the strategy of your organisation and will yield the best results."

Prof Hester Nienaber, Research Professor, Unisa

"*Organisational Diagnosis* contains everything you need to *successfully* conduct and manage OD interventions."

Dr. W. Esterhuizen, SHE Advisor

"Showcasing accumulated local and international exposure and expertise, *Organisational Diagnosis* equips OD practitioners with cutting-edge practices and tools they can implement immediately. It is a practical guide that will enhance the success of *any* organisational diagnosis intervention."

Cecile J. Nel, Industrial Psychologist

"Knowing where you are,*before* you react is vital for organisations, especially in the new world of work - where constant change is the norm. *Organisational Diagnosis* is a complete toolkit that will equip any business leader or manager to determine where they are, what they look like, and then how to plan the road to follow. This book will benefit all employees, no matter their role in an organisation, and it is also essential reading for post-graduate students enrolled in an MBA or a coursework master's programme."

Dr Darelle Groenewald, Coordinator of the Faculty MCom in Business Management, University of Johannesburg

"*Organisational Diagnosis* comes at a time when organisations are challenged by a fast-changing and complex working environment. This practical book offers crucial foundation principles for organisational diagnosis and is an absolute must-read for all academics, professional practitioners and management teams involved or interested in organisational diagnosis."

Dr Michelle F.D Sabbagha, Senior Manager: Client services, Global Markets,
Corporate Investment Banking, Standard Bank

"*Organisational Diagnosis* provides a unique framework that makes it possible to project which interventions will *truly* induce positive change in the workplace."

Dr Joyce Toendepi, Research Specialist, Mandala Consulting

"*Organisational Diagnosis* guides OD practitioners in a practical way through the academically sound principles of organisational diagnosis. By following the methodology in this book, OD practitioners will be equipped to target the *real* challenges of the organisation to unleash its true potential."

Dr Cobus Gerber, Industrial Psychologist, South African Revenue Service

*"**Organisational Diagnosis** offers a best-practice approach, backed by sound research (and many years of seasoned consulting experience!) to help you define, analyse and ultimately find organisational solutions that are vital to the success of your organisation."*

Prof Daneel van Lill, Executive Dean: Faculty of Management, University of Johannesburg

*"**Organisational Diagnosis** provides readers with a thorough overview and clear process on how to do an organisational diagnosis. It offers a comprehensive description of the process to follow, within an academically sound context – which is critical for finding successful solutions to problems."*

Dr Adri Drotskie, MBA Director, Henley Business School

*"The OD experts in **Organisational Diagnosis** offer a fluid mix of theoretical-based advice and practical, step-by-step examples for academic students and organisational leaders alike."*

Elbie Boonzaaier, Organisational Effectiveness, Sibanye Resources

First published in 2017

ISBN: 978-1-86922-705-0 (Printed)
eISBN: 978-1-86922-683-1 (ePDF)

Published by KR Publishing
P O Box 3954
Randburg
2125
Republic of South Africa

Tel: (011) 706-6009
Fax: (011) 706-1127
E-mail: orders@knowres.co.za
Website: www.kr.co.za

Printed and bound: HartWood Digital Printing, 243 Alexandra Avenue, Halfway House, Midrand
Typesetting, layout and design: Cia Joubert, cia@knowres.co.za
Cover design: Marlene de Villiers, marlene@knowres.co.za
Editing & proofreading: Jennifer Renton, jenniferrenton@live.co.za
Project management: Cia Joubert, cia@knowres.co.za
Index created with TExtract / www.Texyz.com

ORGANISATIONAL DIAGNOSIS

Tools and applications for practitioners and researchers

Edited by:

Prof Nico Martins
Dr Ellen Caroline Martins
Dr Rica Viljoen

kr
publishing

2017

TABLE OF CONTENTS

List of tables

List of figures

ABOUT THE EDITORS

Prof Nico Martins

Nico holds a PhD in Industrial Psychology and is registered at the Health Professions Council of SA (HPCSA) as a psychologist and as a chartered HR practitioner at the SA Board for People Practices (SABPP). Over and above his own research, a number of the researcher's masters and doctoral students have conducted further research into organisational culture, focusing on the assessment of sub-cultures; the relationship between organisational culture and concepts such as organisational commitment, employee satisfaction, perceived leader emotional competency, personality type, and occupational health; and employee engagement. This collaborative research has led to the validation of assessment tools in organisational culture, organisational climate, organisational trust, employee engagement and employment equity.

Nico has attended several specialised programmes in the field at the National Training Laboratories (NTL) in the USA and is an international affiliate of the Society of Industrial and Organisational Psychology (SIOP) in the USA.

He has been a Research Professor at the Department of Industrial and Organisational Psychology at the University of South Africa (Unisa) since 1995, and specialises in the field of organisational psychology. His fields of expertise are organisational development and change. Nico has published over 100 refereed conference papers and academic articles both locally and internationally. He is acknowledged by the National Research Foundation (NRF) as a seasonal researcher. He has presented papers at more than 50 national and international conferences based on work done at various national and international companies.

Together with Ellen Martins, Nico started Organisational Diagnostics CC more than 20 years ago. They have participated in over 500 qualitative and quantitative organisational survey projects and have surveyed Southern African and international organisations. He has extensive knowledge in the fields of organisational assessments and interventions, and is the co-editor and author of several books and chapters in his field of expertise.

Dr Ellen Caroline Martins

Ellen holds a D Litt et Phil in Information Science, which focused on an inter-disciplinary study in Knowledge Management, Organisational Behaviour and Organisational Development on the topic of combating knowledge loss in organisations by identifying the organisational and behavioural factors that would enable knowledge retention. Her other qualifications include a Masters of Information Science (cum laude), which focused on the influence of organisational culture on creativity and innovation, the Advanced Programme in Organisational Development (with distinction), and a BBibl (Hons) with distinctions in Research Methodology and Information Science. All these qualifications were obtained at the University of South Africa on a part time basis.

Ellen started her career as a secretary at the University of the Free State and at Natref, Sasolburg, after completing a Secretarial Diploma at the Free State Technical College in Bloemfontein (now the Technikon Free State). While working, she continued her studies and obtained a BBibl degree at Unisa. She then worked as a retriever at the Rand Afrikaans University Library for five years and as librarian at the Institute of American Studies Library (RAU, now University of Johannesburg) for two years. In 1992 Dr Nico Martins and she started an Organisational Development Consultancy – Organisational Diagnostics. For the past 25 years she has specialised in the field of organisational diagnosis and in particular organisational surveys, survey software and training.

She is an inter-disciplinary researcher and author who has published 19 articles, five chapters in books, mostly as first author, and has presented papers at eight international conferences and a number of South African conferences. Her work focuses on knowledge retention, surveys and research methodology, organisational culture, creativity and innovation, and age generation groups. She was the Highly Commended Award Winner of the 2012 Emerald/EFMD Outstanding Doctoral Research Awards in the Knowledge Management category. Her article entitled, *"Organizational and behavioral factors that influence knowledge retention"*, published in the Journal of Knowledge Management was chosen as a Highly Commended Award Winner at the Literati Network Awards for Excellence in 2013.

As a member of the Organisational Diagnostics team she has participated in more than 500 organisational surveys, conducted various focus groups and interviews, presented survey software training workshops on 81 occasions, and co-presented workshops in various organisations on conducting organisational surveys, as well as on "Solving the Millennial Dilemma", in recent years.

Ellen has also become an online mentor to post-graduate students at the Department of Industrial and Organisational Psychology, Unisa, mentoring students in writing up their research, developing their critical thinking skills and professional competence.

Dr Rica Viljoen

Rica research, teaching and service activities reflect her interest in multi-national leadership, inclusivity, OCD and sustainability. Her research has been published and presented internationally, reaching over 42 countries. She is adjunct faculty at the Henley Business School, South Africa, which is affiliated with the Reading University. Rica is a Senior Research Fellow at the University of Johannesburg. As a master OCD practitioner she focuses on large-scale organisational change and development. She is also the managing director of Mandala Consulting, a niche organisational change and development company that specialises in transformational processes, organisational research and spiral dynamics.

Rica's corporate career was in banking, where she held an executive organisational change and development role. She is accredited by numerous professional bodies such as the South African Board of People Practices (SABPP), the Institute of People Management (IPM), the Institute for Management Consultants South Africa (IMCSA) and the American Psychological Association

Division 13 (APA). She was awarded the IPM CEO award in 2016 for her contibution to the field of study nationally and internationally. She also accepted the role of Ambassador to the IPM in 2016.

Rica enjoys writing, and together with authors such as Dr Loraine Laubscher, Dr Don Beck, Profs Ronnie Lessem and Alexander Schieffer, she continues to publish oral histories, multi-cultural narratives and auto-ethnographic works. Her interest in organisational research centres around ensuring that untold stories are heard.

ABOUT THE CONTRIBUTORS

Dr Adéle da Veiga

Adéle holds a PhD in Information Technology, and has been employed at Unisa in the School of Computing as a senior lecturer since 2014. Her research projects relate to information security culture and privacy, with related empirical studies in industry. She obtained an NRF-Y rating in 2016 from the National Research Foundation. She has publications in national and international accredited journals and in proceedings of peer-reviewed conferences. Prior to her academic career she was employed in the industry for 16 years, where she specialised in information security, information security governance, audit, risk management and privacy. She holds a Certified Information Systems Auditor (CISA), a Certified Information Privacy Technologist (CIPT) certification and a Certified Ethics Officer (EthicsSA reg no. EO 572) certification. Her e-mail is daveiga@unisa.ac.za.

Aden-Paul Flotman

Aden-Paul is an Industrial Psychologist and registered Coach with a MA degree in Industrial and Organisational Psychology. He is also a PhD student and Senior Lecturer in the Department of Industrial and Organisational Psychology at the University of South Africa. Aden-Paul has a keen interest in exploring inter-cultural dynamics from a systems psychodynamic perspective, language use as manifestation of leadership anxiety dynamics, somatic intelligence and emotional toxicity in organisations. He has contributed chapters to local and international academic texts on management, international human resource management and global inter-cultural communication. His e-mail is flotma@unisa.ac.za.

Prof Ophillia Ledimo

Ophillia is registered with the Health Professions Council of South Africa as an Industrial Psychologist and is a registered social worker. She holds a Doctorate in Industrial and Organisational Psychology and is a Full Professor and Chair of the Department of IPO. She has led the Research Ethics Committee for the department of IPO and supervised Masters and Doctoral students to the completion of their degrees. She published articles and presented papers at international and national academic forums and was awarded a Research Award by the College of Economic and Management Sciences (Unisa). Prior to joining Unisa, Prof Ledimo worked for Ford in the Human Resource Department, managing the Employee Assistance Programme. Previously she worked for the Brunnel Institute of Social Sciences of South Africa (BIOSSA) as an Organisational Development Consultant, where she was responsible for training, organisational development programmes and assessment/development centres. Prof Ledimo has consulting experience in the field of organisational development and psychological assessments within the public and private sectors. Her e-mail is manetom@unisa.ac.za.

Claude-Hélène Mayer

Claude-Hélène is an adjunct professor at the Institute for Therapeutic Communication and Language Use, European University Viadrina, Frankfurt (Oder), Germany and a Senior Research Associate at the Department of Management, Rhodes University, South Africa. She holds a Ph.D. in psychology (University of Pretoria, South Africa), a Ph.D. in management (Rhodes University, South Africa), a doctorate in political sciences (socio-cultural anthropology, Georg-August University, Germany), and a habilitation (European University Viadrina, Germany) in psychology with focus on work, organisational, and cultural psychology. She has published several monographs, text collections, accredited journal articles, and special issues in her research areas which include mental health, conflict management/mediation, and women in leadership in transcultural and diverse organisational contexts.

Nene Molefi

Nene was born in Soweto and is the CEO of Mandate Molefi HR Consultants, a company with a track record that spans over 16 years.

Her versatility and experience in partnering with boards and executive committees has positioned her well to work with large scale culture change, transformation and leadership development projects.

Over the past 18 years, Nene has gained a reputation both locally and internationally as a thought leader in diversity and inclusion, values driven leadership and transformation. She is a regular presenter at conferences around the world, including Malaysia, Bangladesh, the USA, Zimbabwe and Zambia. She has authored numerous publications, including a chapter in the 'Leadership Perspectives from the Front Line'. She is an expert panellist for a Diversity & Inclusion Benchmark Tool, and is a member of the Diversity Collegium, which is a think tank of globally recognised diversity experts.

Nene is an associate lecturer for GIBS on Global Diversity and Unconscious Bias, as well as an associate lecturer on Transformation Strategy for Stellenbosch Business School.

Nene is committed to Social Entrepreneurship and her community. She sits on the board of Meals on Wheels, which is a non-profit organisation that provides food to the homeless and those in need in South Africa. Her e-mail is nene@mandatemolefi.co.za.

PREFACE by Ellen Caroline Martins

Imagine you were experiencing a need to measure trends over time such as employee satisfaction, commitment or engagement; your organisation was experiencing certain issues such as receiving many customer complaints; people were leaving and there was excessive absenteeism; management needed information for strategic planning; you needed a realistic baseline and benchmark for future assessments; or major changes were taking place and the impact thereof needed to be monitored. These are some of the reasons why an organisation would consider an organisational diagnosis.

If you have been tasked with getting an organisational diagnosis off the ground to address concerns experienced in the organisation, this book will help you to embark on your endeavour and provide you with the necessary advice, tools and applications to conduct a successful diagnosis. Organisational diagnosis consultants who are wondering what aspects are important to consider within the South African and other working environments, will find helpful advice and guidance from the highly experienced and knowledgeable authors of the different chapters in this book.

Broadly speaking, readers will come to understand how to diagnose concerns/problems and leverage untapped possibilities in the organisation in order to improve and be successful in a competitive, fast-changing world. The book consists of 13 chapters, which covers most of the core concepts in conducting an organisational diagnosis. What follows is an overview of these chapters.

Chapter 1: Planning and coordinating an organisational diagnosis

This chapter starts with the justification for conducting a diagnosis, before the focus moves on to how to frame the organisational diagnosis project in terms of describing the project and linking it to the business, planning and coordinating a successful diagnosis project, and acquiring the resources needed to conduct the diagnosis. The chapter ends with an outline of the structure of the book and a detailed organisational diagnosis action plan. In this book, the authors use the term "survey consultant/s" to refer to the person/people involved in organisational diagnosis.

Chapter 2: Preparing and involving all stakeholders

This chapter provides a definition of stakeholders. It also discusses identifying and managing stakeholder resistance to the process and preparing stakeholders for, and involving them in, the process. A successful organisational diagnosis process depends on the practitioner's ability and skills in stakeholder collaboration. The practical case study in this chapter provides awareness of resistance in an organisation to the implementation of an organisational diagnostic project. The lessons in this case study can help practitioners, managers and consultants to act proactively in the process.

Chapter 3: Developing and sourcing assessment instruments

The next step in the diagnostic process, which is to decide on the assessment tools you are going to use, is discussed in chapter 3. This chapter provides guidelines on the qualitative and quantitative approaches that are applicable during an organisational diagnosis. The methods of data collection and the role of the data collection methods to determine organisational issues are discussed, with specific emphasis on their benefits and limitations. There are many survey tools and assessment instruments available, and one of the decisions to be made is whether to use an existing instrument or develop a new one. The types of survey instruments and applications that are available, how to develop tools for surveys, focus groups and interviews are examined. Document analysis and observation as a data collection tool is also briefly discussed. These different methods should allow survey consultants and managers to select, choose and apply them in practice, as they are based on sound knowledge.

Chapter 4: Survey administration process

An essential aspect of the organisational diagnostic process is the implementation of a survey. This chapter provides an indication of possible ways to attract participants, the sampling process and survey distribution methods (online or paper-based). Insight into the benefits and limitations of the various methods in the execution of surveys can assist you with implementing successful organisational diagnostic projects, while knowledge regarding best practices in paper and online surveys can enable you to make sound decisions in your role as a survey consultant or manager. In addition, an overview of managing the survey process and the data management and data cleaning process is outlined.

Chapter 5: Data gathering in groups - an inclusive way of gathering rich data

In chapter 5 the qualitative data gathering method of focus groups is discussed. This data gathering method provides rich data that can significantly assist the phenomenological, ethnographic, integral and collaborative researcher with weaving a colourful tapestry of understanding of a social phenomenon. Various options such as the world café methodology are introduced. Ethical considerations are considered and advice is incorporated on how to conduct an effective focus group. Different ways of documenting and analysing data are considered, and the results of actual focus groups are shared. The chapter concludes with the methodology of collaborative inquiry, where the participants of the group themselves become co-researchers. Criteria are discussed for conducting quality focus groups and ethical considerations.

Chapter 6: Analysing and interpretation of results

You are now at the stage where you will try to make sense of the data you have received. Chapter 6 is concerned with discovering what is going on in the organisation and why. The analysis of quantitative (survey based) results are discussed, followed by a qualitative analysis and lastly the integration of results from a mixed method approach. The value and applications of the benchmarking of results, through statistical analysis (quantitative data) and the use of content analysis (qualitative data), are explored. Examples of how to portray the results in the form of graphs and tables are provided.

Chapter 7: Follow-up process - clarifying survey results

The feedback process following a research survey can be a daunting and intimidating task, even for the most experienced consultant or survey specialist. In Chapter 7, a number of steps are proposed and discussed that can help to support you in the feedback process. This chapter focuses on the value of conducting focus groups and interviews to support, verify and check the accuracy of the quantitative survey results. Both these techniques have their advantages and disadvantages. You will learn, through using a combination of various survey techniques, how the survey consultant can minimise the disadvantages and be able to produce a professional, valid and verified report.

Chapter 8: Report writing and feedback

Chapter 8 examines how to compile a report and present it to the organisation. What to include in different levels of reporting, how to present the results, balancing expectations and reality, and linking the results to an organisational diagnostic model, are discussed. Feedback to different stakeholder groups is discussed and the case studies presented provide interesting information on the value of feedback and the implementation of interventions.

Chapter 9: Action planning and learning

Chapter 9 presents a detailed look at assessing what to do with the results and how to implement the change you desire. As so many organisations and leaders are aware, the most compelling action plans can stall at the point of delivery due to stubbornly ingrained patterns of behaviour. These can be embedded in both individuals and entire organisations. This chapter looks at the action planning and learning process. This begins with visioning sessions with leadership that establish the tone of the action planning going ahead, followed by survey feedback sessions that serve as a mirror for the organisation. Action learning is examined in more detail, as well as what it means to be a learning organisation. Detailed case studies are presented and key shining gems and common pitfalls are highlighted. Throughout this chapter, the emphasis is on relationships and communication, as these are the backbone of successful action planning.

Chapter 10: Conducting multi-cultural research - insights gained from theory and practice

The importance of taking multicultural dynamics into account when doing research is considered in chapter 10. Autographic notes are shared from actual research projects in global settings that illustrate the importance of understanding the fine nuances in diverse cultures. Various theoretical approaches to describe multicultural dynamics are presented. Grounded theory, integrated with systems thinking, is positioned as a research methodology that adequately deals with the dynamics and complexity of conducting multicultural research. Systems thinking methodology is uniquely integrated to visually describe systems dynamics in multicultural settings. The Benchmark of Engagement (BeQ) and narrative stories are used as data gathering methods to provide rich data of not only individual, but also cultural dynamics in social systems. The chapter concludes with a comparison of the findings of different multicultural environments, where the BeQ was used extensively to describe systemic dynamics. The author hopes that this chapter leaves the reader with not only an awareness of the gifts that conducting ethnographical research provides, but also stimulates interest in conducting multicultural research in more than a quantitative way.

Chapter 11: The organisational and psychological impact of organisational diagnosis

This chapter provides insights into the organisational and psychological impact of organisational diagnosis. Firstly, it refers to the significance of organisational diagnosis, its nature and role, and its influence as an intervention. The psychological impact of organisational diagnosis is described, taking the organisational participants, the consultant-employee relationship, and the organisational system into account. In this context, the chapter deals with the themes of risk and change and their management with regard to organisational diagnosis. Furthermore, it refers to the consultant as a diagnostic tool in organisational diagnosis and the concepts of transference and counter-transference from a psychoanalytical perspective. Finally, some guiding questions for diagnostic reflection are provided for practitioners in the field.

Chapter 12: Ethical and privacy considerations for research

In this penultimate chapter, the ethical and privacy considerations that research practitioners should follow when conducting research are discussed. Consultants should be aware of the ethical codes, industry standards and regulatory requirements that apply to research projects so as to protect the research participants, themselves and the organisation. The concept of ethics and the relevant ethical values that must be embedded in research activities are discussed, and practical examples of the ethical values are provided to aid organisations to embed them in research projects. The concept of privacy is discussed in more detail, focussing on the requirements of the Protection of Personal Information Act and how the conditions apply to research projects. Attention is given to aspects that must be considered to establish the risk profile of a research project in order to ensure that necessary controls are implemented to minimise or mitigate the identified risks. The ethical values and privacy considerations are summarised in an ethics and privacy checklist for organisations.

Chapter 13: A few conclusions

The initial 12 chapters provide a comprehensive overview of the phases of organisational diagnoses in the South African context and the international research that the authors have consulted on in the field. In chapter 13 the focus is on the most important learning points, a brief introduction (overview) to some typical interventions survey consultants can propose to follow after a survey effort, and the changing role of the survey consultant, concluding that survey consultants should be aware of and keep in touch with the changing work environment in which new techniques are constantly being tested and applied.

In summary, the editors hope that reading this book will help you to realise the following key points of an organisational diagnosis:

- Try to understand how the organisation works by identifying causes of problems, using the right tools and applications, and focusing on the right solutions.
- Align your diagnosis (survey) with the strategic goals and the business process.
- Have an investigative attitude when collecting and interpreting data.
- Focus time and attention on the survey process and spend energy on trying to identify and fix the right problem.
- Remember that it is a social process - involve people; consider their cultural differences, the psychological impact of the diagnosis, ethics and privacy.
- Create success by gradually developing a consensus about the problem and about possible solutions.
- Follow through with a learning and action planning process towards implementation.

CHAPTER 1

PLANNING AND COORDINATING AN ORGANISATIONAL DIAGNOSIS

by Ellen Caroline Martins

INTRODUCTION

An organisational diagnosis begins with a conversation about a concern that management (executive team or line management) have about their organisation. The managers' first description of the problem is usually called the presenting problem (Centre for Industrial and Organisational Psychology).[1] In this book, readers will come to understand how to diagnose concerns/problems and leverage untapped possibilities in the organisation in order to improve and be successful in a competitive, fast-changing world. This chapter starts with the justification for conducting a diagnosis, before the focus then moves on to how to frame the organisational diagnosis project in terms of describing the project, and linking it to the business, planning and coordinating a successful diagnosis project and acquiring the resources needed to conduct the diagnosis. The chapter ends with an outline of the structure of the book and a detailed organisational diagnosis action plan. In this book the authors use the term "survey consultant/s" to refer to the person/people involved in organisational diagnosis.

JUSTIFICATION FOR CONDUCTING A DIAGNOSIS

Management of an organisation usually become aware of a need to conduct an organisational diagnosis when they have an underlying feeling or notion that they need to collect data as proof of their initial statement about the presenting problem or concern experienced in the organisation, and to pinpoint the areas of concern. This type of evaluation may be aimed at particular issues, units or demographic groups. The organisation might find itself in a crisis situation, such as key people leaving, excessive absenteeism and costs, unmanageable environmental demands, pressure from above, or conflict between work groups, which all relate to organisational behaviour research.[2]

Other reasons why an organisation would conduct a diagnosis are that there might be a need to compare employees' attitudes and opinions with those in other organisations by conducting regular surveys to determine trends. An organisation might want to conduct a diagnosis to improve satisfaction and performance, measure soft factors to improve management, understand how employees see things, gain input for future decisions (for example to gather data on employee preferences that will influence future management decisions in areas such as training programmes), as part of a change intervention required in the organisation, to monitor organisational change and improvement, or to improve customer service. Self-assessment and the use of the resulting data can become a way of life in stimulating and guiding desirable changes.[3]

When the need or concern has been realised, the organisation will contact a survey consultant (either internal or external) and set up a meeting to discuss the symptoms of the problem as it presents itself in the organisation. A good way to get the conversation going is to start with broad enquiries, such as why the person contacted the survey consultant to come and why at this particular time. During the discussion you need to assess how to respond in a helpful way by providing information that will help the client think about the problem and by making suggestions about how the client can go back to the organisation with their own helpful interventions and suggestions.[4] The survey consultant also needs to determine whether the client and others in the organisation are ready and willing to engage in a diagnostic process that the survey consultant might suggest at this stage, but propose more formally at a follow-up meeting. Sometimes a survey consultant might respond to a tender or an invitation to submit a proposal. This is usually followed up with either a meeting as discussed above, or a presentation to the organisation.

During this first contact between the client and the survey consultant, it is important that the survey consultant displays the necessary expertise right from the outset. The role of the survey consultant at this first meeting, regardless of whether the person is an internal or external person, is not to come on too strong as the expert or doctor, but to ask the right and clarifying questions, summarising, checking consensus and gaining an understanding of the symptoms of the problem as explained by those at the meeting. During this first meeting, the survey consultant should try to understand the type of organisation and the health or illness of the organisation, as discussed in section 3.

During this justification phase, several meetings might take place before the diagnostic process itself kicks off. Gallant and Rios[5] state that the outcomes of the justification phase (which they term the entry and contracting phase) are to:

1.   develop a solid working relationship between the client and the survey consultant;
2.   decide whether to go forward with the consultation and diagnostic proposal as such;
3.   prepare a written contract or proposal for the diagnosis process and consultation; and
4.   build the foundation for the remaining phases of the diagnosis.

Block (cited in De Klerk)[6] argues that it is a mistake to assume that the client makes a decision to use survey consultants based purely on rational reasons. The client will consider whether they can trust the survey consultant as someone who can help solve the organisational problems and at the same time be considerate of their position and person.

Discussing and exploring the situation with the client in the first meetings will provide justification for the organisational diagnosis. After the initial meeting, the survey consultant might be asked to prepare a proposal and present it to the client. It is important that the survey consultant builds a framework for the diagnosis that will be proposed to the client.

FRAMING THE DIAGNOSIS PROJECT

Framing the diagnosis project is an important step that enables the survey consultant to determine the relevance and rigour of the diagnosis that he or she wants to propose to the client and accomplish, should the go-ahead be given. Asking reflective questions helps to clarify the survey consultant's thoughts and proposed diagnosis, which should indicate to the client that the proposed diagnosis was well developed and will add value to the business as well as have an impact on solving the presenting problem. The main steps involved in the framework are describing the project, framing the diagnosis project in terms of strategy and the business, and having an impact on the organisation. These steps are outlined as an organisational diagnosis project map in table 1.1, which can guide a survey consultant in framing the project correctly.

Table 1.1: Organisational diagnosis project map (adapted from Yost & Ryan)[7]

Relevance and rigour	Reflection questions
Project description	
Project focus	• What is the presenting problem? • How does the cultural context (involving the demographics of the organisation and ethnic groupings) affect the focus of the project?
Scope of the project	• What is the scope of the project?
Objectives	• What are the objectives of the diagnosis?
Method	• What is the method?
Outcomes	• What do I want to accomplish?
Framing the diagnosis project	
Framing the project	• How does the project link to the business strategy (business initiatives)? • How can I (the survey consultant) frame the project to focus not on problems, but on untapped potential in the organisation?
Link to the business	• How does this diagnostic project add value to the organisation? • What is my competitive advantage (value add) for the organisation/business? • What are my strategic differentiators? • How can I leverage change in the business to do high-quality research?

Key stakeholders (Who are they, why is this diagnostic (research) project valuable to them?)	• Who are the key decision-makers in the organisation? • Who will be my contact in the organisation to understand the priorities and culture of the organisation? • Who are the key stakeholders who will need to support this project? • Have I contacted them and documented the deliverables, the method and the scope of the work?
Having an impact	
The impact I want to have on the organisation Leveraging the changing nature of work Framing the results	• What do I hope will happen inside the organisation when the project is done? • Have I designed the diagnosis project with implementation in mind? • Have I approached the project design considering the pace of organisational change today? • How might I alter my approach to the project to reflect the changing nature of the workplace? • Have I considered how technological advances can aid or impede what I am planning? • Have I considered the cross-cultural applicability of the research? • What might be the 2 or 3 most critical findings? • Have I built in "next steps"? • How do I plan to give feedback on the results to the organisation?
Being rigorous	
Being diligent, attentive, careful, accurate, methodical, thorough and precise	• Have I thought of alternative scenarios for findings and ways to assess what is really going on in the organisation? • Are my measures valid and reliable? • How can I achieve more rapid execution without sacrificing quality? • How can I be more efficient in conducting the diagnosis? • What are the limits (time, length, numbers)? • Have I planned for likely objections? • Have I built in ways to assess or eliminate alternative explanations?
Invited back for more	
Project conducted successfully	• How will I provide all of my deliverables with the highest quality? • Have I built in ways to bring this project to closure? • Have I discussed "next steps" and future areas of untapped potential? • How will my diagnosis project make my customer more successful?

Framing the organisational diagnosis project as reflected above will enable the survey consultant to prepare a proposal that is presented to the client for discussion and approval to continue with contracting and carrying out the organisational diagnosis.

Project description (problem, scope, objectives, method, outcomes)

The project focus relates to the presenting problem and cultural context. The presenting problem in light of the underlying concerns of managers has already been discussed. In Africa, the **African context** needs to be considered as it is quite different from that of the Western world, with their accompanying American individualistic, humanistic values.[8] Srinivas[9] sees the African culture context as traditionally embodying a respect for the person as part of society and valuing social interaction and interdependence as central to life in the community. Msila[10] discusses the concept of ubuntu and, in relation to the African workplace culture, argues that "*Ubuntu* and its principles based on humanising values should lead to people-centeredness". This implies that everyone in the organisation should be involved and cognisance should be taken of diversity in an organisational diagnosis to encourage people-centeredness (see chapter 10 for conducting a diagnosis in multicultural settings). An organisational diagnosis can be threatening, unsettling and scary to the emotional life of the employees and the organisation, thus it is important for any survey consultant to be aware of this and the possible impact on the organisation (see chapter 11 for a discussion of the psychological impact of an organisational diagnosis). A diagnosis is one of the phases of the action research process and therefore cannot be introduced as a single activity (see chapter 13 for the action research process).

The health or illness of the organisation plays a role in the focus of the organisational diagnosis project. In adopting the terminology of individual psychology, organisations have at various times been described as "healthy" or "unhealthy", while organisational cultures have been described in terms of psycho-pathological types such as inadequate, paranoid, immature, emotionally unstable, compulsive and sociopathic. Although this approach to classifying organisations could drive an organisational diagnosis in the sense that it sets out to diagnose neurotic or unhealthy features of the organisation, the disadvantage of such an approach is that it becomes locked into the taxonomy of other disciplines which are inappropriate and obsessed with the negative aspects of company functioning. Furthermore, such a focus is directed toward the "ill" or "sick" organisation rather than a balanced focus on what is healthy in the organisation.[11]

The **scope** of the project needs to be determined by specifying what the main topic of the diagnosis is going to be (organisational culture survey, organisational climate survey, employee satisfaction survey, leadership assessment, etc.) and what the particular issues are on which data will be gathered. Surveys are the most common method of gathering data in an organisational diagnosis. Borg and Mastrangelo[12] point out that there are usually two reasons to conduct an employee survey: measurement and change. It was in the 1970s that the trend to use employee surveys as an intervention method emerged. The core idea was to feed the survey data back into the organisation during special workshops to explain the data further and obtain involvement from staff. Today these survey feedback sessions are one of the most important methods for organisational development and might be built into the scope of the organisational diagnosis project. The survey consultant thus needs to think about the best approach and methods to conduct the diagnosis within the scope of the project.

Another aspect to be considered is whether the entire organisation should be involved in the diagnosis, or only certain levels or units, and whether the focus is internal only, external only, or both. Management should provide an indication of whether they would like to see comparisons of different units, gender groups, age groups, job levels, tenure (years of service groups), geographical regions, or other differentiators which are important to the specific organisation. In some instances survey consultants work not only locally, but also internationally. The international perspective is discussed in chapter 10.

The **objectives** of an organisational diagnosis are its particular purposes or hoped-for outcomes,[13] which will be determined after discussion and engagement with the client. The purpose and objectives need to be agreed on and approved by the client. It is important to make the objectives realistic by pointing out what can and cannot be accomplished and what is required in terms of resources and commitment.[14] The objectives are also a safeguard for the survey consultant to ensure that the organisation's expectations are managed correctly. Table 1.2 provides an example of a diagnosis purpose and objectives.

Table 1.2: Example of purpose and objectives of an organisational diagnosis (Author)

Purpose and objectives of the organisational diagnosis
The purpose can be summarised as follows: • To understand how employees feel about the issues that affect them and the organisation. • To enable management to identify concerns and needs. • To inform the organisation's decision-making processes on related policy and management issues.
The following questions may be asked to formulate the objectives of an organisational climate survey: • Do employees understand the vision and mission and values? • Do employees experience organisational practices such as diversity, employment equity and employee relations as fair? • How do employees perceive management and their integrity? • How do employees experience organisational practices such as the work environment, learning and development, teamwork, and rewards and recognition? • What are the relations between, or impact of, employee engagement and the measured dimensions? • How do the results of the departments/business units compare to the overall results of the organisation? • Are there significant differences in the perceptions of the various biographical groups, i.e. job roles, language, gender and departments/business units? • How can the results be used for strategic planning and future benchmarking?

Once the purpose and objectives have been defined, the next step is to consider the **methods** to be used to obtain the information that might provide answers to the objective questions.

The **methodology** to be used in the organisational diagnosis is extremely important because it forms the baseline of the entire data-gathering process, with the aim of resolving the presenting problem or determining the reason for the diagnosis. The methodology chosen will imply which data collection methods can be used. Broadly speaking, the survey consultant may choose a quantitative, a qualitative or combined approach (mixed method) to conduct the diagnosis. A quantitative approach uses the survey method, whereas a qualitative approach uses focus groups, interviews, document/artefact/archive analysis and observation. These methods are discussed in chapters 3, 4 and 5.

At this early stage in the planning process, the survey consultant should already determine the data collection method(s) to be used in the diagnosis. To make this decision, you should be aware of the benefits and limitations of each method. Martins and Martins[15] summarise some of the benefits and limitations of surveys and focus groups based on the work of other researchers.[16] These are displayed in table 1.3 below. In chapter 3 of this book the pros and cons of interviews, document/artefact/archive analysis and observation are discussed.

Table 1.3: Benefits and limitations of diagnosis methods to collect data (adapted from Martins & Martins[17])

Methodology	Quantitative	Qualitative			
Method to collect data	**Survey**	**Focus groups**	**Interviews**	**Document/ artefact/ archive analysis**	**Observation**
Benefits	• Produces quantifiable, reliable data, usually generalisable to a larger population • Provides pivotal information for business decisions	• Flexible method that can be adapted as required • Relatively inexpensive because it does not require expensive equipment or extensive research staff • Data provides details about behaviour, opinions and attitudes	• Flexible method that can be adapted in the process to gain clarity of information shared	• Relatively inexpensive because it takes minimal time • Information gathered may add depth to quantitative data	• Observing a situation is good for explaining what is going on • Heightens the observer's awareness of significant social processes and allows for experiencing and observing people's emotions

Methodology	Quantitative	Qualitative			
Method to collect data	Survey	Focus groups	Interviews	Document/ artefact/ archive analysis	Observation
Limitations	• Ignores the effects of variables not included in the measurement • Lacks depth and richness of data that it presents	• As a method on its own it is not appropriate for statistically describing large populations • Reliability may be affected because the information gathered is subjective and based on the opinions of individuals	• Expensive because it takes a considerable time • Subjected to interviewee response bias	• Comparison across time may be difficult • Financial or personal records may contain sensitive or blurry information, making it difficult to interpret	• Takes time, requires skills and experience • Observer bias in that confusion might arise between actual observation and own observer interpretation

Awareness of the benefits and limitations of the different data collection methods should enable the survey consultant to determine which method(s) or combination thereof will produce the required data in the most effective way.

The survey consultant may consider using an **organisational model** to guide the organisational diagnosis. Using an organisational model offers a systematic approach to collecting data, minimises bias in what was collected, directs the way for data analysis and provides a common vocabulary for people to use.[18] Survey results have more power if they can be presented through a conceptual framework or model.[19] Most survey consultants have some idea of a model in their head when they conduct an organisational diagnosis. The model used depends on the situation and the survey consultant's style, as well as the way in which the situation is viewed. There are several well-established models to choose from.

There are, however, risks involved in using a diagnostic model, such as *appropriateness* in fitting the client's presenting problem, *substantiveness* in terms of the research support for the model, and *sophistication* of the model in terms of merely categorising symptomatic data or whether it posits cause-and-effect relations that will allow deductions about root causes and show predictive capability.[20] (Refer to chapter 3 for more information about organisational models.)

The survey consultant should consider the **outcomes** to be accomplished by conducting the diagnosis. From a practical point of view, it is good to think of the entire organisation as your ultimate client. This means that whatever interventions are made, they must be guided by whatever estimates can be made of their impact on the total organisation. For example, consider whether you would like to be part of a process to help a company close a plant in a community that will clearly be harmed by such an action, or whether you would like to engage in a project where one manager is trying to win a political battle over another. The survey consultant should ask him or herself what would be best for, and benefit, the entire organisation. It might be best for the survey consultant not to consult and engage with an organisation whose function or purpose in society is destructive to society, unethical or in conflict with their own values.[21]

The survey consultant might ask more specifically what the outcomes of the survey will focus on. Examples of possible outcomes might be to manage change, improve employee satisfaction, improve performance, improve understanding of the vision or strategy, instil new leader and manager behaviours,[22] reduce employee turnover or understand the organisational culture. Sometimes the possible outcomes can be very specific, such as to separate facts from opinions, identify areas of opportunity, obtain unbiased management information, obtain a bottom-up view of the organisation or simply conduct a reality check for the organisation. At this point the survey consultant should have a clear picture of the focus and scope of the project, and he/she should have determined the objectives, decided which methods and model to use in the diagnosis and what outcomes he/she would like to accomplish.

The next step in the project map is to frame the diagnosis project in terms of the strategy, linking it to the business and identifying key stakeholders.

Framing the diagnosis project and linking it to business

Linking the organisational diagnosis to the business strategy and their initiatives requires an understanding of the organisational culture, norms and terminology[23], and finding out what the business initiatives and key priorities are (finding the energy in the organisation). Christelis[24] states that a well-defined strategy gives a "business the absolute focus that is so important for success". Strategy keeps it from being distracted. Do not, for instance, suggest a diversity initiative if it is not connected to the organisation's strategic goals. A diversity initiative might be a moral imperative to Human Resources, but not a business imperative.[25] If, however, you can point out how it connects to the business strategy and why it will help to resolve the presenting problem, it should make sense to the business. According to Borg and Mastrangelo,[26] business issues that are important to organisations, such as performance, strategy implementation, or innovation, can complement issues that are important to the individual employee, such as satisfaction with work aspects.

Linking the organisational diagnosis project to the strategy by focusing on untapped **potential** is a way of linking the project to the business. A practical example might be to conduct a focus group and include appreciative enquiry as a tool to discover the following:

1. Here is where your organisation could be.
2. Here are the problems in the way. Do not ignore them, but focus on the potential.

A survey consultant needs to constantly look for ways to add value, both in the initial phase of linking the organisational diagnosis to the business and during the organisational diagnosis process. Frodsham[27] reiterates as follows: "If the client does not see the value in what you are doing, your efforts will not have the intended effect and any improvements will not be sustained. So go from pushing to asking, and always talk in terms of what the business needs."

The survey consultant can get straight to the heart of things if he or she can offer a cost-effective service and build good relationships with the people in the organisation. It is important to point out your strategic differentiators which separate you from other consulting organisations (your competitive advantage); in other words by pointing out to the organisation and focusing on your skills and abilities in terms of:

1. evaluating problems and potential;
2. measuring "soft" issues (putting numbers to them - statistics);
3. a research-based focus, which includes quantitative and qualitative methods;
4. your experience and publications in the field;
5. a business-focused approach ("talk the business language"); and
6. aligning your efforts with the organisation's priorities.

Another aspect that the survey consultant needs to consider is leveraging change in the workplace to do high-quality research. Employee surveys might signal that change is needed and also what form such change should take. In turbulent markets it might require both internal and external customer audits to gather information effectively to guide policy or strategy development.[28]

Identifying the **key stakeholders** is another important aspect in framing the diagnosis project. Muswaka,[29] in a chapter about employee engagement in a South African context, is quoted as follows: "Key stakeholders contribute to the success of the company and a socially responsible business attends to the legitimate interests of all its key stakeholders." The organisational diagnosis must be positioned to satisfy the needs of many diverse and sometimes conflicting demands and needs. The stakeholders in a South African context might consist of board members, regulators, union members, executive management teams, line management, rank and file employees, and certain special functions such as the legal department or information and data security protection official/officer. Changes within or outside the organisation, such as reliance on new technology, increased focus on corporate governance/compliance, information and data security protection, may also lead to changes in the stakeholders that need to be considered and who need to be engaged with[30] in order to get buy-in at all levels that affect the organisation.

As an organisational diagnosis survey consultant, make sure that the decision-makers in the organisation know what you can do to align your efforts with their priorities.[31] Also determine who the actual client of the project is going to be so that you do not end up working for several clients whose goals are in conflict. Usually the contact client approaches the survey consultant or manager initially, intermediate clients get involved in early meetings or planning next steps, primary clients own a problem for which they need help, and secondary clients may or may not be directly involved with the survey consultant or manager, but they will be affected by the outcomes of the survey.[32]

It is useful to think about the final **impact** that you as the survey consultant would like to have on the organisation in the early planning stages of the process. Some reflective questions about the impact the survey consultant would like to have on the organisation, leveraging the changing nature of work and framing the results of the diagnosis project have been listed in the organisational diagnosis project map under the heading: *"having an impact"*, but are not discussed here in detail (see table 1.1). These aspects and others, such as being rigorous and conducting the project successfully (to be invited back for more), will become clear in the rest of this book. We can conclude that framing the project in the form of an organisational diagnosis project map as described above will guide the entire project from beginning to end, and enhance the possibility of completing it successfully.

PLANNING AND COORDINATING AN ORGANISATIONAL DIAGNOSIS

Some people who do not have experience of an organisational diagnosis project might think that all that is needed is to compile a questionnaire and distribute it to employees to gather data. Those with more experience will know that the project needs to be planned carefully, requires many thoughtful decisions, and consists of quite a number of activities. It requires resources such as people with certain skills, and involves timing, scheduling and has cost implications. To begin the organisational diagnosis project, you first need to plan the activities and tasks that will have to be completed. The next step is to decide who will complete which tasks and what skills are required.

Organisational diagnosis action plan

The detailed organisational diagnosis action plan of Martins[33] is included as a typical example of the planning of main activities, tasks to be carried out in each activity, start and end dates, and who is responsible for each task in the process (see exhibit 1.1 at the end of this chapter).

The 14 main activities of the organisational diagnosis action plan cover setting up the project, planning the schedule, formulating the strategic position, conducting personal interviews, facilitating focus groups, developing and compiling the organisational assessment questionnaire(s), formulating electronic and paper-based procedures, integrating the information/data collected, conducting preliminary analysis, conducting additional focus groups, writing the report, discussing the report with strategic role players, giving feedback to employees and carrying out action planning and evaluation. Some of these aspects were touched on in the discussion on Framing the Diagnosis Process, but the chapters in the rest of this book deal with the aspects in more detail. The organisational diagnosis action plan is used during the project to keep track of the process from beginning to end. The resources that are required to conduct an organisational diagnosis and that should form part of the planning and coordinating phase of the project are discussed below.

People, roles and skills required

Some organisations use internal consultants to conduct internal organisational diagnoses. These consultants are located in the human resources department or form part of a specialised Organisation Development (OD) consulting department. The internal consultants typically have a variety of clients within the organisation, rendering a service to both line management and staff members. Other organisations rely heavily on external survey consultants who are not members of the client organisation, but typically work for a university, a consulting firm or themselves.[34] Internal consultants have the advantage of ready access to and relationships with their clients. They know the organisation's culture and sources of power, have access to information, and enjoy a basic level of trust and rapport. Disadvantages of internal consultants are that they might become overly cautious due to their strong ties to the organisation, particularly when powerful people in the organisation can affect their career. They may also lack certain skills and experience in facilitating the organisational diagnosis process.

External consultants are free to select the clients they want to work with according to their own criteria, and they often have a higher status which enables them to probe difficult issues and assess the organisation more objectively, but it might be expensive for the organisation to make use of their services and expertise.[35] External consultants also draw from a broader business perspective gained from their experience with various clients in many sectors, and add value by bringing new ideas and best practices along to clients. The ability to benchmark in respect of other organisations is another big advantage of external consultants.[36]

Both internal and external consultants must address issues of confidentiality, and must rely on valid information and internal commitment for their success. They both risk project termination and fill a third party role.

Cummings and Worley[37] state that the advantage of having both internal and external consultants is including them in an internal-external consulting team; both parties can share the workload while using their complementary consulting skills. They phrase it as follows: "External consultants can combine their special expertise and objectivity with the inside knowledge and acceptance of internal consultants."

The role of the external survey consultant team will be to liaise with the client project/consultant team and to conduct the organisational diagnosis, focusing on the tasks as specified in the organisational diagnostic plan (see exhibit 1.1). In general, the skills required of an organisational diagnosis survey consultant team consisting of both internal and external consultants encompass communication skills, building relationships with the management team and the organisation's project team, taking time to build the consulting team by confronting individual differences, and establishing their roles within the team, which requires an understanding of emotions and their impact on the consultants' effectiveness (emotional intelligence). Conducting the organisational diagnosis also requires skills such as survey development (which comes from experience, not just education), identifying and compiling action plans, consulting on implications, planning implementation of indicated remedies,[38] knowledge of ethical and legal issues related to organisational diagnosis (see chapter 12 for a detailed discussion), technical survey administration skills, understanding and interpreting survey results, statistical skills, report writing skills and presentation skills.[39]

The client (key person) needs to put together an internal project team that will be responsible for planning and coordinating the organisational diagnosis in the organisation. Depending on the size of the organisation, this internal coordinating project team might consist of a small number of people who run all activities out of a central office or they might have coordinators in different geographical regions. Some of the tasks that the team needs to carry out are liaising with the survey consultant team and with the line managers in the organisation in positioning the diagnosis process and driving the project within the organisation. One person might be assigned to coordinate all communication activities, while another might make sure that the IT infrastructure for running the online survey is in place and aligned with the logistics for paper-pencil surveys. Yet another person might be an expert on organisational questionnaire content. An important task of the project team is to ensure that the milestones of the organisational diagnosis project are reached. It is therefore important that the right combination of people with the right mix of skills be assembled in the organisation to ensure that the project is completed successfully.[40] Other resources that are required to complete the project successfully are time and money.

Planning the time and cost

The project planning phase might include a broad timeline plan of the main components of the organisational diagnosis project, stipulating the number of weeks that each component might take. If the timeline can be displayed visually, it will give decision-makers and the project team in the organisation an idea of how long each phase should take from the start to the end of the project. A list of main components might comprise the following and there might be overlap between the different components (which might be displayed in table format):[41]

1. Positioning and design of organisational diagnosis
2. Planning and preparation
3. Survey administration and data analysis
4. Preparing follow-up processes
5. Feedback of results
6. Actions and implementation
7. Evaluation

The broad timeline could be included in the survey consultant's proposal for acceptance and approval purposes. Exhibit 1.1 can be used to plan the timelines in detail.

Picking the right time to conduct an organisational diagnosis is an important decision to ensure the success of the project. Bad timing would be, for example, to conduct a survey during peak holiday periods, during busy seasons in the organisation, or during plant shutdowns. In South

Africa, April, July, October and December/January are usually not good months to conduct a diagnosis. It is also good to be aware of religious and public holidays to avoid, for example, not arranging questionnaire completion facilitation sessions, focus groups or interviews on those days.

The main cost of an organisational diagnosis is the people involved in the process. A diagnosis cannot be conducted without individuals to plan, design and administer it. This involves the cost of the survey consultants to the organisation for conducting the diagnosis, as well as indirect costs to the organisation in making people available for the diagnosis. On the organisational side, people are involved in the project coordinating team, which takes time and effort, as well as on the participating side, for example meetings, attending focus groups and personal interviews, and completing the surveys.

A tip that might help survey consultants to negotiate their costing is to tell the client what they can do and what it will cost, to offer them baseline components that cannot be done without and alternatives/options to choose from, while at the same time pointing out the benefits of each option (what they will get from a certain option and what they will lose if they don't do it). The cost of each phase of the project can be added to the steps in exhibit 1.1.

SUMMARY

An organisational diagnosis process usually begins with a concern or a problem as it presents itself in the organisation. When management feel the need to get to the bottom of the problem, they will contact a survey consultant (either internal or external) to assist the organisation in diagnosing the "health and illness" of the organisation. Discussing and exploring the situation with the client in the first meetings will provide justification for the organisational diagnosis. Framing the diagnosis project is an important step that enables the survey consultant to determine the relevance and rigour of the diagnosis that he or she wants to propose to the client and accomplish, should the go-ahead be given.

The diagnosis project is framed in terms of the description of the focus, scope, objectives, methods and outcomes. The diagnosis project is linked to the business strategy and initiatives, and the value of the diagnosis to the organisation, the strategic differentiators of the survey consultant, and key stakeholders are highlighted. Framing the project in the form of an organisational diagnosis project map will therefore guide the entire organisational diagnosis project from beginning to end, and enhance the possibility of completing the project successfully. Planning and coordinating an organisational diagnosis is based on a detailed organisational diagnosis action plan that describes who, when and what needs to be done to carry out the project. The resources include the people, their roles, the skills required, the timeline, and timing and cost involved in an organisational diagnosis.

OVERVIEW OF ORGANISATIONAL DIAGNOSIS PROCESS IN RELATION TO THE REST OF THE CHAPTERS

In the diagram below, the chapters that deal with the steps of a typical organisational diagnosis process are shown (figure 1.1):

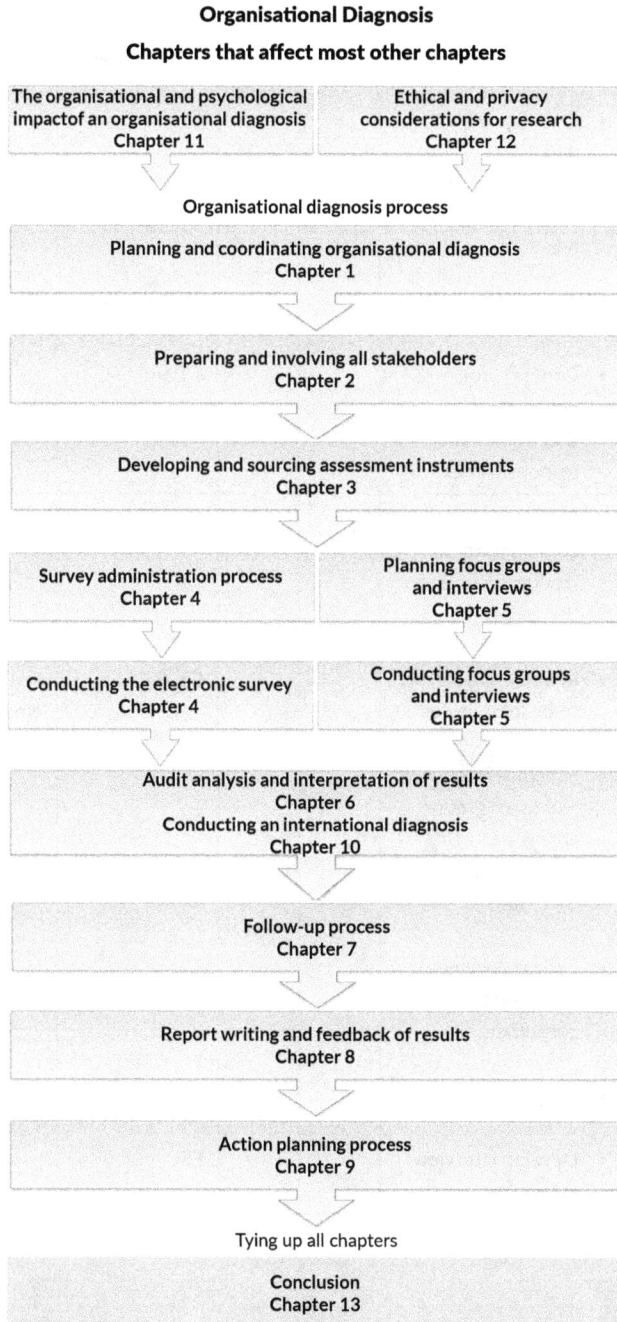

Organisational Diagnosis

Chapters that affect most other chapters

The organisational and psychological impactof an organisational diagnosis Chapter 11	Ethical and privacy considerations for research Chapter 12

Organisational diagnosis process

Planning and coordinating organisational diagnosis
Chapter 1

Preparing and involving all stakeholders
Chapter 2

Developing and sourcing assessment instruments
Chapter 3

Survey administration process Chapter 4	Planning focus groups and interviews Chapter 5

Conducting the electronic survey Chapter 4	Conducting focus groups and interviews Chapter 5

Audit analysis and interpretation of results
Chapter 6
Conducting an international diagnosis
Chapter 10

Follow-up process
Chapter 7

Report writing and feedback of results
Chapter 8

Action planning process
Chapter 9

Tying up all chapters

Conclusion
Chapter 13

Exhibit 1.1: Detailed organisational diagnosis action plan[42]

Action	Activities	Start date	End date	Responsibility	Comments	Cost
1. Project setup	• Sign contracts			Procurement and ESC Organisation	ESC Include union	
	• Schedule initial dates			CT and ESC		
	• Establish project team			CT and ESC		
	• Clarify roles			CT and ESC		
	• Confirm project deliverables, timeframes and responsibilities			CT and ESC		
2. Schedule planning	• Plan communication/ marketing around the survey			CT and ESC		
	• Identify role players to be interviewed			CT and ESC	Include employees at all levels	
	• Schedule interviews and focus groups			CT		
	• Identify documents for review			CT		
	• Collect documents and hand to survey consultant			CT		
	• Review documents			ESC		
	• Develop interview schedules			ESC		

Action	Activities	Start date	End date	Responsibility	Comments	Cost
3. Strategic positioning	• Design workshop on strategic positioning of the survey			ESC		
	• Decide who should attend the workshop and invite role players			ESC and CT	Include union	
	• Conduct workshop			ESC		
	• Develop broad OD model to be used as framework for survey results and integration			ESC	Use a model that is applicable to the organisation	
4. Conduct personal interviews	• Conduct interviews			ESC		
	• Collate information			ESC		
	• Identify themes			ESC		
5. Facilitate focus groups	• Conduct focus groups			ESC	Ensure facilitators are allocated according to language group	
	• Collate information			ESC		
	• Identify themes			ESC		
6. Develop and compile organisational assessment questionnaire	• Present themes to project team			ESC		
	• Develop draft questionnaire (dimensions and statements) and align to vocabulary of XYZ			ESC	Include ±20 employees at all levels	

Action	Activities	Start date	End date	Responsibility	Comments	Cost
6. Develop and compile organisational assessment questionnaire (continued)	• Test questionnaire for face validity			ECS		
	• Present questionnaire to project team for face validity			ESC	Project team needs to approve draft questionnaire	
	• Conduct pilot study			ESC		
	• Finalise questionnaire			ESC		
	• Submit questionnaire to executive team for sign-off			ECS		
	• Set up software for programming the questionnaire			ECS		
7. Distribute questionnaire:	• Communicate on importance and process of survey			CT		
Electronically	• Draft invitation			ESC	Top management to approve	
	• Distribute questionnaires electronically			ESC		
	• Track response rate			ESC	ESC team needs to ensure validity of data	
	• Encourage participation (managers)			ESC		
	• Data cleaning			ESC		
On paper	• Arrange sessions to facilitate questionnaire completion			CT		

Action	Activities	Start date	End date	Responsibility	Comments	Cost
7. Distribute questionnaire: (continued)	• Conduct session • Capture questionnaire data			ESC ESC		
8. Integrate the information	• Analyse data • Conduct statistical analysis			ESC ESC	Conduct validity and reliability analysis as the first step	
9. Conduct preliminary analysis	• Interpret the results, compile graphs and tables, compile first draft • Discuss the results with project team and other specialists to identify areas that need to be explored further • Draft initial high-level report			ESC ESC and CT ESC		
10. Conduct additional focus group discussions to explore certain issues in greater depth	• Conduct further focus groups/ discussions • Integrate focus group findings into initial report • Discuss findings with multidisciplinary team, prepare recommendations and finalise report			ESC ESC ESC	Only if needed to clarify results	

Action	Activities	Start date	End date	Responsibility	Comments	Cost
10. Conduct additional focus group discussions to explore certain issues in greater depth (continued)	• Prepare PowerPoint presentation on the findings • Submit report to XYZ			ESC ESC and CT		
11. Discuss and digest report with strategic role players	• Distribute report electronically to strategic role players • Schedule workshop/meeting to discuss report • Identify next steps			CT ESC CT	Include all levels and union	
12. Feedback to employees	• Provide feedback to employees • Review and identify learning insights (project team)			ESC and CT CT	All departments to be included	
13. Actions	**Action planning** • Plan actions: company-wide and global • Plan actions: in functions, areas, subsidiaries • Plan actions: locally, in work groups			CT CT CT	Conduct action planning workshops	

Action	Activities	Start date	End date	Responsibility	Comments	Cost
13. Actions (continued)	**Implementing actions** • Monitor and control actions and implementation			CT		
	• Conduct reporting within management lines			CT		
14. Evaluation	• Position the evaluation (goals, timing, criteria)			CT		
	• Decide on mix of methods			CT		
	• Decide on and construct measurement instruments			CT		
	• Collect and analyse data			CT		
	• Present results			CT		
	• Conduct follow-up evaluation processes			CT		

Legend for roles

CT = Coordinating team

ESC = Employee satisfaction consultant

REFERENCES

Borg, I & Mastrangelo, PM. 2008. *Employee surveys, tools, and practical applications. Employee surveys in management: theories, tools, and practical applications.* Cambridge, MA: Hogrefe.

Centre for Industrial and Organisational Psychology. 2010. *Advance Programme in Organisational Development: Module 3: The Process of Organisational Development.* Pretoria: University of South Africa.

Christelis, N. 2016. *The art of the arrow: how leaders fly.* Randburg: KR Publishing.

Church, AH & Waclawski, J. 2001. *Designing and using organizational surveys: a seven-step process.* San Francisco: Jossey-Bass.

Consultancy.UK. [2017]. External versus internal consultants. [Online]. Available: http://www.consultancy.uk/consulting-industry/external-vs-internal-consultants [Accessed February 2017].

Crossman, A. 2013. *An overview of qualitative research methods.* [Online]. Available: http://sociology.about.com/od/Research/a/Overview-Of-Qualitative-Research-Methods.htm [Accessed 28 December 2013].

De Klerk, F. 2016. The organisation development process, in *Fundamentals of organisation development*, edited by N Martins & D Geldenhuys. Cape Town: Juta: 139-168.

Fink, A. 2003. *The survey handbook, the survey kit.* 2nd edition. Thousand Oaks: Sage:vol 1.

Frodsham, J. 2001. Staff consulting: gaining credibility and influence as an internal consultant. *Performance in Practice: A Newsletter by and for ASTD Members*, Fall:2.

Furnham, A & Gunter, B. 1993. *Corporate assessment: auditing a company's personality.* London: Routledge.

Gallant, SM & Rios, D. 2006. Entry and contracting phase, in *The NTL handbook of organization development and change: principles, practices, and perspectives*, edited by BB Jones & M Brazzel. San Francisco: Pfeiffer:177-191.

Katz, JH & Miller, FA. 2001. Moving beyond "diversity programs" to a way of life. *Performance in Practice: A Newsletter by and for ASTD Members*, Fall:2.

Kraut, AI. 1996. Planning and conducting the survey: keeping strategic purpose in mind, in *Organizational surveys*, edited by AI Kraut. San Francisco: Jossey-Bass:149-176.

Madigral, D & McClain, B. 2012. *Strengths and weaknesses of quantitative and qualitative research.* [Online]. Available: http://www.uxmatters.com/mt/archives/2012/09/strengths-and-weaknesses-of-quantitative-and-qualitative-research.php [Accessed 28 December 2013].

Martins, EC & Martins, N. 2015. Combining focus groups and quantitative research in organisational diagnosis, in *Leading issues in business research methods: for researchers, teachers and students*, edited by S Geringer & J Mendy. Reading: Academic Conferences and Publishing:vol 2.

Martins, N. 2016. Organisational diagnosis, in *Fundamentals of organisation development*, edited by N Martins & D Geldenhuys. Cape Town: Juta:167-203.

Msila, V. 2015. *Ubuntu: shaping the current workplace with (African) wisdom.* Randburg: Knowres.

Noolan, JCA. 2006. Organization diagnosis phase, in *The NTL handbook of organization development and change: principles, practices, and perspectives*, edited by BB Jones & M Brazzel. San Francisco: Pfeiffer:192-211.

Routledge, M. 2003. The African context: organisational development in African cultures, with particular reference to the NGO sector, in *Organisational development: new models and methods for Southern Africa*, edited by A Moerdayk & C van Aardt. Glosderry: New Africa Books:122-133

Van Tonder, C & Dietrichsen, P. 2008. The art of diagnosis, in *Organisation development: theory and practice*, edited by C van Tonder & G Roodt. Pretoria: Van Schaik:133-166.

Viljoen, R. 2016. Engagement in diverse workspaces: an African and international application, in *Employee engagement in a South African context*, edited by H Nienaber and N Martins. Randburg:KR Publishing:101-126.

Yost, PR & Ryan, AM. 2004. *Relevance and rigor in organisational research.* Workshop presented at Society for Industrial Organisational Psychology. Los Angeles. 14 April.

ENDNOTES

1.   Centre for Industrial and Organisational Psychology, 2010: 28.
2.   Kraut, 1996: 150.
3.   Borg & Mastrangelo, 2008; Kraut, 1996: 151.
4.   Centre for Industrial and Organisational Psychology, 2010: 8.
5.   Gallant and Rios, 2006: 177.
6.   Block, 2006 cited in De Klerk, 2016: 138.
7.   Yost & Ryan, 2004.
8.   Routledge, 2003: 125.
9.   Srinivas cited in Routledge, 2003.
10. Msila, 2015: 20.
11. Furnham & Gunter, 1993: 6-12.
12. Borg &Mastrangelo, 2008: 6-7.
13. Fink, 2003: 101.
14. Borg & Mastrangelo, 2008: 44.
15. Martins & Martins, 2015: 158-159.
16. Crossman, 2013; Madrigal & McClain, 2012.
17. Martins & Martins, 2015: 158-159.
18. Noolan, 2006: 195.
19. Lawler, Nadler & Cammann cited in Noolan, 2006: 195.
20. Van Tonder & Dietrichsen, 2008: 149.
21. Centre for Industrial and Organisational Psychology, 2010: 10.
22. Church & Waclawski, 2001: 34.
23. Frodsham, 2001: 2.
24. Christelis, 2016: 88.
25. Katz & Miller, 2001: 2.
26. Borg & Mastrangelo, 2008: 7.
27. Frodsham, 2001: 2.
28. Furnham & Gunter, 1993: 15.
29. Muswaka, 2014 cited in Viljoen: 2016, 134.
30. Barber, Beres & Lee, 2007 cited in Borg & Mastrangelo, 2008: 30.
31. Frodsham, 2001: 2.
32. Centre for Industrial and Organisational Psychology, 2010: 28.
33. Martins, 2016: 196-199.
34. Cummings & Worley, 2015: 52.
35. Cummings & Worley, 2015: 54.
36. Consultancy.UK, 2017
37. Cummings and Worley, 2015: 54.
38. Cummings & Worley, 2015: 54; Kraut, 1996: 33-34.
39. Fink, 2003: 117-120.
40. Borg & Mastrangelo, 2008: 61-63.
41. Borg & Mastrangelo, 2008: 68.
42. Martins, 2016: 196-199.

CHAPTER 2

PREPARING AND INVOLVING ALL STAKEHOLDERS

by Ophillia Ledimo

INTRODUCTION

Organisational diagnostic processes require the active participation of all stakeholders to be successful. Practitioners and consultants in this field of organisational diagnosis and surveys thus need to understand the relevant stakeholders in the organisations and engage them properly in the process. This chapter provides a definition of stakeholders, discusses identifying and managing stakeholder resistance to the process, and outlines how to prepare stakeholders for, and involve them in, the process. The practical case study in this chapter provides awareness of resistance in an organisation to the implementation of an organisational diagnostic project. The lessons in this case study can help practitioners, managers or consultants to act proactively in the process.

STAKEHOLDER DEFINITION IN ORGANISATIONAL DIAGNOSIS

It is important to understand the term "stakeholder". The following description should help identify stakeholders when conducting an organisational diagnosis. The term "stakeholder" refers to persons, groups or organisations that should be taken into account by leaders, managers and employees. Stakeholder theory recognises that organisations are obliged to engage all their stakeholders; not only their shareholders but also other interest groups such as customers, employees, suppliers and the wider community.[1]

The survival and profitability of an organisation depends upon its ability to fulfilll its economic and social purpose, which is to ensure that each stakeholder group continues as part of the organisation's stakeholder system.[2] Bryson[3] indicates that the concept "stakeholder" has assumed a prominent place in public and non-profit management theory and practice during the last 20 years, especially in the last decade. According to Hult, Mena, Ferrell and Ferrell,[4] organisations have relationships with a multitude of stakeholders who have different rights, objectives, expectations and responsibilities.

Organisations can choose between different status categories to define a stakeholder, namely (a) an exclusively claimant definition; (b) an exclusively influencer definition; and (c) allowing that a stakeholder can be either or both of these two things.[5] Definitions of what it is to be a stakeholder are divided into "claimant" definitions, requiring some sort of claim on the services of an organisation; "influencer" definitions, requiring only a capacity to influence the business of the organisation; and "combinatory" definitions allowing for either or both of these requirements.[6]

Familiarise yourself with the following definitions, of the concept, "stakeholder":

1. All parties who will be affected by, or will affect, [the organisation's] strategy[7].
2. Any person, group or organisation that can place a claim on the organisation's attention, resources or output, or is affected by that output[8].
3. People or small groups with the power to respond to, negotiate with, and change the strategic future of, the organisation[9].
4. Those individuals or groups who depend on the organisation to fulfilll their own goals and on whom, in turn, the organisation depends[10].

The most common definitions broadly view stakeholders as any groups or individuals who can affect, or is affected by, the organisation or its project.[11] In the context of organisational diagnosis, stakeholders are defined in a similar vein as individuals, groups and organisations that are actively involved in, or whose interest may be affected by, the execution or completion of the diagnostic process. All these definitions highlight the fact that stakeholders are identified as groups that have a relationship with the organisation. Therefore, stakeholders have an interest in the organisation's operations and performance because of their relationship with the organisation.

STAKEHOLDER IDENTIFICATION

Stakeholder engagement and identification during the organisational diagnostic process is critical to help minimise resistance to planned organisational audits and to achieve goals. The question may be asked: How can you identify the relevant stakeholders? Also: Why is it necessary to identify stakeholders?

Why it is necessary to identify stakeholders? The purpose of stakeholder identification and management is to facilitate the understanding of survey practitioners of, and thereby the ability to manage in, increasingly unpredictable external environments. Saeed and Wang[12] indicate that organisational diagnosis is an exercise that checks the organisation's current health; a complete diagnosis not only checks the current health, but also suggests corrective measures. Getting an accurate picture of the organisation's health assessment requires the involvement of all the relevant stakeholders, therefore meeting the demands of all stakeholders is necessary during the diagnostic process.[13]

How can you identify the relevant stakeholders? Identifying who the stakeholders really are in the specific organisation is different from relying on generic stakeholder lists. Wolfe and Putler[14] emphasise that the desired result of stakeholder management is to more closely align corporate priorities and actions with stakeholder needs. This can help survey consultant specialists to recognise the uniqueness of the stakeholders in the organisation's context and clarify their significance for the future of the organisation.[15] Creating this alignment produces a good fit between the organisation and its environment, thereby increasing the probability of the organisation's success.[16]

The process of identifying stakeholders involves taking into account their needs and requirements – an essential part of a successful organisational audit process. It is recommended that practitioners should explicitly focus on stakeholder requirements in their approach to organisational diagnosis.[17] According to Aaltonen and Sivonen,[18] successful organisational diagnostic projects show exceptional stakeholder management and potentially follow the process of stakeholder identification, classification, analysis and management approach formulation. Knowledge of the relevant stakeholders is critical during the diagnostic process because it enables the practitioner to identify weaknesses and swiftly act accordingly.[19]

Internal and external stakeholders

The critical step in stakeholder identification is outlining internal and external stakeholders of the organisation. According to Hult et al.,[20] based on the boundaries of what constitutes a stakeholder, stakeholders can be categorised as primary or secondary. Roloff[21] describes internal stakeholders as those who have a direct stake in the organisation, and external stakeholders as those who have a representational stake.

Internal stakeholders are those who are formally members of the organisation, i.e. they can therefore, they can be expected to support and participate in organisational processes. According to Aaltonen and Sivonen,[22] they are often referred to as primary stakeholders or business actors. Primary internal stakeholders bear some risk as a result of having invested some form of capital – human, financial or something of value – in an organisation.[23] A shareholder, an employee or a union member is a stakeholder of the organisation in which they work or hold shares.[24]

In comparison, consumers, suppliers, nongovernmental organisations, social movements and other civil society actors need to formulate a stake in the organisation to qualify as stakeholders; they are normally described as external or secondary stakeholders. Hillman and Keim[25] argue that external stakeholders are not formal members of the organisation, but may affect or be affected by the diagnostic process. These stakeholders claim to speak on behalf of the public or a particular minority group in society.[26]

The ways in which the different types of stakeholders relate to an organisation vary; an organisation can be viewed as a set of inter-dependent relationships among primary and secondary stakeholders. Stakeholders such as shareholders, employees, trade unions, communities, political organisations, suppliers and consumers take their roles only in relation to a company that serves as a focal organisation.[27] While it may be easy to identify primary stakeholders, it is always a challenge for survey consultants to define who qualifies as secondary stakeholders and, more precisely, which stakeholders should not be ignored by the organisation.

Attributes and characteristics of organisational stakeholders

Stakeholders can be identified by their possession of at least one of the three relationship attributes: power, legitimacy and/or urgency. Hult et al.[28] describe the relationship attributes as follows:

1. **Power** refers to the degree to which an actor can impose their will in the relationship by accessing coercive, utilitarian or normative means. In practice, many organisations involve the chief executive officer (CEO) or other members of senior management driving the survey process.

2. **Legitimacy** is defined as a generalised perception or assumption that the actions of an entity are desirable, proper or appropriate in some socially constructed system of norms, values, beliefs and definitions. For example, the union buying into the survey is important as it is a representative of the employees.

3. **Urgency** relates to the extent to which stakeholder demands press for immediate attention. It is based on both time sensitivity (the extent to which the managerial delay is unacceptable to the stakeholder) and criticality (the importance of the demands to the stakeholder). For example, if the management team needs information to reduce a high staff turnover.

In the context of organisational diagnosis, the legitimacy of a stakeholder's claim is used as an appropriate criterion to determine the urgency of the claim and the (potentially threatening) power of the stakeholder.[29] In the process of identifying stakeholders, Roloff[30] suggests that the legitimacy of a stakeholder can be used as a criterion to establish the stakeholder's explanation of why they have a stake in the organisation. If their explanation is approved as reasonable by the practitioner and the general public, their claims are legitimate. In some cases legitimisation can only be determined by public reasoning. The public can determine who the stakeholders are and evaluate their characteristics, namely their potential to harm the organisation, and the legitimacy and urgency of their claims.[31]

Stakeholder identification is characterised by the analysis of stakeholders conducted by the focal organisation or, in this case, by survey practitioners. Wolfe and Putler[32] state that the literature agrees on the major steps involved in stakeholder analysis. Use these steps in your checklist of stakeholder analysis:

1. Identify stakeholder groups (employees, owners, communities, customers, union leaders).
2. Determine which stakeholders are salient (are powerful and have legitimate and urgent claims).
3. Evaluate or assess the priorities of individuals in the salient stakeholder groups.
4. Develop priority-based clusters (place individuals into groups with relatively homogenous priorities).
5. Cross-classify priority-based and role-based stakeholder groups.
6. In cases in which cross-classification indicates that role-based stakeholders are diffused quite broadly across priority-based clusters, profile the latter to determine a set of demographics or other characteristics that members have in common.

The last two steps are used to determine the priorities that should be handled when communicating with salient stakeholders and the media vehicles that should be used to accomplish this communication.[33] Stakeholder analysis is important during the organisational diagnostic process because it allows practitioners to collect information/data from internal and external stakeholders, and disseminate findings and recommendations to the relevant stakeholders to improve performance.[34]

The purpose of the diagnosis for all stakeholders is to develop a shared understanding of the organisation and to determine whether change is required. Begin the stakeholder analysis by identifying the relevant role-based stakeholder groups and then determining the relevant interests (in other words the "stakes") of individuals in each identified stakeholder group.[35] Self-interest provides a natural reason to assume that individuals in a role-based stakeholder group would employ a similar lens when perceiving their stakes, and thus be fairly homogenous in their views of a particular issue. Employees may view their stakes in a particular issue through a lens of self-interest concerns with wages and job security, while shareholders may view the stakes for the same issue through a lens of their own self-interest concerns regarding earnings and dividends.

MANAGING STAKEHOLDER RESISTANCE

To enable practitioners and managers to manage stakeholder resistance during the survey, it is important to first understand the nature of stakeholder resistance. This section describes the types of strategies and methods that practitioners and managers can apply to manage the resistance.

The nature of stakeholder resistance

Ackermann and Eden[36] argue that stakeholders can be identified according to the multifarious nature of the demands they can make on the organisation. Literature suggests that organisations are business entities through which a number of different actors (stakeholders) accomplish multiple and often incongruent objectives.[37] During the organisational diagnostic process, practitioners have a moral obligation to look after stakeholder interests. Given the disparities between the interests and expectations of these various stakeholders, you are unlikely to fulfill all the demands of each stakeholder group.[38] For this reason, stakeholders may offer resistance as a form of expressing their dissatisfaction. A typical example of resistance is the case of a parastatal company that had to deal with resistance during the implementation of the organisational diagnostic survey. Employees refused to take part in the survey and embarked on a strike because they were concerned about the consultation and feedback processes of the company when conducting surveys. Below is a detailed description of this case study for a practical insight into stakeholder resistance.

A case of resistance in a parastatal company in South Africa

An organisational diagnostic (OD) consulting firm was appointed to conduct an organisational diagnosis for a South African parastatal company in the form of a climate survey covering three years. The first year of the climate survey was successful, with the facilitation of focus group sessions, the development and pilot of the climate survey, administration of the survey and feedback to management.

   The second year of the survey saw a multitude of problems, however, including resistance from employees and unions who boycotted the scheduled climate survey completion sessions. Sessions that had already started were disrupted and consultants were threatened should they continue with the process. All the depots of the company embarked on a strike that prevented the consultants and human resource (HR) practitioners from accessing the organisation. As a result of the strike, which lasted more than three weeks, the company was unable to operate as a business. The scheduled sessions were cancelled and the climate survey was delayed for more than a month. This affected the company financially because it lost working hours when the employees embarked on their strike, and the company had to pay the consultants for the planned climate survey completion sessions.

After several meetings with management, staff and union representatives, the OD manager and HR practitioners realised that the staff and unions were concerned that they had not been consulted in the planning and implementation aspects of the second phase of the climate survey. The staff and unions indicated that they also had not received feedback on the first phase findings of the climate survey; the consultants had agreed to provide feedback on the findings of the first phase to all stakeholders and depots before implementing the second phase of the climate survey.

Finally, once feedback sessions were held with all stakeholders on the first phase of the climate survey, the second phase could be implemented successfully. The OD manager, HR practitioners and the consulting firm further conducted further feedback sessions on the findings of the second phase of the climate survey before beginning the third phase.

The following are some of the **critical lessons** consultants learned in this process:

- Excluding employees and unions as key stakeholders can disrupt the organisational diagnostic process.
- The OD manager, HR practitioner and consultants need knowledge and understanding of their stakeholder requirements.
- Collaborating with stakeholders and complying with their requirements, such as engaging with them and providing feedback, resolved resistance to the climate survey in this organisation.
- Constant consultative sessions with stakeholders are critical during the organisational diagnostic process.
- Resistance to the organisational diagnostic process has financial and operational implications for the organisation.

The lessons learnt from this case are noteworthy for survey consultants, practitioners, managers and consultants who are planning to conduct successful organisational diagnostic processes in their organisations. The purpose of stakeholder engagement and management in organisational diagnostic processes is to facilitate an organisational understanding of the increasingly unpredictable external and internal environments, thereby facilitating the organisation's ability to manage its processes in these environments.[39] As a manager or practitioner, you are expected to understand the concerns of stakeholders, including shareholders, employees, customers, suppliers, lenders and the society, and to develop objectives that these stakeholders would support. Stakeholder requirements are then strategically woven into the diagnostic processes at both the technical and management levels.[40]

When stakeholders support organisational objectives, it assures long-term organisational success. Stakeholders who feel ignored and misunderstood are inclined to place limits on the implementation of organisational objectives. Bowie[41] emphasises that when managers make organisational decisions they should respect the wellbeing of stakeholders and not only treat them as a means to achieving organisational objectives. Therefore, in order to realise their objectives without resistance, management and practitioners should understand the needs of stakeholders.

The different types of stakeholder resistance are outlined in figure 2.1:

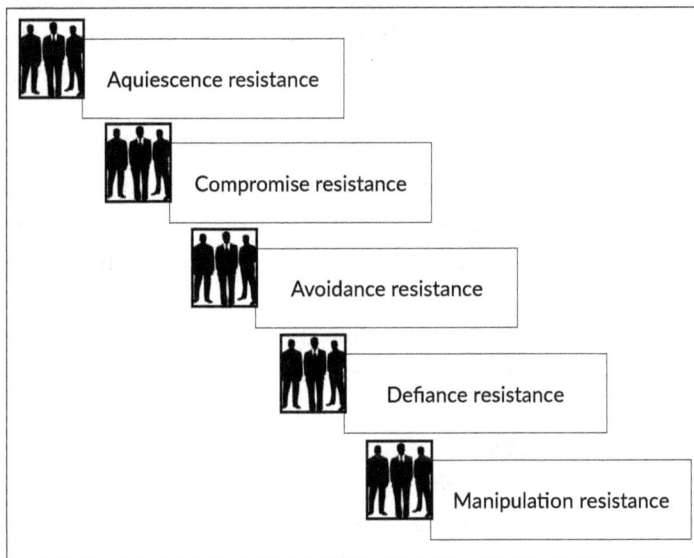

Figure 2.1: Forms of stakeholder resistance during organisational diagnosis

The following forms of resistance strategies indicate the ways stakeholders put pressure on or resist organisational processes:[42]

1. *Acquiescence resistance* can take alternative forms, including habit, imitation and compliance.
2. *Compromise resistance* includes balancing, pacifying and bargaining with the organisation.
3. *Avoidance resistance* is when stakeholders conceal their nonconformity, buffer themselves or escape using the organisational rules and expectations.
4. *Defiance resistance* as an active form of resistance to organisational processes can manifest itself as non-participation, challenge or attack.
5. *Active manipulation resistance* refers to a purposeful and opportunistic attempt to co-opt, influence or control organisational processes.

Organisations and survey consultants need to manage stakeholders irrespective of who they are. Stakeholder management can be considered a knowledge structure that determines how practitioners and managers selectively perceive, evaluate and interpret attributes of the environment.[43] Stakeholders who are perceived as "marginal" or "dependent" should be monitored. If they are classified as "non-supportive" or "dangerous" to the organisation's OD processes, it is important to adopt a strategy of (self-) defence.[44]

Engagement of stakeholders in organisational diagnostic processes

In order to engage stakeholders during surveys, organisations need to handle the demands of their internal and external stakeholders. Wolfe and Putler[45] suggest that the use of a knowledge structure can facilitate information processing and decision making in response to stakeholder demands. All stakeholder theories contain three separate elements in stakeholder management. Mason and Simmons[46] describe these descriptive, instrumental and normative elements:

1. The *descriptive* element identifies the expectations particular stakeholder groups have of the organisation, how organisations respond to these expectations, and the implications for both parties when their expectations are met, such as when survey consultants meet with internal stakeholders (through focus groups or interviews) to clarify the latter's expectations of the survey to be done.
2. The *instrumental* element demonstrates how effective stakeholder management can make a significant contribution to the organisation's efficiency, effectiveness and reputation. For example, consultants can use the cooperation of stakeholders to facilitate the successful implementation of the survey.
3. The *normative* element uses equity as an ethical basis for stakeholder management (via organisational justice dimensions) to assess stakeholder satisfaction with organisational diagnostic philosophy, processes and outcomes. For example, when consultants ask stakeholders to give feedback of their perception of the survey process and then use this feedback to enhance the implementation process.

The descriptive element involves a description of how organisations operate; the instrumental element examines how stakeholder management can contribute to the achievement of the organisation's goals; and the normative element provides an ethical rationale for approaches to stakeholder management.[47]

Practitioners normally adopt the strategies presented in figure 2.2 to handle stakeholder resistance during the survey, starting from the most passive response strategy to the most active response strategy at the end of the continuum.[48]

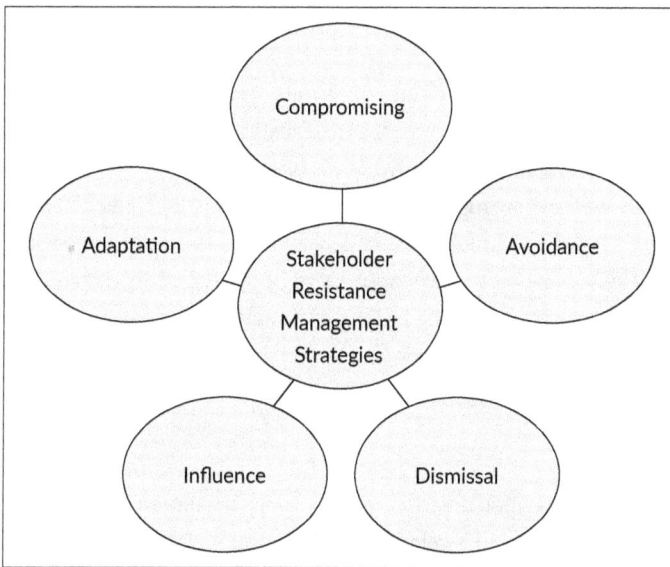

Figure 2.2: Stakeholder resistance management strategies during organisational diagnosis

The following is a detailed description of the five stakeholder resistance management strategies:

Adaptation strategy

The adaptation strategy obeys the demands and rules presented by stakeholders. This strategy argues that to cope with the demands and achieve the objectives of the diagnostic process, it is better to adjust to the stakeholders' requests and pressures. This strategy is relevant in situations when the claims of stakeholders are seen as legitimate and stakeholders have excessive power in the organisation.

Compromising strategy

The compromising strategy is used when practitioners negotiate with stakeholders, listen to their claims about the diagnosis process, and offer possibilities and arenas for dialogue. Survey consultants can facilitate reconciliations and offer rewards as an opportunity to open the project to the stakeholders. Stakeholder resistance usually arises out of conflict between the objectives of the diagnostic process and the interests of stakeholders, however this strategy encourages parity between the interests of the organisation and its stakeholders. As the power and legitimacy of stakeholders' claims increase, survey consultants should get actively involved in and enact more active strategies, such as the compromising strategy.

Avoidance strategy

With the avoidance strategy, practitioners loosen attachment to stakeholders and their claims to shield themselves. This occurs when managers transfer the responsibility of responding to the claims to another actor in the project network. Survey consultants who adopt this strategy are likely to be ineffective in managing resistance because it isolates stakeholders. Isolation means that the practitioners avoid resistance from the stakeholders as they buffer themselves against the presented claims. The avoidance strategy appears to be an option for organisations that transfer the responsibility of managing resistance to the consulting company because it is more capable of responding to claims.

Dismissal strategy

The dismissal strategy occurs when practitioners ignore the presented demands of stakeholders and do not take into account stakeholder-related pressures and their requirements in the execution of the project. Survey consultants who enact the dismissal strategy ignore the demands and pressures posed by stakeholders, for example, practitioners may argue that it is not necessary to take into account such claims for the efficient execution of the diagnostic project.

Practitioners may not be aware that they have chosen the dismissal strategy, because they may be enacting it due to a lack of knowledge or experience. The dismissal strategy is usually used in situations where the claims of stakeholders are not legitimate and stakeholders who exert pressure do not have much power in the diagnostic process.

Influence strategy

The influence strategy means that a practitioner is embarking on the process of proactively shaping the values and demands of stakeholders. It occurs when practitioners share information actively and build relationships with all stakeholders. The intended effect of the influence strategy is to neutralise the stakeholders' resistance and to proactively shape their demands. This strategy involves sharing information actively and innovatively, opening the project to stakeholders, having a dialogue with multiple stakeholders, and building active and non-adversarial, long-term relationships with stakeholders.

Practitioners using the influence strategy proactively aim to influence the stakeholders' perception of the rationale of the survey process, spread information about the process, and utilise informal networks of employees in the organisation. Where practitioners use this type of a strategy, previous knowledge or experience and continuous learning from stakeholder-related resistance is beneficial, as this supports the practitioners' capability to take into account and forecast potential stakeholder resistance.

The above strategies suggest that in the face of stakeholder resistance during an organisational diagnostic process, survey practitioners may choose to respond to it in various ways, ranging from passive adaptation strategies to active influence strategies. These responses are determined mainly by the power of the stakeholders exerting the resistance, the legitimacy of the resistance presented by the stakeholders, the content used by stakeholders to support their resistance, and the ways and means the stakeholders use to advance their resistance. Roloff[49] highlights that practitioners and managers of the focal organisation need to decide on an interaction strategy for each stakeholder, therefore they need to consider the assumptions inherent in the conceptual models they adopt, how these assumptions channel their thinking, and what other perspectives are available.[50]

Value of the competence of survey consultants, practitioners and managers in stakeholder management

In addition to the application of the different strategies, the experience of the survey consultant is critical in order to deal with resistance and management's response to resistance. It is important to note that not all stakeholders are likely to resist the organisational diagnostic process. The roles of survey consultants are discussed in chapter 1.

When survey consultants encounter influential, cooperative stakeholders who are powerful role players with urgent and legitimate stakes, collaboration with them is advised.[51] They should not overlook stakeholders who are affected by the organisational diagnostic process in favour of those who can affect its successful execution. It is important to determine which groups of stakeholders deserve or require management attention, and which do not. In practice, the amount of attention practitioners and management devote to a particular stakeholder depends on their combination of power, legitimacy and urgency.[52] Practitioners tend to overemphasise the demands of powerful stakeholders and to ignore marginal and vulnerable stakeholder groups, as this is the most pragmatic way of ensuring the organisation's effectiveness in the short term, rather than solving the problem, which would take longer. In the long term, uncertainties about future social, economic and ecological developments lead to the insight that it is advisable to take into account the needs of marginal stakeholders, as their impact on the organisation's performance is critical.[53]

In order to ensure that the survey process is regarded as credible and valuable; all stakeholders should be treated as important participants. Scott and Lane[54] propose that managers and practitioners should create and nurture a sense of identity and "groupness" in particular stakeholder groups through impression-management activities such as self-promotion and exemplification. These initiatives can create a unified and positive image in targeted stakeholder groups. Roloff[55] is of the opinion that if an organisation wants to be effective, it should pay attention to all stakeholders, and not only to those that can affect or be affected by the achievements of the organisation. This can help who predict the future environment and independently develop plans for the organisation to exploit its position. This approach to stakeholder management actively designs a new direction for the organisation's response. It takes into account how the organisation can affect the environment and how the environment can affect organisational initiatives.

Practitioners need to understand the priorities of and the ability to deal with identifiable stakeholders as any group that can affect or is affected by the achievement of an organisation's objectives. Management must have the support of those who can affect the organisation and understand how the organisation would affect others.[56] Understanding stakeholder relationships can enable the organisation to achieve its objectives, which in turn can lead to its survival. This offers strategic and cognitive efficiency advantages over conceiving of an organisation's environment as being composed of innumerable individuals and institutions.[57] These advantages are attributed to stakeholder management because they derive from an organisation's provision of a systematic approach for conceptualising, comprehending and analysing external environments.[58] It is an approach that emphasises active management of the organisation's environment, relationships and the promotion of shared interests. This implies that the organisation is focusing on relatively few identifiable stakeholders, as opposed to numerous individuals and institutions, and provides a simplified and more easily comprehended representation of the organisation's world. Therefore, stakeholder management should be responsive to the concerns of managers and practitioners who are buffeted by unprecedented levels of environmental turbulence and change.

CONCLUSION

A successful organisational diagnosis process depends on the practitioner's ability and skills in stakeholder collaboration. Survey practitioners, managers and consultants should be proactive in minimising resistance from stakeholders by using knowledge of the different types of stakeholders and forms of resistance during an organisational diagnosis. It is also essential to develop competence in engaging the stakeholders to prevent resistance.

REFERENCES

Aaltonen, K & Sivonen, R. 2009. Response strategies to stakeholder pressures in global projects. *International Journal of Project Management*, 27:131–141.

Ackermann, F & Eden, C. 2011. Strategic management of stakeholders: theory and practice. *Long Range Planning*, 44:179–196.

Asif, M, Searcy, C, Zutshi, A & Fisscher, OAM. 2013. An integrated management systems approach to corporate social responsibility. *Journal of Cleaner Production*, 56:7–17.

Blair, MM. 2005. Closing the theory gap: how the economic theory of property rights can help bring "stakeholders" back into theories of the firm. *Journal of Management and Governance*, 9:33–39.

Bowie, N. 1999. *Business ethics: a Kantian perspective*. Oxford: Blackwell's.

Bryson, J. 1995. *Strategic planning for public and non-profit organizations*. San Francisco, CA: Jossey-Bass.

Bryson, MJ. 2004. What to do when stakeholders matter. *Public Management Review*, 6(1):21–53.

De Castro, JO, Meyer, D, Strong, KC & Uhlenbruck, N. 1994. Government objectives and organizational characteristics: a stakeholder view of privatization effectiveness. *The International Journal of Organizational Analysis*, 14(4):373–392.

Eden, C & Ackermann, F. 1998. *Making strategy: the journey of strategic management*. London: Sage Publications.

Freeman, RE. 1984. *Strategic management: a stakeholder approach*. Boston, MA: Pitman.

Hillman, AJ & Keim, GD. 2001. Shareholder value, stakeholder management, and social issues: what's the bottom line? *Strategic Management Journal*, 22:125–139.

Hult, GTM, Mena, JA, Ferrell, OC & Ferrell, L. 2011. Stakeholder marketing: a definition and conceptual framework. *AMS Review*, 1:44–65.

Johnson, G & Scholes, K. 2002. *Exploring corporate strategy.* Harlow, England: Pearson Education.

Kaler, J. 2002. .Morality and strategy in stakeholder identification. *Journal of Business Ethics*, 39:91–99.

Mason, C & Simmons J. 2014. Embedding corporate social responsibility in corporate governance: a stakeholder systems approach. *Journal of Business Ethics*, 119:77–86.

Nutt, P & Backoff, R. 1992. *Strategic management of public and third sector organizations: a handbook for leaders.* San Francisco, CA: Jossey-Bass.

Oliver, C. 1991. Strategic responses to institutional processes. *Academic Management Review*, 16(1):145–79.

Phillipson, J, Lowe, P, Proctor, A & Ruto, E. 2012. Stakeholder engagement and knowledge exchange in environmental research. *Journal of Environmental Management*, 95:56–65.

Roloff, J. 2007. Learning from multi-stakeholder networks: issue-focussed stakeholder management. *Journal of Business Ethics*, 82:233–250.

Saeed, BB & Wang, W. 2014. Sustainability embedded organizational diagnostic model. *Modern Economy*, 5:424–431.

Scott, SG & Lane, VR. 2000. A stakeholder approach to organizational identity. *Academic Management Review*, 25:43–62.

Wolfe, RA & Putler, DS. 2002. How tight are the ties that bind stakeholder groups? *Organization Science*, 13(1):64–80.

ENDNOTES

1. Asif, Searcy, Zutshi & Fisscher, 2013.
2. Hillman & Keim, 2001; Blair, 2005.
3. Bryson, 2004.
4. Hult, Mena, Ferrell & Ferrell, 2011.
5. Ackermann & Eden, 2011; Bowie 1999; Kaler, 2002.
6. Kaler, 2002:97.
7. Nutt & Backoff, 1992:439.
8. Bryson, 1995:27.
9. Eden & Ackermann, 1998:117.
10. Johnson & Scholes, 2002:206.
11. Ackerman & Eden, 2011; Aaltonen & Sivonen, 2009.
12. Saeed & Wang, 2014.
13. Asif et al., 2013; Aaltonen & Sivonen, 2009.
14. Wolfe & Putler, 2002.
15. Ackerman & Eden, 2011.
16. Wolfe & Putler, 2002.
17. Freeman, 1984; Roloff, 2007; Asif et al.,2013.
18. Aaltonen & Sivonen, 2009.
19. Olivier, 1991; Saeed & Wang, 2014.
20. Hult et al., 2011.
21. Roloff, 2007.
22. Aaltonen & Sivonen, 2009.
23. Hillman & Keim, 2001; Hult et al., 2011.

24. Roloff, 2007.
25. Hillman & Keim, 2001.
26. Blair, 2005; Roloff, 2007.
27. Roloff, 2007.
28. Hult et al., 2011:49.
29. Bowie, 1989; Kaler, 2002; Wolfe & Putler, 2002
30. Roloff, 2007.
31. Mason & Simmons, 2014; Freeman, 1984.
32. Wolfe & Putler, 2002:65.
33. Wolfe & Putler, 2002.
34. Saeed & Wang, 2014.
35. Wolfe & Putler, 2002.
36. Ackermann & Eden, 2011.
37. Hult et al., 2011.
38. Blair, 2005; Olivier, 1991.
39. Saeed & Wang, 2014; Wolfe & Putler, 2002.
40. Asif et al., 2013.
41. Bowie, 1999.
42. Oliver, 1991.
43. Scott & Lane, 2000; Wolfe & Putler, 2002.
44. Roloff, 2007.
45. Wolfe & Putler, 2002.
46. Mason & Simmons, 2014:79–80.
47. Mason & Simmons, 2014.
48. Aaltonen & Sivonen, 2009:138–139.
49. Roloff, 2007.
50. De Castro, Meyer, Strong & Uhlenbruck, 1994.
51. Roloff, 2008; De Castro et al 1994.
52. Hult et al, 2011.
53. Phillipson et al., 2012.
54. Scott & Lane, 2000:50.
55. Roloff, 2007.
56. Freeman, 1984.
57. Wolfe & Putler, 2002.
58. Wolfe & Putler, 2002.

CHAPTER 3

DEVELOPING AND SOURCING ASSESSMENT INSTRUMENTS

by Ellen Caroline Martins and Ophillia Ledimo

INTRODUCTION

In the organisational diagnosis process, developing and sourcing assessment instruments are important because the instrument or tool used to collect data will determine whether you will be able to solve the problem(s) identified in the organisation and fulfill the purpose of embarking on the diagnosis in the first place. In the previous chapters an overview of the diagnosis process, the purpose and scope of the diagnosis, involving and preparing stakeholders, and dealing with resistance were discussed. The next step in the diagnostic process is to decide on the assessment tools that you are going to use. In this chapter the methods of data collection and the role of the data collection methods to determine organisational issues are discussed. There are many survey tools and assessment instruments available, thus one of the decisions to be made is whether to use an existing instrument or develop a new one. The types of survey instruments and applications that are available, how to develop tools for surveys, focus groups and interviews are discussed, while document analysis and observation as a data collection tool is also briefly examined.

METHODS OF DATA COLLECTION APPLICABLE TO QUANTITATIVE AND QUALITATIVE RESEARCH

Organisational diagnosis provides individual- and organisational-level data for context-specific, goal-oriented planning, and promotes a process of organisational improvement.[1] The purpose of the description of qualitative and quantitative approaches in this chapter is to guide you as survey consultants and managers in the decision-making process when preparing an organisational diagnosis strategy. Qualitative and quantitative approaches differ in terms of their organisational diagnostic methods, orientation and execution.[2] The following table 3.1 indicates the differences between the two approaches that you need to consider when developing your diagnostic plan:

Table 3.1: Differences between qualitative and quantitative approaches (compiled by O Ledimo)

Dimensions	Qualitative	Quantitative
Evaluations	Deals with subjective data	Evaluates objective data
Focus	Focus is flexible and exploratory	Focus is complex and structured, and tests hypotheses
Methods	Interviews, observer-as-participant observation, focus groups, documents and archival data	Questionnaires, surveys, instruments and inventories
Investigation	Conducts the investigation to achieve an insider's view	Conducts the investigation from the outsider's perspective
Process	Process is dynamic and changeable	Process is stable in nature
Approach	Data collection is wide, hence the approach is holistic	Data collection is structured, hence the approach is particularistic
Focus	Focus is more on the validity and representation of the data	Focus is on the reliability of the data and measuring instrument
Sample	Collects data from small sample groups	Collects data using large samples

Despite their disparities, it is feasible for you to integrate these two approaches during the diagnostic process. Flick[3] argues that these approaches should be regarded as complementary methods, not rivalries. Combining qualitative and quantitative approaches within the same process of the organisational diagnosis enables survey consultants to gather comprehensive data and to verify results.

Quantitative approach in organisational diagnosis

Quantitative approaches provide an assessment with predefined categories, which are useful for comparisons.[4] According to Welman, Kruger and Mitchell[5], a quantitative approach is used to gather data from large groups, such as a representative cross-section of the employees of a large organisation or of a large group of employees. This approach of data collection method is, in practice, considered to have high levels of validity and reliability.[6] This implies that, as a survey consultant, you can use a quantitative approach when you require structured and controlled methods to conduct an objective, valid and reliable diagnosis of an organisation.

Quantitative methods of data collection that you can adopt in your organisational diagnostic strategy are questionnaires, surveys, instruments and inventories. Written questionnaires are useful methods for the collection of self-reporting data. Paul[7] indicates that a questionnaire is an impersonal written instrument which "carries both the instructions and questions to respondents, and provides space for them to complete their answers", i.e. the questionnaire is more than simply a list of questions or forms to be completed. Disadvantages of the questionnaire include questionable data quality related to nonresponse bias, accuracy and completeness.[8] Despite these limitations, there are methods to increase return rate; these include follow-up contacts, general delivery and pickup.

Salkind[9] says that "survey" is a broad term that often includes interviews, questionnaires, instruments or inventories. Therefore, you can use a survey to estimate opinions, attitudes, and characteristics of a large number of individuals, based on data collected from some of those individuals.[10] Instruments and inventories are questionnaires that have stood the test of time.[11] These tools are designed mainly to measure particular attributes and have been demonstrated to do so with sound validity and reliability.[12] Instruments and inventories are also recommended in organisational diagnosis because they can assist you to assess specific attributes and behaviours within an organisation. These methods are also discussed in detail later on in this chapter.

Qualitative approach in organisational diagnosis

A qualitative approach can offer you as an organisational survey consultant the possibility for an open, descriptive dialogue.[13] Sandelowski[14] indicates that data collection, using a qualitative approach, is typically directed at discovering the who, what and where of events or experiences. A qualitative approach is descriptive, hence it is concerned with the meaning that individuals attach to things in their lives. It is also a flexible approach; this implies that this approach is reflexive in nature. Literature suggests that qualitative approaches can (and should) be readily changed to match the fluid and dynamic demands of the immediate diagnostic situation in multicultural settings.[15] It is essential to note that in practice, qualitative methods of data collection are regarded as being high on validity and low on reliability when compared to the quantitative approach.

Smith[16] describes a qualitative approach as a process of exploring, describing and interpreting the perceptions and experiences of the participants during organisational diagnosis. This approach of organisational diagnosis now allows survey consultants and managers the option to choose from an increasing array of theoretically and technically sophisticated methods.[17] When you consider the application of qualitative methods of data collection, it is imperative to know that these methods are used to obtain data from small groups and not larger samples, such as a group of interviewees or a focus group. Qualitative data can be used to confirm or reject the quantitative results, because it provides rich data that can give additional contextual information that quantitative data does not render.

Qualitative data collection methods that you can choose in your diagnostic process include interviews, observer-as-participant observation (see discussion on *Observation data collection*) focus groups, documents and archival data. Observer-as-participant observation is a type of unstructured observation in which the survey consultant identifies himself/herself as a diagnostician and interacts with the participants in the social process, but makes no pretence of actually being a participant.[18] A focus group is a group in-depth interview that allows the group members to express their opinions on a specific set of open questions.[19] Data collection techniques in a qualitative approach may also include observations of targeted events and the examination of documents and artefacts.[20] The use of archival and documentary data is an unobtrusive data collection technique because a review of available documents and records can provide you with insight into the behavioural patterns in an organisational system. Archival data often contains a lot of information that is not directly related to the constructs of interest; despite this disadvantage it is an unobtrusive measure or investigation of organisational issues.

In the next sections of this chapter, we provide a detailed description of the different types of qualitative data collection methods that you can use during organisational diagnosis.

Triangulation of the diagnostic approaches and methods

Organisational diagnosis comprises three key components: process, interpretation and methods.[21] These components also include aspects of the diagnostic process that you should follow, namely: contracting, data gathering, and feedback of the data to the organisation. In general, the rigour and variety of methods used for data collection should be maximised within the practical constraints of your organisational diagnosis consultation.[22] Therefore, the particular data collection methods used for an organisational diagnosis are chosen based on the diagnostic model of the consultant and perceived organisational needs. Inauen, Jenny & Bauer[23] indicate that organisational diagnosis is guided by scientific principles of data collection methods, where sources of errors should be minimised during the process.

Qualitative and quantitative research approaches are essential when determining the assessment and evaluation instruments that you can use for data collection during organisational development and consultation. Paul[24] argues that the choice of particular data collection methods depends on the nature and scope of the diagnosis and the unique contribution of each method. A precondition of any data collection method during the process of organisational diagnosis is systematic planning that has clear concepts, roles or a detailed plan with realistic goals.[25] The question you need to ask is: What is the purpose of data collection using these two approaches? Organisational diagnosis engages quantitative and qualitative methodologies of scientific inquiry for the purpose of describing and interpreting the organisation's social reality. Linking quantitative and qualitative data collection methods can ensure that you enhance the overall effectiveness of the diagnostic process. The following section covers the two approaches and their methods of data collection.

ROLE OF DATA COLLECTION METHODS TO DETERMINE ORGANISATIONAL ISSUES

Triangulation of data collection and the role that data collection plays in the organisational diagnostic process are discussed below.

Data collection triangulation

Survey consultants employ scientific methodologies to collect data and generate an organisational diagnosis.[26] Inauen et al.[27] highlight that the different data collection methods should be systematically combined and triangulated in order to determine the critical and relevant issues in an organisational diagnosis. Triangulation refers to the process of combining several data collection methods in the same diagnostic process, as per figure 3.1.

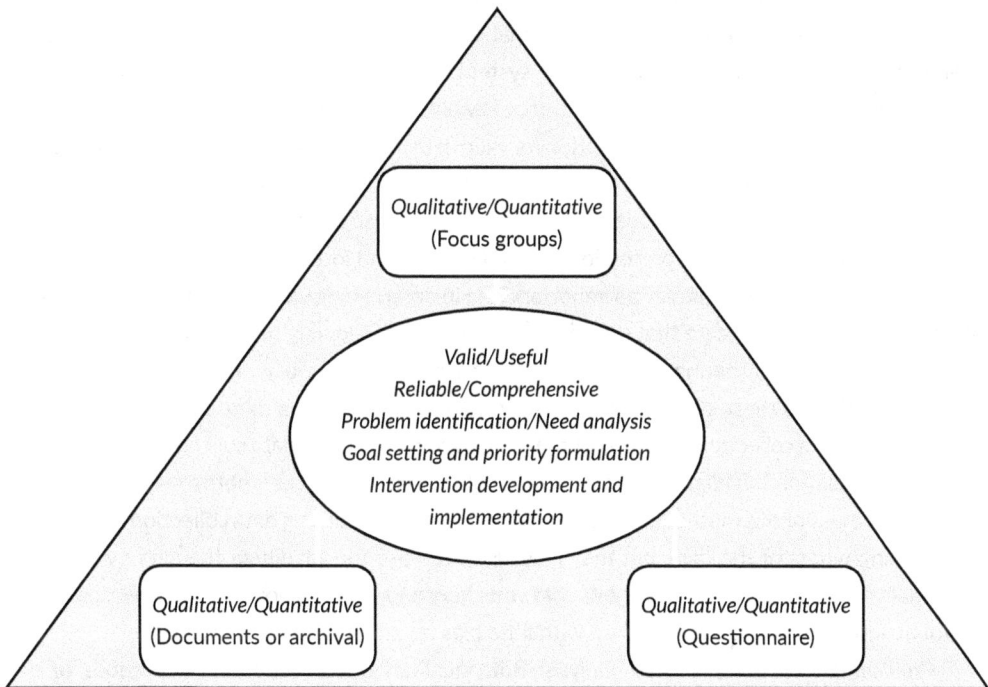

Figure 3.1: Data collection methods triangulation during organisational diagnosis (compiled by O Ledimo)

Figure 3.1 provides an overview of how different data collection methods can be used as a mixed method in the same organisational diagnosis to collect data. A mixed-method technique implies that both quantitative and qualitative approaches can be used in the process of organisational diagnosis, using the process of triangulation of the data collection methods. For example, you can start by collecting primary data with focus groups (qualitative). Secondly, collect secondary data using archives (qualitative), and thirdly, collect primary data using a survey (quantitative). When conducting an organisational diagnosis project on employee engagement, you can start data collection first through archives, use the data to identify engagement trends for a focus group session as the second data collection method, and use focus group data to develop a survey questionnaire (key aspects to assess). Finally, you can use the survey to collect data on employee engagement. This implies that your diagnosis will be based on three methods of data collection in this project, namely archives, focus groups and surveys.

Data collection methods play a critical role in the diagnostic process because they provide you with valid and useful information, data for problem identification and need analysis, comprehensive and detailed information, data for goal setting and priority formulation, intervention development and implementation.

Role of data collection methods

The following is a discussion of these various roles of data collection methods.

Valid and useful information: Organisational diagnosis is the process of generating valid and useful information about an organisational system.[28] Data collection methods in the diagnosis process can help you to obtain 'good data', that is valid, reliable and representative. It is therefore imperative to use methods of data collection for valid data for the diagnosis that can lead to dramatic organisational improvement. While instruments and inventories are ideal for valid and reliable data collection in the diagnosis, they have limitations. Most of these tools are very expensive to acquire and they also require qualified professionals to administer and interpret them.[29]

Data collection methods play an important role in determining valid organisational problems.[30] Mouton and Marais[31] indicate that questionnaires have the following main advantages: increasing validity of the data gathering process and reducing interviewer bias, despite being relatively inexpensive. Due to these obvious advantages, the questionnaire is a more popular method than interviews for data collection. In terms of the observation method of data collection, Terre Blanche, Durheim and Painter[32] highlight that the validity of observers' inferences is both a major strength and a major weakness of this method. Inferences made by observers during data collection may improve the meaningfulness of the data, but they may also decrease the validity of the data by increasing the impact of consultant bias[33]. Methods that you choose for the diagnosis should therefore gather useful quantitative and qualitative data with little bias regarding representativeness.

Problem identification or need analysis: Both qualitative and quantitative methods of data collection enable survey consultants to be able to identify important problems in the organisation as a system and to make specific recommendations[34]. Organisational diagnosis is seen as a general, complete system evaluation process, rather than a specific sub-unit focused one.[35] The purpose of organisational diagnosis is to establish a widely shared understanding of the organisation's problems and, based on that understanding, you should be able to determine whether interventions are necessary.[36] Without careful diagnosis and using appropriate data collection measures, decision-makers may waste effort by failing to spell out the root causes of problems.[37]

Inventories and instruments are available for organisational diagnosis to assess problems or an organisational need in the areas of organisational culture, trust, engagement, employee satisfaction and commitment. You can use surveys in the diagnosis process because they play a critical role in problem identification and need analysis. Surveys that are carried out in organisations for diagnosis are usually conducted for the following reasons:[38]

1. Assessing employees' attitudes towards organisational processes or systems.
2. Investigating employees' opinions about the organisation and its practices.
3. Gathering information related to employees' characteristics.
4. Getting input from employees about their organisational perceptions or their behaviour.

Comprehensive and detailed information: An ideal organisational diagnosis should be organisation-wide in scope and more complex in the description of the organisational reality[39]. Consequently, it is important to use multiple methods of data collection. The number and types of methods used must be sufficient to meet the requisite variety of the system under investigation. When you increase the number and variety of methods, you may also increase the time and expense of conducting an organisational diagnosis[40]. Multiple methods of data collection can lead managers, survey consultants, as well as their client organisation to develop a more in-depth understanding of the social realities of their organisation as a system[41]. Tetteh[42] argues that organisational diagnosis data collection should provide a comprehensive picture of the organisation by identifying the gaps between today (where the organisation finds itself now) and tomorrow (where it wants to be in the future). Data collection tools exist to assist the survey consultants in making decisions to reduce the gaps between the current and future state of your client organisation.

Document analysis can assist you in conducting a comprehensive analysis, using resources such as the organisation's website, performance reports, personnel data, data on productivity and labour records[43]. Paul[44] suggests that these 'traces' of a system's behaviour can lead to modifications in previous understandings of the system, or they can introduce completely new topics and processes for consideration in the diagnosis. The observer-as-participant method of data collection can help survey consultants to gain a detailed comprehension of the typical organisational processes, work roles and general working conditions[45].

Goal setting and priorities formulation: Organisational diagnosis data collection methods are initially needed for retrieving information regarding needs in an organisational context, as well as for setting priorities and for rational, goal-oriented planning[46]. The data collection process is critical because it provides consultants and managers with useful information that represents a basis for informed and competent decision-making and organisational development[47]. For you to effectively diagnose, you should apply data collection methods and approaches that will serve your needs.

Intervention development and implementation: The results of the data collection methods are useful, not only for intervention planning, but also for engaging organisational members in the implementation process[48]. Using relevant methods of data collection makes it possible to use the feedback of results as a key intervention for participation and motivation of organisation members.[9] The data collection process is essential because it can contribute to managerial decision-making, just as it can provide a solid foundation for recommendations by organisational and management consultants[50]. Tetteh[51] affirms that organisational diagnostic tools help organisations to identify the 'gaps' between 'what is' and 'what ought to be' to know the state of health of the organisation and whether it is getting better or worse.

ASSESSMENT OR MEASUREMENT IN ORGANISATIONAL DIAGNOSIS

The intent of measurement in organisational diagnosis differs from the measurement of objects like rulers, scales, gauges and thermometers. When something is measured, a limit is set in some way to constrain the data so that it may be interpreted and compared to a particular quantitative or qualitative standard. In organisational diagnosis we measure concepts, ideas, opinions, feelings, or other intangible entities[52]. For example, we might attempt to measure the satisfaction levels of employees, or the way in which things are done in the organisation (the organisational culture), or the degree to which diversity is accommodated in the organisation.

Surveys, focus groups and interviews as methods of data collection to measure these intangible entities involve the use of measurement instruments or tools that consist of a questionnaire or questions to be answered by people from whom the data is gathered. Each data collection method requires a different type of questionnaire, framework or guide. Questions that the survey consultant might ask are:

1.   Should I use an existing or customised questionnaire, or should I develop a new questionnaire?
2.   What are the types of questionnaires that are available and where and how can I obtain the questionnaire/s?
3.   How do I develop a questionnaire for a survey?
4.   How do I develop a framework for focus groups?
5.   How do I develop an interview guide for interviews?
6.   What types of document/artefact analyses and observation methods can I consider?
7.   What do I need to take into account when conducting document analysis or observation?

These questions will be answered in the rest of this chapter.

Choice of instrument – using an existing or customised or new questionnaire

Leedy and Ormrod[53] state that "measurement instruments provide a basis on which the entire research effort rests". They use the example of a building with a questionable foundation being unsafe for habitation and argue that in the same way, "a research effort employing faulty measurement tools (will) provide little of value in solving the problem under investigation". In our experience we have found that the use of existing questionnaires that were not validated or new questionnaires that were not well designed could/might add little value in identifying real issues and achieving 'positive' results. Typical examples of such questionnaires that have not been validated or [scientifically] well designed would be those found in popular magazines that you can use to test your personality, stress levels, strengths and weaknesses, and so on. It would be unethical for organisations to base their decision-making on results from these types of questionnaires which do not adhere to scientific or ethical guidelines for the development of assessment instruments. (See chapter 12 for a discussion of the ethical and privacy considerations for research.) In organisational diagnosis, if the measuring instrument is not valid and reliable, the research effort might turn out to be invalid for management to base their decision-making on the outcome (results) of the instrument and it might have undesired outcomes for the organisation. Below we will discuss the validity, and reliability of measuring instruments, followed by some thoughts on using existing, customised or newly developed questionnaires.

Validity and reliability of instruments

In an organisational diagnosis you should provide evidence that the instruments you use are valid and reliable for the purpose of the diagnosis[54]. In the South African context it is also important to ensure that the questionnaire you intend to use is valid and reliable for the specific population (for example industry or sector or race groups) in which you intend to use it. Moerdyk[55] cautions that in a multicultural country such as South Africa, with its numerous language and ethnic groups, it is necessary to take differences into account in order to conduct fair assessments. Invariance testing is a statistical method that is used to determine if a questionnaire measures equally among various biographical or regional groups. It might be advisable to determine whether the chosen questionnaire has been subjected to invariance testing and that it measures equally for the groups you intend to survey[56].

The validity of a measuring instrument is "the extent to which the instrument measures what it is actually intended to measure"[57]. Saunders, Lewis and Thornhill[58] refer to measurement validity in terms of a scale or measuring instrument. This means that the findings of your questionnaire actually represent the reality of what you are measuring, which presents you with the problem of why you should collect the data in the first place if you actually knew the reality of what you are measuring. This problem can be overcome by looking for other relevant evidence that supports the answers you find when using the questionnaire. The relevance is determined by your own judgement and the nature of the core research or diagnostic question[59].

Evidence that an existing instrument is valid relates to whether the questionnaire has been tested for face –, content –, criterion – and construct validity. Evidence of the validity of an existing survey instrument should be sourced and provided (in the planning phase and the diagnostic report) by the person who is conducting the organisational diagnosis. When developing a new questionnaire, the validity and reliability tests should be conducted as part of the developing process. (These techniques will be discussed later under the section: Developing a focused questionnaire for quantitative research.)

The reliability of a measuring instrument is "the extent to which the instrument yields consistent results when the characteristic being measured hasn't changed"[60]. The instrument must be internally reliable in terms of the measurement of the area of interest and, if appropriate, externally over time and in terms of the relationship between alternative forms of the same instrument[61]. Reliability of a questionnaire has to do with consistency, "in particular, whether or not it will produce consistent findings at different times and under different conditions [different situations], such as with different samples or, in the case of an interviewer-administered questionnaire, with different interviewers"[62]. The reliability of a new questionnaire can only be determined once the data have been collected, but in the case of existing questionnaires, evidence of the validity and reliability might be available in published research articles. In the discussion on designing a new questionnaire, more will be said about the different ways of testing for reliability, such as test-retest, internal consistency (Cronbach's Alpha) and an alternative form[63].

Internal consistency is probably the best way of testing the reliability of a questionnaire. It involves correlating the responses to each question with the responses to other questions in the questionnaire to measure consistency of responses across the questions or across subgroups of questions. Test-retest is difficult because respondents have to complete the questionnaire twice and it is thus not doable in an organisational diagnosis. An alternative form is when so-called 'check questions' are included. This offers some sense of reliability through comparing responses to a group of questions or a question to alternative forms of the question(s). The difficulty with this type of testing is that it is not easy to ensure that these questions are substantially equal. Respondent fatigue or remembering how they answered a previous similar question may affect test results, thus check questions should be used sparingly[64].

An important ethical aspect to consider concerning validity and reliability is that one should not make inappropriate claims of validity and reliability about the questionnaire that you are going to use. It is also unethical to argue that validity and reliability are irrelevant or unimportant and that the only matter of importance is how the respondents perceive the questionnaire. Face validity on its own is not enough proof of a questionnaire's validity[65], but other means of determining validity can also be used, such as having the questionnaire reviewed by a group of subject experts in the specific field relating to the questionnaire context. Thus, it is important to choose a questionnaire with proven validity and reliability, or to do validity and reliability testing of the questionnaire after collecting the data in order to provide proper evidence of validity and reliability. Figure 3.2 provides a clearer picture of what validity and reliability of a research method mean; these aspects are also applicable to a questionnaire used as part of a research method.

Neither valid nor reliable	**Reliable but not valid**
The research methods do not hit the heart of the research aim (not 'valid') and repeated attempts are unfocussed.	The research methods do not hit the heart of the research aim, but repeated attempts get almost the same (but wrong) results.
Fairly valid but not very reliable	**Valid and reliable**
The research methods hit the aim of the study fairly closely, but repeated attempts have very scattered results (not reliable).	The research methods hit the heart of the research aim, and repeated attempts all hit in the heart (similar results).

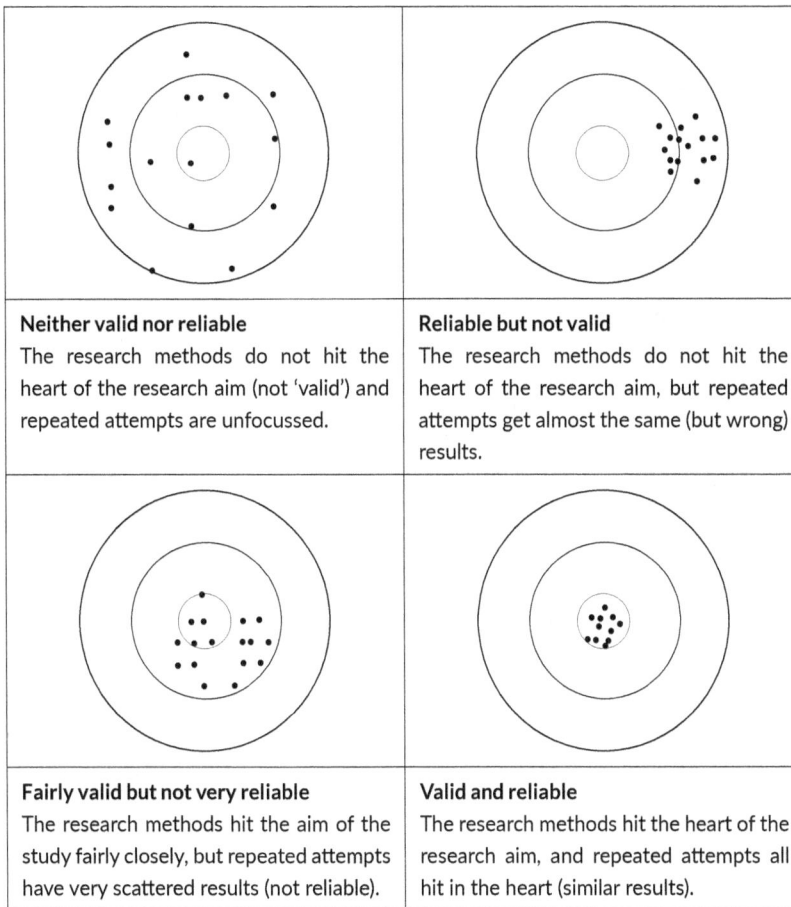

Figure 3.2: Reliability and validity[66]

The top left target indicates that the questionnaire is neither valid nor reliable, while the top right target indicates that the questionnaire is reliable but not valid in measuring what it is supposed to measure. The bottom left target indicates that the questionnaire is fairly valid, but repeated attempts have scattered results making the questionnaire unreliable. The bottom right target shows that the questionnaire is both valid and reliable.

Using existing, customised or newly developed survey instruments

Being aware of the importance of the choice of a survey instrument as outlined above, the next step would be to decide whether to use an existing or customised questionnaire or to develop a new questionnaire. The choice of questionnaire will relate directly to the type of organisational diagnosis that the organisation needs[67] and to keeping the strategic purpose of the diagnosis in mind, as discussed in chapter 1.

1.   Existing questionnaires

The choice of questionnaire will depend on the situation. There is a wide variety of **existing, validated questionnaires**, but these are not always easily available to the organisation. There are some questionnaires that are published in the academic literature and on the internet, but these often need to be tailor-made to suit the needs of the organisation[68]. (See table 3.3 for a list of some South African validated and reliable questionnaires.) There are ethical issues involved and often the questionnaires cannot be used without permission and sometimes have to be purchased from the developer. Two actions are involved in using others' questionnaires. Firstly, a formal request should be sent to the author to obtain the questionnaire, or permission to use the questionnaire if it is already in your possession, unless it is stated that the questionnaire is in the public domain or permission to use the questionnaire is automatically granted[69]. An example of the use of questionnaires that is automatically granted is when a consultant makes use of a survey software system, such as SurveyTracker, which has a library of items and scales on various topics that can be used once the system has been purchased and in return for paying an annual licence fee.

Secondly, the issue of plagiarism needs to be addressed when using a questionnaire that someone else developed or that belongs to another source. It is important to "attribute the material to the source in a manner consistent with the originator's or owner's specification"[70]. It is unethical to provide a survey instrument to a client as if it is your own work if it is from another source or owner[71].

Once a questionnaire has been purchased, it might be used again in the organisation and results might be compared, which provides useful trend data[72]. If a validated and reliable questionnaire belongs to a survey consultancy and they are contracted to conduct the survey, the questionnaire becomes available to the organisation for once-off use.

Existing questionnaires are useful when an organisation wants to change or develop in a certain direction and it turns out that there is a powerful instrument available, which is based on a well-researched model and which has been used extensively and successfully in other organisations. In this case the questionnaire is used in its original form. An example of such a questionnaire is Harrison and Stoke's organisational culture questionnaire[73], which is based on a model that divides an organisation into four organisational cultures (namely power, role, achievement or support cultures). However, an organisational culture instrument that was specifically developed for the South African context might be more beneficial to the organisation hoping to improve its organisational culture, because some international concepts and constructs (dimensions) might not be relevant to South African organisations.

2.   Customised questionnaires

Customisation of an existing questionnaire is possible under certain circumstances, such as adapting the terminology to suit the specific organisation, but not changing the actual meaning of the question, or removing one or two items that are not relevant to the organisation. Sometimes an organisation might need to measure certain constructs (dimensions) or certain concepts that are not covered in a specific questionnaire. To address this need, one or two question items might be added to the existing questionnaire under the relevant dimension. In our experience we have often come across the need to add or remove one or two questions for organisations. It is, however, recommended that the existing dimensions are not altered (too much), as this will affect the validity of the questionnaire. Should the questionnaire have to be changed, it is recommended to conduct validity and reliability tests, making use of statistical analyses such as Cronbach's Alpha (a measure of how well the scale items correlate with each other)[74] and factor analysis, once the data have been collected. Bear in mind that validation can only be conducted when a sufficient number of respondents, based on the number of questions in the questionnaire, has been reached. A ratio of 5 respondents to 1 scale-based question is the minimum requirement, particularly in small sample sizes, in which case findings need to be interpreted with caution. The more acceptable range would be 10 to 1[75]. An example of 500 respondents to a questionnaire with 80 scale-based questions would make the ratio 6 to 1.

Based on our experience, it is recommended that additional dimensions and question items are added at the end of a questionnaire and then analysed separately from the existing questionnaire dimensions and items. In this way validity and reliability are not compromised. Furthermore, if the survey is repeated at a later stage and the objective is to compare results to determine if there has been any change since the previous survey, it is advisable not to change the questions in the repeat survey. The results will then be easily comparable in survey tools and statistical analysis if the structure of the data collected remained the same in the initial and the repeated surveys. See chapter 6 for typical comparisons of results.

3.   Developing your own questionnaire

Sometimes it might be better to **develop your own questionnaire** and create new items that cater exactly to your organisation's needs; it might be the only way to formulate appropriate questions. Involving executives, management[76] and employees in this process can be beneficial in obtaining their understanding, commitment and buy-in for the organisational diagnostic process, and using the results towards improvement or required change.

Consultants sometimes have a substantial number of validated questions from their own database, which could be used in the development of a new questionnaire, suitable for the specific organisation and its needs. This process can shorten the time spent to develop a new questionnaire. Often the results of these items can be compared to benchmark results of other organisations where the items were measured. Although this comparison could detract from the organisation's focus on its own results, it has the advantage of having prior data available that proves the reliability of the items[77]. See chapter 6 where some typical comparative results are portrayed and discussed.

A question that you might pose is: When is it appropriate to draw on others' questionnaires? This question can be answered in the words of Kraut[78]:

"Using one or a few questionnaire items similar to those developed by someone else or attributed to published sources is not plagiarism, especially if the items deal with issues of common, general interest and do so in straightforward prose. There may be an infinite number of ways to ask the same question, but after reading enough examples, they all begin to look very much the same."

Bear in mind that copying portions of another person's questionnaire without obtaining permission and without specifically attributing it to that person, is regarded as plagiarism. This means that it is always safer to stick to the rule of first asking[79].

Other aspects that should be taken into account when developing a new questionnaire are the cost, time, knowledge and effort required in developing a useful tool that will produce meaningful results. Table 3.2 provides an overview of the advantages and disadvantages of the three options of questionnaires that the survey consultant or those who are going to conduct the organisational diagnosis should consider when deciding whether to use an existing or customised questionnaire, or develop a new questionnaire.

Table 3.2: Choice of a survey instrument for organisational diagnosis (compiled by EC Martins)

Choice of instrument	Advantages	Disadvantages
Existing validated questionnaire	• Validity already established: ensures that findings are accurate and actually represent the reality being measured. • Reliable in that it should produce consistent findings at different times and under different circumstances. • Saves time because the questionnaire has already been compiled and tested. • Benchmark results might be available.	• Might be expensive to buy. • Not always readily available and must be sourced or purchased from publishers/developers. • Might not meet your specific survey objectives. • Might require pilot testing in your organisation to test understanding of questionnaire. • Might need to confirm validity and reliability in a different environment.
Customised questionnaire	• Allows for flexibility in terms of measuring additional dimensions or statements. • Saves time as opposed to new design/development.	• Additional dimensions added to the validated questionnaire must be separately analysed. • Changing questions in repeat surveys complicates comparison of data with previous survey(s). • Might require pilot testing in your organisation to test understanding of questionnaire. • Might need to confirm the validity and reliability in a different environment.

Choice of instrument	Advantages	Disadvantages
New questionnaire	• Directly suited to organisation's needs. • Creates an opportunity to engage with executives and senior management, which in turn obtains their commitment to the survey. • Using questions from available question libraries saves time.	• Time consuming and costly to develop. • Requires specific knowledge and expertise on the topic to be surveyed and on questionnaire design. • Requires pilot testing. • Requires validation. • No benchmark results might be available.

When you consider the advantages and disadvantages of the different options of using an existing or customised questionnaire or developing your own, the choice depends very much on the needs of the organisation and what they would like to achieve with the survey. From our experience over many years of conducting surveys, most organisations have preferred to use a valid and reliable questionnaire with minor customisation to suit the needs of the organisation.

DIFFERENT TYPES AND APPLICATIONS OF SURVEYS AND WHERE TO SOURCE EXISTING, VALIDATED QUESTIONNAIRES

In the section below the following question is answered: What types of questionnaires are available and where and how can I obtain them?

In the South African context there are many survey instruments (questionnaires) that have been developed from a scientific research foundation perspective and tested in the South African environment, with evidence of validity and reliability. Table 3.3 summarises some of these instruments, their purpose (or what they measure), the dimensions and main constructs, the method or analyses to ensure validation, and where to find the published articles and contact details of the researchers.

Table 3.3: Some examples of South African developed survey instruments (questionnaires) (Compiled by EC Martins and N Martins)

Assessment instrument/ Questionnaire	Purpose of the study/ Measuring instrument	Dimensions and main constructs	Method/ Analysis	Authors/ Researcher
Employee engagement	To measure employee engagement concurrently at the individual and organisational levels.	• Team • Organisational satisfaction • Customer service • Organisational commitment • Immediate manager • Strategy and implementation	Based on the work of Masey and Schneider, 2008. Questionnaire, Principal Axis Factoring (PAF), confirmatory factor analysis, structural equation modelling (SEM) and invariance testing.	Nienaber, H. & Martins N. (2014) Martins, N. (2015) Martins, N. & Ledimo, O. (2016)
Organisational culture (South African Culture Instrument – SACI)	The SACI measures the extent to which employees identify with the various elements of the organisation's existing and ideal culture	• Leadership • Means to achieve objectives • Management processes • Employee needs and objectives • Vision and mission • External environment • Diversity strategy	Originally based on the work of Schein, 1980. Questionnaire, focus groups and interviews. Used in a number of research projects and by academic students. PAF, SEM invariance testing.	Martins, N. & Coetzee M. (2007) Martins, N. (2014)
Employee and work engagement in multi-cultural settings (Benchmark of Engagement – BeQ)	The BeQ measures the human energy to perform on individual, group and organisational domains while considering multi-cultural worldviews	• I-engage – factors that contribute to employee engagement • We-engage – factors that impact on work engagement • Org-engage – perceptions about organisational doing and being, inclusivity • Multi-cultural aspects as described by spiral dynamics	Based on a doctoral study and a theoretical culture model. Questionnaire, story-telling, focus groups, interviews and workshops, reliability analysis, invariance testing.	Viljoen, RC. (2015) Viljoen, RC. (2016)

Assessment instrument/ Questionnaire	Purpose of the study/ Measuring instrument	Dimensions and main constructs	Method/ Analysis	Authors/ Researcher
Employee satisfaction	To measure employee satisfaction	• Vision and mission • Values • Leadership • Communication • Teamwork • Relationships • Health and safety • Employee equity and diversity • Training • Human resources management • Job satisfaction • HIV/AIDS • Change management	Based on two doctoral studies. Questionnaire, confirmatory factor analysis (CFA), SEM, longitudinal study	Martins, N. & Coetzee, M. (2007) Ledimo, O. & Martins, N. (2014)
Information security culture	Measures the perceptions towards information security to identify what and how to improve the protection (integrity, confidentiality, availability and privacy) of the organisation's information from the threat that human behaviour poses.	• Information asset management • Information security management • Change management • User management • Information security policies • Information security programmes • Trust • Information security leadership • Training and awareness	Based on a doctoral study and a theoretical culture model. Questionnaire, interviews and workshops, PAF, reliability analysis, invariance testing.	Da Veiga, A. & Martins, N. (2015) Martins, N. & Da Veiga, A. (2015)
Change agent identification assessment tool	To identify change agents in large organisations	• Willingness • Commitment • Personality traits • Availability • Facilitator	Based on a doctoral study. Questionnaire, PCA, PAF, and reliability analysis.	Van der Linde-de Klerk, M., Martins, N. & De Beer, M. (2015)

Assessment instrument/ Questionnaire	Purpose of the study/ Measuring instrument	Dimensions and main constructs	Method/ Analysis	Authors/ Researcher
Organisational trust	The measure-ment of organi-sational trust	• Trust relationship • Team management • Work support • Credibility • Organisational trust • Information sharing • Change	Based on extensive studies in SA, doctoral and masters research. Questionnaire, focus groups. PCA, CFA, SEM, reliability and validity.	Martins, N. & von der Ohe, H. (2011) Von der Ohe, H. & Martins, N. (2010)
Organisational climate	To measure organisational climate on a total level as well as the different components of organisational climate.	• Trust • Training and development • Transformation and diversity • Job satisfaction • Leadership • Employee wellness • Communication • Performance management • Remuneration and rewards • Teamwork • Work environment • Organisational image	Based on a number of SA studies, doctoral and masters research. Questionnaire, PAF, CFA, step-wise linear regression and SEM	Castro, ML. & Martins, N. (2010)
Knowledge retention	To identify the factors that would enhance or impede the retention of knowledge in organisations. The focus is based on the knowledge that accumulates over time and through the experience of individual employees.	• Strategic impact of knowledge loss • Knowledge behaviours • Organisational support • People knowledge loss risks • Leadership • Power play • Knowledge attitudes and emotions • Knowledge growth and development • Performance management	Based on doctoral study. Questionnaire, factor analysis, SEM	Martins, EC. & Martins, N. (2011) Martins, EC. & Meyer, HWJ. (2012) Martins, EC. & Martins, N. (2012)

All the instruments listed in table 3.3 can be used in an organisational diagnosis, depending on the purpose of the diagnosis. The questionnaires might also be adapted to suit the specific needs of the organisation, such as terminology changes and other changes as described in the previous section. In the section below, the question about how to develop a new focused questionnaire is answered.

DEVELOPING A FOCUSED QUESTIONNAIRE FOR A QUANTITATIVE SURVEY, INCLUDING A PILOT SURVEY

Developing a questionnaire is a major part of the planning and design phase of the organisational diagnostic process[80]. According to Church and Waclawski[81], a well-developed questionnaire should be successful in measuring what it is supposed to measure, well received by the organisation and actionable, which is not an easy task. It is thus advisable to assemble a **project/design team.** This is discussed below.

Project/design team

Often in practice, in the South African context, the survey design team and the survey project team is one and the same team, as long as they include content and design experts to provide input on the survey content, which should be in line with the purpose of the survey. The project/design team should consist of a mix of members who are either experts or experienced survey consultants in the subject field or in survey design and construction. It is also essential to include the survey sponsor (often a representative from the Human Resources/Human Capital or Organisational Development Department) of the organisation, in the team[82]. If a consultant is contracted as the principal investigator to design a new questionnaire, working closely with such an internal project team is advisable. Other members included in the project team would be an information technology expert responsible for online hosting of the survey, a survey software expert, communication and marketing members to advertise the survey through communiqués by making use of various media, and survey champions. The role of survey champions would be to communicate the survey by word-of-mouth, team meetings and local emails, and to provide feedback and suggestions on the survey to the project team.

Typical members of a survey project/design team are displayed in figure 3.3.

```
┌─────────────────────────────────────────────────────────┐
│                  Project/Design Team                      │
│            headed by the principal investigator           │
└─────────────────────────────────────────────────────────┘
```

Content and design experts	Survey sponsor	Technology and survey software experts	Communication and marketing experts	Survey champions

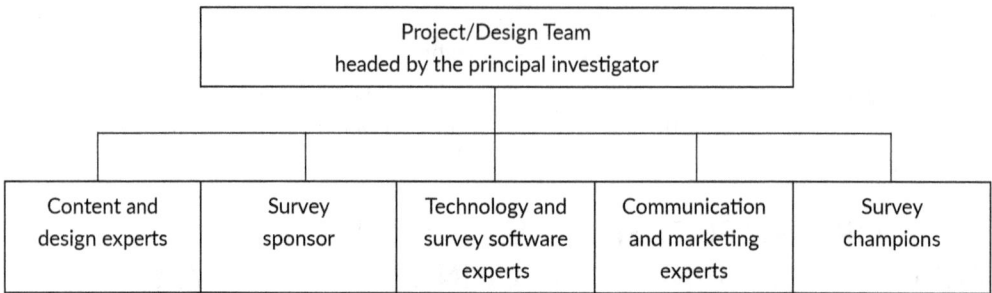

Figure 3.3: Survey project/design team in the South African context (adapted from Church and Waclawski[83])

The project/design team as displayed in figure 3.3 must be briefed regarding their roles and deliverables and the purpose and objectives of the survey[84]. They must participate in the timeline and action planning of the survey process. At this stage, questionnaire development can begin, which is discussed in the section below.

Questionnaire development

Questionnaire development involves three processes, namely: construction from a conceptual perspective, construction from a technical perspective and, a testing phase, comprising pre-testing and pilot testing processes. These aspects are portrayed in figure 3.4.

The survey project/design team is the core of the survey development process that has to clarify the purpose of the survey, involve different people in the organisation, and use different methods to develop the content of the questionnaire from a conceptual perspective. The technical structure of the questionnaire pertains to writing well-designed questions, selecting scale formats, and designing the structure and layout of online and paper versions in different languages, if required. Once the questionnaire has been finalised from both a conceptual and a technical perspective, the questionnaire has to be pre-tested and pilot tested to finalise the questionnaire that will be administered in the organisation. These main components are discussed in more detail below.

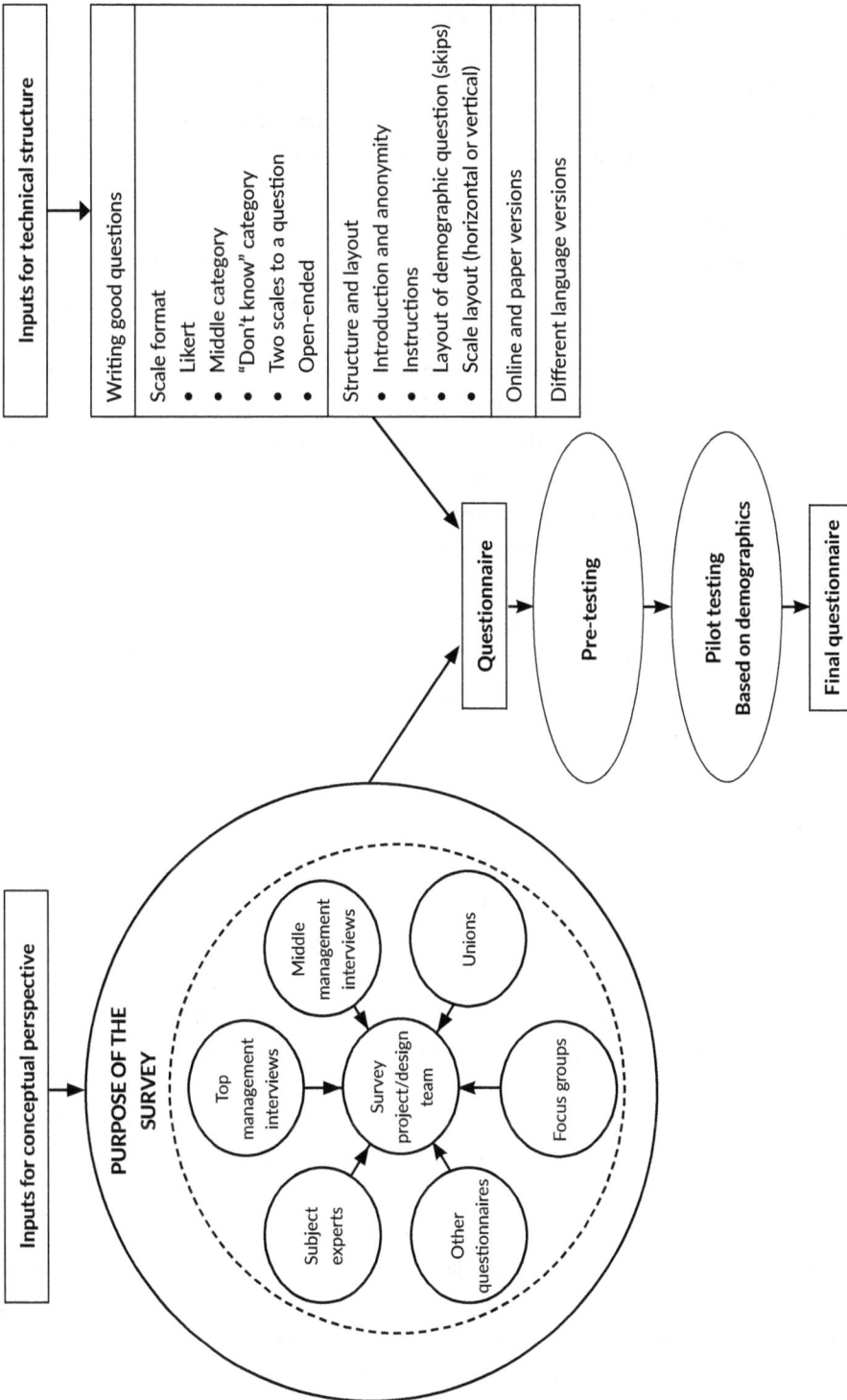

Figure 3.4: Developing a focused questionnaire for a quantitative survey (Compiled by EC Martins)

Questionnaire development from a conceptual perspective

The survey's intended **purpose** is the guiding force in deciding which topics should be covered in the survey[85]. In the case of newly developed questionnaires as well as in the case of customising questionnaires, the consultant should ensure that it fulfills the organisation's purpose for the project[86].

The project/design team must **identify the areas** that need to be measured in the survey. This is where the contributions of subject experts and other stakeholders come into play. Interviews with top and middle management will help the project/design team to identify key issues. Information can be gathered in focus groups from employees who are representative of the workforce in terms of levels, race, gender and business units within the organisation. In the South African context it is also imperative to include the unions from the start of the survey process, because they can easily jeopardise its successful completion by influencing their members not to participate if the union representatives are not well-informed and in agreement with the survey content and process. The authors of this chapter were involved in an organisational diagnosis for a manufacturing company, which was stopped by the union because they felt they were not sufficiently involved in the survey process. This had the effect of delaying the project for more than two months.

The process of involvement must be facilitated carefully so that the focus of the sessions remains on obtaining input for the questionnaire and not allowing it to turn into a debate or an argument[87]. It is, however, important to realise that the purpose of including stakeholders is not for each group to decide what should be included and what not, but to provide input on key issues experienced in the organisation.

There are two different approaches that might be followed to compile the questionnaire:

1. Compile a first draft of the questionnaire based on the purpose of the survey, previous experience, other questionnaires and a database of questions, if available. The next step would be to update the topics and question content based on the information gathered from various stakeholders to ensure that key aspects/issues are covered in the questionnaire.
2. First conduct the interviews and focus groups to identify key topics and then consider other questionnaires and input from subject experts to compile the questions. You should conduct these sessions with a theoretical model as background. This is to ensure that all the relevant aspects pertaining to the constructs to be measured are covered and that irrelevant concepts or issues are not introduced. See chapter 5 on planning and conducting of focus groups and interviews.

Borg and Mastrangelo recommend that it is always better to assemble a solid first draft of the questionnaire (once the key topics have been identified), rather than beginning with "spontaneous ideas made by workshop participants". To the novice, questionnaire development might appear to be easy, but it is best to work with people who have extensive knowledge and experience of the subject field and questionnaire design, in order to avoid pitfalls, mistakes and shortcomings[88].

The final version remains with the survey sponsor and the questionnaire must be approved by top management (executive team).

One of the most important sources to use in questionnaire development is **other questionnaires**. If some questions from other questionnaires are used, the source must be acknowledged and referenced to in the documentation (report) (see the discussion about using existing, customised or newly developed survey instruments).

In the early stages of developing a new questionnaire the following questions come to mind[89]:

1. What topics should be included?
2. What topics are of a sensitive nature or not important enough to measure and should therefore be left out?
3. How should the questions be formulated?
4. What demographics should be included?
5. Should the questionnaire be translated into other languages?

Once the information has been gathered from different stakeholders, summarised and integrated, the key topics to be measured in the survey from the organisational perspective can be identified. Typical topics that can be measured are:

1. levels of trust;
2. managerial competences;
3. employment equity processes:
    *   recruitment
    *   promotion
    *   learning and development;
4. policies and procedures;
5. skills development ;
6. relationships;
7. the organisational climate;
8. gender equity;
9. racial equity; and
10. employee wellness.

There is an unvoiced assumption amongst some researchers that any organisational survey should cover a minimum set of topics such as satisfaction with salary and promotion. However, when a survey is intended to bring about organisational change and development, these types of topics might be counter-productive because they are often unsupportable[90], and the consultant and project/design team need be aware of this potential pitfall.

An important part of organisational diagnosis is to use a **theoretical model** to gain better insight into the circumstances and current functioning of the organisation[91], and to understand organisational phenomena and how the organisation is managed to improve overall effectiveness and performance[92]. Models are developed within a conceptual framework and describe the relationship between different components of the organisation, their context and effectiveness[93]. However, it should be realised that a model is only a partial representation of a phenomenon (conceptual framework). The most obvious aspects of the model are emphasised[94], but the model helps to understand and improve organisational performance. There is no single best model. The consultant can choose a model that lends itself to understanding the particular situation, and he or she must understand the model thoroughly. It should be appropriate to the culture of the client organisation and it must be sufficiently comprehensive to enable data to be gathered about the organisation[95].

Models can inform the project/design team about the dimensions that can be measured in an organisational diagnosis. Examples of assessment frameworks and models that might be used are listed in table 3.4.

Table 3.4: Assessment frameworks and models which assess the organisational effectiveness of a total organisation[96]

Name of framework or model	Reference
Porter, Lawler and Hackman's Model of Individual Performance in Organisations	Porter, Lawler & Hackman (1976)
Weisbord's Six-Box Model	Weisbord (1976)
The Nadler-Tushman Congruence Model for Organizational Analysis	Nadler & Tushman (1977)
The 7-S/8-S Framework	Waterman, Peters & Phillips (1980); Higgins (2005)
Tichy's Technical Political Cultural (TPC) Framework	Tichy (1983)
The Causal Model of Organizational Performance	Burke & Litwin (1992)
The Balanced Score Card	Kaplan & Norton (1992)
The South African Excellence Model for Local Government	Nel & Haycock (2005)
The High Performance Model	Wiley (1996)
High Performance Framework	De Waal (2010)

As mentioned earlier in the discussion about using existing questionnaires, in many instances the measuring instruments available might not cover the aspects you intend to measure. The survey consultant then needs to investigate the various available assessment frameworks and models. Olivier[97] compiled an interesting comparison of the approaches to organisational effectiveness of different assessment frameworks or models, as per table 3.5 below.

Table 3.5: Comparison between assessment frameworks and models and traditional approaches to organisational effectiveness[98]

Assessment framework or model	Traditional approaches to organisational effectiveness				
	Goal approach	Systems resource approach	Internal processes approach	Strategic constituencies approach	Conflicting values approach
Porter, Lawler and Hackman's Model of Individual Performance (1976)	√	X	X	X	X
Weisbord's Six-Box Model (1976)	X	X	√	√	X
The Nadler-Tushman Congruence Model (1977)	X	X	√ .	X	X
The 7-S (1980 and 8-S Framework (2005)	√	X	√	X	X
Tichy's TPC Framework (1983)	X	X	√	X	X
The Burke-Litwin Causal Model of Organizational Performance (1992)	X	X	√	X	X
The Balanced Score Card (1992)	X	X	√	√	X
The South African Excellence Model for Local Government (1997)	√	X	√	√	X
The High Performance Model (2010)	X	X	√	√	X

Once the purpose of the survey has been clarified and information has been gathered to inform the key topics of the survey, the questionnaire must be developed. Related to question design is the **length of the questionnaire**. In our experience, a questionnaire that consists of about 80 content questions and some demographic questions is a reasonable length to complete within a reasonable time. If the questionnaire is too long, respondents might become tired and might be prone to answer the questions quickly without carefully thinking about their responses. If the questionnaire is too short, you may not be able to measure the different dimensions of the survey adequately and to make meaningful interpretations from the results. The rule of thumb is that each dimension must consist of at least five items[99].

Questionnaire development from a technical structure perspective

The aspects involved in developing the questionnaire from a technical perspective, namely writing well-designed questions and statements; deciding on the format; coming up with a structure and layout (including the demographical/biographical questions); creating different versions for completion (online or paper), and translation into different languages, are displayed in figure 3.4 and are discussed below.

1. Writing well-designed questions

Questionnaires may consist of different types of questions and statements that require an answer from the people who are completing the questionnaire. Biographical and demographical questions are usually stated as questions (eg: "In which business unit do you work?"). Some questions might require a yes/no answer (eg: "Have you received information security training in the last 12 months?"), and some questions might be phrased as statements (eg: "I am satisfied with the way my work performance is evaluated"). Although there are other formats of questions such as questions that require multiple answers, for example selecting more than one option from a list of items (eg: "Please select which of the following training courses you have attended in the past 12 months"), the above mentioned formats are used most commonly in organisational diagnosis.

Writing well-designed questions is important in compiling questionnaires and the wording of each question needs careful consideration to ensure that the responses are valid, in other words that the questions measure what you think they do[100]. Table 3.6 below is a checklist of aspects to be aware of when formulating questions:

Table 3.6: Checklist for question and statement wording (adapted from Saunders et al.[101])

• An item should be brief, concise and to-the-point (long items are difficult to understand).
• Use simple words and avoid jargon or abbreviations.
• Items should preferably be **stated positively** (negatively phrased items that include the word "not" are difficult to understand).
• Items should only measure **one concept** (items that include the word "and" usually include more than one concept and should be avoided).
• Any customised items, or items not drawn from a valid pool of question items, should be pre-tested.
• Items should not 'talk down to' respondents as if they would not understand the items.
• Avoid questions that require specialised knowledge.
• Avoid ambiguous questions such as "How do you feel about the company's mission?"
• Avoid sensitive, personal or threatening issues that might cause offence.
• Avoid biased items that imply a specific answer (eg: "Many people believe that too little money is spent on our Public Health Service. Do you believe this to be the case?" To this question, respondents are more likely to answer "yes".)
• Avoid negatively positioned questions that have a double negative (eg. "My manager is not irresponsible about his duties." Rather use: "My manager is responsible about his duties").
• Avoid double-barrelled questions that touch on more than one issue, yet allow for only one answer (e.g. "How satisfied are you with your salary and job conditions?" Rather formulate two separate questions. Furthermore, you might need to explain what you mean by "job conditions" by providing examples (eg working hours, holiday entitlement, sick leave).

2. Scale format

The most common scale used in questionnaires for organisational diagnosis is the Likert scale, where respondents are required to rate a statement such as "I trust my manager" on a scale from "strongly agree" to "strongly disagree". The Likert scale makes it possible to calculate an overall average per statement or per dimension (consisting of a number of statements), as well as an overall average for the entire measurement. Borg and Mastrangelo[102] state that virtually any questionnaire that aims at measuring employees' attitudes or opinions can be expressed in a Likert format. Various Likert scales ranging between 5-, 7- or 9-point can be used, however, the 5-point scale is the preferred choice. Krosnik and Fabrigar[103] argue that a 7-point scale does not help to make the responses more reliable or valid. Offering more categories would lead to data that only seems more precise, but Sudman, Bradburn and Schwartz[104] indicated in experiments with scales ranging between 0 and 100 that respondents mostly picked the "simple" numbers such as 0, 25, 50, 75 or 100. On the other hand three categories can cause problems because it is too simplistic and respondents may feel that it attempts to manipulate their judgement. Furthermore, almost all employee survey benchmark values currently available are on a 5-point scale[105]. Experience with the development of questionnaires in the South African context has shown that most organisations prefer a 5-point scale. The main reason is that most employees are familiar with a 5-point performance appraisal scale.

Sometimes Likert scales with four categories, omitting the middle unsure/undecided value, are used to force a decision on whether respondents tend to agree or disagree. Yet some respondents might not have a clear opinion and would then choose a possible agree or disagree category, or they might skip the item[106], hence leading to incorrectly expressed data or no data, which might lead to a skewed interpretation of results. On the other hand, respondents might lean toward selecting the middle option as a convenient way of avoiding the issues. It is difficult to determine whether respondents who selected the middle option had a mixed opinion, an escapist response or no opinion[107]. In practice it makes sense to interpret the middle category results as part of the disagree/strongly disagree group, which indicates areas of concerns or challenges that need to be addressed. If the respondents are unsure (middle category) it indicates that they either do not have information to make a decision or that low-trust levels might exist in the organisation.

Some people request that a "don't know" option should be used as part of the scale, but experimental research by Krosnick et al.[108] showed that "attraction to no-opinion options was found to be greatest among those respondents lowest in cognitive skills" or those who devoted little effort to the process. "Don't know" options also imply that respondents should be reasonably sure to give the right answer, whereas in employee attitude and opinion surveys there are no right or wrong answers.

In summary, "don't know" responses remain difficult to interpret. It is better to try and make sure that most items measure issues where almost any employee has an opinion or attitude, and that the items are formulated so that most employees are able to answer the items[109].

Some questionnaires include two Likert type scales per item, such as an agree-disagree scale and an importance scale ranging from not important to very important. Although the importance scale might add another additional perspective on the survey results, Borg and Mastrangelo[110] are of the opinion that it "yields little "actionable" information". The authors also find that the use of the two Likert scales per item does not yield favourable results. Respondents do not always use the importance scale with discretion; most of the times they indicate that all constructs are equally important for the organisation.

Open-ended scales that allow respondents to enter comments in text format have become quite popular, especially with online surveys. The value of the comments is that it provides additional explanatory information that cannot be provided by scale category items. In other words, it gives the respondents an opportunity to complement the information collected by the closed questions[111]. Examples of comment questions are:

- If there is anything else you want to remark on regarding the climate of the organisation, please use the space below.
- What do you appreciate most about working at Company ABC?
- What can be done to make Company ABC a better place to work?

Drawbacks and risks of open-ended questions, if answered on paper, are that the handwriting is not always clear, or sometimes might be written in another language as opposed to English, which means that it must be deciphered, corrected and transcribed. Data capturing is expensive because data capturers charge per key stroke and it takes a lot of time to capture. Online entry of comments is easy, but line spacing must be limited in the survey design to reduce long pages of comments, which are difficult to interpret.

The value of open-ended comments relates to the possibility of picking up on general tendencies, which can be used in support of closed question results. It is best to provide the comments verbatim (original words) and leave it to the respective work groups or managers to interpret[112]. The analysis and interpretation of open-ended questions can be time consuming. Just think of the amount of data produced if 1,000 participants completed a few open-ended questions. In such an instance it is advisable to use well-trained data-capturers to capture paper responses and software packages such as ATLAS.ti to analyse the open-ended questions.

3.   Structure and layout of the questionnaire

The first part of the questionnaire is the **cover page and introduction**, which explains the purpose of the questionnaire. It also provides information on the number of questions, how long it will take to complete the survey, confidentiality aspects, the different sections (i.e. demographical questions, scale-based questions that measure the main topic of the questionnaire), **instructions** on how to complete the survey, and contact details for content-based queries and for any online technical errors that might occur.

In both online and paper versions of the questionnaire, the **demographic** items, such as gender, age, race, business unit, department, level, tenure, and so forth, can be placed after the introduction page. In online versions the responses to essential demographic items can be set as a "must complete" scale, which will not allow the respondent to continue with the survey if the question is not answered. The essential items, such as business unit and level, can be decided on by the project/design team. "Must complete" must be used with care because respondents might become annoyed if they are forced to complete questions and exit from the survey. In paper versions one would have to rely on the willingness of the respondents to complete the demographic questions.

Online surveys make it possible to control the flow of the survey, based on the responses entered by setting up "skips" to certain questions. If, for example, respondents have to select their business unit in the business unit question, each category could be set to skip to the particular question containing the departments of each business unit. This is particularly useful in large organisations with complex structures.

Most survey software packages allow you to define the number of columns, scale choice flow from left to right or top to bottom, and number of scale categories. A software package such as SurveyTracker allows for unlimited pages and questions per survey and up to 300 scale-choices per scale. Many different scale types can be designed, such as fixed sum, forced ranking, semantic differential, yes/no and true/false. The scale types most often used in organisational diagnoses are the single response (Likert/ordinal), multiple response and write-in text scales. Examples of these scales are displayed in table 3.7.

Table 3.7: Scales for organisational diagnosis questionnaires (adapted from Training Technologies[113])

Scale	Description	Example
Single response – ordinal	Provides a series of possible choices from which respondents are to select only one response.	1 What is your job level? ○ Executive ○ Manager ○ Non-managerial employee
Single response – Likert	Provides a series of possible choices from which respondents are to select only one response.	1 I trust my colleagues. ○ Strongly disagree ○ Disagree ○ Unsure ○ Agree ○ Strongly agree
Write-in response-text	Write-in areas in which the respondent may enter their verbatim responses.	1 Please provide any suggestions you have for management to make company ABC a better place to work ------------------------- -------------------------
Yes/No		1 Do you have a disability? ○ Yes ○ No

4.   Online and paper versions

In the South African context, depending on the type of organisation, the survey can be conducted online if all employees have access to computers, or a combination of online and paper versions can be used. Some survey software allow for an accessibility version of the questionnaire for respondents who have visual impairment. The accessibility version of the survey contains a simplified high-contrast layout that is modified from the original survey layout. You can offer both versions of the survey to your respondents and they can then select their preferred version for completion[114].

5.   Different language versions

In the South African context with its 11 official languages, it is sometime necessary to translate the English questionnaire into one or two African languages, such as Zulu and Sotho. Sometimes European languages such as Portuguese and French are required if the survey is conducted in a Southern African environment with a global context, such as the banking environment where banks have branches across Africa. Using many languages can quickly increase costs,[115] however, another issue that needs to be considered is the fact that some concepts in English are not easily translated into the African languages. Borg and Mastrangelo[116] mention that the main requirement for translating a questionnaire is for the items to be equivalent in the different language versions. Blind translations (eg by computer) are insufficient because the meaning of an item could be changed. An alternative method of data collection that may be considered is to have only an English version of the questionnaire and then conduct facilitated questionnaire completion sessions with facilitators who can speak the different required languages, and who then translate the questions that are not clearly understood by the respondents. This is also a costly method and the pros and cons have to be weighed up to decide on the best way to address the language issue.

Questionnaire pre-testing by an expert group

Pre-testing of the questionnaire is an important aspect from a content point of view in terms of validity. Several experts[117] agree that pre-testing a questionnaire is essential. The questionnaire may be reviewed by a small group of five to ten subject experts within the organisation to establish if it has content and face validity (a judgement that the items really measure the dimensions and appear to make sense.)[118]

The process of pre-testing usually goes through several versions of design, review and adaptation. The experts could be asked to comment on the representativeness and suitability of your questions and to make suggestions on the structure of the questionnaire[119]. The survey consultant/project team should carefully consider all the comments of the respondents who participated in the pre-test because they are often insightful and helpful, but they need not accept all comments[120]. Once the data have been collected, the reliability of the questionnaire can be tested by means of Cronbach's Alpha (see discussion on *Validity and reliability of instruments*), and the validity of the questionnaire in terms of structure of the questionnaire items can be tested and confirmed via factor analysis[121].

Pilot testing

The last step in the design phase is the pilot test. The purpose of the pilot test is to refine the questionnaire so that respondents will experience no problems in understanding and answering the questions[122]. A pilot test is the only opportunity in which people who were not directly involved in the planning, development and construction of the questionnaire will have to provide their unbiased feedback[123].

To conduct the test, a representative sample is selected from different groups comprising the actual participants of the organisation (such as genders, race groups and job levels). Explain the purpose of testing the questionnaire, i.e. fine-tuning it but not measuring their opinions. After the session the completed questionnaires will be collected, evaluated and refined, and then destroyed. While the test respondents are completing the questionnaire, observe them from a distance to evaluate how long it takes them to complete the questionnaire[124].

After completing the questionnaire, the following questions can be discussed in a focus group by working through the questionnaire, page by page:

1. What was your general reaction to the questionnaire?
2. Were the instructions clear?
3. Which, if any, questions were unclear or ambiguous?
4. In your opinion were any major topics omitted?
5. Was the layout of the questionnaire clear and attractive?
6. Do you think your co-workers will have any difficulty completing the questionnaire?
7. Any other comments[125].

Misunderstandings should be explored and participants should be asked for suggestions[126]. After the focus group discussion, the project team should work through the comments and do the final fine-tuning of the questionnaire.

Final questionnaire

The last step in the process of questionnaire development is to obtain final approval and sign-off from the executive team. Once final approval has been obtained, the online version of the questionnaire can be tested. Focus groups can also be used to explore the needs and expectations of employees when a new questionnaire is developed by the project team members, and then the survey will be ready to implement.

DEVELOPING A QUALITATIVE FRAMEWORK FOR FOCUS GROUPS

The idea behind the focus group method is that group processes can help participants to explore and clarify their views in ways that would be less easily accessible in a one-on-one interview[127]. Depending on your diagnostic objective, the focus group can be used alone or in conjunction with other methods. Focus groups can also be used to explore the needs and expectations of employees when a new questionnaire is developed.

Focus groups allow information to emerge and be formed in an interactive process of dialogue and discussion, whereas employee surveys are an efficient way of gathering data on predefined issues[128]. The data obtained from the focus group sessions are particularly effective in providing information about how people think, feel, or act regarding a specific issue under assessment. A focus group is a type of in-depth interview accomplished in a group context. This session presents characteristics defined with regard to the proposal, size, composition and interview procedures.

Establishing a focus group sample

In planning for the focus group sample, a chronological plan should be developed, including the following activities: development of the participants' representative lists, identification of the participants' characteristics, drafting of a list of the potential participants, and recruiting the participants.

An important determinant of the **number of groups** is the number of different subgroups of populations required for the diagnosis. In an organisational context, the different stakeholders are the different subgroups which can be considered, such as employees, management, union, community and service providers/clients. The more homogeneous the groups in terms of background and perspectives, the smaller the number of groups needed[129].

It is important to note that a single group is never enough, therefore a single group can be divided into groups with different segments based on the various **characteristics of the existent population** in the organisation[130]. You can have four or more groups representing employees, management, union, consumers, community and clients of your organisation. A single focus group should not be used during the diagnostic process, because the facilitator can come across a "cold" group, where the participants are quiet and reluctant to participate. Multiple focus group sessions are essential because they can be representative of the characteristics of the population in the organisation.

Characteristics of the population in the organisation are not limited to the stakeholder groupings, but include biographical factors such as age, gender, job level, educational level, language and tenure. These factors can also be used to determine a **participant list** in a focus group session. When selecting the participants, an issue is the bias of the sample, which is not the same as reliability[131]. You should be able to determine whether the participants on the list possess the indispensable characteristics to participate in the focus group sessions.

When deciding on the **size of your focus group,** you should be mindful that the group must be small enough so that everybody has an opportunity to share their perceptions, but be diverse enough to be able to provide the different perceptions on the issue being investigated. In terms of the number of participants in the sessions, the usual approach is to use groups comprising 6 to 10 individuals. This is a quick and relatively easy way to set up a group[132].

Selection and recruitment of the sample from the population should be based on organisational members who are capable of providing more significant information[133]. It is advisable that you recruit sample participants of individuals who do not know each other; participants who know each other socially or professionally have difficulty concentrating on the topic of the diagnosis. They may also be inhibited from expressing their perceptions because of their fear of other participants that they do not trust.

Facilitation of focus groups

The facilitation of focus groups requires competent survey consultants who have interpersonal skills and knowledge of group dynamics. Facilitation should aim to cover the maximum number of important aspects of the issue under diagnosis; provide data that is as specific as possible; promote interaction that explores the participants' feelings in some depth; and take into account the personal context in which the participants generated their responses to the issue[134].

The process flow of the focus group sessions should include the duration, introduction, setting group norms, purpose of the focus group, data capturing, duration of sessions and closing remarks. Differing approaches by facilitators may cause bias in the data, thus the following process flow of the sessions should be the same for all focus group sessions:

The duration, venue and seating of each session are critical in data collection. Focus group sessions normally last between one and two hours each. Normally, there is no break during the session because it is a short period. In terms of the venue, it should be conveniently located and easily found by the participants. It should foster an appropriate disposition of the participants and be equipped with audio-visual facilities. The participants should be seated at a U-shaped table, with each participant's name visible to the others, and with the facilitator seated at the head of the table, in front of the participants.

The **beginning of the sessions** should be similar in nature, independent of the degree of involvement adopted by the facilitator[135]. Initially, the facilitator introduces the topic in an honest and quite generic way. The first round of questions allows for a quick answer (10 to 20 seconds), and it enables the identification of characteristics that the participants have in common. Introductory questions introduce the general topic of discussion, and provide the participants with an opportunity to contemplate previous experiences[136].

The facilitator presents some basic **group norms or rules**, such as only one person speaks at a time; lateral chats should not take place; everybody should participate, and so forth. Participants are also informed that the session will be recorded.

A list of **topics or a line of questioning** may be used to conduct the sessions, because the topic guide lists words or sentences that remind the facilitator of the topics of interest. You should have a broad or open-ended question that can be discussed in the focus group sessions. Transition questions move the conversation towards the key questions that focus on the diagnosis[137]. They usually vary from two to five questions and are the ones that require more attention. This approach seems more spontaneous to the participants and is more appropriate when the facilitator(s) treat all the sessions in the same way. The same line of questions should be used for a series of sessions with the aim of obtaining similar content, which allows for a more efficient analysis of data and eliminates language differences. Use of the topic guide is most appropriate when the facilitators of the focus group sessions are not always the same.

The main method of **obtaining or collecting the data** is from the recording. Audio-visual recording is fundamental to assure the quality of the data[138], while flip chart notes can help you to record the discussion. A scribe is helpful so that the facilitator can focus on the process. The fundamental data produced by this technique are the transcripts of the group discussions and the facilitator's reflections and explanations. Group dynamics can provide useful information that individual data collection does not provide[139]. A focus group is useful for gaining insight into a topic that may be more difficult to gather data on through other data collection methods. Focus groups can usefully be viewed as the qualitative counterpart to the quantitative survey, in that they are typically used in a qualitative approach to obtain a broad range of information about events[140].

The facilitator should use ending questions when **closing the session.** They should consider everything that was said up to that point, allow the participants to consider all the comments shared in the discussion, and identify the most important ones. The facilitator also has to summarise in two to three minutes the key questions and main ideas that emerged during the discussion. It is important to confirm with the participants if the summary is appropriate or captured the discussion accurately[141]. Following the summary and final questions, the facilitator can briefly explain the purpose of the diagnosis, and then convey appreciation to the participants for sharing their perceptions.

Pros and cons of focus groups

When considering focus groups as a method of data collection, you need to be familiar with their benefits and limitation in a diagnostic process (Krueger and Morgan)[142]. Table 3.8 below presents the benefits and limitations of focus group sessions:

Table 3.8: Focus group benefits and limitations[143]

Benefits of focus groups	Limitations of focus groups
• They are comparatively easier to drive or conduct. • They allow topics to be explored and hypotheses to be generated. • Data can be collected from the group interaction, which concentrates on the topic of the researcher's interest.	• They are not based on a natural atmosphere. • The researcher has less control over the data that are generated. • It is not possible to know if the interaction in the group contemplates group or individual behaviour.

Benefits of focus groups	Limitations of focus groups
• It has high "face validity" (data). • It is a low cost method in relation to other methods. • It promptly supplies the results (in terms of evidence of the meeting of the group). • It allows the researcher to increase the size of the sample of the qualitative studies.	• The data analysis is more difficult to perform. The interaction of the group forms a social atmosphere and the comments should be interpreted within this context • It requires well-trained interviewers. • It is an effort to assemble the groups. • The discussion should be conducted in an atmosphere that facilitates dialogue.

In addition to the above benefits, Kitzinger[144] indicates that some potential advantages of focus groups methods during diagnosis are the following:

1. They do not discriminate against participants who cannot read or write.
2. They can encourage participation from those who are reluctant to be interviewed individually (such as those intimidated by the formality and isolation of a one-to-one interview).
3. They can encourage contributions from people who feel they have nothing to say or who are deemed to be "unresponsive participants" (but engage in the discussion generated by other group members).

However, the limitations of focus groups are that they are susceptible to facilitator bias, discussions can be dominated or side-tracked by a few individuals, data analysis is time consuming, and they need to be well-planned in advance[145]. Focus groups also do not provide valid information at the individual level and the information are not representative of other groups in the organisation. (For a practical application of focus groups see chapter 5.)

DEVELOPING A QUALITATIVE INTERVIEW GUIDE FOR INTERVIEWS

Face-to-face interviews can be used for multiple purposes, including the exploration of organisational questions[146]. Interviews are designed to describe and provide meaning to central themes in the life world of the subjects. According to Inauen et al.[147], interviews are used to gather information on working conditions, demands and resources, tasks and organisation of work, processes, context, and background stories.

The main task in an interview is to understand the meaning of what the interviewees say. As a survey consultant you need to know that the interview as a method of data collection has limitations. It takes time to conduct, and the possibility of interviewer effects, as well as interviewee social response bias, is present[148]. While it is more costly in terms of time and money than a survey, it is more flexible. You can change or adapt your interview during the process of the interview to get clarity or more information. When you develop an interview guide in your diagnostic strategy, it is essential to determine the type of interview, interview schedule questions, and competence of the interviewers.

Types of face-to-face interviews

Interviews provide the interviewer with the opportunity to establish a rapport with the respondent and to ask probing questions to improve accuracy, completeness, and meaningfulness[149]. There are four types of interviews that you can choose from for your organisational diagnosis[150]:

1. Informal, conversational interview: This type of interview has no predetermined questions; the aim is to remain as open and adaptable as possible to the interviewee's views and priorities. During the interview the interviewer "goes with the flow".
2. General interview guide approach: The guide approach is intended to ensure that the same general areas of information are collected from each interviewee. This provides more focus than the conversational approach, but still allows a degree of freedom and adaptability in obtaining the information from the interviewee.
3. Standardised or open-ended interview: The same open-ended questions are asked to all interviewees. This approach facilitates faster interviews that can be more easily analysed and compared.
4. Closed or fixed-response interview: All interviewees are asked the same questions and are requested to choose answers from the same set of alternatives. This format is useful for those not experienced in interviewing.

The type of interview used enables interviewers to cover data collection dimensions at factual and meaning levels[151]. It is usually more difficult to interview at a meaning level because interviews are used particularly for getting the story behind the interviewee's experiences, hence Leedy and Ormrod[152] argue that an interview can be used to pursue in-depth information around the topic or issue under diagnosis. You can use the interview as an alternative method to conduct a follow-up to your survey or questionnaire answers, and to further investigate their responses.

Interview schedule

Your schedule is based on the purpose of the organisational diagnosis. As a survey consultant, you should be able to describe the entire diagnosis to interviewers because they need to know more than simply how to conduct the interview itself[153]. When you use interviewers to collect your data, they should know and understand the background of the diagnosis and why the diagnosis is important. It is also imperative to explain the sampling logic and process, because a naïve interviewer may not understand why sampling is so important and why the sample is limited to a few participants[154]. The responsibility of a survey consultant is to prepare the interviewees for the process.

Construction of a useful interview schedule requires experience, skill, thoughtfulness and time; this can assist in enhancing the validity and reliability of the interview. The following are some of the areas that can be covered when you prepare an interview schedule for an organisational diagnosis[155]:

1. Behaviours: what an individual has done or is doing.
2. Opinions/values: what an individual thinks about the topic or issue.
3. Feelings: what an individual feels rather than what he/she thinks.
4. Knowledge: to get facts about the topic.
5. Perceptions: what people have seen, touched, heard, tasted or experienced.
6. Background/demographics: the standard background questions, such as age, education, gender, job level or years of service.

When properly constructed, interview questions can be used as a scientific tool to obtain data from individuals[156]. Interview questions are ideal when the focus of the diagnosis is to assess the perceptions of organisational members, which is the aim of most organisational diagnostic projects. Before an interviewer can ask interviewees about controversial issues, the interviewer must first ask about some facts relating to the diagnosis. Your schedule can also intersperse fact-based questions throughout the interview. An interview schedule should include questions about the present before asking questions about the past or future. Open-ended rather than closed-ended questions in the interview schedule can help in gathering detailed data[157]. When concluding the interview, it is important that the last questions should allow interviewees to provide any other information they prefer to add and to give their impressions of the interview.

Competence of interviewers

Preparation of the interview requires that you ensure that interviewers are competent through training and experience. It is important to organise in detail and rehearse the interviewing process before beginning the formal diagnosis, therefore it is essential to first pilot the interview[158]. Interviewers need to be aware of the ways in which they can inadvertently bias the results and they must understand why it is important not to be biased[159].

In your preparation as a survey consultant of the organisational diagnostic project, you need to answer the following questions:

1. Did I choose a setting or venue with the least distraction?
2. Did I explain the purpose of the interview to the interviewers?
3. Did I address ethical considerations such as anonymity or confidentiality?
4. Did I explain the format of the interview to the interviewers?
5. Did I indicate the duration of the interview (or that it normally takes an hour)?
6. Did I prepare interviewers to provide their contact information to the interviewees?
7. Did I prepare interviewers to allow the interviewees to clarify their interview doubts?
8. Did I prepare a method for recording data, such as taking notes or voice recording?

Once you are able to answer the above questions (as your checklist), it means that you are well-prepared.

Language proficiency of the interviewers and interviewees is also important when preparing the interview schedule, as the South African society is diverse, with 11 official languages. As a survey consultant, you should be familiar with the language proficiency of the members of the client organisation; you can also work with the help of a translator. In chapter 2 on stakeholder engagement, we shared a case study of a parastatal organisation that faced challenges with the organisational diagnostic process because of stakeholders' resistance. In this organisation, language was another contributory factor that affected the diagnostic process because most employees at the operational level could not read or write. Facilitators proficient in the official languages were helpful in explaining and communicating with employees in their mother tongue so that they could understand and participate in the diagnostic process. Interviewers can only be effective in the data collection process when they communicate with the interviewees in a language that they are conversant in.

DOCUMENT OR ARCHIVE ANALYSIS AND OBSERVATION

Qualitative methods of data collection in organisational diagnosis may include document, artefact or archive analysis, or the observation of people in certain situations.

Document/archive analysis

Analysis of documents, artefacts or archives can be classified as the analysis of secondary data, according to Noolan[160]. Examples of collecting secondary data in organisational diagnosis are reviewing written company policies, handbooks, financial reports (such as profit/loss, return on investment, support system cost, stockholders and dividends), personnel records (such as job descriptions, recruitment, transfers, promotions, exit or debriefing data, attendance, absenteeism, turnover rates, grievances), minutes of meetings (such as board meetings), time records and government regulatory reports[161], and artefacts such as project plans, business cases and risk assessments. Noolan[162] refers to people drawing up responsibility charts of the networks of people they work with (sociograms), which are other forms of data collection.

Information collected from different documents in the organisation, as well as information in the public domain (such as newspaper articles and other media reports about the organisation), might be used in conjunction with information gathered from an organisational survey for an additional perspective to the interpretation of what is happening in the organisation.

Advantages of document analysis are that it is relatively inexpensive and minimal time is needed to collect the data because they should be available in-house. Top management has a preference for quantifiable performance data as opposed to more qualitative data, but document analysis data may add depth to quantitative data. Drawbacks are "selective editing" of records and susceptibility to changes in record keeping over time, thus making comparisons difficult. Financial and personnel records might contain "mushy measurements" (sensitive or blurry information) which makes it difficult to interpret the data. Data gathered from the public domain (media reports) might not be credible as they could be presented from a media sensation point of view[163]. The consultant/project team needs to be aware of the drawbacks in order to collect meaningful data, which will enhance other forms of data collection as described in this chapter.

In a project with which the authors were involved, the survey results, financial results, document analysis and communication patterns were part of the diagnostic process. A team of various subjects experts, such as statisticians, financial experts, strategic planning experts, media consultants, and of course the survey consultants, were part of the project team. The purpose of the project was to determine the organisation's current level of performance and the impact of its leadership. The final report to the board of directors was very comprehensive and assisted them in pinpointing issues from a relationship, leadership, financial, communication and strategic perspective. A comprehensive and integrated intervention plan was then presented.

Observation data collection

Leedy and Ormrod[164] define an observation study as follows: "A type of quantitative research in which a particular aspect of behaviour is observed systematically and with as much objectivity as possible". The behaviour is quantified in some way, for example each occurrence of the behaviour is counted to determine its overall frequency. Observation in qualitative studies is unstructured, free flowing and flexible, allowing the observer to take advantage of unforeseen data sources as they surface. Observational studies can be divided into two broad types, namely: participant observation (the aim is to become an accepted member of the participant community) and non-participant observation (the observer stands back from a situation and observes from a distance)[165]. Brewerton and Millward[166] caution that "observation is a highly skilled activity which should not be considered lightly", however, as part of a focused organisational study, there is no reason why observation as an instrument should not be used, if it will elicit the evidence you want. The data collected will depend on the purpose (research question) of the observation. In organisational diagnosis, observation works best if the observer does not participate in the activities being observed[167].

Observation might be useful when determining the dynamics of socialisation in a group or a team, such as interaction patterns in an open-plan office, in meetings and other forums. The purpose would be to identify strengths and weaknesses within the group/team/area dynamics. Knowledge obtained from the observation could be used as the basis for intervention design[168]. Other applications of observation and some advantages and drawbacks are displayed in table 3.9.

Table 3.9: Applications of observation, advantages and drawbacks (adapted from Brewerton & Millward; Leedy & Ormrod; Saunders et al.)[169]

Examples of observation applications
- Examination of interview dynamics (eg selection or performance appraisal)
- Dynamics of socialisation in groups
- Interaction patterns in meetings, group forums or open-plan offices

Advantages	Drawbacks
• Observing a situation is good for explaining "what is going on". • It heightens the observer's awareness of significant social processes. • Some observation opportunities afford the observer the opportunity to experience the emotions of those who are being observed. • Virtually all data that are collected are useful. • Data collection might be simplified by using coding or a checklist scheme.	• Observation takes time. • Observation requires skill and experience. • The observer role can be demanding at a level which is not suited to all researchers. • The closeness of the researcher to the situation can lead to observer bias. • There can be high levels of role conflict (eg. "colleague" versus researcher). • The observer might not know what is most important to observe, or may influence what people say or do. • Data recording is often difficult for the researcher. • The observer might confuse actual observations and his or her interpretation of them (bias).

Observer bias must be taken into account and managed. Saunders et al.[170] argue that we have a propensity to colour our interpretation of what we believe to be true. As an observer, you must thus be careful not to confuse your actual observations with your interpretation of them, which means you need to be objective in your record keeping and your interpretation of what you have seen or heard, as it may change over the duration of the observation study[171].

CONCLUSION

This chapter provides guidelines on qualitative and quantitative approaches which are applicable during an organisational diagnosis. The different methods of data collection have been described, with specific emphasis on their benefits and limitations. How to approach a quantitative survey assessment and develop a new questionnaire was discussed in practical terms. These different methods should allow survey consultants and managers to select, choose and apply them in practice, as they are based on sound knowledge.

REFERENCES

Babbie, E. 1998. *The practice of social research*. 8th edition. Belmont, CA: Wadsworth.

Bolarinwa, OA. 2015. Principles and methods of validity and reliability testing of questionnaires used in social and health science researches. *Nigerian Postgraduate Medical Journal* 22: 195-201.

Booysen, S. 2003. Designing a questionnaire, in *Intellectual tools: skills for the human sciences*, edited by D Rossouw. 2nd edition. Pretoria: Van Schaik: 127–142.

Borg, I & Mastrangelo, PM. 2008. *Employee surveys in management: theories, tools, and practical applications.* Cambridge, MA: Hogrefe.

Brewerton, P & Millward, L. 2001. *Organizational research methods: a guide for students and researchers.* London: Sage.

Castro, M & Martins, N. 2010. The relationship between organisational climate and employee satisfaction in a South African information and technology organisation. *SA Tydskrif vir Bedryfsielkunde* 36(1): 1-9.

Centre for Industrial and Organisational Psychology. 2010. *Advanced programme in organisational development: module 3: the process of organisational development.* Pretoria: University of South Africa.

Christensen, LB. 1994. *Experimental methodology.* 6th edition. Boston: Allyn & Bacon.

Cummings, GT & Worley, CG. 2008. *Organisational development and change.* Ohio: South-Western Learning.

Church, AH & Waclawski, J. 2001. *Designing and using organizational surveys: a seven-step process.* San Francisco, CA: Jossey-Bass.

Coetzee, M. 2016. Core theories and models, in *Fundamentals of organisation development*, edited by N Martins & D Geldenhuys. Cape Town: Juta: 82-130.

Da Veiga, A & Martins, N. 2015a. Information security culture and information protection culture: a validated assessment instrument. *Computer Law & Security Review* 3(12): 243-256.

Da Veiga, A & Martins, N. 2015b. Improving the information security culture through monitoring and implementation actions illustrated through a case study. *Computers and Security* (49): 162-176.

De Waal, A. 2010. Achieving high performance in the public sector: what needs to be done? *Public Performance & Management Review* 34(1): 81-103.

Evans, JR & Mathur, A. 2005. The value of online surveys. *Internet Research* 15(2): 195-219.

Flick, U. 2009. *An introduction to qualitative research.* 4th edition. London: Sage.

Foxcroft, C & Roodt, G. 2005. *An introduction to psychological assessment in the South African context.* 2nd edition. Cape Town: Oxford University Press.

French, LW & Bell, CH. 1999. *Organisational development: behavioural sciences interventions for organisation improvement.* 6th edition. Upper Saddle River: Prentice Hall.

French, WL, Bell, CH Jr. & Zawacki, AR. 2000. *Organisational development and transformation: managing effective change.* 5th edition. New York: McGraw-Hill.

Furnham, A & Gunter, B. 1993. *Corporate assessment: auditing a company's personality.* London: Routledge.

Gregory, JR. 2007. *Psychological testing: history, principles and applications.* 5th edition. Boston: Pearson Education.

Hair, JF, Anderson, RE, Tatham, RL & Black, WC. 1995. *Multivariate data analysis.* 4th edition. London: Prentice-Hall.

Harrison, R & Stokes, H. 1992. *Diagnosing orgnizational culture.* Amsterdam: Pfeiffer.

Harrison, R. 1993. *Diagnosing organizational culture: trainer's manual.* Amsterdam: Pfeiffer.

Harrison, MI. 1994. *Diagnosing organizations: methods, models, and processes.* 2nd edition. Thousand Oaks, CA: Sage.

Inauen, A, Jenny, GJ & Bauer, GF. 2011. Design principles for data- and change-oriented organisational analysis in workplace health promotion. *Health Promotion International* 27(2): 275- 283.

Jankovicz, AD. 1991. *Business research projects for students.* London: Chapman & Hall.

Kitzinger, J. 1995. Introducing focus groups. *British Medical Journal* 311: 299-302.

Kraut, AI. 1996. Planning and conducting the survey: keeping strategic purpose in mind, in *Organizational surveys*, edited by AI Kraut. San Francisco:Jossey-Bass: 149-176.

Krueger, RA. 1994. *Focus groups: the practical guide goes applied research.* Thousand Oaks, CA: Sage.

Ledimo, O & Martins, N. 2014. A longitudinal study of employee satisfaction during the process of transformation in a water utility organisation. *Problems and Perspectives in Management* 12(4): 172-180.

Lee, TW, Mitchell, TR & Sablynski, CJ. 1999. Qualitative research in organizational and vocational psychology, 1979-1999. *Journal of Vocational Behaviour* 55(2): 161-187.

Leedy, PD & Ormrod, JE. 2010. *Practical research: planning and design.* 9th edition. Boston: Pearson.

Martins, EC & Martins, N. 2011. The role of organisational factors in combating tacit knowledge loss in organisations. *Southern African Business Review* 15(1): 49-69.

Martins, EC & Martins, N. 2012. *A model development strategy to determine factors that influence knowledge retention in organisations.* 11th European Conference on Research Methods in Business and Management, 28-29 June. University of Bolton, UK.

Martins, EC & Meyer, HWJ. 2012. Organisational and behavioural factors that influence knowledge retention. *Journal of Knowledge Management* 16(1): 77-96.

Martins, N. 2014. Factorial invariance of the South African culture instrument. *Problems and Perspectives in Management* 12(4): 242-252.

Martins, N. 2015. Testing for measurement invariance for employee engagement across sectors in South Africa. *Journal of Contemporary Management* 12: 757-774.

Martins, N & Coetzee, M. 2007. Organisational culture, employee satisfaction, perceived leader emotional competency and personality type: an exploratory study in a South African engineering company. *Journal of Human Resource Management* 5(2): 20-32.

Martins, N & Da Veiga, A. 2014. *The value of using a validated security culture assessment instrument.* The 8th European Conference on IS Management and Evaluation, 11-12 September. University of Ghent, Belgium.

Martins, N & Da Veiga, A. 2015. *An information security culture model validated with structural equation modelling.* 9th International Symposium on Human Aspects of Information Security & Assurance, 1-3 July. Lesbos, Greece.

Martins, N & Ledimo, O. 2016. The measurement of employee engagement in government institutions. *Risk Governance and Control* 6(3): 18-25.

Martins, N & Von der Ohe, H. 2011. A longitudinal study of the role of trust during change. *Journal of Psychology in Africa* 21(2): 301-306.

Moerdyk, A. 2009. *The principles and practice of psychological assessment.* Pretoria: Van Schaik.

Mouton, J & Marais, HC. 1990. *Basiese begrippe: metodologie van die geesteswetenskappe.* Pretoria: Raad vir Geesteswetenskaplike Navorsing.

Mouton, J & Marais, CH. 1994. *Basic methodology of the social science.* Pretoria: Human Sciences Research Council.

Morgan, DL. 1988. *Focus groups as qualitative research.* Beverly Hills: Sage.

Neuman, WL. 2000. *Social research methods: qualitative and quantitative approaches.* 4th edition. Boston, MA: Allan & Bacon.

Neuman, WL. 2007. *Basics of social research: qualitative and quantitative approaches.* 2nd edition. Boston: Pearson.

Nienaber, H & Martins, N. 2014. An employee engagement instrument and framework building on existing research. *Mediterranean Journal of Social Science* 5(20): 485-496.

Noolan, JCA. 2006. Organization diagnosis phase, in *The NTL handbook of organization development and change: principles, practices, and perspectives,* edited by BB Jones & M Brazzel. San Francisco, CA: Pfeiffer:192-211.

Olivier, BH. 2014. *The development and validation of an assessment framework for measuring the organisational effectiveness of a metropolitan municipality in South Africa.* Unpublished D.Admin thesis. University of South Africa, Pretoria.

Paul, J. 1996. Between-method triangulation in organizational diagnosis. *The International Journal of Organizational Analysis* 4(2): 135-153.

Salkind, JN. 2009. *Exploring research.* 7th edition. New Jersey: Pearson Education International.

Sanchez, PM. 2007. The employee survey: more than asking questions. *Journal of Business Strategy* 28(2): 48-56.

Sandelowski, M. 2000. Focus on research methods: whatever happened to qualitative description? *Research in Nursing & Health* 23: 334-340.

Sashkin, M & Prien, EP. 1996. Ethical concerns and organizational surveys, in *Organizational surveys*, edited by Al Kraut. San Francisco: Jossey-Bass: 381-403.

Saunders, M, Lewis, P & Thornhill, A. 2009. *Research methods for business students*. 5th edition. Harlow: Prentice Hall.

Smith, J. 2015. *Qualitative psychology: a practical guide to research methods*. 3rd edition. London: Sage.

Terre Blanche, M, Durrheim, K & Painter, D. 2006. *Research in practice: applied methods for the social sciences*. Cape Town: University of Cape Town Press.

Tetteh, VK. 2012. *Organisational diagnosis – a management tool for change in the telecommunication industry*. Master's dissertation. Kwame Nkrumah University of Science and Technology, Kumasi.

Training Technologies. 2008. SurveyTracker E-mail/Web User's Guide. USA.

Van der Linde-de Klerk, M, Martins, N & De Beer, M. 2015. The factorial validity and reliability of a change agent identification assessment. *South African Journal of Labour Relations* 39(1): 114-130.

Van Tonder, CL & Roodt, G. 2004. *Organisational development: theory and practice*. Pretoria: Van Schaik.

Viljoen, RC. 2015. *Organisational change and development: an African perspective*. Randburg: KR Publishing.

Viljoen, RC. 2016. Engagement in multi-cultural environments: reflections and theoretical development, chapter 3 in *Employee Engagement in a South African Context*, edited by N Martins & H Nienaber. Randburg: KR Publishing.

Von der Ohe, H & Martins, N. 2010. Exploring trust relationships during time of change. *SA Tydskrif vir Menslikehulpbronbestuur* 8(1): 1-9.

Welman, JC & Kruger, SJ. 2001. *Research methodology for the business and administrative sciences*. 2nd edition. Oxford: Oxford University Press.

Welman, C, Kruger, F & Mitchell, B. 2009. *Research methodology*. Cape Town: Oxford University Press.

Wiley, JW. 1996. Linking survey results to customer satisfaction and business performance. In *Organizational surveys*, edited by Al Kraut. San Francisco: Jossey-Bass: 330-359.

ENDNOTES

1. Christensen, 1994; Inauen, Jenny & Bauer, 2011.
2. Smith, 2015.
3. Flick, 2009: 27.
4. Inauen et al., 2011.
5. Welman, Kruger & Mitchell, 2009.
6. Leedy & Ormrod, 2010.
7. Paul, 1996: 136.
8. Flick, 2009; Welman et al., 2009; Newman, 2007.
9. Salkind, 2009.
10. Evans & Mathur, 2005; Sanchez, 2007; Mouton & Marais, 1994.
11. Foxcroft & Roodt, 2005.
12. Welman et al., 2009; Gregory, 2007.
13. Inauen et al., 2011.
14. Sandelowsk, 2000: 338.
15. Lee, Mitchell & Sablynski, 1999; Welman et al., 2009.
16. Smith, 2015: 33.
17. Sandelowski, 2000; Leedy & Ormrod, 2010.
18. Mouton & Marais, 1994, Lee et al., 1999.
19. Welman et al., 2009.
20. Leedy & Ormrod, 2010; Sandelowski, 2000.
21. Harrison, 1994; Paul, 1998.
22. Cummings & Worley, 2008; Harrison, 1994.
23. Inauen, Jenny & Bauer, 2011.
24. Paul, 1996.
25. Flick, 2009; Inauen et al., 2011.
26. Paul, 1996; Van Tonder & Roodt, 2008.
27. Inauen et al., 2011.
28. Paul, 1996.
29. Christensen, 1994; Foxcroft & Roodt, 2005.
30. Inauen et al., 2011.
31. Mouton and Marais, 1994.
32. Blanche, Durheim & Painter, 2009.
33. Smith, 2015; Sandelowski, 2000.

34. Cummings & Worley, 2008.
35. Tetteh, 2012.
36. Tetteh, 2012; French & Bell, 1999.
37. Tetteh, 2012.
38. Neuman, 2007; Salkind, 2009; Leedy & Ormrod, 2010.
39. Paul, 1996.
40. Christensen,1994.
41. Paul, 1996.
42. Tetteh, 2012.
43. Inauen et al., 2011.
44. Paul, 1996.
45. Kitzinger, 1995; Inauen et al., 2011.
46. Inauen et al., 2011.
47. Tetteh, 2012.
48. French, Bell & Zawacki, 2000.
49. Inauen et al., 2011.
50. Tetteh, 2012.
51. Tetteh, 2012, 25.
52. Leedy & Ormrod, 2010.
53. Leedy & Ormrod, 2010: 91.
54. Leedy & Ormrod, 2010.
55. Moerdyk, 2009: 11.
56. Martins, 2015.
57. Leedy & Ormrod, 2010: 92.
58. Saunders, Lewis & Thornhill, 2009.
59. Saunders et al., 2009: 372-373.
60. Leedy & Ormrod, 2010: 93.
61. Brewerton & Millward, 2001: 89.
62. Saunders et al., 2009: 373.
63. Saunders et al., 2009: 373.
64. Saunders et al., 2009: 374.
65. Sashkin & Prien, 1996: 391.
66. Bolarinwa, 2015.
67. Furnham & Gunter, 1993: 31.
68. Borg, Mastrangelo & Mastrangelo, 2008: 78.
69. Sashkin & Prien, 1996: 388.
70. Kraut, 1996: 388.
71. Kraut, 1996, Sashkin & Prien, 1996.
72. Kraut, 1996.
73. Harrison & Stokes, 1992; Harrison, 1993.
74. Sashkin & Prien,1996.
75. Hair, Anderson, Tatham & Black, 1995.
76. Kraut, 1996.
77. Kraut, 1996.
78. Kraut, 1996: 388-389.
79. Kraut, 1996.
80. Kraut, 1996.
81. Church & Waclawski, 2001.
82. Church & Waclawski, 2001: 53.
83. Church & Waclawski, 2001.
84. Church & Waclawski, 2001.
85. Kraut, 1996; Borg & Mastrangelo, 2008.
86. Borg & Mastrangelo, 2008.
87. Borg & Mastrangelo, 2008.
88. Borg and Mastrangelo, 2008: 154.
89. Borg & Mastrangelo, 2009: 153.
90. Kraut, 1996.
91. Jankovicz, 1991; Coetzee, 2016.
92. Chawane, Van Vuuren & Roodt, 2003 cited in Coetzee, 2016: 84.
93. Cummings & Worley, 2005 cited in Coetzee, 2016: 84.
94. Mouton & Marais, 1990.
95. Noolan, 2006.
96. Olivier, 2014.
97. Olivier, 2015.
98. Olivier, 2014.
99. Hair et al., 1995.
100. Saunders et al., 2009.
101. Saunders et al., 2009: 384.
102. Borg & Mastrangelo, 2008.
103. Krosnik & Fabrigar, 1997, cited in Borg & Mastrangelo, 2008: 111.
104. Sudman, Bradburn & Schwartz, 1996, cited in Borg & Mastrangelo, 2009: 111.
105. Borg & Mastrangelo,2009.
106. Borg & Mastrangelo,2008.
107. Borg & Mastrangelo, 2008.
108. Krosnick et al., 2002, cited in Borg & Mastrangelo, 2008: 113.
109. Borg & Mastrangelo, 2008.
110. Borg & Mastrangelo, 2008: 116.
111. Borg & Mastrangelo, 2008.
112. Borg & Mastrangelo, 2009.
113. Training Technologies, 2008.
114. Training Technologies, Inc, 2008.
115. Borg & Mastrangelo, 2008.
116. Borg & Mastrangelo, 2008.
117. Babbie, 1998; Booysen, 2003; Welman & Kruger, 2001.
118. Neuman, 2000; Saunders et al., 2009: 394.
119. Saunders et al., 2009.
120. Booysen, 2003.

121. Borg & Mastrangelo, 2008.
122. Saunders et al., 2009.
123. Church & Waclawski, 2001.
124. Borg & Mastrangelo, 2008; Kraut, 1996.
125. Borg & Mastrangelo, 2008: 164; Saunders et al., 2009: 394.
126. Kraut, 1996.
127. Kitzinger, 1995.
128. Salkind, 2009; Inauen et al., 2011.
129. Salkind, 2009.
130. Inauen et al., 2011.
131. Welman et al., 2009.
132. Kitzinger, 1995.
133. Salkind, 2009.
134. Wellman et al., 2009.
135. Newman, 2007.
136. Leedy & Ormrod, 2010.
137. Kitzinger, 1995.
138. Leedy & Ormrod, 2010.
139. Cummings & Worley, 2008; Lee et al., 1999.
140. Sandelowsk, 2000.
141. Newman, 2007.
142. Krueger, 1994; Morgan, 1988.
143. Krueger, 1994; Morgan, 1988.
144. Kitzinger, 1995: 300.
145. Wellman et al., 2009; Newman, 2007.
146. Terre Blanche et al., 2006; Salkind, 2009.
147. Inauen et al., 2011, 27.
148. Wellman et al., 2009; Smith, 2015.
149. Smith, 2015; Paul, 1996.
150. Leedy & Ormrod, 2010; Flick, 2009; Newman, 2007.
151. Wellman et al., 2009.
152. Leedy & Ormrod, 2010.
153. Lee et al., 1999; Salkind, 2009.
154. Terre Blanche et al., 2006.
155. Cummings & Worley, 2008; Harrison, 1994; Tetteh, 2012.
156. Smith, 2015.
157. Leedy & Ormrod, 2010.
158. Inauen et al., 2011.
159. Newman, 2007; Paul, 1996.
160. Noolan, 2006: 205.
161. Centre for Industrial and Organisational Psychology, 2010: 28; Noolan, 2006: 205.
162. Noolan, 2006.
163. Centre for Industrial and Organisational Psychology, 2010.
164. Leedy & Ormrod, 2010: 108.
165. Brewerton & Millward, 2001: 96.
166. Brewerton & Millward, 2001: 96, 98.
167. Saunders et al., 2009.
168. Brewerton & Millward, 2001.
169. Brewerton & Millward, 2001: 97-98; Leedy & Ormrod, 2010: 147; Saunders et al., 2009: 299
170. Saunders et al., 2009.
171. Leedy & Ormrod, 2010

CHAPTER 4

SURVEY ADMINISTRATION PROCESS

by **Ellen Caroline Martins and Ophillia Ledimo**

INTRODUCTION

An essential aspect of the organisational diagnostic process is the implementation of the survey. For this reason, as an organisational survey consultant and manager, you need to be conversant with the administration process of the survey. This chapter provides an indication of possible ways to attract participants, the sampling process and survey distribution methods (online or paper-based). In addition, an overview of managing the survey process, the data management and the cleaning process is outlined to help you determine which are spoilt and which are usable questionnaires.

PROMOTING THE SURVEY

The aim of promoting the survey to organisational members as participants is to increase the response rate. There are several ways in which a survey can be promoted, including an introductory letter and potential incentives.

Introduction/Cover letter: Your survey should include a cover letter with an introduction. It is mostly characterised by information relating to the purpose of the survey, the reason why it is important for the participants to participate in the survey, the time required to complete the survey, ethical considerations such as anonymity or confidentiality, and instructions for completing and returning the survey. You can also add information to prepare participants regarding the timelines for returning the survey. In addition, it is essential to, in the cover letter, include the contact details of the administrator of the organisational diagnostic projects, such as name, telephone number and e-mail address. See an example of a cover letter for an electronic survey (Example 1 at the end of this chapter).

Survey incentives: Some practitioners and consultants prefer to encourage participation in organisational diagnostic surveys by using incentives. The purpose of incentives is to reward survey participants for their time and effort in order to increase survey response rates. When you decide on whether to offer an incentive or how much of an incentive to offer, consider the characteristics of your sample population, as well as the length of the organisational diagnostic survey. Incentives include organisational promotional items such as pens, lanyards, magnets, coasters, key chains, bags or a small amount gift card from the marketing department. Some companies use an inter-departmental competition to encourage participation, i.e. the department with the highest response rate receives a promotional gift.

While promoting the survey, it is important to take cognisance of ethical considerations relating to survey participation. One of the ethical considerations is recognising that survey participation is a voluntary choice that requires you to encourage participation without undue pressure or coercion of the participants[1]. Incentives should not be used to coerce or influence participation without providing a choice.

SAMPLING

When you develop a sample for a survey, the aim is to gather quantitative data that describes specific aspects of a given population. The sample survey provides an objective, efficient, and valid method of obtaining the characteristics of an entire population from only a small part of that population[2]. In the case of an organisational diagnosis, as a survey consultant, you need to collect data from organisational members and therefore the data might be subjective. According to Salant and Dillman[3], sample selection depends on the population size, its homogeneity, the sample media, the cost of its use, as well as the degree of precision required. Remember, a sample is a selected portion of the population from which the findings can later be generalised back to the population.

While it is often not possible to know the true population, it is critical that part of your sampling selection is to define the target population as narrowly as possible. In order for you to determine that your survey sample is an ideal one, you should be able to achieve the following aims:

1. Obtaining information from large samples of the population.
2. Gather demographic data that describes the composition of the sample.
3. Be inclusive in the types and number of variables that can be studied, require minimal investment to develop and administer, and are relatively easy for making generalisations.
4. Elicit information about attitudes that are otherwise difficult to measure by using observational techniques.

It is important to note that surveys only provide estimates for the true population, and not an exact diagnosis of the total population[4]. Before you can decide on the sampling type that you will apply in order to perform your diagnosis, you need to consider the following five factors:

1   The desired degree of precision: A survey is used to establish that a postulated effect exists in the sample. Practitioners and consultants must ensure that the number of surveys distributed is sufficient to allow for no-response and for unusable, illegible, and incomplete responses.

2   The statistical power required: The probability exists that the practitioner or consultant might reject the null hypothesis of the organisational diagnosis, given that the alternate hypothesis is true about the issue being assessed.

3   Access to the sample: The ability of the practitioner or consultants to gain access to the sample participants; sometimes it is not ideal to have a large sample that is inaccessible. You will need to decide who you want to include in your sample and how you will reach them.

4   The degree to which the population can be stratified is essential, hence determining a sample size requires that the population can be stratified according to sector, size, or technology level.

5   The selection of the relevant units of analysis. In an organisational diagnosis you must decide whether the respondents to a survey will be individuals, departments, offices, or the entire organisation.

Types of samples

A complete sample uses every member of the group of interest (the population or audience, which could for example be all employees employed at an organisation). The complete sample is used most often with either small populations or with a survey distributed electronically, because it costs less to distribute to more people electronically than with paper surveys. Inviting all employees in an organisation to participate in a survey is ideal in the sense than everyone is allowed the opportunity to decide whether they want to participate or not. They then feel part of the survey process and feel that they are given a "voice" in that their opinions as employees (as a group) are heard.

If the organisation decides that a sample must be selected, the people selected to be part of the sample must be selected at random; they must have an equal (or known) chance of being selected. There are two main methods of sampling, namely probability and non-probability sampling.

Probability sampling ensures that all members of the population have an equal opportunity for participating in the survey[5]. This method entails the following:

1.   **Simple random sampling** uses random selection to ensure that all members of the group of interest have an equal chance of being selected to participate in the survey. Random sampling is the most common sampling method.

2.   **Stratified sampling** (proportional and disproportional), this method allows the population surveyed to be divided into groups ("strata"). In stratified sampling, you first indicate a subgroup (or strata) from the audience list (for example, the Department field) and randomly select a proportionate number of respondents from each stratum to get the sample. For example, if you had a target population of 10,000 with 40% of the people in Accounting and 60% in Sales and a sample size of 1,000, the list would be divided into an Accounting list of 4,000 and a Sales list of 6,000. Then 400 Accountants and 600 Sales people would be randomly chosen from their respective lists. This gives each element in the strata an equal chance of being selected for the sample and maintains the population proportion desired[6].

3.   **Systematic selection** (interval sampling) is used when a stream of representative people is available. In systematic sampling, every X number of individuals is selected. Software such as SurveyTracker determines the size of the audience list and then the size of the desired samples, divides the numbers and comes up with the interval. A random audience member is then selected and every X respondents following until the desired total is reached. If the audience ends, SurveyTracker continues from the top of the audience - if it encounters members it has selected, it skips to the next member[7].

4. ***Clustered sampling method*** is used when the population of interest is large and geographically widely dispersed. Clusters within the population are randomly selected. Cluster sampling (also called Area Sampling) includes people who meet a certain criteria. This is most often done to save money when the criteria are based on a specific location. Software such as SurveyTracker does this by allowing you to set criteria from which it will select a random sample. If your target population is greater than or equal to the size of the audience after the criteria have been established, SurveyTracker conducts a complete sample on the filter (set of criteria)[8].

Purposive (non-probability) sampling methods is sampling with a purpose in mind, usually interest in particular groups[9]. Purposive sampling is appropriate when the survey consultant wishes to select unique cases that can provide special information[10]. If, for example, the purpose of the diagnosis is to determine the degree to which the organisation retains the knowledge and expertise that accumulates over time through the experience of its individual employees and that is critical to the organisation's overall functioning and competitive advantage, it might be appropriate to limit the sample to supervisory and management levels. The reasoning here would be that they would have a sound understanding of knowledge retention behaviours, influencing factors and the strategic impact that the knowledge loss could have on their organisation, which might not be the case with lower levels in the organisation[11]. Other examples of purposive sampling are discussed below.

1. ***Convenience sampling*** occurs where participants are those to whom the researcher has relatively 'easy access. This is typically the sampling technique which many organisations use. They invite all employees with e-mail and access to the internet to participate in the survey. However, the survey consultant must still ensure that a representative sample, based on the objectives of the survey, is obtained. Consult the guide (Example 2 at the end of this chapter) which can be used to ensure that you obtain a sufficient overall sample, as well as for specific biographical groups.
2. ***Snowball sampling*** is applied when participants who meet the survey requirements recommend others with the same characteristics. This method is used when trying to access populations which are difficult to reach.

You can decide on the method that is suitable for your survey project, to ensure that the participants are representative of the total population of the organisation.

SURVEY SOFTWARE PACKAGES (THEIR ADVANTAGES AND DISADVANTAGES)

You can program the survey into an online survey software programme, such as SurveyGizmo, Survey Monkey, SurveyTracker or Zoomerang. Once you have launched the survey, administering it requires less manpower, time and resources than paper completion surveys would cost. Benefits of online survey programmes are that they are relatively low-cost (or free for basic packages) and enable you to design your own survey. You can use their available tutorials and templates on their websites that can assist you with designing and formatting your survey[12].

The software packages also have instructions for collecting participants' responses, sending reminders, and analysing the results. Glascow[13] indicates that the following are the main benefits of using survey software packages:

1. They are very low in cost.
2. They provide you automation and real-time access to the survey.
3. Less time needed to administer and distribute the survey.
4. They are convenient for participants who are technologically knowledgeable.
5. Design flexibility: surveys can be programmed even if they are very complex.
6. When there are no interviews, participants may be more willing to share information, knowing that the process is safe and confidential.

As an organisational development manager or survey consultant, you can encourage the organisation to buy the software, especially when the organisation intends to conduct a number of surveys on a regular basis. You can also visit their respective websites for more information about designing or administering surveys on SurveyGizmo, Survey Monkey, SurveyTracker, Zoomerang or other software packages. Typical criteria that you can use to evaluate survey software programmes are displayed in table 4.1.

Table 4.1: Criteria to evaluate survey software (adapted from Rivera; Schindler[14])

Software criteria	Business experience	Respondent experience	Help and support
• Themes/tools to make surveys attractive (design features) • Types of questions and response scales • Question creation/review collaboration • Supports Captcha fields • Supports passwords • Distribution methods (web, e-mail, flash disk, smart phones) • Offline data collection • Export data in CSV, Excel or text format • Send response reminders • Reporting features in the form of graphs and tables • Export report as PDF, or PowerPoint, or Word	• Suitability for small, middle size or large businesses • Ease of use • Upgrade annual plan • Competitive price • Fully customised branding • Supports kiosks	• Partial data submission • Progression bar • Single page survey • Save and continue later (might require respondent identification) • Easy data submission • Skip-page logic	• Phone support • Email support • Searchable FAQs and blog

It is advisable to test survey software in terms of the survey design, distribution, data collection and reporting facilities, the business experience, respondent experience and the help and support that is available. The criteria displayed above are by no means a complete list of aspects that must be considered. Each software programme has its own advantages and disadvantages, so it will depend on the needs of the survey consultant and the organisation as to which survey software tool or programme will be most suitable to purchase. If an organisation does not conduct regular surveys it is more cost effective to rather make use of survey consultants, because conducting a survey requires quite a capital layout as well as trained survey experts with survey and statistical knowledge.

SURVEY DISTRIBUTION METHODS

During the planning phase of the organisational diagnosis the consultant must discuss the various options of collecting the data with the project team in order to determine which methods will be suited to the particular organisation. The main methods of data collection with a quantitative questionnaire are web-based, which requires a computer or smart phone and internet access, or paper-based. Martins[15] investigated whether web-based and paper-based organisational surveys can be regarded as equivalent techniques of data collection in the same survey. The organisation had limited access to the internet and due to the complex geographical placement of various units, both distribution methods were used. Overall, 1,295 employees participated in the survey. Of these, 396 completed the web-based survey and 899 completed it on paper. The SurveyTracker software package was used for the web survey. Confirmatory Factor Analysis (CFA) in a Structural Equation Modelling (SEM) framework was used to determine if web-based and paper-based methods can be considered equal. It was "concluded that web-based and paper-based surveys can be considered equal with respect to similar factor structure, with equal factor loadings and equal variances of the factors and equal co-variances between the factors. The results may therefore be combined in a single analysis without compromising measurement validity"[16].

The consultant should have the means to host the survey within the organisation or to make use of a service provider who can offer the survey hosting, administration and reporting services. Sometimes the organisation has its own survey software and means to administer the survey, however in the South African context we have found that there is often a lack of trust among employees in organisations, who fear that they might be identified and victimised if the survey is hosted in-house. It is then better if the survey can be hosted by the survey consultant on a remote server, and if the consultant team can administer and facilitate the paper completion process (see discussion on *paper distribution*). In the section below, different methods of conducting online web-based data collection and paper-based methods are discussed.

Data collection methods using technology

The most common technique to complete a survey online is by using a **computer with an internet connection**. Each employee in the sample will receive an email invitation (see example 1) containing a URL link to the survey. By clicking on the link the survey will appear in the web-browser, and the participant completes the questionnaire by clicking the radio buttons for the answers that the person selects. At the end of the questionnaire the person will click on 'submit' and receive a confirmation message that the data have been submitted.

It is also possible to set up a **kiosk** of a number of computers or laptops to allow people who do not have access to computers the opportunity to complete the survey online (polling station method). This usually works well in situations where staff members fear that they might be identified based on the IP address of their computer if they complete the survey on their own computer or laptop.

Although not often used in organisational surveys, some software packages like SurveyTracker make it possible to complete a survey by using a **USB thumb drive** (flash disk) containing the survey, which is plugged into any computer. You would then use Windows Explorer to locate the survey.exe file and to display the survey. Once completed, the data is stored on the USB and later the administrator would transfer the data into the software programme. The USB can be passed around to different participants and you could also have a couple of USBs circulating to collect the data.

The latest technology is **smart phone** completion and **application (app)** completion. The process of completion is the same as described above for computer web-browser completion. The mobile-friendly survey is fitted to your phone's screen in a vertical, zoomed-in layout or rotated in a landscape format. Below is a picture (figure 4.1) of what a survey looks like in a vertical display on a smart phone.

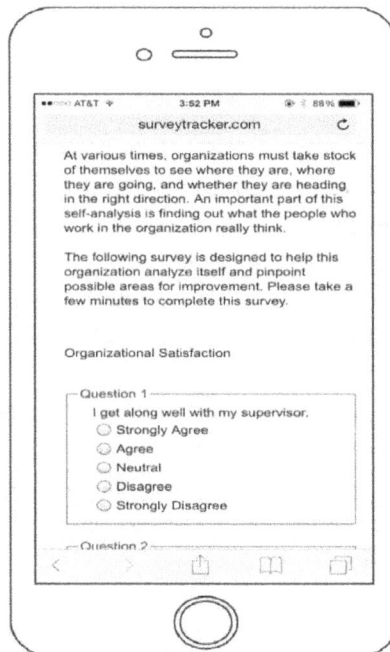

Figure 4.1: Display of a survey screen on a smart phone

The smart phone option might work well when employees have a phone that is supported by their employer, as smart phone owners would not want to use their own phone data to complete the survey for the organisation. This is also a very practical option for employees who travel a lot and mostly use their smart phones for their internet access. Some organisations, such as the mining industry, use iPads in protective covers to conduct surveys underground.

IT support and helpdesk

Information Technology (IT) and helpdesk support while the survey is administered, is important. The consultant should liaise with the IT support team in order to ensure that they will be able to assist survey participants with internet connection and browser difficulties for the duration of the survey administration process. The IT team needs to be informed of aspects such as the survey hosting process, web-browser requirements, troubleshooting information for web-browsers, contact details of the consultant IT team for survey and server support issues, and how to deal with frequently asked questions, such as: how anonymity is ensured in surveys which do not require personal details, whether the participants can save the survey and resume completion at a later stage or not, and how multiple submissions of the same data are prevented. The 'save and resume' option is usually linked to the name of the person and requires password set-up, which does not allow for anonymity, so this needs to be explained to the project team during the design and planning phase of the project (the stage when it is decided which methods will be used and why). A good practice is to supply the help desk with a survey guide booklet which they can use to answer questions or look for solutions to possible problems participants might encounter.

Paper distribution

The distribution of paper surveys can be twofold, namely postal or group administration. The *postal administration* allows you to administer your survey to a large sample distributed over various geographical areas. It is easy and cost efficient. When there are no interviewers, participants seem to be more willing to share information. The limitation with postal surveys is the low response rate and it is not appropriate for low literacy audiences. When choosing a postal survey administration method, Kelly, Clark, Brown and Sitzia[17] suggest the following:

1. Prepare all the necessary mailing materials, including the cover letter, survey, envelope, and a self-addressed stamped envelope. You can also check with your company's mail service to see if they have registered with the post office for 'business reply mail'. This will allow you to print your company's indicia on the reply envelopes and to pay return postage only for those surveys that are actually returned to you.
2. Make sure to format the survey so that questions and respective response options do not break across pages.

3. If you have the time and resources, you could send a postcard or a brief letter of introduction, announcing that the survey will follow shortly. This will help to increase the response rate of your survey.
4. Allow three to four weeks for respondents to complete and return the survey via mail.
5. Develop a method for tracking completed surveys.

The **group administration** is ideal to eliminate the challenges of unreturned survey questionnaires when using the postal administration. This type of survey affords you the opportunity to collect data immediately from participants. While it is applicable for participants who can competently read and write, this method is also ideal for participants with a low literacy level. Referring to the case study of a company shared with you in *chapter 2*, this company had several employees who had limited English proficiency. The project team had to assemble a team of facilitators to conduct group administration of the survey in the 11 official languages. In a diverse sample population, participants can be grouped based on their respective home languages for facilitators to interpret questionnaires statements for them. The following are factors that you need to consider in group administration of the paper surveys:

1. Recruit skilled facilitators who are proficient in the participants' home language.
2. Facilitators should be trained in administering the survey and have an understanding of each of the items.
3. Interpersonal skills of the facilitators are critical for creating a positive environment that allows participants to feel valued and respected during the process.
4. To ensure consistency of the administration process, all facilitators should follow the same guidelines provided to them.
5. Adherence to the time limits is important, but participants should not be rushed by the facilitators. They must be afforded an opportunity to reflect on their responses.
6. Facilitators should also comply with ethical considerations such as confidentiality, anonymity and voluntary participation.
7. After completion, facilitators can ensure that completed surveys are collected in a secure manner.

The advantage of paper-based completion is that it allows participants who do not have access to computers and the internet the opportunity to participate in the survey[18]. The limitation of group administration using facilitators might be that others may feel embarrassed to indicate that they need assistance to complete the surveys and decline to participate. Another limitation is the cost involved in using facilitators.

Despite the method of paper administration you may choose, you need to be cognisant that securing a high response rate to the survey is difficult to control[19].

Combination of data collection methods

In most organisations it is possible to use a combination of survey and data collection methods, depending on the needs of the organisation, but it requires a well-planned process and clear communication between all stakeholders involved. In South Africa the online web- and paper-methods in combination are the most popular methods. Some organisations have production units with employees who do not have computer skills and computers, which requires the paper-pencil mode.

The question might be asked whether people should be given a choice in which mode they would like to complete the survey, however this might lead to people completing the survey more than once. Although organisations might trust their employees' integrity in this regard, measures to prevent it from happening as far as possible must be discussed in the project team and must be put into place in order to prevent multiple completions. If people who do not have access to computers are given no choice, they might complain that they are treated as 'second-class citizens' by being given 'cheap' paper questionnaires and that the white-collar employees are favoured. From a financial perspective, a paper-based survey completion is more expensive than an online survey completion, especially when a consulting company has the questionnaire printed on shiny paper in full colour, and employees might regard it as money wasted. Borg and Mastrangelo[20] advise that the company should communicate that paper questionnaires are being used despite the fact that it is more costly than online data collection because the survey should be available and accessible to all employees, regardless of where they work and their working environment.

In South African organisations both paper and online methods are often used in combination in order to accommodate workers who have access to computers as well as those who do not work on computers. Table 4.2 portrays the positives and negatives of online and paper methods.

Table 4.2: Online and paper-based data collection (adapted from Church & Waclawski and Perkins in Martins[21])

	Positives	Negatives
Internet-based website response (includes USB, thumb drive and smart phones)	• Data collection and processing are quick and immediate. • Enhanced error correction at entry if screening methods are employed. • Easy to administer on network and users can log in via laptops or desktops whenever they like. • Can be easy to change at last minute. • Variety of interactive formats and programming techniques available. • Perceptions of being cutting-edge and in alignment with e-business mentality. • Quicker analysis of data and feedback. • More regular surveys can be conducted.	• Response requires a computer or laptop • Requires computer literacy (and familiarity) on part of respondents • Requires network access and connectivity • Confidentiality highly suspect due to the nature of the ID systems often used • Potential for multiple responses from single individual unless tracked (cookies can be activated to prevent multiple response submissions) • Can require significant time for initial set-up and debugging, even with the existing 'engines'

	Positives	Negatives
Internet-based website response (includes USB, thumb drive and smart phones) (continued)	• Anonymity can be protected • Fewer human resource services required – less photocopying of instrument, typing and verification of data	• System error, server problems, network traffic or limited bandwidth can crash entire process and frustrate respondents • Less sophisticated systems can be problematic (for example, cutting write-in text off at too few characters; not allowing user to save partially completed survey to finish later, or to submit a form if incomplete)
Paper-and-pen or -pencil response	• Most intuitive survey approach to data collection • Allows great flexibility regarding types of items and scales • Participants work directly on the survey document • Moderate level of confidentiality (concerns regarding handwriting can be an issue) • Easy to change at last minute • Can be completed anywhere, at any time, in any order • Lower risk, fewer uncertainties with technical glitches	• Costly to print in large booklets • Costly to administer via mail • Response burden can be high with long documents • Data processing is costly, complex, time-consuming and more prone to errors due to hand entry or scanning process • May require good writing skills • Appears 'low tech'

More recently, technology such as cell phone completion of an organisational survey has started to become part of the combination of methods being used, especially in organisations where some staff members possess company cell phones, such as agents who work in the field and not in an office. The combination of different methods of data collection appears to be the preferred way of conducting a survey these days, because it creates the impression that the company cares about the different needs of their employees. Furthermore, it creates the opportunity for more employees to participate, thus sufficient data is received to ensure a scientifically sound survey outcome.

MANAGING THE SURVEY PROCESS

Once the forthcoming survey has been communicated to employees, face-to-face meetings have been conducted in the different business units in order to generate excitement about participating in the survey, and posters and pamphlets or other means of communication have been dealt with, the survey is ready to commence. The processes of managing the online and paper-based surveys are discussed below.

Online survey process

An online survey resides on a web-server and usually the data are stored in a file on the server, from where the administrator can download the data. The first step in the online survey process is that the survey consultant should test the online survey, download the test data and import it into the survey software. Following this step would be that the client needs to test the survey on their side. Usually the project team, including the IT person responsible for the internet browser and network connections, should test the survey internally by answering the questions and submitting the test data. When testing is completed, the project team should notify the consultant, who will then download the data and ensure that it reads into the survey software system correctly. Test data then needs to be removed from the hosting server and the client is informed that the survey is ready to commence. This means that the email invitations containing the survey link can be distributed to invite employees to complete the survey online. The IT department distributes the email invitations and must ensure that these emails will not be filtered out as "spam" and that the web survey displays properly on the screen[22]. The survey consultant might be requested to distribute the email invitations when it is important that the consultant and the survey process are visibly viewed as independent due to trust issues in the organisation. Access to the survey is usually obtained by clicking on the link in the e-mail. The internet browser should then display the survey. After selecting the answers to questions and completing open-ended questions, the responses are submitted (by clicking on the 'submit' button).

The survey consultant then needs to download the data at regular intervals and compile a response rate feedback report, which is sent to the client. It is good practice to look through the data immediately after each download in order to identify problems such as duplicate submissions and to compile a true reflection of the response rate for the client.

1.   Response rate feedback report and monitoring response rates

There are different ways of compiling a **response rate feedback report**, but it works best if the consultant speaks to the client project team in order to determine what information they would require to give feedback to the organisation. Mostly the response rate from the different business units and different job levels are important, particularly because interventions based on survey results can be implemented at these levels. Response rates relating to age generation categories, race and gender groups might also be of interest to ensure that sufficient numbers of staff members per category have participated in order to be representative of each category. A representative sample per category provides a sound basis for forming conclusions from the results of the different categories during the analysis and reporting phase. It is advisable that the client provides the survey consultant with at least the actual number of staff members per business unit and per job level. The percentage of participation per category can then be calculated, based on the actual staff complement and the actual participation.

It is important that the project team actively encourages participation in the survey for the duration of the survey administration process. This can be done by sending the response rate feedback report to the managers of each business unit and requesting them to encourage their staff members at their meetings to participate in the survey. Most survey software packages have a functionality whereby managers can also obtain the response rates in *real time* by clicking on a link. The only problem with this is that the data have not yet been verified and cleaned (as discussed in the section *Data Management and Cleaning* below), thus an incorrect picture may be portrayed.

In most surveys, the **response rates** of electronic surveys are usually the highest within the first day after data collection starts, and then decreases exponentially over the rest of the period that the survey is live (active). The question is often asked what percentage of responses would be regarded as sufficient to be representative of the organisation's population and to make meaningful interpretations. The higher the response rate (regardless of administration mode – online or paper), the better, because it will enable the survey consultant to drill down in the data of smaller biographical groups. Borg and Mastrangelo[23] state that according to literature and their survey experience over a period of 20 years, the response rates of employee surveys have an enormous range, between 7% and 100%. They use a value of 80% as a rule-of-thumb target in online employee surveys. Edwards et al.[24] reported that, according to their literature review, response rates lie between 35% and 80%. In our experience as survey consultants we have had an organisation with a 100% response rate. In this particular case there was an extensive marketing and awareness campaign driven from the top, and then driven on all levels to participate in the survey. An interesting case was a parastatal organisation that conducted three employee surveys over a period of six years (biannually). The response rate of the first survey was 34%, but the response rate of the second survey dropped to 22% as a result of low morale of employees during a restructuring phase. The response rate increased substantially to 47% in the third survey, when the organisation was more stable. This example indicates that survey participation is related to the present climate experienced in the organisation. In order to determine if sufficient responses have been received per biographical/geographical group, the guidelines as discussed under *Promoting the Survey* can be used.

2. Sending reminders

Based on each response rate feedback report, the project team can send regular **reminders** to employees during the survey administration process in order to encourage participation. The reminders might consist of the following aspects:

- Survey title and a concise, attention grabbing subject line.
- The purpose of the survey.
- How to access the survey.
- The due date.
- How to get help for technical support or information about the survey itself.

The same branding and key words as in the survey invitation and other survey advertising material must be used in order to minimise confusion. The tone of each consecutive reminder can be designed to read increasingly urgently. In table 4.3 below are examples of three reminders:

Table 4.3: Reminder messages (adapted from the Australian Bureau of Statistics)

Example of first reminder: E-mail for an employee satisfaction survey.

Subject line: **How satisfied are you with the pulse in our organisation?**

Dear Employee,

Last week we sent you a survey, asking for your opinion on a number of aspects in the organisation. If you have already completed and submitted the survey, thank you for your valuable input. If not, please **complete your survey** [link to survey], **and submit your response by** [date].

Your response is much appreciated as it will help us to plan and implement interventions where needed. If you have any questions, please contact the survey consultant at [e-mail address] or [phone number].

Regards,

[CEO name]

Example of second reminder: E-mail for an employee satisfaction survey.

Subject line: **Your participation is vital in evaluating the pulse in our organisation**

Dear Employee

Two weeks ago we sent you a survey, seeking your evaluation of our organisation. If you have already submitted your survey, thank you for your valuable input. If not, please **complete your survey** [link to survey], **and submit your response by [the new date of submission]**.

We have extended the due date because your particular responses are vital in helping us to obtain a sufficient number of respondents to inform our decision-making. If you have any questions, please contact the survey consultant at [e-mail address] or [phone number].

Regards,

[CEO name]

Example of third reminder via SMS:

Sender name: [Survey Manager]

Message: Remember to complete your employee satisfaction survey by [date], or contact us

at [phone number] for help. [CEO Name]

The first reminder can be e-mailed about four days after the start date of the survey. If the survey runs for three weeks, a reminder can be sent out once a week. The dates for sending out reminders must be included in the survey project plan.

Other methods of reminding employees of the survey can be used, such as pop-ups about the survey on the computer screen that pop up as a reminder every morning when an employee starts his/her computer. Most organisations have very creative means of encouraging survey participation and the survey consultant can explore it together with the project team, who could make use of the IT and Marketing divisions for assistance. In some instances companies run competitions per Department or Business Unit.

Experience has shown that most surveys run for two to three weeks, depending on the size of the organisation. We have found that the participation rate determines whether the survey can cut off on the set cut-off date or whether an extension should be granted. The probable extension period should be built into the project plan.

Paper data entry (capturing)

After collecting the completed paper questionnaires, the data needs to be manually captured, either in an Excel spreadsheet format or in the software itself. In figure 4.2 below is an example of raw data that were captured directly from the paper documents to an Excel spreadsheet.

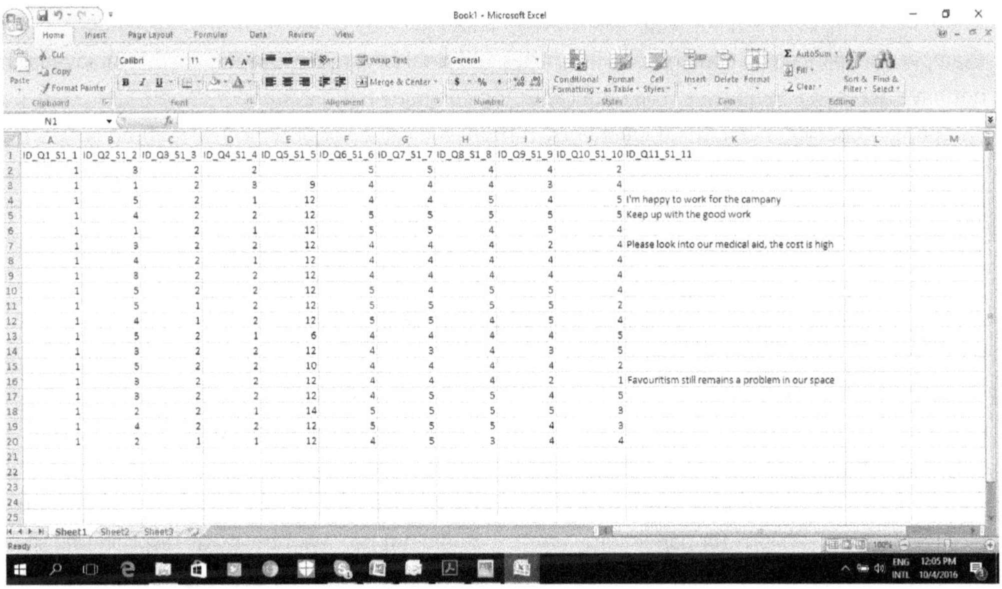

	A	B	C	D	E	F	G	H	I	J	K
1	ID_Q1_S1_1	ID_Q2_S1_2	ID_Q3_S1_3	ID_Q4_S1_4	ID_Q5_S1_5	ID_Q6_S1_6	ID_Q7_S1_7	ID_Q8_S1_8	ID_Q9_S1_9	ID_Q10_S1_10	ID_Q11_S1_11
2	1	3	2	2		5	5	4	4	2	
3	1	1	2	3	9	4	4	4	3	4	
4	1	5	2	1	12	4	4	5	4	5	I'm happy to work for the campany
5	1	4	2	2	12	5	5	5	5	5	Keep up with the good work
6	1	1	2	1	12	5	5	4	5	4	
7	1	3	2	2	12	4	4	4	2	4	Please look into our medical aid, the cost is high
8	1	4	2	1	12	4	4	4	4	4	
9	1	3	2	2	12	4	4	4	4	4	
10	1	5	2	2	12	5	4	5	5	4	
11	1	5	1	2	12	5	5	5	5	2	
12	1	4	1	2	12	5	5	4	5	4	
13	1	5	2	1	6	4	4	4	4	5	
14	1	3	2	2	12	4	3	4	3	5	
15	1	5	2	2	10	4	4	4	4	2	
16	1	3	2	2	12	4	4	4	2	1	Favouritism still remains a problem in our space
17	1	3	2	2	12	4	5	5	4	5	
18	1	2	2	1	14	5	5	5	5	3	
19	1	4	2	2	12	5	5	5	4	3	
20	1	2	1	1	12	4	5	3	4	4	

Figure 4.2: Data captured in an Excel spreadsheet

The columns relate to each question in the survey (Column A is question 1, etc.) and each row contains the responses of one individual respondent to each question in the survey. The code that is captured in each cell relates to the category that was selected. For example, if column C contains the data of the question: "What is your gender?" and there were three categories, the code value of each category would be 1 for "male", 2 for "female" and 3 for "do not want to disclose":

- ○ Male
- ○ Female
- ○ Do not want to disclose

An example of a Likert type scale coding is as follows:

1 = Strongly disagree

2 = Disagree

3 = Unsure

4 = Agree

5 = Strongly agree

Based on the individual's selected answer, the particular code must be entered in the cell relating to the question. The codes are not shown on the online version of the questionnaire, as they are programmed in the survey software. The survey consultant must make sure that for the paper completed version, the coding for each question category is provided in an MS Word format as an example to refer to during the capturing process.

The data capturers should ensure that the codes are typed correctly. We usually make use of a data capturing company for large quantities of paper surveys collected from organisations in, for example, the mining and construction industries and local government, where many employees do not have access to computers. The data capturing company has a system of double capturing, i.e. two people/operators would independently capture the same set of data. The method is referred to as double key entry. The second person is responsible for verifying discrepancies between the second and first entries. Macey[25] states that the accuracy of double key entry is guaranteed by service providers to be in excess of 99%, but in practice it is 100% accurate.

Final cut-off, response feedback and data consolidation

On the day of the official cut-off date of the survey, the survey consultant would prepare a response rate feedback report of the online data collected. The online survey should then be removed from the web so that employees at the organisation cannot access the survey to complete it after the cut-off date. Unless a manual tracking system of participants per business unit was kept during facilitated group sessions for paper completion, it would not be clear how many respondents from the different business units and the rest of the biographical categories have responded, before the data has not been captured. Usually the survey consultant might arrange that data capturing of paper questionnaires takes place as they are collected, to cut down on data capturing time after the survey has closed off.

Once the paper questionnaire data have been captured and verified, the data of the different collection methods used in the survey administration process must be consolidated into one database. At this point, the survey consultant and the organisation might get the first clear picture of the overall responses. A final response rate feedback report can be compiled to update the project team on the total data collection status.

DATA MANAGEMENT AND CLEANING

Church and Waclawsky[26] point out that some people think the data that have been captured or collected online are automatically ready for analysis, but this is not the case. The data must be prepared (cleaned), which is the process of identifying and removing the various types of problematic responses that sometimes occur in any data collection process. Borg and Mastrangelo[27] compare data cleaning and eliminating data errors to detective work, stating that it is tedious and detail-focused.

After each download of the online data, the data must be screened for obvious faults or errors. Notes can be kept of the changes made to the data, which are re-applied after each download, and then screening continues on the newly added response data. Because the manually captured data are added to the online data at the end of the survey administration process, it is advisable to screen the entire data file at this stage, before moving forward to the analysis and interpretation process. The screening of data is easily done in an Excel spreadsheet format.

Typical types of common problems or issues must be identified in the data and then either be removed or re-coded (edited). Some of the most common problems (type of issue and examples) and typical solutions are listed below in table 4.4.

Table 4.4: Data cleaning and editing (adapted from Borg & Mastrangelo; Church & Waclawski; Macey)[28]

Type of issue	Examples	Typical solution
Missing, incomplete, or partially completed responses	• Blank rows without data. • First five questions completed, and the rest left blank.	• Delete row(s). • Delete row(s). Partially completed questionnaires should be retained, but if less than 10 percent of the total set of questions is completed, the row of data must be removed.
Duplicate rows of responses	• Two or more rows of the exact same data from beginning to end, indicating that the person accidentally or intentionally submitted online data more than once	• Delete row(s).
Problematic or intentional response patterns	• All middle scores (for example, all 3's) • All extreme scores (for example, all 1's or 5's) • Repeating scores (for example 1,2,3,4,5,1,2,3,4,5,1,2,3,4,5	• Delete row(s). • Delete row(s). • Delete row(s).

Type of issue	Examples	Typical solution
Paper questionnaires with the exact same scores	• Handing in a pack of photocopies of one paper completed questionnaire, together with the rest of the paper completed questionnaires.	• Hard to detect, but might be noticed if manually paging through and checking before capturing, or in the Excel data file if captured one after another and noticing duplicate rows of data, which should be deleted.
Re-coding/Editing of data		
Incorrect responses to biographical or demographical questions	• Selecting wrong business unit; with organisational restructuring occurring frequently in business these days, all employees may not be aware of the official new business unit names.	• Discuss issues with the project team and decide how to handle these issues. There might be ways of verifying the business units based on some of the other biographical questions.
	• More employees classifying themselves as supervisory or management staff members than warranted by the organisational status of levels.	• For example, if all members of the executive team are males, then all females who claim to belong to the executive group must be wrong.

Some errors, such as incorrect responses to biographical or demographic questions might not immediately be detected in the raw data file, but by having a look at response distributions to determine whether patterns fall within expected boundaries. For example, the survey consultant might create cross-tables of gender and levels. If there is a frequency of, for example, '2' for executive females in the cross-table and there are no females on this level, these responses can be located in the data rows and the 'executive' response to the question on levels of these two females can be removed in the data. In the end, any recoding must be done with great care because it does remain speculative[29]. If there are uncertainties that cannot be rectified in a logical way, the consultant can always explain to the client that it is difficult to guess and that errors are removed as far as possible to guarantee the integrity of the data.

Data editing and cleaning require general rules for exceptional handling, which should be followed rigorously, and require experience. It might be useful to keep a record of decisions made that fall outside the scope of the general rules. For example, the authors conducted an annual employee satisfaction survey for six consecutive years for a South African organisation with just over 1,000 staff members. In the first year one of the directors noticed in the first response feedback report that there were way too many people who selected his particular department, he had only 20 staff members reporting to him. It then turned out that some of the agents working in the field were under the wrong impression that they belonged to his department. Their responses thus had the potential of skewing the departmental results. It was decided to retain their responses to all questions, but to remove the departmental code of all the respondents who selected that particular department. In this way their responses would still be included in the overall results, but not linked to a particular department. Upon immediate investigation after the discrepancy was noticed, it turned out that only two of the actual staff members from that department had completed the survey and their particular department selection was obviously removed with the rest of the codes for that department. The 18 staff members who had not completed the survey were then requested to complete the survey the day after the official cut-off date, so that a departmental report could be generated for the department. In the years to follow, when the same survey was repeated, the rule became that staff members from that particular department would complete their surveys on the day after the official cut-off date.

One needs to maintain a record of changes made to data records, particularly where recoding of survey responses was required[30]. These aspects might even be included in the survey reporting to the organisation to explain how discrepancies, if any, were dealt with in the most reasonable way. Once the data have been cleaned, the next phase is the analysis and reporting phase which will be discussed in chapter 6.

CONCLUSION

This chapter should be able to assist you in the administration of surveys. The knowledge regarding best practices in paper and online surveys can enable you to make sound decisions in your role as a survey consultant or manager. Insight into the benefits and limitations of the various methods in the execution of surveys can assist you in implementing successful organisational diagnostic projects.

REFERENCES

Australian Bureau of Statistics. 2010. *Reminder Letters. ABS Forms Design Standards Manual.* Retrieved October 3, 2016, from http://www.nss.gov.au/nss/home.NSF/533222ebfd5ac03aca25711000044c9e/6ec35906bf-3d2a4fca257a760007d6e1/$FILE/Survey%20Practice%20Guide%20Survey%20Reminders.pdf

Borg, I. & Mastrangelo, P.M. 2008. Employee surveys in management: theories, tools, and practical applications. Cambridge, MA: Hogrefe.

Church, A.H. & Waclawski, J. 2001. *Designing and using organizational surveys: a seven-step process.* San Francisco, Calif: Jossey-Bass.

Evans, JR. & Mathur, A. 2005. The value of online surveys. *Internet Research,* 15(2):195-219.

Kelly, K., Clark, B., Brown, V. & Sitzia, J. 2003. Good practices in the practice and conduct reporting of survey research. *International Journal in Quality Health Care,* 15(3):261-266.

Leedy, DP. & Ormrod, EJ. 2010. *Practical research: planning and design.* (9th ed.). New Jersey: Pearson Education International.

Macey, WH. 1996. Dealing with the data: collection, processing, and analysis, in *Organizational surveys,* edited by Al Kraut. San Francisco: Jossey-Bass:149-176.

Martins, EC. 2010. *Identifying organisational and behavioural factors that influence knowledge retention.* PhD dissertation. Pretoria: University of South Africa.

Martins, N. 2010. Measurement model equivalence in web- and paper-based surveys. *South African Business Review* 14(3):77-107.

Pennsylvania State University. *Example 2: Program Evaluation, Tipsheet #60. How to determine a sample size.* [Online]. Available: http://ucanr.edu/sites/CEprogramevaluation/files/143304.pdf [Accessed 16 March 2017].

Rivera, A. 2016. *The best survey software of 2017: get actionable insights with survey software.* [Online] Available. http://www.toptenreviews.com/business/software/best-survey-software [Accessed: 14 February 2017].

Schindler, E. 2016. *The best online survey tools of 2016.* [Online] www.pcmag.com/article2/0,2817,2494737,00.asp [Accessed: 14 February 2017]

Training Technologies. 2008. SurveyTracker E-mail/Web User's Guide. USA.

Uys, T. & Puttergil, C. 2003. Sampling, in *Intellectual tools: skills for human sciences*, edited by D Rossouw. 2nd edition. Pretoria: Van Schaik:107-116.

Watson, J. 2001. *How to Determine a Sample Size: Tipsheet #60, University Park, PA: Penn State Cooperative Extension.* Available. http://www.extension.psu.edu/evaluation/pdf/TS60.pdf [Accessed 16 March 2017]

ENDNOTES

1.   Glascow, 2005
2.   Frankel & Frankel, 1988.
3.   Salant & Dillman, 1994:54.
4.   Salant & Dillman, 1994.
5.   Leedy & Ormrod, 2010.
6.   Training Technologies, 2008.
7.   Training Technologies, 2008.
8.   Training Technologies, 2008.
9.   Leedy & Ormrod, 2010.
10. Uys & Puttergil, 2003.
11. Martins, 2010.
12. Evans & Mathur, 2005.
13. Glascow, 2005.
14. Rivera, 2016; Schindler, 2016.
15. Martins, 2010.
16. Martins, 2010:77-7.
17. Kelly, Clark, Brown & Sitzia, 2003:266.
18. Leedy & Ormrod, 2010.
19. Kelly et al., 2003.
20. Borg & Mastrangelo, 2008:226.
21. Church & Waclawski, 2001; Perkins, 2004 in Martins, 2010:81-82.
22. Borg & Mastrangelo, 2008:207.
23. Borg & Mastrangelo, 2008.
24. Edwards, et al., cited in Borg & Mastrangelo, 2008.
25. Macey, 1996.
26. Church & Waclawsky, 1998.
27. Borg & Mastrangelo, 2008.
28. Borg & Mastrangelo, 2008; Church & Waclawski, 1998; Macey, 1996.
29. Macey, 1996.
30. Macey,1996.

Example 1: Cover Letter

Dear Employee,

It is important for Exco to understand the satisfaction levels of our staff members. In an attempt to understand what is important to our employees and to identify any possible concerns of our staff members, Co ABC, in conjunction with Organisational Diagnostics, is conducting a survey. To help us in arriving at this point, we would like to urge staff members to take the time to complete the questionnaire which is available on the link to an independent website, given below.

Participation is on a voluntary basis. Participation is also anonymous and confidential – no one will know the answer you selected.

Should you experience any technical difficulties, please contact Ellen/Anthea at Organisational Diagnostics on 011 432 2006 or send an e-mail to nicellen@iafrica.com.

The questionnaire will be available on the following web-link http://www.orgdia.co.za/survey/CoABC/empsat.htm from xxxxx to xxxxx. Every employee at Co ABC is hereby invited to complete the questionnaire during this period.

What does the questionnaire consist of?

Section 1:

Biographical Information: These questions are designed to gauge the feelings of different groups within Co ABC. The information on race and gender, for instance, would ensure that any concern by any groupings in this regard is appropriately addressed.

Section 2:

Questions on how you perceive/experience the working environment (your perception regarding satisfaction/dissatisfaction).

Questions you might have regarding the survey.

Following are answers to some of the questions you might have regarding this project.

Why do I need to complete the questionnaire?

Your participation is vital in gaining an accurate reflection of the perceptions of all employees. This study will only be relevant if you participate. The results will enable management to determine whether we are moving towards achieving our goals.

What will happen to my answers?

The results of the survey will be used to make Co ABC a place where you can learn and grow; where your differences and concerns are appreciated, valued and addressed; and your ideas sought, tested and used.

Can I really be honest?

Yes! Please answer each question as honestly as possible, because your views are essential. All information supplied will be treated strictly confidentially by Organisational Diagnostics, which will be conducting the analysis. To ensure this, the questionnaire will be completed on a web-based platform and the results will be analysed collectively, where it is impossible to identify individuals. The survey is totally confidential and I urge you to use this opportunity to give your opinion.

How long will it take to complete the questionnaire?

It will only take ± 20 to 30 minutes to complete.

Will I get feedback?

Feedback will be given to you by Organisational Diagnostics via focus groups and by means of your management. Thank you in advance for your willingness to participate in the survey.

Sincerely,

PENNSTATE

Cooperative Extension

Example 2: Program Evaluation
Tipsheet #60

How to Determine a Sample Size

I want to survey a large group of people. What size should my sample be? Twenty percent? Thirty percent?

AVOID

There is no set percentage that is accurate for every population. What matters is the actual number or size of the sample, not the percentage of the population. Consider a coin toss: the first few times you flip the coin, the average result may be skewed wildly in one direction (say you got 5 tails in a row), but the more times you flip the coin, the more likely that the average result will be an even split between heads and tails.

So, if you surveyed 20% of a group of 300 program participants to produce a sample of 60 people, you would **under represent** the population, since there is a fairly large chance in a small group that the respondents you choose will vary from the whole population. On the other hand, 20% of 30 000 county residents (a sample of 6 000) would be a wastefully large sample and not significantly more accurate than a sample of 400.

USE

There are five steps in deciding a sample size. If you are familiar with them, select a sample size, using the tables in Appendices 1 and 2 at the end of the Tipsheet. To use a formula, move to Appendix 3. If you wish to review the five steps before selecting a sample size however, read on.

Steps in selecting a Sample size

An appropriate sample size is based on a number of accuracy factors that you must consider. Together they comprise a five step process:

1. Determine **Goals**
2. Determine desired **Precision** of results
3. Determine **Confidence** level
4. Estimate the degree of **Variability**
5. Estimate the **Response Rate**

Step One: Determine Goals

- Firstly, know the size of the population with which you are dealing. If your population is small in number (200 people or less), it may be preferable to perform a **census** of everyone in the population, rather than a **sample**. For a marginally higher cost than a 134-person sample, you can survey the entire population and gain a 0% sampling error. However, if the population from which you want to gather information is larger, it makes sense to rather perform a sample.

- Secondly, decide on the methods and design of the sample you are going to draw and the specific **attributes or concepts** you are trying to measure.

• Thirdly, know what kind of resources you have available, as they could be a limitation on other steps below, such as your level of precision. Once you have this information at hand, you are ready to proceed to the next step.

Step Two: Determine the Desired Precision of Results

The **level of precision** is the closeness with which the sample predicts where the true values in the population lie. The difference between the sample and the real population is called the **sampling error**. If the sampling error is ± 3%, this means we add or subtract 3 percentage points from the value in the survey in order to determine the actual value in the population. For example, if the value in a survey says that 65% of farmers use a particular pesticide and the sample error is ± 3%, we know that in the real-world population, between 62% and 68% are likely to use this pesticide. This range is also commonly referred to as the **margin of error**.

The level of precision that you accept depends on balancing accuracy and resources. High levels of precision require larger sample sizes and higher costs to achieve those samples, but high margins of error can leave you with results that are not much more meaningful than human estimation.

The tables in Appendices 1 and 2 at the end of the Tipsheet provide sample sizes for **precision levels** of 5% and 3% respectively.

Step Three: Determine the Confidence Level

The confidence level involves the **risk** that you are willing to accept that your sample is within the average or "bell curve" of the population. A confidence level of 90% means that, were the population sampled 100 times in the same manner, 90 of these samples would have the true population value within the **range of precision** specified earlier, and 10 would be unrepresentative samples. Higher confidence levels require larger sample sizes.

The tables at the end of this Tipsheet assume a 95% confidence level. This level is standard for most social science applications, though higher levels can be used. If the confidence level chosen is too low, results will be "statistically insignificant".

Step Four: Estimate the Degree of Variability

Variability is the degree to which the attributes or concepts being measured in the questions are distributed throughout the population. A heterogeneous population, divided more or less 50%-50% on an attribute or a concept, will be harder to measure precisely than a homogeneous population, divided for example 80%-20%. Therefore, the higher the degree of variability you expect the distribution of a concept to be in your target audience, the larger the sample size must be to obtain the same level of precision.

To estimate variability, simply take a reasonable guess of the size of the smaller attribute or concept that you are trying to measure, rounding **up** if necessary. If you estimate that 25% of the population in your municipality farms organically and 75% does not, then your variability would be .25 (which rounds up to 30% on the table provided at the end of this Tipsheet). If variability is too difficult to estimate, it is best to use the conservative figure of 50%.

Note: When the population is *extremely* heterogeneous (i.e. greater than 90-10), a larger sample may be needed for an accurate result, because the population with the minority attribute is so low.

At this point, using the **level of precision** and **estimate of variability** you have selected, you can use either the table or the equation provided at the bottom of this Tipsheet in order to determine the **base sample size** for your project.

Step Five: Estimate the Response Rate

The base sample size is the number of responses that must be returned to you when you conduct your survey. However, since not everyone will respond, you will need to increase your sample size and perhaps the number of contacts you attempt to take into account for these non-responses. To estimate the response rate that you are likely to get, you should take into consideration the method of your survey and the population involved. Direct contact and multiple contacts increase response ratio, as does a population which is interested in the issues involved, or connected to the institution conducting the survey, or limited or specialised in character. You can also look at the response rates that may have occurred in similar, previous surveys.

When you have estimated the expected response percentage, then divide the base sample size by the response percentage. For example, if you estimated a response rate of 70% and had a base sample size of 220, then your final sample size would be 315 (220/0.7).

Once you have established this, you are ready to commence with your sampling!

One final note about response rates: the past thirty years of research have demonstrated that the characteristics of non-respondents may differ *significantly* from those of respondents. Follow-up samples may need to be taken of the *non*-respondent population to determine what differences, if any, may exist.

Appendix 1 Example: 5% Error and Qualification.
Appendix 2 Example: 3% Error and Qualification.
Appendix 3 Example: An Equation for Determining Final Sample Size

REFERENCES:

Blalock, H. M. 1972. Social Statistics. New York: McGraw-Hill Book Company.

Israel, G.D. 1992. "Determining Sample Size." Program Evaluation and Organizational Development, IFAS, University of Florida. PEOD-6.

National Science Foundation, Research and Development in Industry: 1992, NSF 95-324. Arlington, VA.

Smith, M.F. 1983. "Sampling Considerations in Evaluating Cooperative Extension Programs." Cooperative Extension Serve, IFAS, University of Florida. DRAFT.

Taylor-Powell, E. May 1998. "Sampling." Program Development and Evaluation, University of Wisconsin Extension. G3658-3.

Sudman, S. 1976. Applied Sampling. New York: Academic Press.

Warmbrod, J.R. 1965. "The Sampling Problem in Research Design." Agriculture Education Magazine. pp 106-107, 114-115.

Yamane, T. 1973. "Statistics: an Introductory Analysis." New York: Harper & Row.

Jeff Watson, Research Assistant, Cooperative Extension & Outreach. The reference citation for this Tipsheet is: Watson, Jeff (2001). How to Determine a Sample Size: Tipsheet #60, University Park, PA: Penn State Cooperative Extension. Available at: http://www.extension.psu.edu/evaluation/pdf/TS60.pdf

Appendix 1: Tables[a] for Finding a Base Sample Size[b]

+/- 5% Margin of Error[c]

Sample Size

Variability					
Population	50%	40%	30%	20%	10% [d]
100 [e]	81	79	63	50	37
125	96	93	72	56	40
150	110	107	80	60	42
175	122	119	87	64	44
200	134	130	93	67	45
225	144	140	98	70	46
250	154	149	102	72	47
275	163	158	106	74	48
300	172	165	109	76	49
325	180	173	113	77	50
350	187	180	115	79	50
375	194	186	118	80	51
400	201	192	120	81	51
425	207	197	122	82	51
450	212	203	124	83	52
500	222	212	128	84	52
600	240	228	134	87	53
700	255	242	138	88	54
800	267	252	142	90	54
900	277	262	144	91	55
1,000	286	269	147	92	55
2,000	333	311	158	96	57
3,000	353	328	163	98	57
4,000	364	338	165	99	58
5,000	370	343	166	99	58
6,000	375	347	167	100	58

	Variability				
Population	50%	40%	30%	20%	10% [d]
7,000	378	350	168	100	58
8,000	381	353	168	100	58
9,000	383	354	169	100	58
10,000	385	356	169	100	58
15,000	390	360	170	101	58
20,000	392	362	171	101	58
25,000	394	363	171	101	58
50,000	397	366	172	101	58
100,000	398	367	172	101	58

Qualifications

a) This table **assumes a 95% confidence level**, identifying a risk of 1 in 20 that actual error is larger than the margin of error (greater than 5%).
b) Base sample size should be **increased** to take into consideration potential non-response.
c) A **five percent margin of error** indicates willingness to accept an estimate within +/- 5 of the given value.
d) When the estimated population with the smaller attribute of concept is less than 10%, the sample may need to be increased.
e) The assumption of normal population is poor for 5% precision levels when the population is 100 or less. The entire population should be sampled, or a lesser precision accepted.

Appendix 2: Tables[a] for Finding a Base Sample Size[b]

+/- 3% Margin of Error[c]

	Variability				
Population	50%	40%	30%	20%	10% [d]
2,000 [e]	714	677	619	509	322
3,000	811	764	690	556	341
4,000	870	816	732	583	350
5,000	909	850	760	601	357
6,000	938	875	780	613	361
7,000	959	892	795	622	364
8,000	976	908	806	629	367

	Variability				
Population	50%	40%	30%	20%	10% d
9,000	989	920	815	635	368
10,000	1000	929	823	639	370
15,000	1034	959	846	653	375
20,000	1053	975	858	660	377
25,000	1064	984	865	665	378
50,000	1087	1004	881	674	381
100,000	1099	1014	888	678	383

Qualifications

a) This table **assumes a 95% confidence level**, identifying a risk of 1 in 20 that actual error is larger than the margin of error (greater than 3%).
b) Base sample size should be **increased** to take into consideration potential non-response.
c) A **three percent margin of error** indicates willingness to accept an estimate within +/- 3 of the given value.
d) When the estimated population with the smaller attribute of concept is less than 10%, the sample may need to be increased.
e) The assumption of normal population is poor for 3% precision levels when the population is 2,000 or less. The entire population should be sampled, or a lesser precision should be accepted.

Appendix 3: An Equation for Determining Final Sample Size

$$n = \frac{\left(\dfrac{P\left[1-P\right]}{\dfrac{A^2}{Z^2} + \dfrac{P\left[1-P\right]}{N}} \right)}{R}$$

Where:

n = sample size required

N = number of people in population

P = estimated variance in population, as a decimal: (0.5 for 50-50, 0.3 for 70-30)

A = Precision desired, expressed as a decimal (i.e. 0.03, 0.05, 0.1 for 3%, 5%, 10%)

Z = Based on confidence level: 1.96 for 95% confidence, 1.6449 for 90% and 2.5758 for 99%

R = Estimated response rate, as a decimal

Source: Adapted from Watson (2001).

CHAPTER 5

DATA GATHERING IN GROUPS – AN INCLUSIVE WAY OF GATHERING RICH DATA

by **Dr Rica Viljoen**

INTRODUCTION

In this chapter the qualitative data-gathering method of focus groups is discussed. Focus groups can be used in various research designs that are underpinned by different research philosophies. This data-gathering method provides rich data that can significantly assist the phenomenological, ethnographic, integral and collaborative researcher in weaving a colourful tapestry of understanding of a social phenomenon. Various options to this method, such as world café methodology, are introduced, and advice is incorporated on how to conduct an effective focus group. Different ways of documenting and analysing data are considered, while the results of actual focus groups are shared. The chapter concludes with the methodology of collaborative inquiry, where the participants of the group themselves become co-researchers. Criteria are discussed for conducting quality focus groups and ethical considerations.

Sparkes[1] explains that a researcher can use auto-ethnographic tales to reflect on personal experiences in the actual writing of research results. The author makes use of this approach to share some experiences of focus groups in multicultural settings in this chapter. Auto-ethnographical notes will be indented and presented in a smaller font.

> I was sitting in the midst of 15 elderly men from Marikana. It was difficult to connect with the participants. They seemed aloof and disinterested. It was dark still, and the outside temperature was close to -6 °C. After what felt like thirty minutes, an elderly gentleman joined the group, and spoke quite animatedly to them. He told me to continue asking the questions that I wanted. To my disbelief, a passionate conversation started. After the two hours scheduled for the session was done, the participants could not be stopped and still wanted to share their thoughts. Later I asked the elder what he had told the group to say. He explained that he was a chief in the local village and that the group would always wait for him to appear. He explained how collectivism worked, and that permission from the elder was crucial. Tongue in the cheek he told me that he had the lowest job title of all the participants. That day I learned not to underestimate the worldview of research participants.

Focus groups can be used as a data-gathering method in numerous research strategies. It is particularly effective in exploring social system dynamics. Different research philosophies that will result in specific research strategies for which focus groups provide congruent and rich data are presented below.

PHILOSOPHY

Introduction

Creswell[2] describes five different qualitative strategies from which the prospective researcher can choose. These are a narrative study, a phenomenological study, a grounded theory study, ethnography and case-study methodology. In selecting an approach, the unit of study is important. According to Creswell, the unit of analysis in phenomenology and in ethnography is often on the group domain. Focus-group inquiries or interviews are viewed as appropriate ways of gathering data in a phenomenological study.

Although focus groups can also be used in case studies, or as an additional voice for validating an auto-ethnography in a narrative study, they are mostly used in studies that explore a specific phenomenon. Viljoen-Terblanche[3] highlights the importance of focus groups in a mixed methods study, yet even then, she explains, such groups have a phenomenological nature. For the purpose of this chapter, phenomenology, and to a lesser degree ethnography, is positioned as a philosophical stance.

True to the phenomenological stance, the author will speak from the first person in this chapter.

Phenomenology

Phenomenology does offer ways of understanding not offered by other research methodologies.

> *"In contrast to the scientific method it is both poetic and interpretive. . . ."*
> —Chambell, unknown in Viljoen-Terblanche[4]

Through the methods of phenomenology, readers come to apprehend the means by which phenomena, which originate in human consciousness, come to be experienced as features of the world. The aim of phenomenology, as propounded by Husserl[5], is to study human phenomena without considering questions relating to the causes, the objective reality, or even the appearances of these human phenomena. Ultimately, the intent is to study the way in which phenomena are experienced in consciousness, therefore phenomenology seeks to understand the ways in which human beings construct meaning. A human being's experience of the world, upon which his or her thoughts about the world are based, is, however, inter-subjective, because the world is experienced with and through others. The meanings that are created have their origins in human actions[6]. Thus, the purpose of phenomenology is to describe the experiences of one or more individuals of the phenomenon in question[7]. Rich, multicultural sensitive data is rendered by this paradigm.

As a result of the complex interrelationships that were studied at a deeper level of understanding[8] in social systems studies[9] in order to generate greater knowledge about the phenomenon of Inclusivity, phenomenology was adopted as the research philosophy for this study.

Phenomenology, which is sometimes considered to be a philosophical perspective, as well as an approach to qualitative methodology, is dedicated to "describing the structures of experience as they present themselves to consciousness, without resource to theory, deduction or assumptions from other disciplines such as the natural sciences"[10]. It is a school of thought in terms of which the emphasis is on subjective experiences and interpretations of the world. In other words, the phenomenologist seeks to understand the way in which the world appears to others[11].

Phenomenology has its roots in the work of Husserl[12] who believed that the objectivism of science precluded an adequate apprehension of the world. From the work of Husserl, Schutz[13] distilled a sociological approach, and endeavoured to describe the way in which subjective meanings gave rise to an apparently objective social world. Traditionally, philosophy includes at least four core fields or disciplines, namely, ontology, epistemology, logic and ethics. In phenomenology the following statements would explain the contribution of each of these core fields[14]:

1. Ontology is the study of beings or their being – what is.
2. Epistemology is the study of knowledge – how we know.
3. Logic is the study of valid reasoning – how we reason.
4. Ethics is the study of right and wrong – how we should act; and
5. **Phenomenology is the study of our experience – how we experience.**

Despite the fact that phenomenology has a theoretical orientation, it does not generate deductions from propositions that may be empirically tested[15]. Phenomenology rather operates on a meta-level, and demonstrates its premises through descriptive analyses of the procedures of the self, and the situational and social settings. Phenomenology is the study of the contents of consciousness – phenomenon – and phenomenological methods are ways in which these contents may be described and analysed[16]. Focus group data is particularly meaningful to the phenomenological?

WHAT IS A FOCUS GROUP?

A focus group defined

The American Heritage® Dictionary of the English Language[17] defines the focus group as "a small group selected from a wider population and sampled, as by open discussion, for its members' opinions about or emotional response to a particular subject or area, used especially in market research or political analysis". Kruger and Casey[18] define a focus group as "a carefully planned series of discussions designed to obtain perceptions on a defined area of interest in a permissive non-threatening environment". A focus group is a data-gathering method that is applied during qualitative research to understand the attitudes of the participants towards the research questions. Powell et al.[19] described a focus group as a group of individuals selected and assembled by researchers to discuss and comment on, from personal experience, the topic that is the subject of the research.

In literature focus, groups are sometimes referred to as organised dialogue[20], interaction[21], social events[22], collective endeavours[23], participant groups[24], and human mandalas[25]. In this chapter the terms "focus groups" and "group interviews" are used interchangeably. Further, alternative creative ways of gathering data in groups are introduced such as round-table groups[26], collaborative inquiry methods,[27] appreciative inquiry[28] and listening posts[29].

Powell and Single[30] define a focus group as: "A group of individuals selected and assembled by researchers to discuss and comment on, from personal experience, the topic that is the subject of the research." It should be planned carefully[31], and can be described as a planned series of discussions intended to gather insights on a defined area of relevance in a lenient non-threatening environment. Krueger[32] explains that participants had to respond to ideas, questions or comments in a planned manner that facilitated interaction in a neutral space that was close to real-life properties.

Human communication is characterised by metaphor[33]. Techniques such as storytelling and art can thus be integrated with great effect into conducting a focus group. Bateson[34] also highlights the transformational effect of becoming conscious of our own metaphors, and states that the actual research can have an impact on a social system. The focus group can therefore have positive unintended systemic implications.

A focus group is not the following:

1. A discussion or a debate – it is rather a dialogue
2. A therapy group
3. A problem-solving group – rather it is an opportunity to collaborate
4. A conflict resolution group
5. A training group – rather it is a data-gathering group that studies a specific phenomenon from different angles.

Mouton[35] explains that the purpose of a focus group is to bring together participants who were identified as having a specific profile. The participants can be homogenous along specific criteria and heterogeneous along others. A limited number of questions are posed to the focus groups. In focus groups, unlike in interviews, an additional dimension for interpretation is presented, namely the interaction between team members. The skilled focus group facilitator will also interpret the group dynamic, what is not being said, and the silences, and try and make sense of the non-sense in the group, especially if the researcher has adapted a psychoanalytical lens[36].

Criteria for a focus group

Patton[37] states that there are no rules for sample size in qualitative inquiry, and explains that "sample size depends on what you want to know, the purpose of the inquiry, what is at stake, what will be useful, what will have credibility and what can be done with available time and resources". He[38] explains that validity, meaningfulness and insights generated from qualitative inquiry have more to do with the richness of information and the observational/analytical capabilities of the researcher than the sample size. Babbie[39] refers to Freud, who established the field of psychoanalysis based on fewer than ten client cases over a long period of time.

MacIntosh[40] recommended that six to ten participants take part in a focus group. Others, such as Goss and Leibach[41] state, that it may consist of up to 15, while Kitzinger[42] prefers to work with as few as four participants. One can have a longitudinal design where the researcher meets with the same group several times. Alternatively, one meeting with each of several groups can be held[43]. A focus group typically lasts between one and two hours. It is best if a location is chosen that is neutral[44], although it also could be conducted in rented facilities, at the home of the researcher or participant, or in the workplace.

The researcher should attempt to identify a diverse group with appropriate knowledge of the research question or problem area. It is important to make the participants feel at ease. This statement may impact the combination of participants for a specific session. Here, Morgan[45] underlines the fact that people with similar characteristics or understanding of the topic at hand may feel more comfortable than if it were not the case. Participants may be invited by word of mouth[46], through posters or advertising[47], or key informants may be used. Social networks may also be applied. Sometimes incentives such as gift vouchers are offered. Typically, a focus group is arranged six to eight weeks in advance.

The setting up of the physical space

The actual location is important for the focus group. The researcher should ensure that there is enough parking space, that there is easy access if public transport is used, and that the venue is large enough to host all the participants. Bion[48] explains that one can create psychological safety through the contracting of boundaries of time, space and content. For market research and political science research, psychological safety is critical. Here tables may be placed in front of the participants to create a sense of safety, and observers may look on from behind one-sided mirrors. However, in groups where it is important to create a sense of discomfort that is facilitated into a trust group, all tables may be removed. Initially anxiety is created in this way, however through the contracting of the boundaries of time, space and content, authentic voices are often heard. In the case of working with rural groups, one can form a circle under a tree. In all the cases described here, the researcher should sit at eye-level with the participants so as not to create a power dynamic. By sitting with people on the grass or floor in rural settings, one is quickly embraced as one of them and deep inclusive conversations can take place.

The facilitator should ensure that all necessities are provided, such as markers, flipchart paper, and name tags. Notepads and pens may also be provided. A computer with the presentation may be set up, and the interview schedule may be printed. A list of all the participants should be available. It is helpful to place a large clock in a space that all can see. Refreshments may be provided. The facilitator must be there in time to welcome the participants and to arrange the room in a way that is conducive such, as a U-curve with everyone at one table. An audio tape-recorder and/or a video-recorder may be used to capture the session. Cellular phone applications such as Evernote and Audionote provide easy access to recording facilities. The author always takes post-it notes with her, which are used when it is important to note down the views of individual participants during certain parts of the group interview. Participants are then requested to generate one idea per post-it note so that these individual voices are not lost. These notes can either be displayed on a shared work space, or be kept for data analysis later in the process. Blank sheets of paper can be used for similar effects. If a specific framework or model forms the theoretical underpinning of a focus group, a laminated poster that displays it can be placed on the wall, in the middle of the room or on the floor; basically in any shared open space. Alternatively, it may be projected on a proxima/light projector. In the last scenario, a laptop or other electronic device is also required. The facilitator can also use graphic facilitation skills to construct a mind map or visually present different viewpoints as the session progresses. In this case a large white or brown sheet of paper can be attached to an open wall, and with special markers a rich visual picture will emerge.

Posing questions

Good questions start with "how?" and "what?" as they provide a descriptive answer. The facilitator should ask follow-up questions and probe for additional information[49]. The questions should be aligned with the research questions of the research study. It is good practice to formalise a focus group schedule. In the writing up of research results in the actual dissertation or thesis or compilation of an organisational report, the researcher must attach this framework as an appendix.

Questions may include: "What did you learn?" – "What was the biggest surprise?" – "Who is in charge?" – "Who can gain most?" – "Why?" – "What is left unsaid in the organisation?" – "What are the unwritten rules of inclusion?" – "What are you still curious about?" – "If you could ask leadership one question what would it be?" – "What will you tell someone who is going to pick up from where you leave off?" and "How do things work here?"

The facilitator should steer away from leading the group, and opposing views should be welcomed. The principles of dialoguing are useful, and can easily be incorporated in a group interview. In the book *Organisational Change and Developments: An African Approach*, Viljoen[50] describes the processes and principles of dialoguing in depth. LeBarOn[51] is quoted to emphasise that there has to be a spirit of inquiry, release, witness, engagement, creative action, perspective and acknowledgement in a dialoguing session. The importance of adopting an ethnographic mindset with openness to explore different viewpoints by participants is stressed, and the following statement is added: "This approach develops personal and collective insights into the thinking processes, particularly when responses are conditioned and biased by needs, fears and desires, and are distorted by culture, race or gender."[52]

A thought-provoking statement that hits close to home may be made at the beginning of the session. This may include: "We all must agree here", or "It seems that the more the system tries to adapt, the more it stays the same". The group is then allowed to dialogue on the theme for a set period of time. Building on Viljoen[53], the following questions may be effective for the purpose of dialoguing: "Who are you?"; "Where are you now?"; "Where must you be?"; "What can we do to make a difference?"; "What if we replaced your exco-team with the exco-team of a successful firm in another industry?"; and "If an international shareholder took over your company, why should they keep you?" Ultimately, the purpose of dialogue is to understand the underlying assumptions of the phenomenon under study. Participants are encouraged to build on the statements of other members, and to inquire into the underlying network of beliefs that uphold a specific perception or reality.

The role of facilitator

The facilitator is sometimes called a moderator in focus group literature. Here the words 'facilitator' and 'researcher' are used interchangeably. Participants have their own preconceptions about the facilitator[54], which may affect the degree to which the facilitator is able to achieve rapport with the participants' diversity factors, such as race, gender, ethnicity, age, socio-economic class and occupation. These comprise some of the significant factors that may affect the relationship that comes into being during a focus group[55].

> After a large-scale research project in Morila, Yatela and Sadiola in Mali, the head of the union passionately told the author: "For a woman you speak sense". It dawned on her that if she wanted to save a lot of time in gaining credibility in a system, she needed to be very aware of diversity dynamics in that context. Moving forward she always used a male researcher in that multicultural environment where Boko Haram was active and fundamentalism was at the order of the day.

As the researcher becomes a more familiar presence, participants are less likely to behave uncharacteristically[56]. During a focus group the researcher himself or herself becomes the research instrument, and is given the opportunity to enter into the world of the respondent[57]. Questions should be framed in a way that the group understands[58] and are posed in the language of the case organisation[59].

The facilitator should ensure that everyone is at ease, and that there is a clear understanding as to the purpose of the group. Questions should be posed, and debates should be stimulated. Open-ended questions work the best for focus groups. It is critical that the facilitator must be able to deal with the different personalities, diversity of thought and the different worldviews of the group. The facilitator must also test for understanding or probe for details, and the group conversation should be focused on the task at hand. Everyone should be able to participate and have a voice, and the facilitator should keep a neutral stance at all times. Personal opinions of the facilitator are not shared during a focus group; and it is important to listen consciously, and to not give too much direction to the dialogue. More than one facilitator may be assigned to a focus group. In this case it is very critical to contract roles and responsibilities. The roles may, for example, be split between facilitation and recoding. The facilitator should be well-trained in the specific methodology that is applied, for example appreciative inquiry or collaborative inquiry.

Questions are asked within an interactive group setting in which participants are free to engage with other group members[60]. This allows the researcher to study people in a setting that is more natural than the one-on-one interview. This option may be used together with techniques such as participant observation in order to gain access to cultural and social data and tacit knowledge[61]. This method has a high apparent validity, is low in cost and is less time-consuming than individual interviews[62]. Conversely, however, the researcher has less control over a group than in a one-on-one interview situation. Time may be wasted on issues irrelevant to the topic, and data may be difficult to analyse because such data may be either culture-specific and topic-specific or specialised within the context of the organisation. The data obtained from groups are not necessarily representative of the whole population. The issue of observer dependency (as in other qualitative research forms) should be addressed in the analysis.

> At three o clock one morning, before a shift started in a big mine group in Ghana, the research team left the camp to meet with the participants of a study on behaviour-based safety, for the first focus group. There were 15 participants in the group. To the team's dismay no one responded to any of the questions asked, and all were very with-holding. Even our Twi-speaking translator could not manage to get the group to participate in the focus group. I felt totally disillusioned. After the session one of the participants asked if he could speak to me personally. He apologised for the perceived failure of the session and advised that I ask permission from the local nanna (the elder in the village) to do the work there. He also explained that I greeted people from the left to the right, and in Ghana it was done the other way round. He further explained that by only speaking to 15 people that day, I excluded others and that it was important to them that everyone should be included. We made a lot of cultural mistakes that day. We arranged to speak to the nanna straightaway. The next morning more than two hundred and twenty participants arrived in time for the focus group. They explained that the nanna told them that if you pushed a good man up a tree, he would bring fruit for everyone, and this was a good initiative. We explained that we really would like to hear all the voices, divided the group into small groups each with a researcher, and conducted a mass focus group in the chop shop (the cafeteria). The results were deep and meaningful. We also handed out blank sheets of papers at the end of the session and invited people to anonymously say whatever they wanted in relation to the research question. To our surprise we got all the forms back from the empty box provided for this purpose. All the forms had names on. On trying to find out why people would respond so honestly and then still add their names to it, when the invitation was to do so anonymously, I was told that if a person wanted to say something, he must not be scared to add his name to it. Although our research design targeted only 30 per cent of the population, we ended up by speaking to 98 per cent. It became very clear that in Ghana it is important to speak up respectfully about things that were important to you.

Typically, no documents are distributed beforehand or handed out before a focus group. The researcher attempts to gain insight into the research questions during the discussions, and to explore the research topic whilst studying the effectiveness of the group dynamics for additional data. The output may represent the impressions of the facilitator or researcher, and may be supplemented by similar statements on the part of other group members. The nature of the data that are collected include views, mental models, opinions, preferences, inclinations and feelings in respect of the topic at hand.

Informed consent

It is good ethical practice to ensure that before the actual focus group takes place research participants are briefed about the intent of the research, the conditions about it (such as confidentiality and anonymously), and how the results will be communicated.

The following is a typical example of an invitation to participate in a focus group:

> Dear All
>
> Thank you for your willingness to participate in this research, and for taking time to attend this working supper.
>
> I contacted your line manager, (xxxx), and she indicated that she was in favour of this session.
>
> We will start the session with something to eat, and in the next half hour the focus group discussion will be conducted. This will probably last for an hour.
>
> Please note that the session will be recorded as it is almost impossible for a scribe to record all the voices at the same time. Photos will be taken during the session. A group photo will be taken afterwards.
>
> For more information, please contact me on 082 345 6789.
>
> Thank you for participating.
>
> Kind regards,
>
> The survey consultant

The informed consent forms should be carefully filed for research purposes.

Taking of photos and taping of conversations

From an ethical perspective, it is important to always contract with the participants before focus group conversations are taped or photos are taken. In Peruvian culture it is believed that a camera is capturing the soul of a person, and taking photos is not allowed. For Bequia islanders, a photo can be used as part of a voodoo ritual. A photo is viewed as more potent than hair or blood. The multicultural researcher should be aware of local beliefs and practices. In emerging economies and rural environments, the author should make field notes rather than record conversations due to the limiting impact that it has on the group dynamic and depth of conversations. The author also tries to minimise the props and use of electronic devices in such settings. The same principle applies in organisations, especially in cases where trust is compromised. It is good practice to then incorporate more researchers in the inquiry; one researcher may be appointed to study the group process only, while another may act as facilitator. The author sometimes allocates different participants, or different parts of the room to different researchers. At the end the notes and observations are consolidated.

The actual focus group may be video-recorded or audio-taped with the permission of the group. The recordings are then transcribed. Observations made by the researcher during the facilitation of the focus group may also be considered. It is important not only to make detailed notes of what is said during the interview, but the researcher must also pay attention to what is not said. Unconscious group dynamics can be studied, and group process comments as described by Bion and Cilliers[63] may also be considered. The researcher may also reflect on his or her own emotions.

> In a rural village close to Harare, Zimbabwe, local women participated in a focus group as part of a collaborative inquiry process. Although the author worked with a translator, and had a basic understanding of the local language Swahili, very soon the group started to act out their response to the questions that were posed in a drama or a gestalt. The author was deeply touched by the ability of the unschooled women to respond in metaphor, and this session is still fondly remembered as a day when drama transcended the boundaries of language, age and nationality, and women connected at a deep soulful level. Not one of the participants, and surely not the researcher, was left untouched by the depth of experience and humanity of these local women.

Conscious listening

Zinker[64] advised the use of phenomenological listening. This way of listening places emphasis on a person's terms rather than on an effort to interpret them. The focus shifts from the content of what is said to the process that is used to say it. Bateson[65] distinguishes between the primary process thinking and the language-based purposive thinking. Metaphoric primary process thinking is integrated with linear thinking. As one individual in a focus group becomes more alert, it may lead to a new pattern of interaction with others. By altering one's initial communication, a different response can be achieved[66]. Changes in an individual's thinking can thus lead to systemic change in the social system.

CREATIVE TYPES OF FOCUS GROUPS

Round-table discussion

A round-table discussion may be classified as a focus group that is formed with the purpose of exploring specific issues[67]. An effort is made to form a community of inquiry[68], and, although facilitated leadership is shared, a crisis of meaning is explored[69]. A round-table discussion provides the added dimension of interactions among members. For the purpose of qualitative research a round-table session may be facilitated in an informal and impromptu manner, although the conversation can be influenced by six to eight open-ended questions which typically are distributed via e-mail before the actual discussion group. Hard copies (prints) of the questions are distributed to all the group members at the beginning of the discussion. No formal discussion statements are introduced, and minutes are kept to record conversations[70]. Dialoguing may be used to explore underlying mental models, beliefs and assumptions.

As Addison[71] correctly states, the division between the data-gathering phase and the data-analysis phase is forced as it is innately integrated, and analysis would already have taken place during the gathering phase. However, ultimately, content analysis is carried out on the output of the different data-gathering efforts.

> During one round-table conversation it became quite clear that the group was not going to answer the questions. Initially, the author thought that all the participants were introverted, and therefore reflective. Very quickly she could, however, see that there was a lot of extroverted energy in the room. She tested the hypothesis that the group could be collectivist. This was not the case as most of the participants were from first-world environments and visibly expressive. It was a question of trust. The direct line manager was also in the group. Later it became clear that although she invited people to disagree with her, she kept grudges, and the participants were concerned about career-limiting reactions. The author gave everyone a few post-its, and asked them to write one idea per post-it in an anonymous way. On the clustering of the post-it stickers it became clear that participants were scared to speak publicly, but did not mind sharing in-depth feelings on the post-its. The direct line manager was exposed – not by one specific person, but by most of the group. Jung[72] said that if something is silenced too long, it will come out as a cry. That day the group cried out loudly.

Collaborative inquiry: When groups are conducting research inquiries

Introduction

Groups come together to participate in the powerful methodology of collaborative inquiry, conducting systemic, holistic, human inquiry and facilitating adult learning[73]. Lived experiences form the basis of such an inquiry. This methodology assists in the facilitation of meaning-making and is additional to a research methodology. It also creates transformation and the building of theory for public discourse.

Collaborative inquiry is a methodology that can be used for social innovation, integral theory and organisational behaviour. Brooks and Watkins[74] also underline the applicability of this methodology to the construction of new knowledge in the fields of education, community development and organisational studies. It differs from action research as it rests heavily on an evolving inquiry paradigm that acknowledges participation and democracy in the actual research process. It demystifies research and can be viewed as an inclusive research methodology. Research participants are consulted in the actual design and the conducting of the inquiry. Heron[75] believes that, from an ethical perceptive, participants have a right to participate and to share their own value in the process. Reflexivity plays a large role in this research methodology.

In collaborative inquiry, the underlying belief is that collecting data and experiments cannot lead to a full understanding of the human experience in a specific social system. Bray et al.[76] defined collaborative inquiry as: "A process consisting of repeated episodes of reflection and action through which a group of peers strive to answer a question of importance to them." Research is done with people rather than on them[77]. This means that each participant becomes a co-researcher and can impact the entire research design. The definite line between the researcher and the subject is eroded in this approach.

The process of collaborative inquiry

One of the tenets of collaborative inquiry is that the cycle of participation and learning is repeated. It typically starts with the formation of a collaborative inquiry group,[78] and specific attention is given to the creation of a true learning group. The group must then act on the inquiry question through the repetition of cycles of action and reflection until the process of meaning-making is reached where knowledge is constructed. This is a very fluid process. The stages can overlap, and are not always distinct. Bray et al.[79] stated that typically a collaborative inquiry group consists of five to twelve people who form part of the inquiry group. The facilitator initiates the group, but soon shifts into a co-inquirer or a co-learner in the group where leadership is shared.

Research philosophy

During a collaborative inquiry a hermeneutic phenomenological ontology is adapted. It is assumed that learning is an act of interpretation where lived experiences of the research participants are the objects of attention. Bray, et al.[80] explain that this research methodology is "a dialogical act of interpretation between the interpreter and what is interpreted. The outcome is a fusion of horizons from which new meaning emerges... the experience is fused with the perspective of the experience". The assumption is made that participants cannot escape their own human condition, but rather learn about it through their embodiment thereof. Habermas[81] explained that through intersubjective communicative competence, the defining of the "...life-world as represented by a culturally transmitted and linguistically organised stock of interpretative patterns: culturally transmitted" meaning-making occurs. As participants make meaning of their lived experience, their personal horizons and the horizon of the actual inquiry merge into a new understanding of the phenomena under study. In collaborative inquiry a participatory epistemology is adapted.

The forming of the group

The first step is to form a collaborative inquiry group. Unlike than conventional research where research questions are theory driven, a collaborative inquiry group is formed from a deep-rooted personal experience. Typically, it occurs when there is an imbalance experience in the researcher's inner state of being[82]. Such a group is highly dependent on the initiator's feeling that such an inquiry is important. The initiator invites others to participate, and obtains institutional consent where needed. Participant consent is obtained. The establishment of the physical context of the inquiry is important, as is the spirit of the place.[83] It is important that participants, who are incorporated in the inquiry, represent different views on the topic. Various techniques can be used to describe diversity of thought early on. Personality type analysis, as described by Jungian typology[84], can help learning styles, as described by Kolb[85]. This can be shared or team roles can be facilitated. The author uses the psychological map[1] to describe world views and thinking systems during this phase of the research. The group is oriented around the research inquiry, which typically takes two to three meetings.

Once participants commit to the inquiry, the inquiry question is formulated. What typically happens during this phase is that the individual learning interest transcends into a group question. Brain-storming can be used as a technique to create a deeper understanding of the research question, which should be delimited. Typically it is phrased as "How can....?", How do....?; and "What does....?". The inquiry is then designed. At this stage the initiator becomes a co-inquirer. During each step time is allocated for reflection and participants are advised to take reflective notes.

Ultimately, meaning-making should happen. Reason[86] states that a good question to reflect on is: "How can I understand what I have been through?" Mezirow[87] said that meaning-making is the process of interpreting experience and the act of giving coherence to an experience. The process involves interpretation, reflection and contemplation. Themes that emerge from reflective writing can assist greatly in the group's collective learning, while different methods of analyses can assist the participants to make sense of their experience. Drawings, causal diagrams, systems-thinking insights and other forms of visual documentation can be very helpful. Data from reflective journals can add largely to the richness of the ongoing meaning-making process. As the group goes through repeated cycles of action and reflections, "nascent meaning emerges and is further tested, with new meaning continually emerging from the progress"[89] explained.

Storytelling as a data-gathering method

Storytelling is a technique that is under-estimated in terms of the value it can offer to behavioural scientists. Not only can the story of the research inquiry be told, but often the starting points are the personal stories of the participants. Trends and themes trigger similar or contradictory stories in others, and supportive stories assist in minimising cognitive bias[89]. As lived experiences, and not secondary research, are shared, the face validity is enhanced. Insights gained about the inquiry question should be carefully documented. Reason[90] explains that collaborative inquiry "relies primarily on rational verbal reports on experience, but is branching out into imaginative storytelling and the use of metaphor". Reflexivity adds to the validity as it is written for the public arena, and therefore a rigour in the reflective process is required. Storytelling is indeed a valuable technique to be used in groups where the language is not a written one or where cross-cultural research is conducted[91].

In storytelling, the individual story can be shared (auto-ethnography), the story of the culture can be shared (ethnography), and the story of literature can be added. A combination of these three stories form integral research methodology, as described by Lessem and Schieffer[92].

---

1   The psychological map is a tool that describes spiral dynamics or human niches. It is described in the book Organisational Change and Development: An African Perspective by Viljoen (2015).

Hendry[93] expresses a strong view on what he believes should be the new approach to auto-ethnography as follows:

> Through telling our lives we engage in the act of meaning-making. This is a sacred act. Stories are what make us human. Our narratives, be they life stories, autobiographies, histories, sciences, or literature are the tales through which we constitute our identities. We are our narratives. They are not something that can be outside ourselves because they are what give shape to us, what gives meaning. In this sense, I believe they cannot be an object of "research" or study. Who we are is embedded in our stories. We can't step outside ourselves to study something that constitutes who we are. Treating stories as objects of study I would argue is a violation of the sacred "interpretation" dehumanizes and contributes to the very objectification that qualitative researchers have been critiqued. Thus, my primary contention in regard to the future of narrative research is that there is no future unless we radically transform our notion of research in ways that honour the sacredness of our humanness. I would like to consider how we might rethink research not as a scientific act, but as a spiritual act, one that honours the sacredness of our humanity.

In an auto-ethnographic study, sacred stories can find their way into business research projects and other types of research. The sharing of stories is a powerful data-gathering method that can render rich data, and provide and describe contextual multicultural dynamics.

In an ethnographic study, the researcher aims to study the dynamics and behaviour of a culture-sharing group[94]. In this type of approach an intact group that shares a culture is the unit of study. It is important that participants should enter for a long enough period to have shared patterns of behaviour and language. In the beginning, a detailed description of the group is presented. The researcher aims at understanding the way in which the group views cultural concepts such as politics, work life and gender issues. The ethnography ends with a description of the manner in which the group is functioning daily in real life.

Dialoguing as a data-gathering method

Merizow and Viljoen[95] both specify conditions for dialogue – another method that can increase the validity of a collaborative group. Participants should have the freedom to express their voices; there should be an openness to diverse perspectives and a desire to critically reflect on the underlying assumption of ideas. Equal opportunity for participation is critical. Dialogues should be taped and transcribed. Bray et al.[96] stressed the importance of paying careful attention to words that are chosen to express views in the public arena. The group should have a group dynamic where it is safe to disagree from each other, and to truly dialogue. Dialoguing was described in more detail in the paragraph that dealt with questions to pose in a focus group.

Pictures, metaphors and poetry as a meaning-making process

"A picture is worth a thousand words"

—English saying

Pictures, metaphors and poetry can also be applied to elicit group learning. Laubscher in Viljoen[97] explains that at least 65% of people in emerging economies think and speak in metaphor. Laubscher and Viljoen[98] also remind us that a person continues to speak and make sense of the word in the format of the lingo of his or her mother tongue. Numerous languages in Africa and other emerging economies are analogue or metaphoric of nature. Richardson[99] states that "poetry can assist to problematize reliability, validity and 'truth'... it lets us hear, see and feel the world in new dimensions. Poetry is thus a practical and powerful method for analysing social worlds." Ultimately the purpose of using pictures, metaphors and poetry is to construct meaningful and practical knowledge around the collaborative inquiry question. The author often gives disposable cameras to participants a few weeks before an inquiry, and asks them to take pictures of what touches them the most in their society or about aspects of their daily lives that tell us something about their culture. These photos are then developed before the collaborative inquiry session and form the basis for the conversation.

Reflection as meaning-making process

Reflection forms an integral part of the meaning-making process. Heron[100] described three forms of reflection, namely, descriptive reflection, evaluative reflection and practical reflection. All three of these forms take place during a typical collaborative inquiry group. Descriptive reflection focuses on what has happened, with no evaluation, interpretation or judgement. Heron[101] called this pure phenomenology. Evaluative reflection involves reflection and critique, while practical reflection applies the insights gained to the self. Van Manen[102] claimed that meaning is multi-dimensional and multi-layered. He says: It can never be grasped in a single definition." Zelman[103] described the sense of being a co-operative researcher as "in this flirtation dance, I am part of you . . . I keep my distance".

The richness of Heron's contribution is often under-estimated. Only when the researcher himself or herself emerges in the inquiry and through the actual participatory research, the strength of the collaborative inquiry process is experienced. Yorks[104] underlined the emotion that collaborative researchers often experience – namely, that it seems to be a compelling methodology, but "on the other hand some of it seems a little crazy...".

This methodology is poetically described by Gerdau[105] as:

> "Bubbling up from our beings
> Streams of inquiry coalesce
> Beckoned by a single question
> Only wanderers will solve
> We assembled, five testers of waters,
> Apprentice stream searchers
> Seekers of wisdom
> Of truth and utility....
> Streams of inquiry
> Become streams of meaning..."

Ensuring quality in collaborative inquiry

Bray et al.[106] stated that for collaborative inquirers, consensus is "a methodological issue because of its relation to validation and its integral role in the group learning process". Group members should steer away from premature closure, and rotate leadership. The following question can be asked: "Do we all agree?" Each group member should individually react to this question.

Mezirow and Heron[107] explain that the trustworthiness of collaborate inquiry is strengthened by the repetitive cycles of testing and reflecting. An intense interplay between action and reflexivity is a common praxis in action research, action inquiry, action learning, appreciative inquiry, integral research and collaborative inquiry.

Guba and Lincoln[108] state that "meeting tests of rigor is requisite for establishing trust in the outcome of an inquiry", while Ricoeuer[109] argues that lived experience can be treated as text to be analysed and interpreted. Content analysis can be done on the transcribed data from dialogues. Polkinghorn[110] believed that in narrative research the criterion for validity should concern itself with whether it is well-grounded and supportable. Qualitative probability was introduced by Ricoeuer[111], who explained that validation was not verification; it is argumentative and should be logical. Kirk and Miller in Irvine and Gaffikin[112] consider validity in qualitative research as considering whether "a researcher sees what he or she think he or she sees". Through dialoguing, several voices come together that can minimise self-deceptions. Lincoln and Guba[113] also introduced the authenticity criteria to warrant meaning in qualitative research. They offer four criteria, namely fairness – does the record demonstrate that the viewpoints of participants have been given equal representation?; ontological authenticity – increased awareness among participants of the complexities of the issue at hand; educative authenticity – the existence of evidence that participants have gained increased appreciation for the sources of alternative views around the question at hand; and catalytic authenticity – the willingness of participants to be involved in change. This addressed the criteria of Reason[114] for collaborative inquiry, namely that they produce change in the participants or in the context.

World café methodology

Brown and Isaacs[115] were amazed that in formal group settings little spontaneous conversation happened, but when groups broke for coffee or tea, a lot of informal conversations took place. World Café methodology is built to mirror this more informal behaviour. Viljoen[116] describes this in full in a chapter on inclusivity methodologies in the book *Organisational Change and Development: An African Approach*. World café has the ability to bring all people together in terms of issues that matter. During a world café various tables are set up as can be seen in Figure 5.1 below.

As people share
insights between
tables, the "magic
in the middle" and
a sense of the
whole become
more accessible.

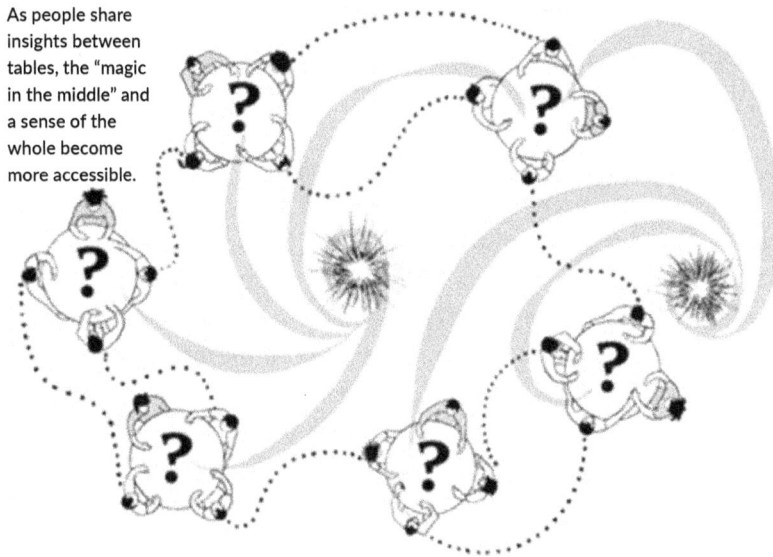

Figure 5.1: World Café methodology.[117]

Each table has a topic of interest and a host is identified per table. The role of the host is to document what the group is saying. The host is not a facilitator, but may participate fully in the conversation. Over a period of time, the facilitator rotates the different cafés. For research purposes it is best if the host remains at the table while the rest of the group rotates. Ultimately the host speaks to everyone and engages on every topic.

The notes of the hosts are collected, and form part of data that are gathered for research purposes.

Appreciative inquiry groups

The process of appreciative inquiry is described in full in the book *Organisational Change and Development: An African Approach*[118]. For the purpose of this chapter it is introduced as a way to find out what is right with the topic under study, instead of what is wrong with it. French and Bell[119] defined appreciative inquiry as qualitative, diagnostic research that focuses on the strengths within organisations, and which assists in co-creating shared understanding and meaning. Four principles apply, namely (i) research of topics must begin with appreciation; (ii) questions and foci must be applicable; (iii) the inquiry into scenarios must be provocative; and (iv) inputs generated must be collaborative and focused positively.

An appreciative inquiry group is a small work group or research group that aims at identifying the most significant growth possibilities latent in the system that could be leveraged. For example, the appreciative inquiry might focus on one of the following:

1. When did people attain the highest motivational levels in the life of the organisation?
2. When did people feel the most fulfilled?
3. What do staff members do to make themselves, their tasks, their team and the organisation successful?

The research inquiry is often a shared effort on the part of both the leadership and the stakeholders of the organisation. The problems and solutions must be relevant so that focus on learning and forward growth can take place[120]. The focus must be client-centric and not expert-centric. In other words, the organisation must be the central focus, and this focus must not be on problems only, but also on strengths. It is important that the right people are in the room. People who are directly impacted on, and those who have a mandate to do something about the task at hand, should participate. Appreciative inquiry can be used as a research strategy in a dissertation or a thesis.

The Cooperrider[121] process of appreciative inquiry can be followed to generate research data. The process usually consists of four phases, namely: discovery ("appreciate what is"); dream ("imagine what might be"; design ("determine what should be"); and destiny ("create what will be")[122]. Types of questions that can be asked include "Why did you join this company in the first place?" or "What made you successful so far on your journey?" This type of questioning, as part of the discovery phase, will result in a sense that there is goodwill in the room and a lot has been achieved so far. During the next phase, the dream phase, the group dream together on what the future may hold. Here the facilitator can introduce creative media such as clay or pastels for drawing. A vision board in the form of a collage can be constructed. Questions that can be posed in this part of the process include "Where do you see yourself in 10 years' time?"; "what is the future that you would like to co-create"; and "what is the best vision for the future for your company?". During the design phase of an appreciative inquiry, questions such as "In what must you invest today to ensure that you build your dream?" should be considered. In the last phase – the destiny phase, the questions should rotate around the actual delivery, and the group can move into business planning mode.

Listening posts

A listening post is a qualitative inquiry method first described by the Organisation for Promoting Society (OPUS). Stapley[123] says that a listening post is created for individual citizens to reflect on their own relatedness to society, and to study what is happening in society at that moment in time. During a listening post, participants can share their preoccupation in relation to various societal roles, and therefore express a part of the unconscious assumptions in this regard. The listening post is seen as a microcosm of society at large. Through the definition of a task boundary, it is possible to evoke experiences similar to the larger society and to observe societal dynamics in the group[124]. Listening posts intend to act as social inputs into a rich experience in societal research. The underlying assumption for a listening post is that the interdependency between participants and the collective unconscious of the group emerge from group processes in the "here and the now". Stapley[125] explains that the rationale of a listening group is to explore the unconscious processes of participants as they make sense of the topic under study. In the group participants can co-create knowledge and gain insight about the phenomenon.

Typically, a listening group is conducted in two one-hour sessions with a 30-minute break in between. The session is facilitated by a convenor, who participates on equal basis with others, and who instils a firm time boundary[126]. During the first session participants are asked to express their own relatedness to the phenomenon under study. After the break, in the second session, the participants can reflect on session one. Participants reflect on the themes of the first session, analyse them, and form a hypothesis regarding the underlying assumptions and dynamics in the group[127]. The trustworthiness of a listening post is achieved through appropriate participant selection, and trained psychodynamic conveners enhance the authenticity of results. During a listening post, participants are enabled to reflect on their own understanding of the phenomenon under study. The group is provided with the opportunity of integrating themes that emerged during the first listening post session. A variety of themes typically emerge from a listening post, from reflections and participant discourse. These themes can add valuable insights to the qualitative researcher.

A REAL-LIFE COLLABORATIVE INQUIRY CASE

The CEO of a large private hospital group and the nursing director wanted to implement an organisational development initiative that could assist nursing staff to improve patient outcomes and their perceptions of care received. The researcher wanted to understand the organisational dynamics better before suggestions for interventions were made. With the support of the nursing director the top 5% of nursing leadership participated in a collaborative inquiry process. Five groups from different regions participated in a facilitated process to understand the systemic dynamics at play that result in patient complaints. Art-based techniques were incorporated in a two-hour session designed on the principles of cooperative inquiry as described by Heron[128]. The data-gathering phase had three cycles.

During the first cycle a world café was facilitated to determine the phenomenon of caring in the organisation. In Figure 5.2 below a typical co-operative inquiry process is visually presented.

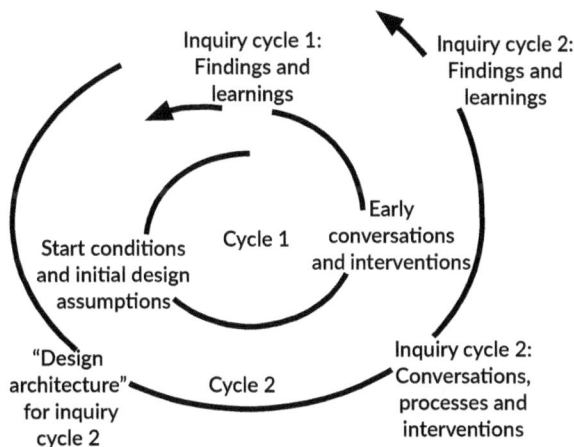

Figure 5.2: Co-operative Inquiry Cycles[129]

Four stations (cafés) were created where groups engaged on the following topics:

1. Why do people say that nurses don't care?
2. What impacts on the perception of the lack of caring?
3. What does non-caring in the organisation look like?
4. How does caring manifest in the nursing team?

During the world café all participants had the opportunity to participate in conversations around the topics. Detailed notes were made of each conversation.

For the second-level inquiry an art-based intervention was used, again in a world café format. Here participants had to draw a day in the life of a nurse, a day in the life of a nursing manager, a day in the life of a doctor, and a day in the life of a patient. Participants were invited to reflect on the feelings that manifest daily at the workplace. In Figure 5.3 and Figure 5.4 below, two of the actual pictures from this cycle are shared.

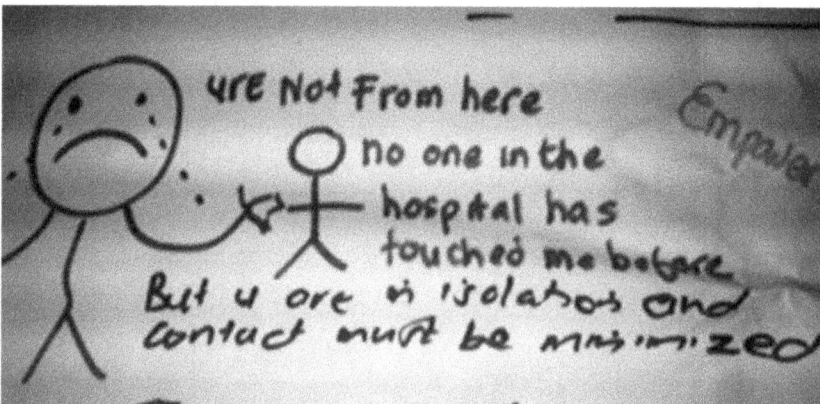

Figure 5.3: Drawing on patient care from co-operative inquiry session

Figure 5.4: Drawing on impact of behaviour on doctors from co-operative inquiry session

During the third cycle of inquiry participants had the opportunity to generate answers to the following questions by confidentially writing one idea per post-it sticker. These stickers were later clustered into themes. The questions emerged as the sessions progressed and focused on issues such as the following:

1. How do we get nurses to "own" caring?
2. How could we build a culture of caring?
3. What do nursing staff need to care?
4. What type of intervention/learning do you prefer?
5. What type of intervention/learning do you dislike?
6. What advice do you have for the nursing director?
7. What are we not saying in the organisation?

The co-operative inquiry results were content analysed, coding was done, themes were identified and the story in figure 5.5 below was presented.

CARING IN THE ORGANISATION – THE SYNTHESIS OF RESULTS

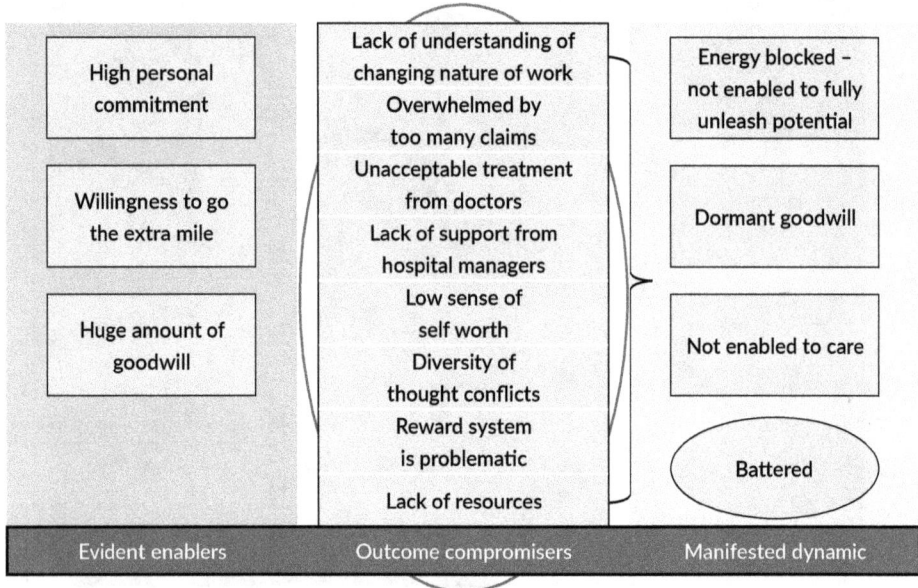

Evident enablers	Outcome compromisers	Manifested dynamic
High personal commitment	Lack of understanding of changing nature of work Overwhelmed by too many claims	Energy blocked – not enabled to fully unleash potential
Willingness to go the extra mile	Unacceptable treatment from doctors Lack of support from hospital managers	Dormant goodwill
Huge amount of goodwill	Low sense of self worth Diversity of thought conflicts Reward system is problematic Lack of resources	Not enabled to care
		Battered

Figure 5.5: Synthesis of co-operative inquiry results

A large scale organisational development process followed to re-author the narrative in the organisation, to enhance the emotional capacity and change the resilience of the nursing management, and to create depth in terms of leadership skills. Through interventions, a new narrative is now (three years later) told in this organisation. The case will be presented in the doctorate of the nursing director, Shannon Nell, documented different initiatives that were implemented, described processes, and policies that were indicated and provides evidence of how emotional intelligence has developed during the transformational journey. She also highlights the shifts in underlying beliefs in the system and presents pre-and post-intervention analysis. Ultimately, she proposes meta-insights into large scale cultural transformational processes.

DATA ANALYSIS

> *"Analysis is the interplay between researchers and data. It is both science and art."*
> —Strauss & Corbin[130]

As Addison[131] correctly states, the division between the data-gathering phase and the data-analysis phase is forced as it is innately integrated, and analysis would already have taken place during the gathering phase. However, ultimately, content analysis is carried out on the output of the different data-gathering efforts.

Themes emerge, and are often expressed, in narrative form. In collaborative enquiry other less conventional ways of constructing knowledge are also accepted. These include the revision of policies of the insights gained from the group learning[132]. Here the individual story is told first, and then the story of the group. Later theory or insights gained are applied to their own story or the group learning. Lessem and Schieffer[133] follow a similar approach with integral research where the individual tells his or her own story, the story of the culture is told, literature and analysis of the situation is added, and ultimately social innovation is facilitated.

In phenomenological studies one does not count the number of times that a theme emerges, but rather a theme is viewed as "the sense we are able to make of the phenomenon, the product of insightful discovery and disclosure. At best a theme is a distillation".[134] Heron[135] acknowledges that it is basically impossible to completely bracket off one's own pre-interpretations. Here the hermeneutical phenomenological stance holds that it is impossible to avoid our own knowledge as our thoughts are always connected to cultural antecedents.

The use of narrative writing, a descriptive use of language, is also an act of interpretation. Van Manen[136] stresses that research and writing are aspects of the same process, while Whyte[137] explained that "although writing is not usually considered a component of research methods…. it seems to me [to be] an indispensable part of the analysis process".

ETHICAL CONSIDERATIONS

The ethical considerations for focus groups are similar to those of other social research projects[138]. It is important to declare up-front what the purpose of the focus group is, and participation should be voluntary. The participants should clearly know what is expected of them, and the objective of the focus group should be understood. It is good practice to set out norms up-front on how to deal with sensitive information and confidentiality in the group. Researchers must anonymise data and participants should be encouraged to ensure the confidentiality of the actual focus group.

ENSURING QUALITY DATA

Quality criteria

In view of the fact that qualitative studies typically are unstructured and rely heavily on the ingenuity of the qualitative researcher, these studies may be criticised as lacking reliability[139]. Stenbacka[140], however, claims that repetitive correctness has value only within those research settings that are dominated by the deductive demand for unconditional inter-subjectivity. Several qualitative researchers argue that qualitative research should aim at defining quality with the help of other concepts, such as "trustworthiness", "reasonableness" and "credibility"[141]. The reliability of research data refers to the extent to which the data that have emerged from the study are consistent and stable both over time and across a range of different respondents[142].

Polkinghorne[143] identifies the following five questions that phenomenological researchers could ask themselves:

1. Did the interviewer influence the contents of the participant's descriptions' in a way that they no longer truly reflect the actual experience?
2. Is the transcription accurate, and does it convey the original meaning of the focus group?
3. In the analysis of the transcriptions, were there conclusions that could have been derived at other than those offered by the researcher?
4. Is it possible to go from the general structural description to the transcriptions and to account for the specific contents and connections in the original examples?
5. Is the structural description situation specific or does it hold true for other situations?

Creswell[144] added the following quality criteria:

1. Does the author convey an understanding of the philosophical assumptions of the phenomenon?
2. Does the author have a clear phenomenon to study?
3. Does the author use congruent procedures of data analysis as described by Moustakas or Van Manen[145]?
4. Does the author convey the overall essence of the participant experience?
5. Is the author reflective?

Often focus group are combined with other types of data collection[146]. The purpose of **triangulation** in qualitative research is to increase both the credibility and the validity of the results. Investigator triangulation (the use of multiple researchers in an investigation), data triangulation (data used from different sources), and methodological triangulation (the use of more than one method to gather data), as defined by Denzin[147], can be used to increase the credibility and validity of the results. Credibility may also be enhanced by *peer debriefing* (critical examination and evaluation by subject matter experts) and by *member checking* (verification of the researcher's interpretations and conclusions with the various groups of participants themselves).

The importance of reflexivity

The acknowledgement of the importance of reflexivity in qualitative research is increasingly documented[148]. Some researchers reflect deeply on the inter-subjective relationships between the researcher and the studies[149]. Marcus and Fischer[150] described various forms of reflexivity and analysed the way in which different strategies served different purposes. They identified the following forms:

1. Sociological reflexivity.
2. Self-reflexivity.
3. Anthropological reflexivity.
4. Feminist reflexivity.

Marcus and Fischer[151] warn that if researchers do not make themselves vulnerable, the self-reflection may be seen as narcissistic. Kirsch and Mortensen[152] agreed that authored-saturated texts may be seen in this way, and added that such texts might be self-indulgent. Alsop[153] quotes Guba, Le Compte, Preissle, Maxwell and Kirsch in stating that although there is such a risk, reflexive text must be incorporated to increase trustworthiness of research results. The author supports this view in that sharing the researcher's cultural and social relationship with the research increases its credibility.

Haraway[154] emphasises that: "Reflexivity is a bad trope for escaping the false choice between realism and relativism in thinking about strong objectivity and situated knowledge in techno-scientific knowledge." Stevens[155] offers a valuable alternative by introducing goal-orientated rather than truth-orientated claims that support cultural logic. The author believes that without critical reflexivity the voice of the researcher is lost, and the valuable lessons that can be learned from the experience are not documented. Further, if the ups and downs of a qualitative journey are not documented as auto-ethnographical notes or a story behind the story, the reader is often not necessarily convinced by the rigour of the research project.

CONCLUSION

In this chapter a synthesis on focus group methods was offered, and various creative ways of conducting focus groups were incorporated. The chapter builds on the philosophy of phenomenology, and touches on ways of conducting focus groups, questions to ask, conscious listening and ways to capture data. Ethical considerations are considered and criteria for conducting effective focus groups are shared.

I deliberately interwove stories relating to various focus groups with examples from history, popular culture, business and politics. These fragments act as examples of challenges that face a qualitative researcher while conducting focus groups.

REFERENCES

Addison, RB. 1989. Grounded interpreted research: an investigation of physician socialization. *In Entering the circle: Hermeneutic investigation in psychology*, edited by MJ Parker & RB Addison. New York: SUNY Press: 39-57.

Alsop, J. 2004. Protean Subjectivities. In *Ethnography Unbound*, edited by SG Brown & SL Dorbin. New York: University of New York Press.

Babbie, E. 2007. *The Practice of Social Research.* 7th edition. Belmont: Wadsworth.

Baily, CA. 2007. *A guide to qualitative field research.* 2nd edition. London: Sage.

Bateson, G. 2000. *Steps to our senses: Body and Spirit in the Hidden History of the West.* New York: Simon & Schuster.

Bion, WR. 1970. *Attention and interpretation.* London: Karnac Books.

Bohm D. 1998: *On dialogue.* London: Brunner-Routledge.

Bray, JN, Lee, JS & Yorks, L. 2000. *Collaborative Inquiry in practice.* London: Sage.

Briggs, CL (ed). 1986. *Learning how to ask: a sociolinguistic appraisal of the role of the interview in social science research.* Cambridge: Cambridge University Press.

Brooks, A & Watkins, KE. 1994. A new era for action technologies: A look at the issues. In *The emerging power of action inquiry technologies: New directions for adult and continuing education*, ed. A Brooks and KE Watkins. San Francisco, CA: Jossey-Bass.

Brown, J & Isaacs, D. 2005. *The world café: shaping our futures through conversations that matter*. San Francisco: Berrett-Koehler.

Bryman, A. 2004. *Social research methods*. Oxford: Oxford University Press.

Burgess, J. 1996. Focusing on fear. *Area* 28(2):130-36.

Chalmers, D (ed). 2002. *Philosophy of mind: classical and contemporary readings*. Oxford and New York: Oxford University Press.

Cilliers, F. 2007. A systems psychodynamic exploration of diversity management. *The experiences of the client and the consultant*. South African Journal of Labour Relations, 31(2): 32-50.

Cooperrider, D, Whitney, D & Stavros, J. 2003. *Appreciative inquiry handbook*. San Francisco: Berrett-Koehler.

Creswell, J. 2013. *Research Design: Qualitative, Quantitative, and Mixed Methods Approaches*. 4th Edition. Los Angeles: Sage Publications

Darroch, V & Silvers, RJ (eds). 1982. *Interpretive human studies: an introduction to phenomenological research*. Washington, D.C.: University Press.

Davies, CA. 1999. *Reflexive Ethnography: A guide to researching selves and others*. London: Routledge.

Flores, JG & Alonso, CG. 1995. Using focus groups in educational research, *Evaluation Review* 19(1):84-101.

French, WL & Bell, CH. 1999. *Organizational development*. New Jersey: Prentice Hall.

Freud, S. 1964. *Jokes and their relationship to the unconscious*. New York: Norton.

Gerdau, J. 1995. *Learning in adulthood through collaborative inquiry*. Dissertation Abstracts International, 56(07), 25247, (University Microfilms No. AAC95-39807).

Gold, R. 1997. The ethnographic method in sociology. *Qualitative Enquiry*, 3(4):387-402.

Gorzelsky, G. 2004. Shifting Figures. In *Ethnography Unbound*, edited by SG Brown & SL Dorbin. New York: University of New York Press.

Goss, JD & Leinbach, TR. 1996. Focus groups as alternative research practice: experience with transmigrants in Indonesia. *The Royal Geographical Society*, 29(2):115-123.

Guba, EG & Lincoln, YS. 1981. *Effective evaluation: Improving the usefulness of evaluation results through responsive and naturalistic approaches*. San Francisco, CA: Jossey-Bass.

Guba, EG & Lincoln, YS. 1982. Epistemological and methodological bases of naturalistic inquiry. *Educational Communication and Technology*, 30(4):233-252.

Guba, EG & Lincoln, YS. 1989. *Fourth generation evaluation*. Newbury Park, CA: Sage.

Habermas, J. 1987 [1981c]. Intermediate Relections: Social Action, Purposive Activity, and Communication. Pp. 263-337 in Jürgen Habermas, *The Theory of Communicative Action. Volume 1: Reason and the Rationalization of Society*, trans. Thomas McCarthy. Cambridge: Polity Press.

Haenfler, R. 2004. Rethinking subcultural resistance: Core values of the straight edge movement. *Journal of Contemporary Ethnography*, 33: 406-463.

Haraway, DJ. 1997. *Modest – Witness@Second – Millinnium.FemaleMan-Meets-OncoMouse. Feminism and Technoscience*. New York: Routledge.

Helenius, R. 1990. *Förstå och bättre veta*. Stockholm: Carlsson.

Hendry, PM. 2007. The Future of Narrative. *Qualitative Inquiry*; 13:498-512.

Heron, J. 1996. *Cooperative Inquiry: Research into the human condition*. London: Sage.

Hoffman, WM. 1991. Business and Environmental Ethics. *Business Ethics Quarterly*, 1(2): 169-184.

Holbrook, B & Jackson, P. 1996. Shopping around: focus group research in North London, *Area, 28(2): 136-142*.

Homan, R. 1991. *Ethics in Social Research*. Harlow: Longman.

Hoppe, MJ, Wells, EA, Morrison, DM, Gilmore, MR & Wilsdon. A. 1995. Using focus groups to discuss sensitive topics with children, *Evaluation Review* 19(1):102-14.

Husserl, E. 1931. *Ideas: general introduction to pure phenomenology*. Translated by WR Boyce Gibson. New York: Humanities Press.

Husserl, E. 1970. *The crisis of European sciences and transcendental phenomenology*. Translated by David Carr. Evanston, Ill.: Northwestern University Press

Irvine, H & Gaffikin, M. 2006. Getting in, getting on and getting out: reflections on a qualitative research project. *Accounting, Auditing & Accountability Journal*, 19(1):115-145.

Jung, CG. 1953. *Collected works*. Princeton: Princeton University Press.

Kasl, E & Yorks, L. 2002. An Extended Epistemology for Transformative Learning Theory and Its Application Through Collaborative Inquiry. *TCRecord Online*. http://www.tcrecord.org/Content.asp?ContentID=10878. Accessed on 15/08/2016.

Khaleelee, O & Miller, E. 1985. Beyond the small group: Society as an intelligible field of study, in M Pines (Ed.), *Bion and group psychotherapy*. London: Routledge & Kegan Paul:354-385.

Kitzinger, J. 1994. The methodology of focus groups: the importance of interaction between research participants. *Sociology of Health* 16(1):103-21.

Kitzinger, J. 1995. Introducing focus groups. *British Medical Journal*, 311: 299-302.

Kirsch, GE & Mortensen, P. 1996. *Ethics and representation on qualitative studies of literacy*. Urbana, IL: NCTE.

Kolb, DA. 1984. *Experiential learning: experience as the source of learning and development*. London: Prentice-Hall.

Kreuger, RA. 1988. *Focus groups: a practical guide for applied research*. London: Sage.

Krueger, R.A. 2002. *Designing and conducting focus group interviews*. Available on http://www.rkruger@tc.umn.edu Accessed on 15/08/2016.

Krueger, DA & Casey, MC. 2000. *Focus groups: a practical guide for applied research*. 3rd edition. California: Sage.

Krueger, RA & Casey, MC. 2008. *Focus groups a practical guide for applied research*. 4th edition. New York: Sage.

LeBaron, M. 2005. *Bridging cultural conflicts: a new approach for a changing world*. San Francisco: Jossey-Bass.

Lessem, R & Schieffer, A. 2010. *Integral Research*. Ashgate: London.

Lankshear, AJ. 1993. The use of focus groups in a study of attitudes to student nurse assessment'. *Journal of Advanced Nursing*, 18:1986-89.

Lincoln, YS & Guba, EG. 1985. *Naturalistic inquiry*. Newbury Park: Sage Publications.

Lincoln, YS & Guba, E. 1986. But is it rigorous? Trustworthiness and authenticity in naturalistic evaluation. *New Directions for Program Evaluation, 20*:15-25.

Marcus, GE & Fischer, MMJ. 1986. *Anthropology as cultural critique*. Chicago: University of Chicago Press.

Marshall, C & Rossman, GB. 1999. *Designing qualitative research*. 3rd edition. London: Sage.

MacIntosh J. (1981) 'Focus groups in distance nursing education', *Journal of Advanced Nursing* 18:1981-85.

Marton, F. 1994. Phenomenography. In *The international Encyclopedia of Education*, 2nd edition, edited by T Husén & TN Postlethwaite. Oxford: Pergamon. 8:4424–4429.

Merton, RK & Kendall, PL. 1946. The Focused Interview. *American Journal of Sociology* 51: 541-557.

Mezirow, J. 1978. Perspective transformation. *Adult Education*, USA, XXVIII.2:100-110.

Mouton, J. 2001. *How to succeed in your Masters and Doctoral studies. A South African Guide and Resource Book*. Pretoria: Van Schaik.

Mouton, J & Marais, HC. 1992. *Basic concepts in the methodology of the social sciences*. Pretoria: Human Sciences Research Council.

Moustakas, C. 1990. *Phenomenological research methods*. Thousand Oaks, CA: Sage.

Morgan, DL. 1988. *Focus groups as qualitative research*. London: Sage.

Morgan, DL. 1997. *Focus groups as qualitative research*. London: Sage.

Morgan, DL & Spanish, MT. 1984. Focus groups: a new tool for qualitative research. *Qualitative Sociology*, 7:253-70.

Morgan, DL & Kreuger, RA. 1993. When to use focus groups and why. In Morgan DL (ed.). *Successful Focus Groups*. London: Sage.

Munodawafa, D, Gwede, C & Mubayira, C. 1995. Using focus groups to develop HIV education among adolescent females in Zimbabwe. *Health Promotion*, 10(2): 85-92.

Nahum, T. 2005. Listening post: Global uncertainty and the outbreak of the war in Iraq: February to April 2003. The median group as a potential container for listening posts. *Organisational & Societal Dynamics*, 5(1): 38-56.

Nisbett, R & Ross, L. 1980. *Human inference.*"*Strategies and shortcomings of social judgment*. Englewood Cliffs, N.J.: Prentice-Hall.

Patton, MQ. 1990. *Qualitative evaluation and research methods*. New Bury Park: Sage.

Phenomenology Online homepage. 2004. Inquiry. http://www.phenomenologyonline.com/ Accessed on 07/08/2016.

Polkinghorne, DE. 2005. Language and meaning: data collection in qualitative research. *Journal of Counseling Psychology*, 52:137-145.

Polinghorne, DE. 1989. Phenomenological research methods, in RS Valle & S Halling (Eds.) *Existential-phenomenological perspectives in psychology*. 4160. New York: Plenum Press.

Powell, RA & Potter J. 2006. *Spiritual development for beginners*. Woodbury, Minnesota: Llewellyn Publications.

Powell, RA & Single, HM. 1996. Focus groups, *International Journal of Quality in Health Care*, 8(5): 499-504.

Powell, RA, Single, HM & Lloyd, KR. 1996. Focus groups in mental health research: enhancing the validity of user and provider questionnaires, *International Journal of Social Psychology*, 42(3): 193-206.

Rasmussen, ES, Østergaard, P & Beckmann, SC. 2006 *Essentials of social science research methodology*. Odense: University Press of Southern Denmark.

Reason, P. 1995. *Participation in Human Inquiry*. London: Sage.

Reason, P & Rowan, J. 1981. *Human Inquiry: A Sourcebook of New Paradigm Research*. London: Wiley.

Reitsperger, WE. 1986. Japanese management: coping with British industrial relations. *Journal of Management Studies*, 1:72-87.

Remenyi, D, Williams, B, Money, A & Swartz, E. 1998. *Doing research in business management: an introduction to process and method*. London: Sage.

Ricoeur, P. 1991. Poetry and possibility. In A Ricoeur Reader: *Reflection & Imagination*. (Valdes, M.J. ed.). New York: Harvester Wheat-sheaf: 448-462

Ricoeur, P. 1974. The problem of double meaning as hermeneutic problem and a semantic problem (French original 1960). In *The Conflict of Interpretations. Essays in Hermeneutics* (Ihde D ed.). Evanston: Northwestern University Press.

Richardson, L. 1994. Writing: A method of inquiry, in NK Denzin & YS Lincoln (Eds.), *Handbook of qualitative research*. Thousand Oaks: Sage:516-529.

Rowan. J. 2001. The humanistic approach to action research, in P Reason & H Bradbury (eds.). *Handbook of Action Research*. London: Sage.

Saludadez, JA & Primo, GG. 2001. Seeing our quantitative counterparts: construction of qualitative research in a roundtable discussion. *Forum: Qualitative Social Research*. 2.1. http://www.qualitative-research.net/fqs/fqs-eng.htm Accessed on 07/08/2016.

Saunders, M, Lewis, P & Thornhill, A. 2003. *Research methods for business students*. 3rd edition. London: Prentice Hall.

Schutz, A. 1962. *Collected papers*. The Hague: Martinus Nijhoff.

Schutz, A. 1967. *A phenomenology of the social world*. Evaston. IL: Northwestern University Press.

Smith, JA, Scammon, DL & Beck, SL. 1995: Using patient focus groups for new patient services. *Joint Commission Journal on Quality Improvement*, 21(1): 22-31.

Sparkes, AC. 2002: *Telling tales in sport and physical activity: A qualitative journey*. Human Kinetics: Exeter University.

Spradley, JP. 1979. *The ethnographic interview*. Wadsworth: Thompson Learning.

Stapley, LF. 2006. Global dynamics at the dawn of 2006. *Organisational and Social Dynamics*, 6(1):111-142.

Stenbacka, C. 2001. Qualitative research requires quality concepts of its own. *Management Decision*, 39(7): 551-556.

Stevens, SM. 2004. Debating Ecology. In *Ethnography Unbound*, edited by SG Brown & SL Dorbin. New York: University of New York Press.

Stewart, DW & Shamdasani, PN. 1992. *Focus groups: theory and practice*. London: Sage.

The American Heritage® Dictionary of the English Language. 2007. http://www.bartleby.com/am Accessed on 07/03/2016.

The World Café. 2017. http://www.theworldcafe.com/copyright-use-policies Accessed on 16/01/2017.

Thomas, PN. 2007. *The shift towards consulting psychology in South Africa: Implications for Training*. Unpublished Masters dissertation available at the University of Stellenbosch.

Van Manen, M. 1990. *Researching lived experience*. New York: State University of New York Press.

Viljoen, RC. 2014. *Inclusive Organisational Transformation: An African Approach*. London: Ashgate.

Viljoen, RC. 2015. *Organisational Change and Development: an African perspective*. Randburg: Knowledge Resources.

Viljoen-Terblanche, RC. 2008. *Sustainable organisational transformation through Inclusivity*. www://uir.unisa. ac.za/bitstream/handle/10500/726/ ?sequence=2 Accessed on 31/06/2016.

White, GE & Thomson, AN. 1995. Anonymized focus groups as a research tool for health professionals. *Qualitative Health Research* 5(2): 256-61.

Whyte, W.F. 1991. *Participatory action research*. Newbury Park: Sage

Williams, JA. 1964. Interviewer-respondent interaction: a study of bias in the information interview. *Sociometry*, 27(3):338-352.

Wilson J. 1999. *Internet training: the time is now*. HR Focus.http://www.Hrfocus.com Accessed on 02/07/2016.

Whitney, DK & Trosten-Bloom, A. 2003. *The power of appreciative inquiry: a practical guide to positive change*. San Francisco: Berrett-Koehler.

Zelman, A. 1995. Answering the question: "How is learning experienced through collaborative inquiry?" *Dissertation Abstracts International*, 56(07), 2534.

Zinker, JC. 1987. *Body Process: A gestalt approach to working with the body in psychotherapy*. New York: Gestalt Institute of Cleveland.

ENDNOTES

1. Sparkes, 2002.
2. Creswell, 2013.
3. Viljoen-Terblanche, 2008.
4. Viljoen-Terblanche, 2008.
5. Husserl, 1970.
6. Wilson, 1999.
7. Marton, 1994.
8. Remenyi, Williams, Money & Swartz, 1998: 35.
9. Saunders, Lewis & Thornhill, 2003: 86.
10. Phenomenology online homepage, 2004:1.
11. Marton, 1994.
12. Husserl, 1931; 1970.
13. Husserl, Schutz, 1962; 1967.
14. Chalmers, 2002.
15. Darroch & Silvers, 1982.
16. Vijoen-Terblanche, 2008.
17. The American Heritage® Dictionary of the English Language, 2007.
18. Kruger & Casey, 2000: 5.
19. Powell et al., 1995: 400.
20. Kitzinger, 1994.
21. Kitzinger, 1995.
22. Gross & Leinbach, 1996.
23. Powell & Single, 1996.
24. Thomas, 2007.
25. Laubscher, 2016.
26. Viljoen-Terblanche, 2008; Peck, 1990.
27. Heron, 1996.

28. Cooperrider, 2004.
29. Stapley, 2006.
30. Powell and Single, 1996: 449.
31. Krueger and Casey, 2008: 5.
32. Krueger, 2002.
33. Gorzelsky, 2004.
34. Bateson, 2000.
35. Mouton, 2001.
36. Bion, 1970.
37. Patton, 1990: 84.
38. Patton, 1990.
39. Babbie, 2007.
40. MacIntosh, 1981.
41. Goss & Leibach, 1996.
42. Kitzinger, 1995.
43. Burgess, 1996.
44. Powell & Single, 1996.
45. Morgan, 1988.
46. Burgess, 1996.
47. Holbrook & Jackson, 1996.
48. Bion, 1970.
49. Baily, 2007.
50. Viljoen, 2015.
51. LeBarOn, 2005.
52. Viljoen, 2015: 89.
53. Viljoen, 2015: 90.
54. Moustakas, 2006.
55. Williams, 1964: 340; Viljoen-Terblanche, 2008.
56. Gold, 1997.
57. Spradley, 1979.
58. Briggs, 1986.
59. Viljoen-Terblanche, 2008.
60. Krueger & Casey, 2000.
61. Viljoen-Terblanche, 2008.
62. Marshall & Rossman, 1999.
63. Bion, 1970; Cilliers, 2007.
64. Zinker, 1987.
65. Bateson, 2000.
66. Gorzelsky, 2004: 85.
67. Viljoen-Terblanche, 2008.
68. Peck, 1990.
69. Bohm, 1998.
70. Saludadez & Primo, 2001.
71. Addison 1989.
72. Jung, 1953.
73. Bray, Lee, Smith & Yorks, 2000: 1.
74. Brooks & Watkins, 1994.
75. Heron, 1996.
76. Bray et al., 2000: 6.
77. Heron, 1996; Reason, 1995.
78. Bray et al., 2000: 6.
79. Bray et al., 2000: 47.
80. Bray et al., 2000: 23.
81. Habermas, 1984: 170.
82. Rowan, 2001.
83. Bray, 2000: 57.
84. Jung, 1953.
85. Kolb, 1984
86. Reason, 1998b: 8
87. Mezirow, 1991: 4.
88. Bray, et al., 2000: 90.
89. Nisbett & Ross, 1980.
90. Reason, 1994a: 334.
91. Viljoen-Terblanche, 2008; Viljoen, 2014.
92. Lessem & Schieffer, 2010; Viljoen, 2014.
93. Hendry 2007, p. 495.
94. Haenfler, 2004.
95. Merizow, 1991: 77-89; Viljoen, 2015.
96. Bray, et al., 2000.
97. Laubscher in Viljoen, 2014a.
98. Laubscher & Viljoen, 2014.
99. Richardson, 1994: 522.
100. Heron, 1988.
101. Heron, 1988: 49.
102. Van Manen, 1990: 78.
103. Zelman, 1995: 250.
104. Yorks, 1995: 77.
105. Gerdau, 1995: 345-347.
106. Bray et al., 2000: 118.
107. Mezirow, 1991; Heron, 1985.
108. Guba & Lincoln, 1981: 103.
109. Ricoeuer, 1991.
110. Polkinghorn, 1988.
111. Ricoeuer, 1974.
112. Kirk & Miller in Irvine & Gaffikin, 1986: 21.
113. Lincoln & Guba, 1986.
114. Reason, 1995.
115. Brown & Isaacs, 2005.
116. Viljoen, 2015.
117. The World Café, 2017.
118. Viljoen, 2015.
119. French & Bell, 1999.
120. Viljoen, 2015: 110.
121. Cooperrider, 2003.

122. Whitney & Trosten-Bloom:2003: 6.
123. Stapley, 2006.
124. Khaleelee & Miller, 1985.
125. Stapley, 2006.
126. Stapley, 2006.
127. Nahum, 2005.
128. Heron, 1996.
129. Heron, 1996.
130. Strauss & Corbin, 1998: 13.
131. Addison, 1989.
132. Bray, 2000: 100.
133. Lessem & Schieffer, 2012.
134. Bray, 2000: 102.
135. Heron, 1992.
136. Van Manen, 1990.
137. Whyte, 1991b: 270.
138. Hofman 1991.
139. Bryman, 2004: 284.
140. Stenbacka, 2001.
141. Rasmussen, Østergaard & Beckmann, 2006:117; Helenius, 1990; Lincoln & Guba: 1986; Bryman, 2004:273.
142. Rasmussen, Østergaard & Beckmann, 2006: 133.
143. Polkinghorne, 1989:57.
144. Creswell, 2013:260.
145. Moustakas, 1990; Van Manen, 1990.
146. Reitsperger, 1986.
147. Denzin, 1978.
148. Stevens, 2004.
149. Davies, 1999: 96-104.
150. Marcus & Fischer, 1986, 190.
151. Marcus & Fischer, 1986.
152. Kirsch & Mortensen, 1996: 77.
153. Alsop, 2004.
154. Haraway, 1997: 16.
155. Stevens, 2004.

CHAPTER 6

ANALYSIS AND INTERPRETATION OF RESULTS

by **Nico Martins**

INTRODUCTION

The interesting part of any diagnosis is the interpretation of the results. After all the hard work, you are now at the stage that you will try to make sense of the data you received. The prospect of analysing data can be a daunting task for many survey specialists. This phase is concerned with discovering what is going on in the organisation and why. As discussed in the previous chapters, the data collected can be quantitative or qualitative or a combination of the two; in other words a mixed approach. In the discussion which follows, the analysis of quantitative (survey based) results will firstly be discussed, followed by qualitative analysis and lastly a reference to the mixed method.

PRESENTING QUANTITATIVE SURVEY RESULTS

Before analysing the data it is important to refer back to the purpose of the diagnosis. The way you analyse the data must be focused on the purpose and the research questions you have set. According to Leedy and Ormrod[1], "all research activity is subordinate to the research problem itself". These research questions might be very specific and in a business environment focus on some outputs the organisation wanted to obtain. An example of the purpose of an organisational effectiveness survey is to obtain a better understanding of the organisational effectiveness of Better Work Company.

Some typical objectives are to:

1.   provide a barometer of the status quo;
2.   determine employees' satisfaction/dissatisfaction with the measured dimensions;
3.   identify the root causes affecting organisational effectiveness;
4.   describe the consequences/impact of these causes on:
     *   profitability
     *   customer satisfaction, and
     *   competitiveness
5.   determine if there are any relationships between the levels of employee satisfaction and overall organisational effectiveness;
6.   determine how the various demographic groups experience the organisational effectiveness in the organisation;
7.   make recommendations and propose interventions to improve organisational effectiveness and performance; and

8.   propose recommendations in shaping the organisation to become an Employer of Choice.

The objectives indicate that the survey consultant will need to focus on various analyses; on item -, dimensional -, overall levels and by geographical groups. It also appears as if the survey specialist will need to conduct some advanced statistical analyses to answer some of the objectives. The data received via a survey are not really of any value until they have been analysed and interpreted. When you are interpreting survey results, you are engaging in a process of data synthesis. The intended outcome is an accurate and meaningful distillation of the main themes, trends and issues[2]. The two authors summarise the distillation process as below in figure 6.1.

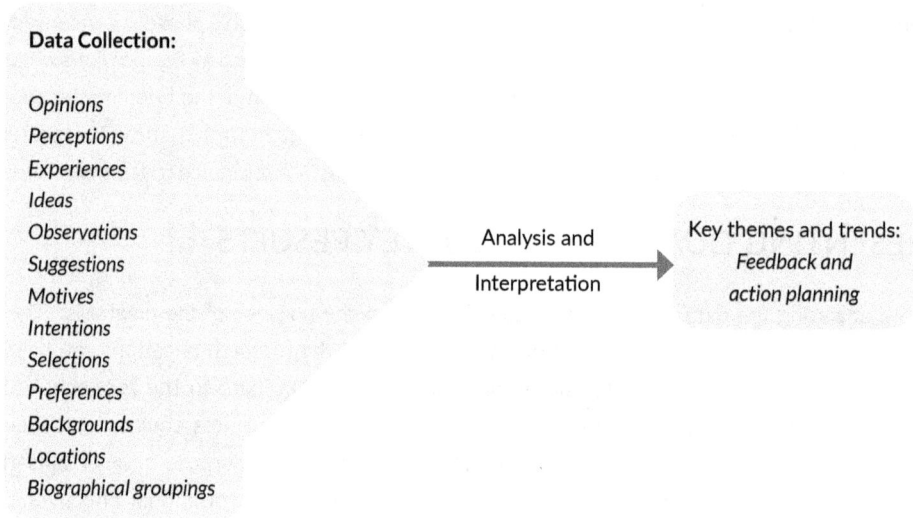

Data Collection:

Opinions
Perceptions
Experiences
Ideas
Observations   Analysis and   Key themes and trends:
Suggestions   Interpretation   Feedback and
Motives   action planning
Intentions
Selections
Preferences
Backgrounds
Locations
Biographical groupings

Figure 6.1: The distillation process (adapted from Church & Warclawski[3])

The above figure can guide the survey specialist to solve the problems through the interpretation of the data gathered[4].

Some pre-requisites before reporting

A novice survey specialist might be tempted to immediately report on the survey results without checking aspects such as the validity and reliability of the survey. It can be very embarrassing if feedback is given regarding a survey and somebody in the audience asks the questions: How valid and reliable is your questionnaire? Does your questionnaire cater for different ethnic groups? The survey specialist must thus ensure that the following aspects are in place and have been verified before the report is written:

1. Was an adequate sample included in the survey? (See chapter 4 for a discussion on sampling.)
2. Was the questionnaire pre-tested in your organisation? (See chapter 3 for a discussion on pre-testing.)
3. Was a valid and reliable questionnaire used in the survey? (See chapter 3.) If not, it might be a good idea to ensure that the validity of the survey is determined by means of factor analysis, and its reliability by means of item analysis (Cronbach's Alpha). Although factor and item analysis do not form part of this book, it is important that the survey specialist familiarise him/herself with these statistical processes or make use of a statistician to assist. The two concepts (validity and reliability) are defined as follows (also see figure 6.2 below):
    - Validity is the extent to which a measure or set of measures correctly represents the concept of the study, such as organisational culture or climate.
    - Reliability is the extent to which a variable (dimension) or set of variables (dimensions) is consistent in what it intends to measure. If multiple measurements are taken, reliable measures will be consistent in their values[5].

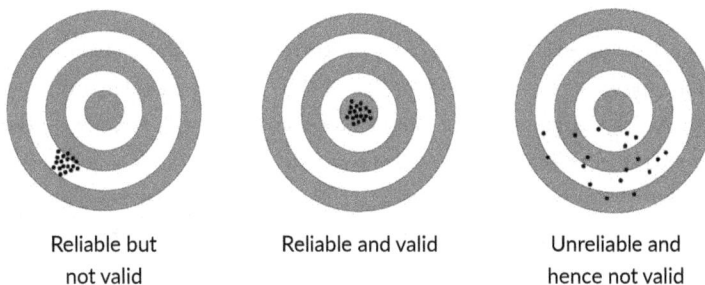

| Reliable but not valid | Reliable and valid | Unreliable and hence not valid |

Figure 6.2: Reliability and validity

4 Is this questionnaire valid and reliable for the specific population and biographical groups measured? If not, it is a good idea to firstly determine the factorial invariance of the questionnaire for various populations. It is interesting to note that most of the validity and reliability studies on employee surveys generally refer to the validity and reliability of the instrument for the total population participating in the particular survey(s)[6]. In substantive research focusing on multi-group comparisons, it is typically assumed that the instrument of measurement operates in exactly the same way and that the underlying construct being measured has the same theoretical structure for each group under investigation. As evidenced in reviews of the literature, however, these two critical assumptions are rarely, if ever, tested statistically[7].

5 Are the results based on a specific organisational diagnostic model? (See chapter 3.)

Reporting the results

Various options are available to the survey specialist to provide overall feedback on the survey results. A number of survey software packages (see chapter 3) are available that can assist with the analysing of results and the compilation of graphs and tables. The question the survey specialist has to answer is: Which method will portray the results in such a way that it becomes easy to understand correctly? If graphs with colour bars and percentages are used, most people will be able to understand and interpret the results. Before portraying the results in tables or graphs it helps to clarify some terms which will be used, such as:

Clarifying terms used in the survey

1. Rationale for using the survey instrument

   It is important to explain to the organisation why the specific survey instrument was used to conduct the survey.

   For instance, was an existing survey instrument used, was the instrument adapted for the organisations, or was a new instrument developed? A typical explanation can be as follows: "The South African Organisational Culture Instrument (SACI), developed by Martins[8], was the primary measuring instrument used in this study. The SACI is a locally-developed survey for the South African context and measures the extent to which employees identify with the various elements of the organisation's existing and ideal culture[9]. It has been scientifically and objectively proven valid and reliable[10] and was therefore appropriate for use in this study.

   The instrument consisted of 89 items but due to operational time constraints imposed by the organisation the questionnaire was shortened to 60 items that were ultimately used in this study. These 60 items were representative of the seven dimensions of the original questionnaire.

   Respondents made use of a five-point Likert scale to rate each statement. A low rating (1) specified that the respondents strongly disagreed and a high rating (5) that they strongly agreed. All factors were scored such that a low score indicated non-acceptance of the cultural dimension, while a high score indicated acceptance[11].

   In addition, biographical and demographic data were requested from each participant and were collected from a section within the survey. No identifying information was requested apart from age, race, gender, region and level in the organisation. Of particular importance to this study, participants were also requested to self-select the generational category, delineated by birth years, into which they fall"[12].

2. Reliability of the questionnaire

   The reliability of an instrument can be defined in terms of the internal consistency with which each item in a scale correlates with every other item, ensuring that a test measuring the same thing more than once has the same outcome results[13]. As explained in chapter 3, it is important that the organisation knows that they are using a reliable instrument.

3. Validity of the questionnaire

    Explain how the validity of items (questions/statements) was evaluated (factor analysis), if a reliable process was followed during data collection, and if the data was analysed, reported and interpreted in a valid, reliable, fair and unbiased manner. Both the reliability and validity are important aspects to discuss, especially when managers or employees start to question the survey results and are trying to discredit the survey instrument or process.

4. A dimension

    A dimension consists of a number of statements or questions which measures a specific concept or construct.

5. The cut-off point

    For the purpose of this analysis the cut-off point of the mean of 3.20 will be used, based on work done by the Human Sciences Research Council (HSRC) of South Africa[14]. Some companies also develop their own in-house benchmarks based on previous surveys conducted, or may use other developed benchmarks.

6. Displaying of results

    Results are given as % agreement (scores of 4 and 5 as a %; or scores of 3 as a %).

7. The mean

    The mean, commonly known as the arithmetic average, is computed by adding up all the scores in the distribution and dividing the total (sum) by the number of scores. The mean for a distribution is the sum of the scores divided by the number of scores.

8. Frequency

    The number of responses for each question/statement.

9. Standard deviation

    A common measure of the dispersion or spread of the data around the mean.

10. Correlation coefficients

    Correlation coefficients measure the relationship between two variables (eg dimensions or statements).

11. Multiple regression analysis

    Predicts outcomes, using one or more predictor variables, for example predicting staff turnover from age, organisational commitment, or employee engagement.

12. T-test

    The T-test compares the results of two groups of participants to determine whether the differences are significant.

13. Analysis of variance (ANOVA)

    A statistical procedure used to determine whether or not there are differences between more than two groups of participants on one or more factors (dimensions). The F-test is used in ANOVA.

14. Structural equation modelling (SEM)

    SEM is a multivariate procedure that combines multiple regression and factor analysis when examining the research hypotheses of causality in a system[15]. SEM is divided into two different parts, namely a measurement model and a structural model. The measurement model deals with the relationships between the measured and latent variables, whereas the structural model only deals with the relationships between the latent variables. It is important if SEM is used to explain how and why it was used. An example is discussed in paragraph 2.4, for instance: In the context of the present study, SEM analysis was performed in order to test the relationship between the variables (dimensions) obtained from the confirmatory factor model.

15. The model or assessment framework

    The model or assessment framework which will be used to display the results are explained. As discussed in chapters 1 and 3, various models or assessment frameworks are available which survey consultants can use to explain the results as well as the relationships between dimensions. It is important that a model or assessment framework is used which supports the purpose of the survey and which is understandable to the organisation.

Displaying the results

Various examples are available to display the results of the biographical groups. Below are a few examples of typical graphs and tables that can be used. Figures 6.3 and 6.4 and table 1.1 portray some overall biographical results of the years of service groups, education level and job levels of participants.

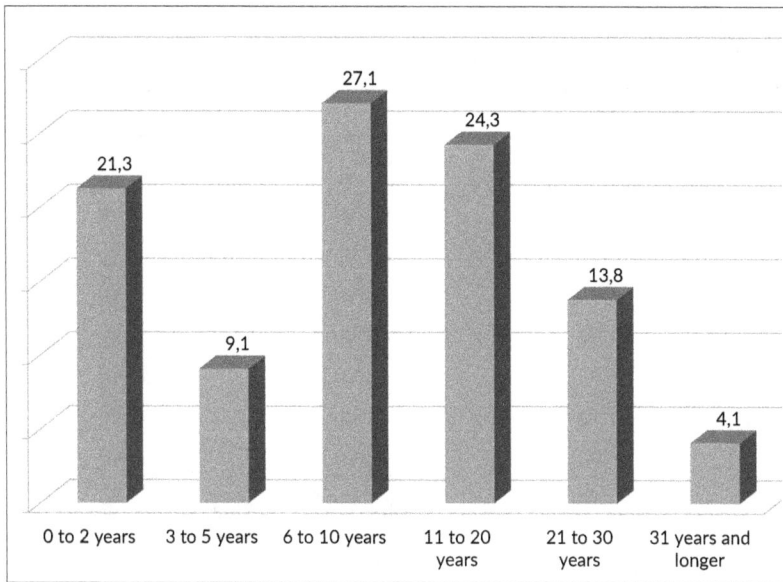

Figure 6.3: Years of service (participants)

It appears from figure 6.3 that most respondents have between 6-20 years of service, with quite a large component of new employees. This already alerts the survey specialist that it appears as if many employees leave the organisation after two years of service. A more in-depth analysis, using the analysis of variance, can be applied to investigate the survey results and to determine why this is happening. The results of the educational levels are displayed below in table 6.1.

Table 6.1: Educational level of participants

Qualifications	n	%
Matric (Grade 12)	163	47.6
Diploma	79	23.1
Degree	68	19.9
Postgraduate degree	32	9.4
Total	**342**	**100.0**

The educational level distribution of the respondents is presented in table 6.1. The results indicate that 163 (47.6%) of the respondents had a matric certificate. The information further indicates that 32 (9.4%) of the respondents had completed a postgraduate degree. This compares well with the proportional distribution evident across the study population, where all levels of qualifications are represented according to the population of the organisation.

In many instances companies also conduct follow-up surveys to compare trends and to determine if their interventions have had the anticipated effects. In figure 6.4 below, the job levels of respondents are displayed over a period of three years.

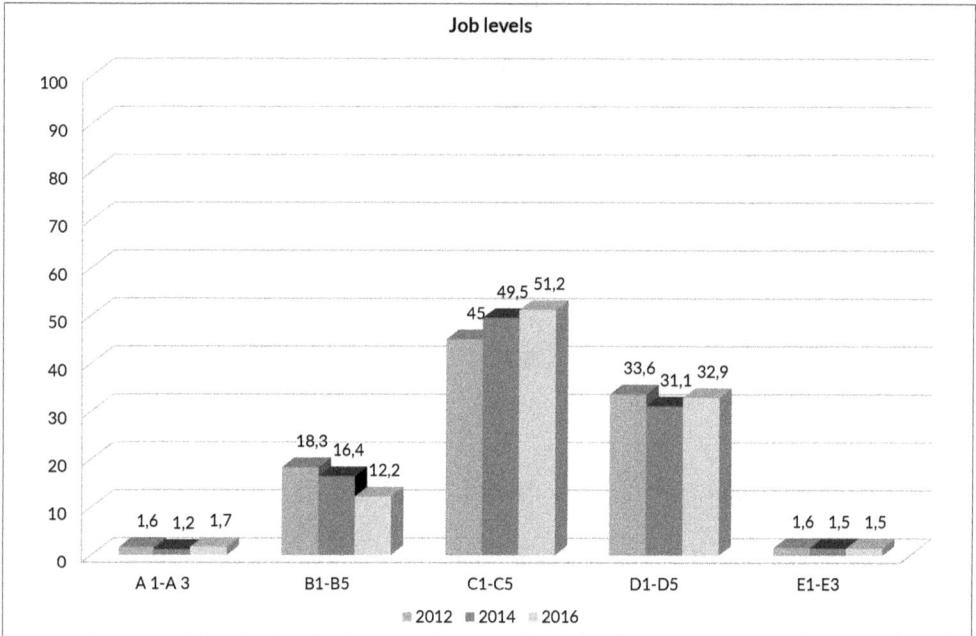

Figure 6.4: Job levels

It is clear from the above results that this company has maintained a very similar employment profile over the four year period.

In displaying the results of the dimensions and statements various options are available. Table 6.2 displays the results by dimension, and table 6.3 by statement, ranked from the highest to the lowest mean score.

Table 6.2: Results of main dimensions

Dimension	Mean		Strongly disagree	Disagree	Unsure	Agree	Strongly agree
Strategic focus	4.35		0.7%	1.5%	5.5%	47.0%	45.4%
Leadership	3.86		4.9%	7.5%	12.3%	47.0%	28.3%
Trust	3.71		4.6%	8.9%	18.0%	48.2%	20.3%
Systems and procedures	3.30		10.4%	19.8%	12.4%	44.0%	13.3%
Work environment	3.01		18.5%	23.1%	7.4%	40.8%	10.2%
Performance management	2.88		20.0%	20.8%	18.9%	32.1%	8.2%

The above results indicate that both work environment and performance management are regarded as developmental areas, if the 3.20 cut-off point is used. It appears as if most respondents are satisfied with the three highest ranked dimensions. In table 6.3 below the results of the individual statements are displayed.

Table 6.3: Results of questions ranked from the highest to the lowest mean score

Question	Mean		Strongly disagree	Disagree	Unsure	Agree	Strongly agree
I regard the organisation as an employer of choice.	4.28		1.0%	2.8%	8.0%	43.6%	44.6%
I believe what my immediate manager says.	4.04		1.4%	6.7%	7.9%	54.0%	30.0%
I am motivated by the example set by my manager.	3.94		1.7%	6.9%	12.6%	53.5%	25.3%
My immediate manager manages a diverse team well.	3.91		4.5%	7.9%	9.8%	47.6%	30.1%

Question	Mean		Strongly disagree	Disagree	Unsure	Agree	Strongly agree
My immediate manager encourages me to develop myself further.	3.88		2.5%	8.4%	12.9%	50.5%	25.7%
I am proud to work for the organisation.	3.84		5.6%	8.9%	12.9%	40.7%	32.0%
My immediate manager leads by example.	3.59		8.6%	12.3%	13.9%	41.6%	23.5%
I trust my immediate manager.	3.49		10.5%	11.6%	16.8%	40.7%	20.2%
I am satisfied with the opportunities for career development.	3.02		17.4%	21.4%	15.3%	33.8%	12.1%
Regular teambuilding opportunities are arranged for our section.	2.86		15.1%	30.7%	14.4%	32.8%	7.0%

The results in table 6.3 provide an example of how the responses to individual questions can be displayed. This ranking table can help managers to compare the results of all questions, and to easily identify specific questions below the cut-off point. The results can also be displayed by statement and by dimension to interpret the results by dimension. With the presentation and discussion of results it also helps if the survey specialist focuses on the most positive and the main developmental statements, as displayed in tables 6.1 and 6.2. This conveys two messages, namely in some aspects the company is doing very well, and in other areas they need to focus on specific future interventions

Benchmark results

Most frequently, when the survey specialist presents the results, the management team is interested to see how they compare to the results of other companies or previous survey results. This comparison value is called a benchmark[16]. The important criteria are that the survey specialist must compare apples to apples and ensure that his/her comparison is applicable to the organisation or industry. In many instances the comparison might be for a specific job level or division. Many companies use their own internal benchmarks, such as repetitive surveys; their own cut-off points (as referred to earlier and in Figure 6. 5 below); or the prognoses of the management team. In other instances companies are only interested in external benchmarks (Table 6.3 below). According to Borg and Mastrangelo[17], picking an optimal benchmark is rarely trivial. If the benchmark is too high it can discourage employees, but if it is too low it can lead to complacency. Experience with the setting of benchmarks has taught the author that it is a good principle to discuss the benchmark with the company survey project team and also to obtain input from the Exco team.

The Spider graph (6.5) below compares the results by dimension, per year with the cut-off point (benchmark).

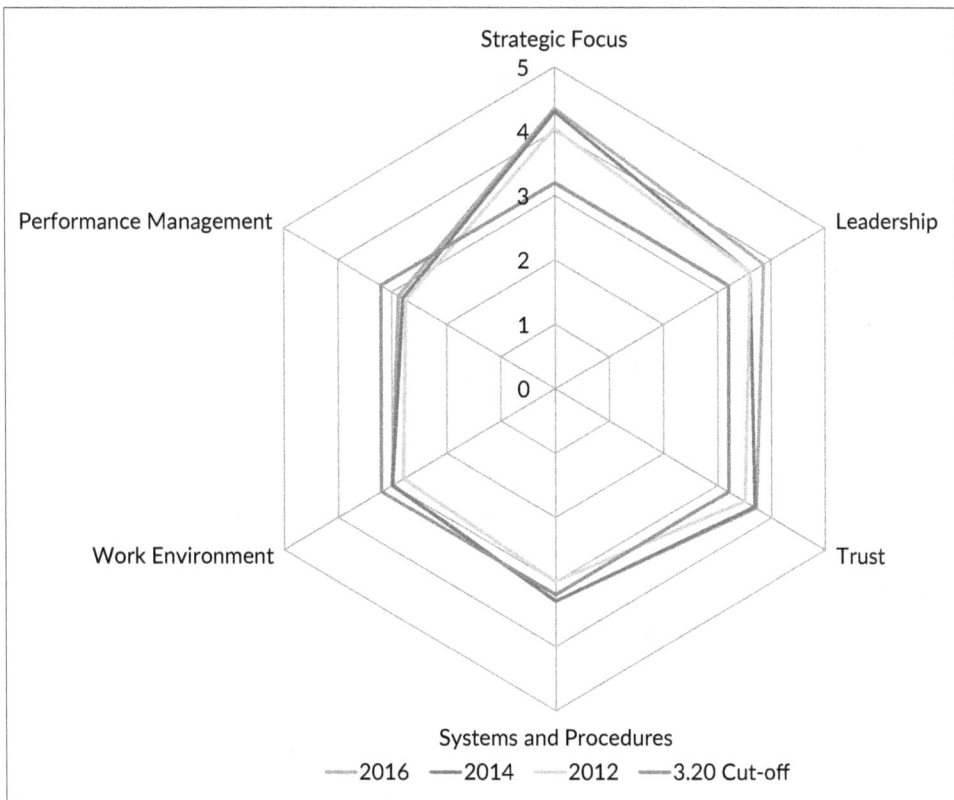

Figure 6.5: Comparing results by year

The Spider graph above clearly shows that the strategic focus is the most positive dimension for all three years, and well above the cut-off point. Performance management and work environment are, however, below the 3.20 cut-off point.

Table 6.4 portrays some external benchmark results. These are summarised overall results and the results in figure 6.6 portray results for specific statements.

Table 6.4: Comparative results of companies

Organisation	Overall index (mean score)
Private company (2015)	3.95
Private company (2014)	3.94
Private company (2013)	3.91
Private company (2015)	3.91
Private company (2013)	3.74
Government (2011)	3.69
Private company (2014)	3.57
Government (2016)	3.27
Government (2012)	3.27
Private company (2012)	3.20
Government (2014)	3.18
Government (2014)	3.14
Private company (2013)	3.09
Government (2012)	3.00
Government (2015)	2.88

The main purpose of these comparisons is to provide the company with some benchmark information of other similar surveys. This can assist the company to determine if they are scoring better or worse than their competitors with regards to a specific dimension or statement. These comparisons can subsequently assist management to decide on the priorities of interventions.

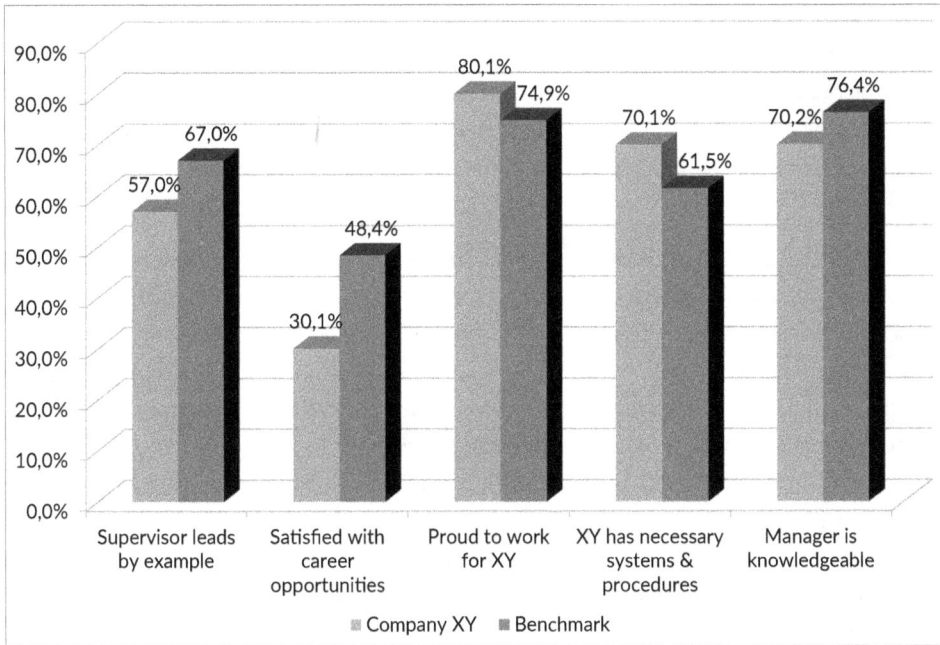

Figure 6.6: Comparative results of benchmark results by statement (% Agree)

The comparisons by division (figure 6.7), as an example, can assist management to compare results internally. This can again assist management to determine where they need to focus with future interventions.

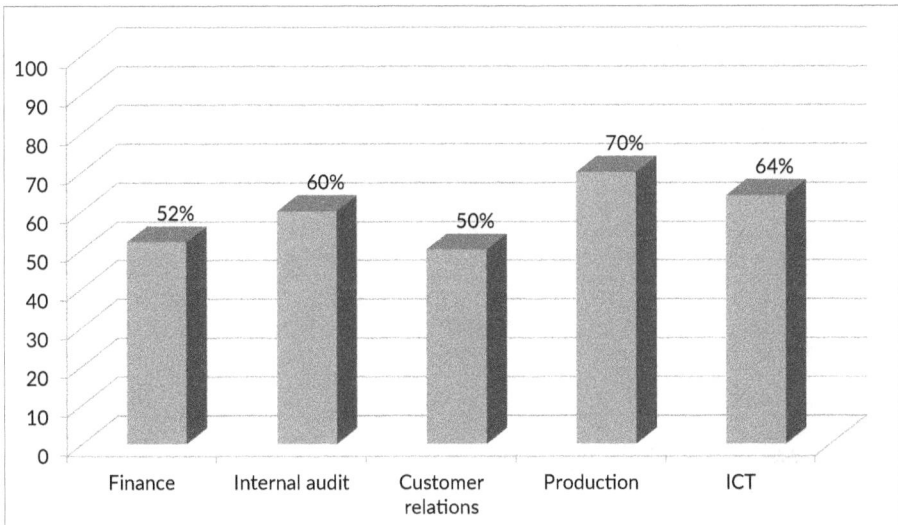

Figure 6.7: Comparison by division

In our example above it appears as if the production division's participants are quite satisfied with the measured concepts, while it does not appear to be the case for the participants from the finance division. The survey specialist might thus propose specific interventions for the finance department, which might not be applicable to the production department.

Statistical data analysis

In most instances the above examples will provide the company with an overview of the results, but no clear indication of where to focus with interventions. The purpose of inferential statistics (T-test, ANOVA, correlation, regression analysis and structural equation modelling) is to answer the following questions:

1   Are you interested in differences between two groups, for example pre- and post-tests, comparing the results of males and females? (T-tests)
2   Are you interested in differences between more than two groups, for example divisions, age groups, race groups? (ANOVA)
3   Do you intend to predict one or more outcome factors, for example predicting individual performance by examining employees' affective reactions to the work environment? (Regression analysis)
4   Do you intend to develop or test a developed model, for example a model to predict employees' intention to leave? (Structural equation modelling)

The purpose of these analyses is to investigate relationships, to draw conclusions and make predictions about future interventions. It is beyond the scope of this book to discuss the various statistical tests and their applications. An example of a model to test if a more positive attitude towards the company correlates negatively with customer satisfaction is portrayed below in figure 6.8[18].

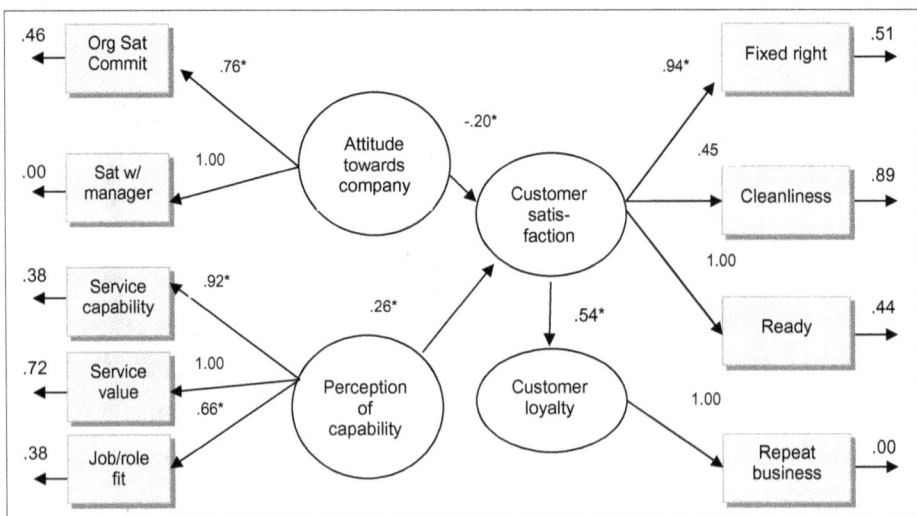

Figure 6.8: A more positive attitude towards the company correlates negatively with customer satisfaction[19]

The above results indicate that the perception of capacity positively correlated with customer satisfaction (.26), but attitude to the company was negatively related (-.20). A more positive attitude towards the company thus did mean that the customer is more satisfied. It might be that in this organisation the focus was more internally than on the customer. These types of analyses can assist management to decide where to focus and not to spend money on the wrong interventions. If the survey specialist is not trained in statistics it might be best to use the services of a trained statistician for these analyses.

In many instances organisations only conduct focus groups or interviews (qualitative analysis), or use both quantitative and qualitative analyses. In the next section, qualitative analysis as a survey collection option will be discussed.

QUALITATIVE ANALYSIS

In chapter 3 the advantages and disadvantages of qualitative analysis were already discussed. In this section the focus will be on the analysis of interviews and focus group data. The planning and coordination of focus groups and interviews are discussed in chapter 5. The value of interviews and focus groups is that they allow the survey specialist to clarify and probe the statistical results[20]. In many instances, management might query the statistical results. This usually happens when the results are not according to their expectations. If this is the case, they will look for reasons why the results are not good enough. Reasons proffered by management, which we have encountered, are:

1. The employees did not understand the questions in the survey questionnaire.
    Answer: Explain the survey development process which included a pilot study (see chapters 1 and 2).
2. The employees answered the questions incorrectly.
    Answer: Again explain the pilot study during which employees of various job levels participated to test their understanding of the questions. Secondly, explain the role of the focus groups and interviews which were used to clarify employees' perceptions and answers.
3. The different language groups did not understand the English questionnaire.
    Answer: Explain the survey collection process and how people from different language groups were accommodated (see chapter 3).
4. The statistical results are not valid.
    Answer: Explain how the quantitative data are supporting the qualitative data (focus groups and interviews). Explain how the reliability and validity of the questionnaire was determined.

The benefit of using a multi-method approach is that it provides the survey specialist confidence that the data are valid[21]. In many survey feedback sessions to management, the multi-method approach confirmed the validity of the data and eliminated any concerns from management (see section 3.2 below).

Analysing and interpreting qualitative data

A number of different analytical traditions within qualitative analysis are available, such as phenomenology, grounded theory and thematic content analysis. For the survey specialist who is not conducting academic research, but needs to report reliable and valid qualitative data, a thematic content analysis might be the most practical analysis process.

Content analysis is a technique used to acquire a richer understanding of the data. It involves identifying the major concepts or issues discussed in an interview or focus group, for example, and then counting the number of occurrences[22]. The six phases of the thematic content analysis process can be summarised as follows[23]:

Phase 1: Familiarisation with the data

During this phase the data are firstly transcribed verbatim and any patterns, ideas and possible coding schemas are noted.

Phase 2: Generating initial codes

The survey specialist now compiles a preliminary coding table based on the interviews or focus group questions asked. An example of such an initial coding framework is portrayed below in table 6.5[24]. The focus of the study was the development and evaluation of a coaching programme to improve safety leadership. Quantitative and qualitative surveys were conducted.

Table 6.5: Initial coding framework – qualitative research[25]

Main category	Sub-categories
101 Safety perceptions	1011 Current perceptions
	1012 Previous perceptions
	1013 Reasons for changes
	1014 Has it changed
201 Challenges in safety leadership	2011 Management tasks
	2012 Behavioural
	2013 Priorities
301 Areas of improvement	3011 Knowledge
	3012 Behavioural
401 Experience of the process	4011 Receiving feedback
	4012 Receiving guidance
	4013 Management commitment
	6013 Applicability to other levels

Phase 3: Searching for themes

After identifying the initial themes, frequencies can now be calculated to determine the prevalence of codes across the data set and in relation to each preliminary theme. See the example below in table 6.6.

Table 6.6: Frequency distribution of codes[26]

Theme description	Sub-code and description	N of responses	% in data	% in theme	N of participants that mentioned it	% of participants (N=4)
101 Attitude towards safety	1011 Current attitude is positive	19	10.7	51.4	4	100
	1012 Previous attitude	12	6.8	32.4	4	100
	1013 Attitude has changed	6	3.4	16.2	4	100
	Sub-totals	37	21	100		100
102 Reasons for changes	1021 Training/increased legal knowledge	6	3.4	31.6	3	75
	1022 Experience with previous accidents	2	1.1	10.5	2	50
	1023 Awareness of legal consequences	7	4	36.8	4	100
	1024 Improved housekeeping	4	2.3	21.1	2	50
	Sub-totals	19	11	100		68.8
201 Challenges	2011 Management tasks	10	5.7	25.6	3	75
	2012 Change employees' mind-set	25	14.1	64.1	3	75
	2013 Competing priorities	4	2.3	10.3	2	50
	Sub-totals	39	22.1	100		66.7
301 Impact	3011 Increased knowledge	3	1.7	7	2	50
	3012 Increased pro-activeness	10	5.7	23.2	4	100
	3013 Increased self-awareness	22	12.4	51.2	4	100
	3014 Improved interaction	2	1.1	4.6	2	50
	1015 Less incidents	6	3.4	14	4	100
	Sub-totals	43	24.3	100		80

Theme description	Sub-code and description	N of responses	% in data	% in theme	N of participants that mentioned it	% of participants (N=4)
401 Manager's experiences	4011 Positive experience	8	3.4	44.5	4	100
	4012 Want feedback	2	1.1	11.1	2	50
	4013 Design of programme	4	2.3	22.2	3	75
	4014 Recommend to other levels	4	2.3	22.2	4	100
	Sub-totals	18	9.1	100		81.3

Phase 4: Reviewing themes

In this phase the themes are refined and the survey specialist also reflects on each theme and how they could be linked together.

Phase 5: Defining and naming themes

During this phase the survey specialist compiles a thematic map of the data. The survey specialist further defines and refines the themes to ensure that they align with the purpose of the survey and the set aims. A typical thematic map is portrayed in figure 6.9[27].

For each theme a detailed analysis (figure 6.9) was conducted and written and the researcher considered how it fitted into the broader overall analysis in relation to the research questions and theory on safety leadership and coaching programmes. The titles or names of the themes were also finalised. The names of the themes were concise, consisted of words that respondents actually used (as opposed to technical terms), and indicated a sense of what the themes were about[28].

Phase 6: Producing the report

In this last phase the report is compiled. The report now focuses on the themes extracted and how they relate to the purpose and aims of the survey. As mentioned earlier, in many instances the purpose of the qualitative data is to support the findings of the quantitative (statistical) analysis.

Integration of the results (mixed-method approach)

As mentioned, a multi-method approach is in many instances used to confirm the validity of the data and to eliminate any concerns from management.

A summary of the findings of the study on safety leadership is portrayed below. These results indicate the value of integrating the results of qualitative and quantitative surveys[29].

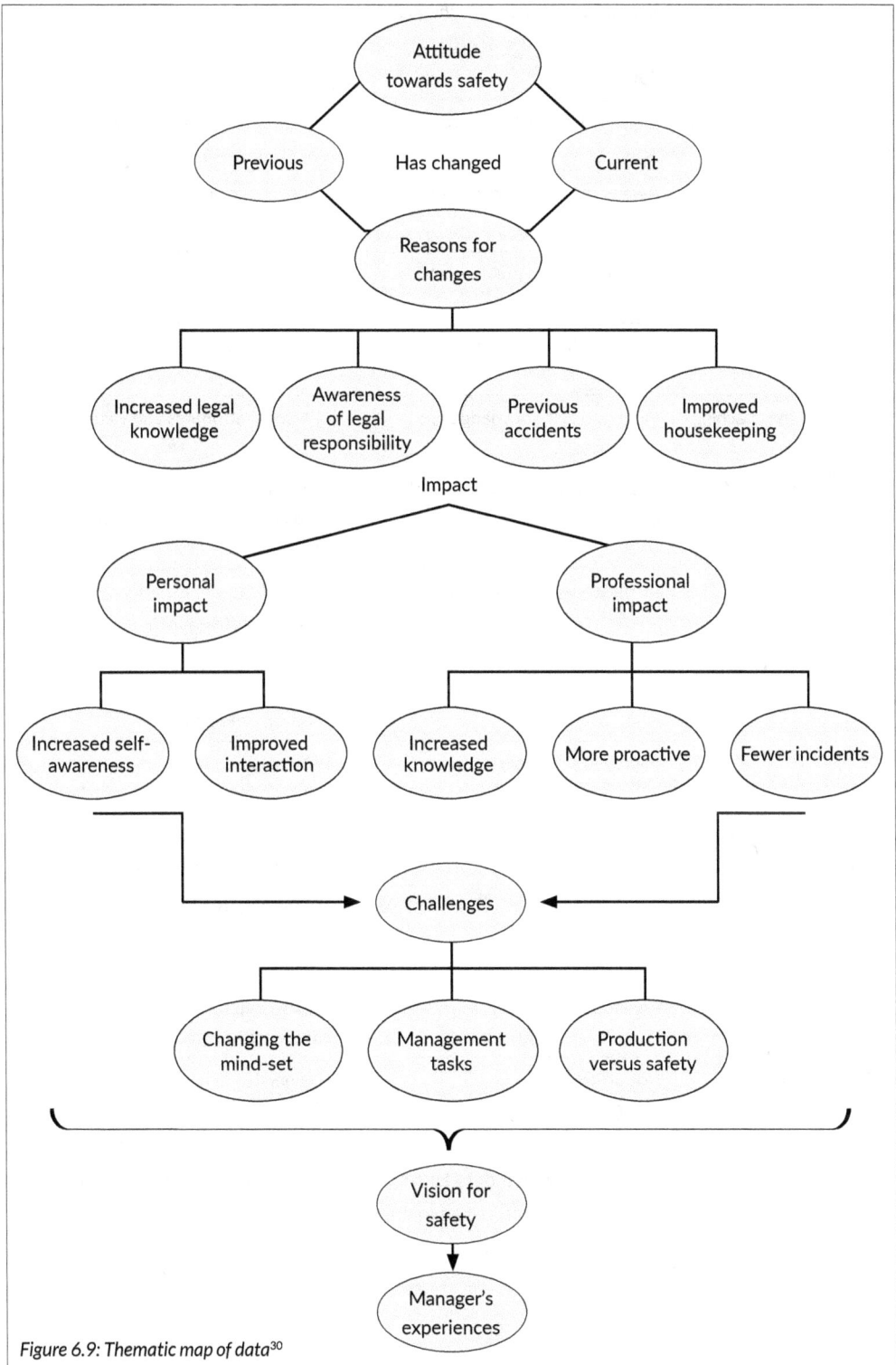

Figure 6.9: Thematic map of data[30]

Table 6.7: Linking the findings of the qualitative results to the quantitative results

Theme	Sub-theme	Safety leadership element
Reasons for changes in attitude (Theme 2)	Increased legal knowledge	Knowledge and experience
	Awareness of legal consequences	Knowledge and experience
	Experience with previous accidents	Knowledge and experience
	Improved housekeeping	Not applicable
Impact of the coaching programme (Themes 3 and 4)	Increased self-knowledge and awareness	Personal attributes and values
	More positive interactions with employees	Leadership behaviours (Collaboration, feedback and recognition)
	Increased legal knowledge	Knowledge and experience (Learning orientation)
	Increased pro-activeness	Leadership behaviours (Action orientation)
	Improved safety performance	Management tasks
Challenges for safety Leadership (Theme 5)	Ensuring compliance with safety procedures	Management tasks Leadership style (transactional)
	Changing the mind-set of employees	Leadership behaviours (Accountability) Leadership style (Transformational)
	Production vs. safety	Leadership behaviours (Business integration)
The vision for safety (Theme 6)	No sub-themes	Leadership behaviours (Vision and values)

The next step is then to use the qualitative data to support the statistical analysis in the reporting of results. The reporting options will be discussed in chapter 8.

CONCLUSION

In this chapter the discussion focused on the analysis of quantitative (survey based) and qualitative results, and then lastly the integration of the two in a mixed-method approach. In the next chapter the follow-up process will be discussed. In many instances organisations use only one approach, either quantitative or qualitative. The discussions in this chapter show the value if both approaches can be used in a diagnosis.

REFERENCES

Borg, I. & Mastrangelo, PM. 2008. *Employee surveys in management: Theories, tools and practical applications.* Toronto: Hogrefe.

Braun, V. & Clarke, V. 2006. Doing thematic analysis in psychology. *Qualitative Research in Psychology* 1(3):77-101.

Byrne, N. 2004. Testing for multigroup invariance Using AMOS graphics: A road less traveled. *Structural Equation Modeling* 11(2):272–300.

Church, AH. & Waclawski, J. 1998. *Designing and using organizational surveys: A seven-step process.* San Francisco: Jossy Bass.

Esterhuizen, W. 2015. *Organisational culture of shift workers in the health care environment.* Unpublished doctoral thesis. Pretoria: University of Pretoria.

Garson, G. (2008). *Structural equation modelling: Stat notes.* North Carolina State University, Raleigh, NC: David Garson & Statistical Associates.

Hair, JF., Black, WC., Babin, BJ. & Anderson, RE. 2010. *Multivariate data analysis.* 7th edition. Englewood Cliffs, NJ: Prentice Hall.

Leedy, PD. & Ormod, JE. 2010.*Practical research. Planning and design.* 9th edition. Boston: Pearson Education International.

Martins, N. (1989). *Organisasiekultuur in 'n finansiele instelling.* (D.Phil-proefskrif). Pretoria: University of Pretoria (Unpublished).

Martins, N. 2014. Factorial invariance of the South African culture instrument. *Problems and Perspectives in Management* (Special issue: South Africa-2) 12(4):242-252.

Martins, N. 2016. Organisational diagnosis, in *Fundamentals of organisation development*, edited by N Martins & D Geldenhuys. Cape Town: Juta:169-192.

Martins, N. & Coetzee, M. 2007. Organisational culture, employee satisfaction, perceived leader emotional compency and personality type: An exploratory study in a South African Engineering Company. *SA Journal of Human Resources Management*, 5(2):20-32.

Martins, N. & von der Ohe, H. 2006. Detecting sub-cultures in an organisation. *South African Business Review*, 10(2):130-149.

Moss, M. *Generational sub-cultures.* (M-dissertation) Pretoria: University of South Africa (Unpublished).

Remenyi, D. 2014. A *dictionary of concepts and issues.* Reading, United Kingdom: Academic Conferences and Publishing International Limited.

Terre Blanche, M., & Durrheim, K. 2002. *Research in practice: Applied methods for the social sciences.* Cape Town: University of Cape Town Press.

ENDNOTES

1. Leedy & Ormrod, 2010: 218.
2. Church & Waclawski, 1998: 150.
3. Church & Warclawski, 1998: 150.
4. Leedy & Ormrod, 2010: 218.
5. Hair, Black, Babin & Anderson, 2010.
6. Martins, 2014: 242.
7. Byrne, 2004: 273.
8. Martins, 1989.
9. Martins & Coetzee, 2007.
10. Martins & Coetzee, 2007; Martins & von der Ohe 2006.
11. Martins & Coetzee, 2007.
12. Moss, 2015, p 20.
13. Terre Blanche & Durrheim, 2002.
14. Martins, 2016: 186.
15. Garson, 2008; Hair et al., 2010.
16. Borg & Mastrangelo, 2008: 298.
17. Borg & Mastrangelo, 2008: 299.
18. Lezotte & McLinden, 2003 in Borg & Mastrangelo, 2008.
19. Lezotte & McLinden, 2003 in Borg & Mastrangelo, 2008.
20. Martins, 2016.
21. Martins, 2016.
22. Remenyi, 2014.
23. Braun & Clarke, 2006.
24. Esterhuizen, 2015.
25. Esterhuizen, 2015.
26. Esterhuizen, 2015.
27. Esterhuizen, 2015.
28. Esterhuizen 2015.
29. Esterhuizen, 2015.
30. Esterhuizen, 2015.

CHAPTER 7

FOLLOW-UP PROCESS – CLARIFING SURVEY RESULTS

by **Nico Martins**

INTRODUCTION

The feedback process following a research survey can be a daunting and intimidating task, even for the most experienced consultant or survey specialist. When the survey results are mostly positive, and they were expected as such, not many critical questions will be asked by the project and management teams. However, when the results are less positive than expected, you can be sure that a number of difficult questions will be posed, either when you are presenting the survey results or when you hand over the report. All of a sudden the validity of the questionnaire, the clarity of the questions, the sample size, the survey distribution, the interpretation of results, and the recommendations will be scrutinised. The question now is if the consultant or survey specialist can build in some steps to ensure that he/she can answer all these questions professionally and with ease.

In this chapter a number of steps will be proposed and discussed which will help not only to support you in the feedback process, but also to ensure the validity and integrity of the survey process.

SESSIONS TO CLARIFY THE RESULTS

Various options can be considered to clarify and confirm whether the survey results are correct. The author proposes that you build these options into your project plan. The most obvious next step after you have conducted the survey and have analysed some results, is to discuss it with the project team. The next step will be to discuss the results with the main sponsor. In many instances that might be the Human Resources Director or even the CEO. After the sessions you can continue with focus groups or interviews to further clarify the survey results (see chapters 3 and 5). The sequence of sessions will obviously depend on the arrangement of the project, as outlined in the project plan or the survey results.

Discussions with the project team

The first discussion is always with the project team. As soon as preliminary results are available, a feedback and discussion session is arranged with the project team[1]. The agenda for such a session can be as follows:

1. Confirm the project scope (this could have been a tender document, a quotation or an internal project scope).
2. Confirm the main purpose of the project.
3. Confirm the aims of the project.
4. Confirm the expected outcomes.
5. Discuss the participation of employees (participation by biographical and geographical groups). Was it representative?
6. Discuss the overall results by dimension.
7. Discuss the detailed results by dimension and statement.
8. Highlight any tendencies noted (specifically high or low results).
9. Discuss the results of the biographical and geographical groups. The input from the project team can be valuable. They can confirm specific tendencies such as high turnovers in departments, newly appointed managers and demographic profiles of departments. The personnel profile of a department can influence the survey results. Think of a department with mostly younger employees (millennials) versus a department with mostly older employees (Baby Boomers). Research indicates that the needs and expectations of the various generational groups differ in many instances[2].
10. Highlight any tendencies noted. Specifically focus on outliers, such as very high or very low results. Check the results with the initial perceptions of the project team.
11. Discuss the possible next steps such as initial feedback to the project sponsor, focus groups or interviews to clarify tendencies, or possibly an additional invitation to groups with low responses to participate again.
12. Discuss any internal or external impacts or changes which might have influenced the results, and which the survey consultants need to take into consideration when they are compiling the recommendations. A number of changes can impact employees' attitudes and subsequently survey results. These changes include events such as: a new CEO or Exco team (structural changes); market changes such as the launch of a new product; human resources changes such as retrenchments; external changes such as new government policies; or international changes such as Brexit. It is important that all of these are discussed to put the results and recommendations to be suggested into the correct perspective.
13. Discuss if more in-depth statistical analysis will be needed to clarify specific results or tendencies.

As can been seen from the above, the main purpose is to have an open and frank discussion of the results and any possible influences, and determining what should be done to ensure that the results are perceived as credible and valid. The purpose is not to alter or change any results (that would be unethical), but to ensure that the results are portrayed and explained correctly and in the correct business context. Organisations, strategies and aims are very different; it is important that the survey specialist takes note of this and incorporates it in the report. A positive result for one organisation might be a developmental issue for another. A typical example might be a well-established organisation with an aging workforce, where learning and development might already be very high. In contrast, the results of a newly established organisation with a number of younger employees might indicate a bigger need for learning and development.

Discussion with the main sponsor

Now is a good time to inform the project sponsor of the results to date. The purpose of this meeting will be very similar to the one with the project team, however now they have been informed and their inputs can be incorporated in the preliminary report and presented to the sponsor. Members of the project team should also be invited to this meeting so that they can provide the organisational context as needed. The same agenda as above can be followed. One of the sub-aims of this meeting will be to obtain approval from the sponsor if additional analysis is required, such as an invitation to low response groups for participation and the conducting of focus groups and interviews. The specific participants for focus groups and interviews can now also be discussed and approval can be obtained. It always helps if the invitation for further participation or other sessions comes from the office of the main sponsor.

A very important objective of this meeting is to ensure that the sponsor understands the results and that he/she will not be confronted with any surprises when the final report is presented. It is also important that the sponsor feels he/she is fully informed and participating in the survey process.

Focus groups and interviews to verify the results

After the first two sessions the target groups for focus groups or interviews would have been clarified. As discussed in chapter 2, a number of aspects need to be considered when conducting focus groups. This chapter will discuss the processes that can be applied to explore and verify survey results.

Focus groups to verify survey results

To explain the focus group process typically used by the author and a colleague, two case studies are presented below.

Case study 1: Focus groups in a metropolitan organisation

After the survey had been administered with a sample size of 6,715 respondents in a metropolitan organisation, the quantitative data were analysed and a second round of focus groups conducted. The **purpose** *of these focus groups was to give feedback on the survey results, verify the results, and explore possible causes and solutions to the challenges that came to light in the quantitative survey results. The groups were asked to confirm the results of the most positive and most challenging outcomes of the survey. They were asked to select an item or items for further exploration and the following two questions were asked:*

---

1. Why is it a challenge to the organisation?
2. How do you propose the challenge can be addressed in order to improve it?

The first question provided clarity and a better understanding of the survey results. The second question possibly resulted in collaboration and feeling part of the organisation in the sense that employees were afforded the opportunity to express their ideas and opinions.

The **research design** of the second round of focus groups was based on the compilation of nine focus groups with a total of 82 participants. The duration of the sessions was two hours, and at least three to five challenges were discussed in each session. Separate focus groups were conducted with the top management team members, the middle management/supervisory levels and lower-level employees, so that each group would feel free to participate without fear of victimisation. All races and genders were represented in all of the groups. Two moderators facilitated the focus groups.

A different method of **data collection** was used in the second round of focus groups compared with the first round (the first round of focus groups aimed at verifying the questionnaire items). Firstly, an overview of the survey results was presented, with a focus on the best and most challenging outcomes of the quantitative analysis. Secondly, participants were informed of the purpose of the focus groups and the ground rules for the session, and the roles of the moderators were explained. Post-it notes and pens were handed out to each member. The first question was asked and members were asked to write down the reasons why they thought the matter being explored was a challenge and possibly provide examples to explain their reasons. The post-it notes were collected, quickly reviewed by the moderators and roughly categorised on the white board/flip chart. The moderator would inform the group of what had been written down. It was then further discussed and clarified, while one moderator added notes on a flip chart. The same process was repeated with the second question.

The methodology that was followed ensured that groupthink, where the dominant voice in the group might influence others to express themselves in the same way, was controlled by affording each person an opportunity to participate without being influenced by another group member. The methodology also lent itself to more data being collected. It was interesting to note that employees often listed the same information without being influenced by other group members, which was a way of verifying the actual causes of the quantitative research outcomes.

During the **data analysis** phase, all the information collected on the post-it notes was typed for each focus group and then finally integrated into one document. An example of a typical challenge, the reasons for it being a challenge, and the possible solutions proposed by the focus group participants are depicted below.

Topic: Communication between departments[3]

Developmental aspects	Reasons and examples of why it is an issue/challenge	Proposed solutions
Q43: There is good communication between departments in our organisation (only 20.1% agreed). Q42: My department (where I work) receives information about what is happening in other departments (only 21.3% agreed).	• Everyone is focused on their own area – don't care about other departments as long as theirs is good. • Big company – number of departments – not easy to communicate, not necessarily dependent on other departments. • Time pressures and deadlines limit communication with other departments. • Lack of communication causes one step forward and two steps back. Is a waste of money. • We do not discuss, after a project, what we could improve on in future.	• Newsletter to communicate what all departments are doing – brief overview – format: electronic in Excel. • Each department should look inwards on how to improve communication within, and if that works, then expand to other departments. • Progress meetings to be held once a week. • "Big picture" project information should be communicated in the beginning (specification sign-off). • Introduce kick-off project meetings and retrospective meetings after finalising a project.

In the second case study a slightly different approach was followed to clarify and understand the survey results in a Namibian organisation and a Middle East organisation.

Case study 2: Focus groups in two international organisations

The focus group design and methodology that were used in the two multicultural organisations are described below in relation to the theoretical discussion on focus groups as a research method.

Purpose and research questions

In both organisations, quantitative organisational assessments were conducted and, in both instances, the survey results created the need for further investigation and understanding of the results. It was proposed that the focus group methodology be used for the main purpose of elaborating and clarifying the organisations' current state of functioning with a focus on the future. The outcome should indicate to the management teams what they are doing well and how to improve their organisational effectiveness.

Taking the guidelines for conducting focus groups into consideration, as well as a positive psychology perspective, the following four questions were formulated and used in the focus groups in both organisations:

1. What are the characteristics of an employer of choice? (Question 1)
2. What excites you about your work (makes you happy) at the organisation? (Question 2)
3. What does the organisation do particularly well? (Question 3)
4. What would you change at the organisation if you had the opportunity? (Question 4)

From the above it is apparent that the first three questions focus on current positive aspects, and the last question has a focus on future improvements instead of focusing on what is wrong or negative in the organisation.

Research design

In both organisations English was the business language, and guidelines on the composition of the focus groups (such as selecting employees from all levels, business units, gender, race and national origins) were discussed with the human resources practitioners. In both instances purposive sampling was used to select and invite participants.

In the Middle Eastern organisation 16 focus groups consisting of 147 participants were conducted, and in the Namibian organisation eight focus groups consisting of 58 participants were conducted. Most of the focus groups consisted of eight to 10 staff members. The duration of each focus group was two hours.

Data collection and moderating

The focus groups were conducted by two professional moderators with consulting and moderating experience. The common factor between the moderators and the participants was that they were from several different national origins (cultures), hence creating an understanding of a multicultural environment.

After a brief introduction, the purpose of the session, the ground rules, and the roles of the moderators were explained. Groupthink and multicultural differences were controlled as follows:

1. Each of the four questions was separately listed on flipchart paper.
2. The participants were requested to write down their answers individually on oval post-it notepaper. In order to maintain confidentiality they were asked not to discuss the answers with their colleagues (figure 7.1).

Figure 7.1: A multicultural focus group writing down their answers

3. The oval post-it notes were collected by the researchers (moderators) and quickly reviewed. The responses were then provisionally grouped by the managerial dimension/ theme identified in the Burke-Litwin[4] model (figure 7.2):

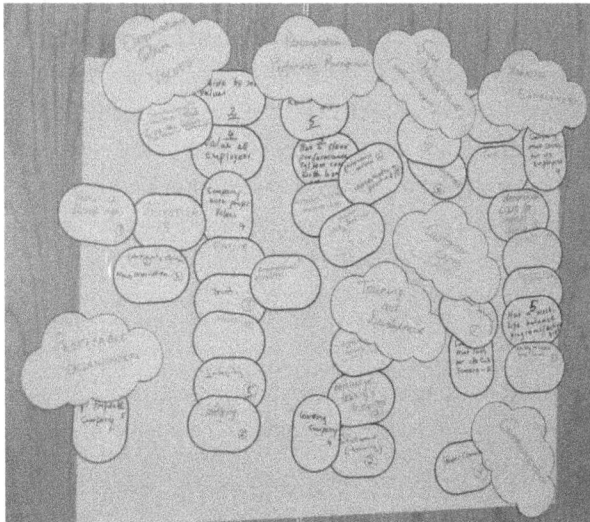

Figure 7.2: Example of data collection

4. All misunderstandings or unclear answer were then discussed. Notes were made on the oval post-it notes, or on separate sheets of flipchart paper. During this phase the contributions made by the dominant participants were facilitated and the participation of those participants who appeared to be shy, was encouraged.
5. The above process was repeated for each of the four questions.

The methodology followed ensured that no one person was permitted to dominate the group and it allowed for all participants to obtain clarification on any of the questions. The sequence of questions also started with more general questions to encourage participation[5].

Data analysis and reporting

A thematic content analysis method was used to analyse the results, which were linked to a diagnostic organisational model. Thematic content analysis is defined by Braun and Clarke[6] as a qualitative diagnostic method for identifying, analysing and reporting on patterns or themes detected in data. In the context of organisational diagnostic approaches, the factual bases of data are established by separating the factual from the non-factual data (which comprise perceptions, skewed facts or interpretations/inferences). Confirmed facts that bear some similarity to one another are then clustered into separate categories, or groups of facts. The categories are then labelled so as to depict accurately the core character of the group of facts and to clearly differentiate one category from another[7].

The relationship between different categories is established by identifying a sufficiently detailed and valid diagnostic model or framework of organisational dynamics that addresses and incorporates the majority of the categories identified during the clustering process. The chosen diagnostic model or framework is then conceptually overlaid on the categorical data, and the cause-effect relationships in the diagnostic model are transferred to the data[8].

The provisional grouping of data per managerial dimension/theme simplified the data-recording process. In line with the research objective, the Burke-Litwin[9] model of organisational performance and change was applied to categorise and analyse those themes regarded as confirmed facts that emerged from the focus group participants. In both organisations the subsequent report, together with recommendations, led to a better understanding of the development areas that were highlighted in the quantitative surveys.

How weaknesses were addressed

The main weaknesses that could have an impact on the focus group research methodology in this research, and as summarised by O'Raghallaigh, Sammon and Murhy[10], were addressed or minimised as outlined below:

Main weaknesses of focus groups as a research method[11]

Weaknesses	Description	How weaknesses were addressed/minimised
Groupthink	The dominant voice in the group might influence others to express themselves in the same way, regardless of whether such expression really reflects their opinion.	• The researchers controlled the possibility of groupthink by using the approach described.
Multicultural groups	Weaknesses related to overcoming cultural and communication barriers, as well as the potential for discrimination.	• Moderators and group members introduced themselves by referring to their cultural background.

Weaknesses	Description	How weaknesses were addressed/ minimised
Multicultural groups (continued)		• Possible discrimination and biases were to a large extent eliminated because responses remained anonymous. • Writing down ideas alleviated the fear in participants who do not speak English as their first language.
Might become "moan and groan" sessions	When discussions focus on what is wrong/ negative in the organisation.	• A positive psychology approach focuses on a positive way of viewing the organisation.
Difficult to assemble and encourage participation	Focus groups can be difficult to assemble and to obtain a representative sample that is willing to participate.	• Human resources assisted in selecting the sample. • By allowing each individual to write down their ideas, a lack of participation resulting from shyness was eliminated.
Loss of control over the data produced	Other than keeping participants focused on the topic, the moderator has less control over the data produced as participants must be allowed to talk to each other, ask questions, and express doubts and opinions.	• After collecting ideas on post-it notes, group discussion was encouraged to further clarify and add more information. This information was captured on a flip chart.
Responses from group members are not independent of one another	It cannot be assumed that participants are expressing their personal views as they may be expressing those that they perceive to be most acceptable to the group.	• Independence of ideas is obtained by having individual participants write down their ideas on post-it notes without influencing each other.
Results are not fully confidential or anonymous	The discussions in focus groups are never fully confidential or anonymous because the content is being shared with others in the group, resulting in some participants deciding to withhold relevant information.	• Collecting the post-it notes and roughly categorising them on the wall ensures confidentiality because participants do not know who wrote down what.
Analysis of the data can be difficult	The open-ended nature of the questions and the wide-ranging responses can make the analysis of the data difficult.	• Initial categorising under "cloud" themes made analysis of the data easier. Secondly, an organisational model was used to categorise the data.

Weaknesses	Description	How weaknesses were addressed/ minimised
Time constraints and complexity of discussions	The time available for discussions in a focus group is limited and this means that some complex issues may not receive sufficient attention and may not be covered adequately.	• The limited number of questions asked (4) and with a specific focus, collecting written ideas and allowing open discussion ensured that topics were appropriately covered.
Requirement for a skilled and experienced moderator	A skilled and experienced moderator is needed for an effective research study.	• Two professionally qualified and experienced moderators were used to moderate the focus groups.

Source: Adapted from O'Raghallaigh et al.[12]

The above two case studies both followed four different steps, namely[13]:

1. Problem identification.
2. Planning.
3. Implementation.
4. Assessment.

The four steps assisted the survey consultants to minimise the weaknesses inherent in focus groups. In both case studies the consultants were able to obtain valuable results to enhance the results of the quantitative data (survey results).

Interviews to verify survey results

According to Breakwell,[14] interviewing is an extremely flexible research tool. Brewton and Millward[15] feel that interviewing can be used at any stage of the research process. They list the following stages where it can be applied:

1. The initial phases to identify areas for more detailed exploration.
2. As part of the piloting or validation of instruments (see chapter 3).
3. As the main mechanism for data collection.
4. As a "sanity check" by referring back to the survey participants to ensure that the interpretations made from the data are representative and accurate.

The types of interviews and how to plan for an interview are discussed in detail in chapter 5. In this chapter, a case study of the application of interviewing to clarify and check the accuracy of survey data in an international organisation will be presented.

In this case study the survey consultants were requested to verify and confirm the accuracy of the results of an organisational climate survey conducted by another consultant group. Both focus groups and interviews were conducted to verify the results. Reference was already made to the focus groups in case study 2. The Burke-Litwin model[16] as a diagnostic framework was used in this project to categorise the data.

Case study 3: Interviews in a Middle East Hotel

Semi-structured probing interviews were used to collect data from the 11 executive managers for the purpose of the current research. In the context of the current study, each of the 11 executive managers was interviewed individually at their offices or in one of the meeting rooms made available. The interviews with the participants were scheduled to last an hour, however the duration of the interviews varied for the different participants. The average time of each interview, however, was 50 minutes. The purpose of the interview was explained, and 15 semi-structured questions were asked of the managers concerned. In 10 instances, scales were added to the questions to enable the researchers to quantify the responses, so that the interviewees' responses could be probed more deeply. As listed below, the interview guide consisted of 15 questions, which focused more strategically on aspects such as: the culture of the hotel company; anticipated future competition; business objectives; the quality of service and the products made available; the professionalism of the staff; work/life balance; the equality of conditions; the service standards; workforce diversity; and the social activities of staff. Opportunities were also given for additional comments.

List of interview questions

1. How would you describe the hotel to a friend (the culture; the way you do things; what you do well; your customer focus)?
2. In general, what outside conditions, such as competition, market changes, and so forth, have the biggest influence on the hotel?
3. Do you think that the hotel is correctly positioned to meet these challenges?
4. Are the hotel's business objectives driven primarily by your customer focus?
5. From your point of view, what do you experience as the best products and services of the hotel?
6. How does the hotel's service and product quality compare to that of your competitors?
7. How do you view the competence and professionalism of the staff?
8. Are decisions made "close to the customer"?
9. How do you experience the balance between work and personal life?
10. Do you think that all the employees are treated equally and fairly?
11. Do the employees understand the service standards?

12. Do the managers in general understand the diverse workforce?
13. Does the hotel cater sufficiently for the recreational and social activities of its staff?
14. If you had the opportunity, what would you change at the hotel to improve the overall performance?
15. Do you have any other comments?

In terms of the focus groups, the following steps were applied in analysing the themes:

1. The facilitator (researcher) and scribe concerned worked together to debrief their impressions and to review the post-it paper responses and notes.
2. All those responses that were regarded as confirmed facts were then coded, according to the Burke-Litwin model, for questions 2, 3 and 4.
3. All the responses (confirmed facts) per dimension were then tabulated, and the frequencies were counted.
4. The tabulated frequencies were summarised per centralised heading under each dimension of the model. The Burke-Litwin model was populated with those core findings that were regarded as causing the effectiveness, or ineffectiveness, of the organisation[17].

The three case studies emphasised the value of focus groups and interviews to verify the accuracy of quantitative data. In addition, the added value of focus groups and interviews is the richness of the data obtained. In multi-cultural environments these two techniques further enrich the understanding of the results.

USE OF SUPPORTIVE INFORMATION TO BACK THE RESULTS

It was mentioned in this chapter that it is important to discuss the context of the survey and possible internal and external influences on the survey results. Sometimes it is necessary to investigate some of these possible influences in more detail to understand the impact on the survey results and to understand possible linkages.

Some of these internal and external influences are briefly discussed below:

1. **Leadership styles.** In many organisations, financial independent franchisees or branches are involved in surveys. Think about companies such as Nandos or KFC with a number of independent franchisees, or large corporates such as Telkom. In these instances separate results are usually compiled for the different regions. If a specific tendency is noted which is different from the main results, it needs to be investigated. In a number of instances, the assessment of leadership styles has provided the answer. For instance, in a study by Martins and Coetzee[18] in an engineering organisation in South Africa, after interpreting the results of the Myers Briggs Type Indicator (MBTI) for senior management, they came to the following conclusion: "These findings could offer a probable explanation for the

experiences of particularly females and support staff regarding the leaders' communication, control and decision-making style, as well as manager-worker relationships as reported by the organisational culture and employee satisfaction survey results. In addition, the findings regarding the perceived emotional competency and dominant task-driven personality type of the leaders, also suggest probable reasons for the negative work/life balance experiences of the directors and associates."

2. **Dissatisfaction of specific employee groups.** In some instances, unions and the bargaining units can have an influence on employees' perceptions. It is always important to take note of their influences and stance regarding any organisational assessments. Bear in mind the impact of the dissatisfaction of employees just before or after the violent confrontations at Marikana and the strike in which 100,000 workers participated across sectors[19].

3. **Organisational initiatives.** Initiatives such as annual salary increases can influence any survey results. It is thus important that the timing of a survey takes such events into consideration. If an organisational diagnosis is after a very positive salary increase or vice versa, this information has to be factored into the survey report. The one solution to this is to conduct the survey at the same time each year.

4. **Turnover trends.** In analysing the results in many instances, specific biographical groups, such as the millennials, might be more dissatisfied than other generational groups. It might, therefore, be valuable to investigate the turnover statistics for the various generations to determine if any specific links can be made.

CONCLUSION

This chapter focused on the value of conducting focus groups and interviews to support, verify and check the accuracy of the quantitative survey results. Both these techniques have their advantages and disadvantages. With the combination of various survey techniques the survey consultant can minimise the disadvantages and be able to produce a professional, valid and verified report. The report and how to compile it will be discussed in the next chapter.

REFERENCES

Anstey, M. 2013. Marikana – and the push for a new South African pact. *South African Journal of Labour Relations* 37(2): 133-145.

Braun, V & Clarke, V. 2006. Doing thematic analysis in psychology. *Qualitative Research in Psychology* 1(3): 77-101.

Breakwell, GM. 1995. Interviewing. In *Research methods in psychology*, edited by GM Breakwell, S Hammond & C Fife-Shaw. London: Sage Publications.

Brewton, P & Millward, L. 2002. *Organizational research methods*. London: Sage Publications.

Burke, WW & Litwin, GH. 1992. A causal model of organisational performance and change. *Journal of Management* 8(3): 523-546.

Martins, N. 2016. Organisational diagnosis, in *Fundamentals of organisation development*, edited by N Martins & D Geldenhuys. Cape Town: Juta: 169-192.

Martins, EC & Martins, N. 2014. *Combining focus groups and quantitative research in organisational diagnosis.* Proceedings of the 13th European Conference on Research Methodology for Business and Management, 16-17 June. Cass Business School, City University, London, UK.

Martins, EC & Martins, N. 2015. Combining focus groups and quantitative research in organisational diagnosis, in *Leading issues in business research methods,* edited by S Geringer & J Mendly. Lightning Source POD.

Martins, N & Coetzee, M. 2007. Organisational culture, employee satisfaction, perceived leader emotional competency and personality type: An exploratory study in a South African engineering company. *Journal of Human Resource Management* 5(2): 20-32.

Martins, N & Coetzee, M. 2009. Applying the Burke-Litwin Model as a diagnostic framework for assessing organisational effectiveness. *SA Journal of Human Resource Management* 7(1): 1-13.

Martins, N & Martins, EC. 2012. Assessing millennials in the South African work context, in *Managing the new workforce: International perspectives on the millennial generation:* 152-180, edited by E Ng, S Lyons & L Schweitzer. Cheltenham: Edward Elgar.

Morgan, DL. 1998. *The focus group guidebook (Focus Group Kit 1).* Thousand Oaks, CA: Sage Publications.

O'Raghallaigh, P, Sammon, D & Murhy, C. 2012. *Using focus groups to evaluate artefacts in design research.* Proceedings of the 6th European Conference on Information Management and Evaluation, edited by T Nagle, University of Cork, Ireland, 13-14 September: 251-257.

Van Tonder, CL & Dietrichsen, P. 2008. The art of diagnosing, in *Organisation development: Theory and practice:* 133-166, edited by CL van Tonder & G Roodt. Pretoria: Van Schaik.

Waclawski, J & Church, AH. 2002. *Organizational development: A data-driven approach to organizational change.* Boston, MA: Jossey-Bass.

ENDNOTES

1. Martins, 2016.
2. Martins & Martins, 2012.
3. Martins & Martins 2015.
4. Burke-Litwin, 1992.
5. Waclawski & Church, 2002.
6. Braun & Clarke, 2006.
7. Van Tonder & Dietrichsen, 2008.
8. Van Tonder & Dietrichsen, 2008
9. Burke-Litwin, 1992.
10. O'Raghallaigh, Sammon & Murhy, 2012.
11. Martins & Martins, 2014.
12. O'Raghallaigh et al., 2012.
13. Morgan, 1998.
14. Breakwell, 1995.
15. Brewton & Millward, 2002.
16. Burke & Litwin,1992.
17. Martins & Coetzee, 2009.
18. Martins & Coetzee, 2007.
19. Anstey, 2013.

CHAPTER 8

REPORT WRITING AND FEEDBACK

by **Nico Martins**

INTRODUCTION

After conducting all the analyses, the next phase is to write the report and present it to the organisation. Organisations usually expect either a written report, a PowerPoint report, or both. This will depend on the initial contract with the organisation. The following scenario is typical of what can happen if the feedback reporting is not carefully planned[1]:

Imagine the following scene. You are at work one day, and are called in to a meeting that your manager feels will be useful and informative to you, so you put aside whatever "mission critical" work you are engaged in and head off for the meeting. Realising that the meeting is just about to start, you gingerly walk down the hall, open the large oak door, and enter the cavernous board room. The myriad armchairs are arranged in a crescent shape around a deep-mahogany coloured table. You take a seat on the left hand side of the table near the front.

During the next five minutes or so, several people (some you know, some from a consulting firm) shuffle into the room and take their seats as well. A professional looking individual enters the room, goes to the front of the table, pulls out a large report, and starts speaking in a language you have never heard before. You do not know what this person is saying. After the first few minutes of the presentation, you being to vacillate between feeling bored and uninterested in what is being presented because you cannot understand it anyway, and you experience anxiety every time the others in the room nod their heads in understanding and astonishment at the speaker's comments. You then ask yourself, "What does this have to do with me and my job anyway? Why am I wasting my time here when I could be doing something important? And why are these consultants getting paid big bucks for this nonsense?"

Usually a number of senior managers, managers and specialists attend the first feedback session. Many organisations ask for a report that they can distribute before the feedback session. The above scenario is something you would prefer to avoid. You do not want the participants to not understand the results, get confused, be overloaded with information and miss your core proposals. It is important to carefully plan the report and the presentation. Not all participants might be familiar with survey terminology, survey processes, the analysis of data, the interpretation of survey results and statistics. It is thus important that the presentation and the report be clear, accurate, and provides an appropriately detailed picture of the organisation that will allow others to plan for action[2]. In this chapter the different level reports will be discussed as well as some case studies which indicate the value of feedback and well planned interventions.

DIFFERENT LEVELS OF REPORTS

A survey project usually concludes with a written report, which will include the purpose, methods, respondents' participation rate, findings and recommendations. A report permits others to also profit from the survey results. A good report summarises the entire project and makes the data available to others, who might use them for the implementation of changes or interventions.

In fact, there are three levels of reports that people in business are usually called upon to produce. There is the macro-level report, the mid-level report and the micro-level report. Each report is designed to provide a different level of detail and achieve a different purpose. These reports will now be discussed briefly:

The macro-level report

The macro-level report is the type of report that is usually prepared for senior management of an organisation. This report may focus more on a summarised analysis and includes the elements that are of most interest to those who must make decisions for the organisation as a whole, such as:

1. the purpose of the survey;
2. the planning that went into the project;
3. the projected and the actual budgets (were you on or over your budget?);
4. an overview of the methodology used;
5. a summary of the geographical groups who participated in the survey;
6. a summary of the overall results of the survey, the statistical analysis, focus groups, interviews or any other analysis done;
7. multi-analysis results (comparative results of geographical of biographical groups);
8. a detailed analysis of any strengths or weakness revealed;
9. comparisons with previous surveys and benchmark surveys;
10. key levers for change;
11. conclusions drawn from the survey ; and
12. suggestions for actions to be taken and a roadmap of priorities.

The mid-level report

The mid-level report is designed for supervisors and other middle management who need the survey data to better oversee the day-to-day functions and activities of the organisation. This report will go into more detail than the macro-level report and will include items such as[4]:

1. the purpose of the survey;
2. the planning that went into the project;
3. the schedule that the project followed;
4. a copy of the survey instrument;

5. the methodology used to analyse the results;
6. a summary of the geographical groups who participated in the survey;
7. a summary table of the overall results;
8. the results of specific groups or departments compared with the overall results;
9. a detailed analysis of any strengths or weaknesses revealed;
10. any pertinent responses to open-ended questions or opportunities to make comments;
11. comparison of results of previous surveys or benchmark data;
12. conclusions drawn from the survey data; and
13. suggestions for actions to be taken in specific departments or areas.

The micro-level report

The micro-level report contains the most detailed presentation. This report is designed to provide complete data and analysis for those who wish to pursue a particular topic or question response further. This report is often aimed at the project team, the project sponsor, internal OD specialist, and the internal survey specialist, who wants to know how others responded to the survey and needs to implement future interventions. This report includes such elements as[3]:

1. the purpose of the survey;
2. the planning that went into the project;
3. the schedule that the project followed;
4. a copy of the survey instrument;
5. a summary table analysis of the survey data;
6. a multi-table analysis of the survey data;
7. analysis of every question in the survey;
8. summary of any strengths or weaknesses revealed;
9. any pertinent responses to open-ended questions or opportunities to make comments;
10. comparison of results of previous surveys;
11. conclusions drawn from the survey data;
12. decisions made for action steps to be taken; and
13. a detailed implementation plan.

A very effective way to write these reports (if you have time), is to do the micro-level report first, then write the mid-level report from that and the macro-level report from the mid-level report. In this way, each report is basically a condensation of the previous one. However, in the real world, there is often not enough time to write all your reports before presenting the results. Often senior management wants to know the results immediately. See Annexure 2 for a summary and comparison of the three levels of reports.

These reports can be in an MS-Word format or in a PowerPoint format. A number of survey consultants produce only PowerPoint reports, which they print and bind. The advantage of a PowerPoint report is its flexibility for presentations. Many organisations follow up the survey with a letter from the CEO thanking them for their participation and explaining the next steps in the process. Some of the results, planned actions and timelines are also provided. This can typically be hosted on the company website or on the company bulletin boards. This makes the results as well as the actions to be taken available to all employees. The action planning process is discussed in chapter 9.

THE SURVEY RESULTS

When presenting the survey results to any of the relevant groups, it is important to ensure that the presentation is clear and understandable. Many consultants use colourful slides to present their results while others focus more on detailed tables and graphs. Many organisations are in favour of a desktop approach to portray the main results on one page (see the example below).

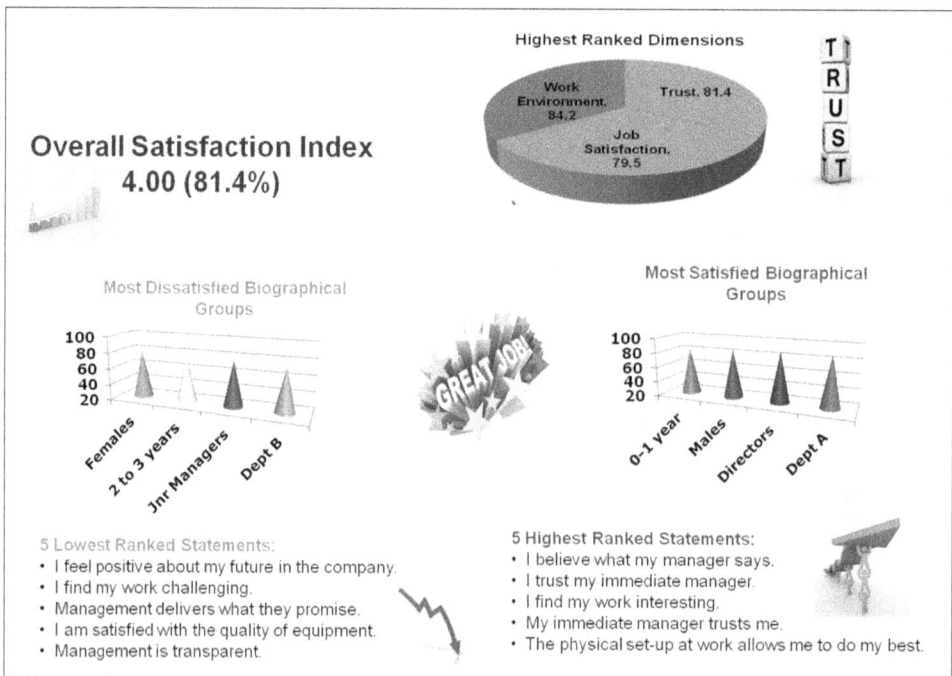

Figure 8.1: Overall results

What is more important, however, is that the audience understands the feedback and that the feedback will lead to some action. Most survey and management books provide various examples of how to portray and explain survey results. See the attached annexure A for the typical contents of a survey report. The following criteria are a guideline that survey consultants can use when they prepare a survey report or presentation:

Objectives
1. Have the objectives of the survey been stated clearly and are they realistic?
2. Is an explanation given of the problem or need that the survey's data are intended to solve?

Survey planning and implementation issues
1. Has the survey population been specified?
2. Are the sample and sampling methods adequately described?
3. Has the questionnaire been translated into other languages to cater for employees who might find it difficult to answer it in English, and translated back into the original language?
4. Was a valid and reliable questionnaire used? If not, was the questionnaire's validity and reliability tested?
5. Has the questionnaire been piloted in the survey population (but with people who were not part of the sample)?
6. Were enough qualified human resources (HR) practitioners/managers/supervisors available to assure quality of the measurements and interviews?
7. Were all the survey team members trained (briefed) in the same way?
8. Were the interviewers able to read questions in a standardised way from the questionnaire?

Survey methodology
1. Was the sample representative of the target population, that is, nobody was left out in the sampling approach?
2. Has the sample size calculation been described in detail, including sample size calculations that are based on different outcomes?
3. Is the sample size large enough for appropriate precision?
4. Was the cut-off point to distinguish between positive and developmental results explained?
5. Was the terminology used in the survey explained?

Survey reporting
1. Were the overall results reported?
2. Have the results been reported on a dimensional and item level?
3. Has the survey questionnaire been provided in the report?

Results
1. Do the results reflect the objectives of the survey?
2. Does the report contain standard information (ie, survey population, date of survey, person conducting the survey)?
3. Have 95% confidence intervals been reported with the statistical analysis?
4. Were sufficient and appropriate statistical analyses conducted to report on the relationships between dimensions (correlation analysis), to report on significant differences (T-tests or ANNOVAs), to report on possible impacts (regression analysis) and to test specific organisational models (structural equation modelling)?

5.   Does the report provide detailed information and discussion of the questionnaire dimensions?
6.   Does the report focus on the results of the various biographical and geographical groups?

Discussion

1.   Does the report include a discussion of results, including limitations of the survey?
2.   If results are compared to a benchmark, is the quality of the benchmark information discussed (e.g., the organisation that conducted the assessment, methods used, sectors or populations included)?

Recommendations

1.   Are recommendations based on the survey results?
2.   Have realistic recommendations been proposed (eg, a solid interpretation of what the data can provide and what it cannot)?
3.   Are recommendations based on science and best practices and not driven by organisational politics?
4.   Are the recommendations useful, that is, could they have been made without the study?
5.   Are the recommendations realistic and supported by a roadmap (a plan) of priorities?
6.   Is a roll-out plan provided of the feedback and proposed actions?

BALANCING EXPECTATIONS AND REALITY

Managers and survey consultants can both be guilty of suggesting that the proposed survey and report with the recommendations will solve all the organisational issues. This is unfortunately not true. An organisational survey has a specific aim and focus; the recommendations will and should only focus on this. Survey consultants should understand that any survey process has the potential of raising anxiety and fear on the part of the respondents, the end users and even the survey sponsor[5]. When providing the feedback, the survey consultant can expect some resistance. This is usually encountered when the results are not as positive as expected or if a specific tendency is not confirmed. The survey consultant can manage this by explaining the survey process and steps taken as discussed in the previous chapter. It also helps if the survey consultant can explain to the audience the typical stages they will experience in the survey feedback and how they and he will address it. An example of this process is portrayed below.

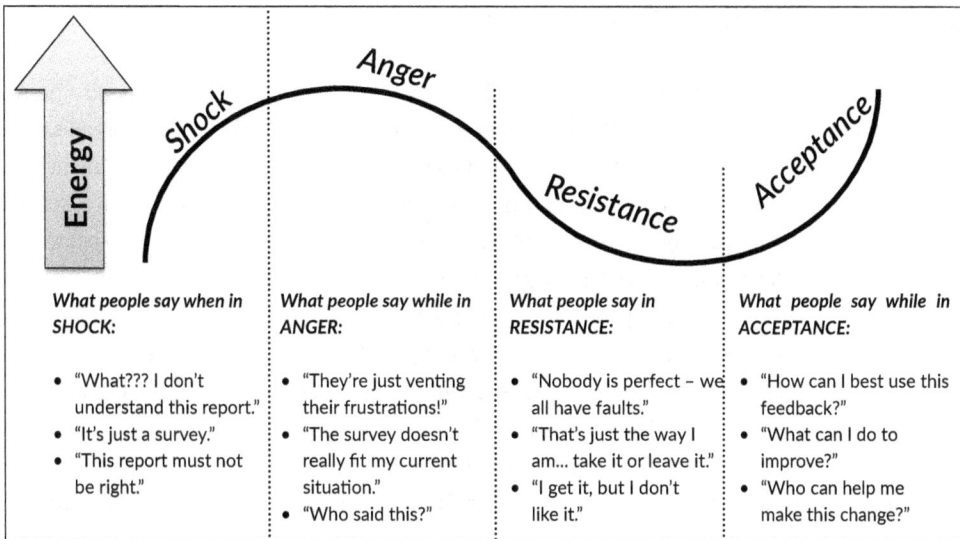

Figure 8.2: SARA – Natural response to feedback[6]

Church and Waclawski[7] propose that the survey consultant presents and discusses this framework with the audience. This will help them to understand that their reactions are normal. A second very important aspect is that the survey consultant must ensure his objectivity and integrity and the confidentiality of the survey respondents. In many instances the author has been presented with the following questions and comments:

1. Can you tell us who the negative people are?
2. What is your experience; are production people always so negative?
3. So what you imply is that women are better trained than men?
4. More manufacturing staff answered the survey thus the results are more developmental?
5. Are you sure your sample was adequate?
6. I assume the results of the IT department are so low because of the attitude of the manager?

In all of the above instances it is important that the survey consultant stays objective and provides only factually correct information without implicating any individual or group. Many survey consultants are registered psychologists, thus is it important that they adhere to the ethical code of the Health Professional Council of South Africa (HPCSA: http://www.hpcsa.co.za). Others are registered with other professional bodies such as the South African Board for People Practices (SABPP: http://www.sabpp.co.za). According to the privacy regulatory requirements in South Africa, it is important for survey consultants to follow the guidelines to protect the privacy of research participants. Personal information is defined by the Protection of Personal Information Act of 2013. This is discussed in detail in chapter 12.

ORGANISATIONAL DIAGNOSTIC MODELS

Organisational diagnostic models and their application were discussed in chapter 1, and a number of advantages of organisational diagnostic models were discussed. The use of organisational diagnostic models is also a very effective method to use to combine qualitative and quantitative results in one overall picture. Many survey consultants use a model because it provides a systematic approach to collecting data, minimises bias of what is collected, constitutes a mechanism for data analysis, and provides a common vocabulary for people to use[8].

The results of an engineering company that requested both an organisational culture and an employee satisfaction survey are portrayed below in figure 8.3. Both quantitative and qualitative analyses were conducted. By applying the adapted Burke-Litwin model of organisational performance and change[9] to identify relationships, list core themes and categorise results, the survey consultants were able to interpret and present the findings relating to the quantitative and qualitative results. According to Coetzee[10], the Burke-Litwin model differentiates between the transactional level of human behaviour and the everyday interactions and exchanges that create the climate of the organisation. The transformational processes are required for actual change in the culture of an organisation. Changes in the transformational factors of the organisational system are usually caused by the interaction with environmental forces for change (both within and external), and therefore require entirely new behaviour on the part of organisations' employees[11]. Changes in the transformational components (external environment, organisational mission and strategy, leadership, culture, individual and organisational performance) affect the transactional components (organisational structure, systems, management practices, task requirements, individual needs and values, motivation and climate)[12].

There are two additional system components that do not form part of the original Burke-Litwin model[13]. These two factors relate to the transactional aspects of the model and were identified by the diagnostic process that formed part of the organisational diagnoses conducted by Martins and Coetzee[14].

1. **Equipment**: This system component refers to the tools required to do the job and the quality of available technology.
2. **Working environment**: This system component refers to facilities such as the buildings, offices, staff cafeteria and recreational facilities for staff.

By including the model populated with the results, the survey consultants were able to discuss the results easily and also indicate the relationships between dimensions. The populated model is also a useful tool to explain the recommendations and where to focus.

The symbols used in the model can be explained as follows: + indicates positive results while the – indicates developmental results.

Figure 8.3 below can now be used as an integrated model to discuss the results, the relationships, and where the organisation might focus its interventions.

The overview of the results helps to portray the most positive dimensions easily:

1. External environment.
2. Mission and strategy.
3. Equipment.
4. Work environment.

The dimensions with mixed results + and - (but are apparently more positive) are:

1. leadership;
2. culture;
3. structure;
4. management practices;
5. departmental climate; and
6. task requirements and skills and abilities.

The dimensions that are mostly developmental are:

1. systems, policies and procedures;
2. individual needs and values; and
3. individual and organisational performance.

It thus appears from the above that the organisation will need to focus on transformational and transactional factors to improve organisational functioning.

```
                        ┌─────────────────────────────┐
                        │ * External Environment      │
                        │ + Positive image            │
                        │ + Good engineering practices│
                        │ + Profitable organisation   │
                        │ + Customer service          │
                        └─────────────────────────────┘
```

* External Environment
+ Positive image
+ Good engineering practices
+ Profitable organisation
+ Customer service

* Leadership
+ Competent & knowledgeable leaders
+ Strong leadership team
- Poor communication and lack of transparency regarding leadership decisions
+ Leaders are accessible
- Poor emotional literacy

* Culture
+ Core culture of professionalism, innovation and creativity
+ Flexible
+ World class solutions
- Lack of information sharing
- Lack of transparency

* Mission and Strategy
+ Clearly defined value and success factors
+ Flexible market dependent strategy
+ Good corporate social investment program
+ Shared values, everybody understands

Management practices
+ Competent managers
+ High standard of ethical conduct
- Unethical behaviour of some managers
- Autocratic behaviour
- Poor people & performance management
- Little recognition or feedback regarding performance

Systems, Policies & Procedures
- No clear performance management process in place
- Talent management is non-existent
- High turnover of staff
- Too much paperwork

Structure
+ Flat & efficient structure
- Insufficient staff
- Poor workload distribution
- Work overload

Departmental climate
+ Relaxed but dynamic working atmosphere
+ High integrity among staff
- Poor teamwork
- Lack of communication between departments
- Self-control is promoted and voicing of opinions is discouraged

Individual needs & values
+ Good job security
- Minimal organisational support for balanced work & personal lives
- Inability of individuals to maintain balanced work & personal lives and still advance in the organisation
- Poor salary structure
- Biased evaluation of performance and/or achievements

Task requirements and Individual skills/abilities
+ Competency based training programmes in place
+ Further education & training is encouraged
- Induction programme needs improvement
- Minimal opportunity for advancement with biased selections

Motivation
+ Job enrichment
- Lack of feedback
- Lack of competitive salaries

Working environment
+ The physical appearance of the building, offices, etc, supports the image of the organisation

* Individual & Organisational Performance
+ Profitable organisation
+ Good customer service
- Inadequate and market misaligned salaries and benefits
- Lack of staff recognition

Equipment
+Equipment is of a standard that supports the functions being performed

Key:	Transformational *	Transactional = All remaining dimensions

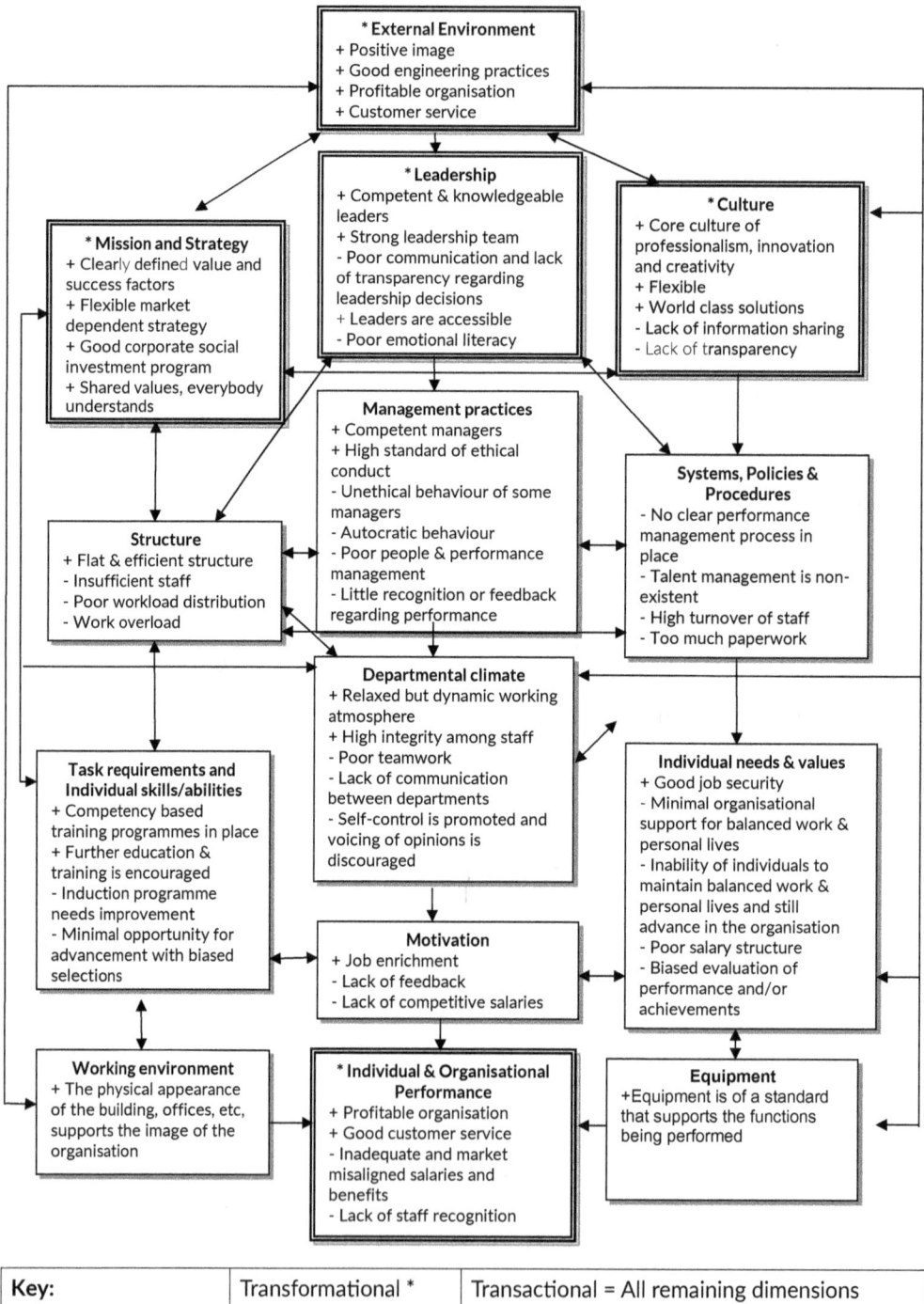

Figure 8.3: Summary of organisational diagnosis outcome (focus groups and surveys)[15]

FEEDBACK TO DIFFERENT STAKEHOLDER GROUPS

One of the worst sins in conducting an organisational assessment is failing to provide feedback to employees. In many organisations the feedback to senior management or to the executive council (Exco) is the first and last feedback. If an organisation goes to the expense and trouble of conducting a survey among its employees, then it needs to communicate the results of that survey to those employees. After all, they deserve the respect of a response after making the effort to complete and return the questionnaire. If no feedback is given it can impact employees' satisfaction levels and their willingness to participate in future surveys[16].

Practical examples may help to illustrate the value of feedback to employees. Two examples are explained below.

Example 1: Comparing the results of two organisations

In an organisational study, the author compared two companies that used an attitude survey to determine the prevailing situation in their organisations and reassessed their organisations after a period of 12 to 18 months. Both organisations operate in the same industrial sector and have the same core business. Both subscribe to the same human resource policies and are guided by the same advisory board. In both cases, the same Likert type scale, validated by means of an overall reliability (Cronbach's Alpha) of 0,983 for the questionnaire, and with an internal consistency for the seven dimensions measuring between 0,776 and 0,868, was used[17].

In the first survey, organisation B measured eight of the nine dimensions of the climate survey, that were measured, significantly more positive than organisation A, with one of the dimensions – relationships and trust – showing no significant difference. The second survey showed the opposite results, with organisation A evaluating all nine dimensions significantly more positively than organisation B. The results of organisation B's two surveys showed no significant improvement.

What could have caused this major turnaround? Reasons for the shift in perceptions of the two organisations were discussed with the management and human resources teams. The main difference in the two organisations was the feedback and discussion processes they used after the surveys.

Feedback: Organisation A

After consultation with management and organisational representatives it was agreed that group feedback meetings would be held based on the work of French and Bell[18], namely:

1. get the right people together;
2. for a large block of uninterrupted time;
3. to work on high priority problems or opportunities that;
4. they have identified and that are worked on;
5. in ways that are structured to enhance the likelihood of;

6. realistic solutions and action plans that are;
7. implemented enthusiastically; and
8. followed up to access actual versus expected results.

It was also agreed to use some of the concepts of the nominal group technique and electronic meetings[19] during the meetings between managers and employees.

The results of the survey would be presented by means of a PowerPoint presentation, allowing all participants to view the results and to participate by asking questions about the survey. The software programme allowed for immediate analysis and feedback on any question, dimension or biographical grouping and, this feedback could be given in the form of graphs or tables during the feedback sessions. Figure 8.4 provides an overview of the process.

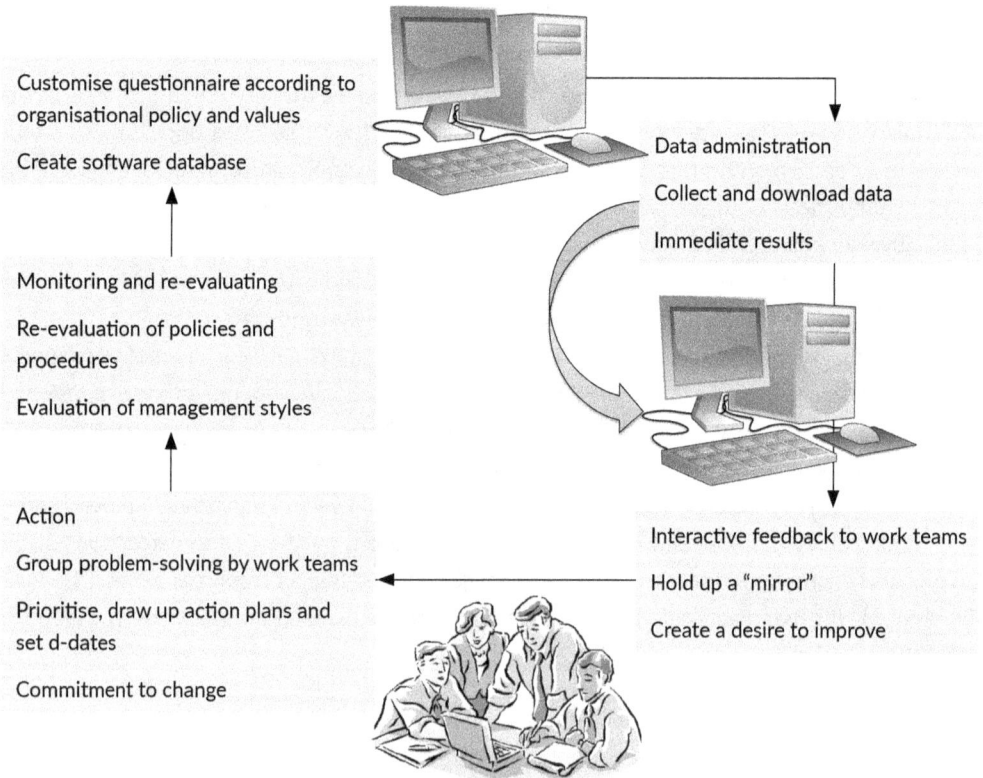

Customise questionnaire according to organisational policy and values

Create software database

Data administration

Collect and download data

Immediate results

Monitoring and re-evaluating

Re-evaluation of policies and procedures

Evaluation of management styles

Action

Group problem-solving by work teams

Prioritise, draw up action plans and set d-dates

Commitment to change

Interactive feedback to work teams

Hold up a "mirror"

Create a desire to improve

Figure 8.4: The survey feedback process (Compiled by N. Martins)

The agenda for the feedback meetings was as follows:

Feedback of survey results:

1. A discussion of problem areas and positive areas.
2. A discussion in teams (management and union representatives together) of the reasons for the problem areas as well as possible solutions.
3. Integration of the problem areas and solutions.
4. Discussion (in groups) of the actions and values needed to address the problem areas.
5. Integration of the actions and values and what this means in practical terms.
6. Prioritisation of the problem areas (actions to be taken).
7. Discussion of realistic due dates and action plans for each problem area identified (in smaller groups).
8. Discussion as a main group of the process of implementation.
9. Decision on follow up and monitoring processes .
10. Feedback of decisions to all employees.
11. Finalisation of the dates for a second audit.

Each team building group consisted of representatives from management, unions, unrepresented employees and various groups with specific problems, as indicated by the results. The problems allocated to the various teams differed and ranged from very important issues, such as the company's promotions and development policy, to day-to-day issues, such as the use of the company's bus by all employees. The diversity of the problems indicated that issues cannot be dealt with in a once-off seminar or workshop, but should be integrated into a way of life practised by human resources and management in general.

Results of the team building sessions: Organisation A

All the groups that had been identified attended the team building sessions. The steps as outlined above were followed and action plans compiled. Where it was too difficult or time consuming to finalise action plans, committees were elected to draw up the action plans.

An action committee was appointed in every geographical area to monitor the implementation of the action plans. Human resources acted in a consultancy, advisory and coordinating capacity. Feedback from the team building sessions indicated the following positive points:

1. Better understanding between management and employees.
2. More open channel of communication between the two groups.
3. Declaration by management that they had used the wrong style of management in the past.
4. Commitment from the union representatives to become involved in solving problems that would ultimately improve productivity.
5. Feeling among team members that they were building something together.
6. Various problems that could lead to strikes and unnecessary misunderstandings were addressed.

The act of building something together appears to generate a feeling of camaraderie, cohesion and *esprit de corps*, as described by Cummings and Worley[20]. These more positive attitudes were confirmed by the results of the second survey and the T-test analysis. As mentioned above, the second survey showed the complete opposite results with, organisation A evaluating all nine dimensions significantly more positive than organisation B.

Feedback: Organisation B

After discussions with organisation B's management team, it was decided to present the results to the management team only. A meeting was arranged at which the results were presented to the management team, which lasted 20 minutes. At this meeting it was decided that management would decide what action should be taken, and when and where this action would be taken. No feedback was given to employees.

Results of process: Organisation B

Employees were reluctant to participate in the second survey and remarked that nothing had changed. It took much negotiation before they agreed to participate, but only if the completed questionnaires would be delivered by courier to the organisation conducting the analysis. The results of the second survey showed no significant improvement over the first results and were significantly more negative than the results shown by organisation A.

The results of the two companies confirm the feelings of Horton and Reid[21]:

The Chow Still Stinks

"The worst sin in conducting employee opinion surveys is failing to act on the results. In the New York Times, Claudia H Deutsch tells of one manager who recalls an employee survey at his company that produced many complaints about the cafeteria. Although management reported the survey's results in the employee newsletter, it did nothing about the cafeteria complaints. 'Before, we could kid ourselves that the bosses did not know how bad the cafeteria was,' the manager said. 'After the survey we knew they just didn't care.'"

Example 2: The results of a longitudinal study

The discussed examples above focused only on the role of feedback. A number of organisational variables as well as external factors can influence organisational survey results. A longitudinal study conducted by Ledimo and Martins[22] on employee satisfaction focused on changes during organisational transformation. The study was conducted among a population consisting of employees in a utility and parastatal organisation based in the Gauteng Province of South Africa. The employee satisfaction survey (ESS) measured employee satisfaction in 2003, 2007 and 2008, using convenience samples. The 2003 sample comprised of 1,140 participants; the 2007 sample involved 920 participants; and the 2008 sample included 759 participants who voluntarily completed the survey. During all three years of study, feedback was given to the Exco team, divisions and employee groups. A very similar process was followed as indicated for organisation A, as discussed above. The organisation subsequently decided to implement a number of organisational transformational interventions based on each year's survey results and the inputs received via the feedback sessions. The following interventions were implemented[23]:

From 2004 to 2006, the company implemented organisational transformation interventions as follows

1. **Strategy**: Organisational strategy was changed and a new HR strategy was developed.
2. **Restructuring**: Corporate services and operations departments were restructured to align with the new organisational strategy.
3. **Policy development**: New policies were implemented for employment equity; talent management; recruitment and selection; career management; disciplinary codes; and performance management.
4. **System:** An IT system was introduced for salaries administration.

Again in late 2007 and early 2008, this organisation introduced the second phase of transformation, focusing on the following:

1. **Policy development**: Policies were formulated on the talent management, career management and performance management strategy.
2. **Training programmes**: Leadership and supervisory development programmes were introduced to train team leaders, supervisors and managers.

The results of the three years of study are portrayed below in table 8.1.

Table 8.1: Mean scores for differences in the years of study for ESS (2003, 2007 and 2008)

ESS dimensions	2003 mean	2007 mean	2008 mean
Vision and mission	2.59	3.22	3.38
Values	3.00	2.97	3.13
Leadership	2.99	2.88	3.13
Change management	2.30	2.47	2.69
Health and safety	3.09	3.12	3.22
Employment equity and diversity	2.29	2.32	2.53
Human resource management	2.11	2.24	2.69
Training	2.91	2.80	3.00
HIV/AIDS	2.58	3.77	3.90
Communication	2.39	2.60	2.86

ESS dimensions	2003 mean	2007 mean	2008 mean
Teamwork	3.10	3.14	3.29
Relationships	2.99	3.01	3.21
Job satisfaction	2.97	3.21	3.37
Total ESS	**2.56**	**2.80**	**3.22**

As can been noted from table 8.1, the results of all dimensions improved in 2008, indicating more satisfied employees. The Kruskal-Wallis statistical analysis was applied to determine if significant differences existed between the three years of study, but only the dimension of health and safety indicated no significant differences. It is also interesting to note that between 2003 and 2007 some dimensions actually obtained lower results, the main reason being that no interventions were implemented for those dimensions.

The 2003 results indicated four dimensions that progressively improved in 2007 and 2008 (namely change management, employment equity and diversity, human resource management and communication). This study again emphasises the value of feedback but added another important dimension to the survey process, namely the identifying of interventions and then the implementation of those interventions. See chapter 13 for an overview of typical interventions.

Comparing the three examples described above, it is clear that one of the worst sins in conducting an organisational assessment is failing to provide feedback to employees. The positive results of the re-assessments, on the other hand, show the value of feedback and the implementation of actions.

SUMMARY

This chapter focused on report writing and feedback of survey results. The case studies presented provided interesting information on the value of feedback and the implementation of interventions. All in all, the conclusion is that feedback, and how it is dealt with, is a very important phase of the survey process, which cannot be neglected nor disregarded.

ANNEXURE 1: EXAMPLE OF REPORT CONTENTS

 Organisational
Diagnostics

Organisational Diagnostic Survey Report

for McDonald Construction

July 2016

Compiled by:
Dr Nico Martins and Dr Ellen Martins
Organisational Diagnostics
P O Box 1550
Glenvista
2058

Tel: 011 432 2006
Fax: 011 507 5671
E-mail: orgdia@iafrica.com
Web: www.orgdia.co.za

CONTENTS:

Executive summary

Exhibits

Exhibit 1:   Scoring system for surveys/audits
Exhibit 2:   Overall results of divisions
Exhibit 3:   Overall results of departments
Exhibit 4:   Overall results of contract of employment
Exhibit 5:   Overall results of gender groups
Exhibit 6:   Overall results of age groups
Exhibit 7:   Overall results of race groups
Exhibit 8:   Overall results of length of service groups

Annexures

Annexure 1:   Biographical information
Annexure 2:   Results of dimensions and statements
Annexure 3:   Comparative results of divisions
Annexure 4:   Comparative results of departments
Annexure 5:   Comparative results of contract of employment
Annexure 6:   Comparative results of gender groups
Annexure 7:   Comparative results of age groups
Annexure 8:   Comparative results of race groups
Annexure 9:   Comparative results of length of service groups
Annexure 10:   Results of correlation and regression analysis

ANNEXURE 2: REPORTING LEVELS

Report items	Macro level	Mid-level	Micro level
• The purpose of the survey	✓	✓	✓
• The planning that went into the project	✓	✓	✓
• The schedule that the project followed		✓	✓
• The projected and the actual budgets (were you on or over your budget?)	✓		
• An overview of the methodology used to analyse the results	✓	✓	
• The methodology use to analyse the results in more detail		✓	
• A summary of the geographical groups who participated in the survey	✓	✓	
• A summary of the overall results of the survey, the statistical analysis, focus groups, interviews or any other analysis done	✓	✓	
• Multi-analysis results (comparative results of geographical and biographical groups)	✓		
• A detailed analysis of any strengths or weaknesses revealed	✓	✓	
• Comparisons with previous surveys and benchmark surveys	✓		
• Key levers for change	✓		
• Conclusions drawn from the survey data	✓		✓
• Suggestions for actions to be taken and to provide a road map of priorities	✓		
• A copy of the survey instrument		✓	✓
• A summary table of the overall results		✓	✓
• The results of specific groups or departments compared with the overall results		✓	
• Any pertinent responses to open-ended questions or opportunities to make comments		✓	
• Comparison of results of previous surveys or benchmark data		✓	
• Conclusions drawn from the survey data		✓	
• Suggestions made for actions to be taken in specific departments or areas		✓	
• Analysis of every question in the survey			✓
• Summary of any strengths or weaknesses revealed			✓
• Any pertinent responses to open-ended questions or opportunities to make comments			✓
• Comparison of results of previous surveys			✓
• Decisions made for action steps to be taken			✓
• A detailed implementation plan			✓

REFERENCES

Borg, I & Mastrangelo, PM. 2008. *Employee surveys in management. Theories, tools and practical applications.* Toronto: Hogrefe.

Burke, WW & Litwin, GH. 1992. A causal model of organisational performance and change. *Journal of Management,* 8(3): 523–546.

Church, AH & Waclawski, J. 1998. *Designing and using organizational surveys: A seven–step process.* San Francisco: Jossy Bass.

Coetzee, M. 2016. Core theories and models in fundamentals of organisation development, edited by N Martins & D Geldenhuys. Cape Town: Juta: 169–192.

French, WL & Bell, CH. 1999. *Organizational development. Behavioural science interventions for organizational improvement.* 6th edition. Englewood Cliffs, NJ: Prentice Hall.

Horton, RT & Reid, PC. 1991. *Beyond The Trust Gap Forging a New Partnership Between Managers and Their Employers.* Homewood, Ill: Business One Irwin.

Jones, BB & Brazzel, M. 2006. *The NTL Handbook of organizational development and change: Principles, practices and perspectives.* San Francisco: Pfeiffer.

Ledimo, O & Martins, N. 2014, 16–17 June. *Conducting a longitudinal study of employee satisfaction during organizational transformation.* 13th European Conference on Research. 16–17 June: 209–216.

Martins, N. 1995. Affirmative action: A consensus approach in analysing employees' perceptions. *Management Dynamics: Contemporary research,* 4(1): 3–5.

Martins, N & Coetzee, M. 2009. Applying the Burke-Litwin model as a diagnostic framework for assessing organisational effectiveness. *South African Journal of Human Resource Management,* 7(1): 144–156.

Rogel, C. 2015. Using the SARA Model to Learn from 360-Degree Feedback. *DecisionWise.* Retrieved from: https://www.decision-wise.com/using-the-sara-model-to-learn-from-360-degree-feedback/ [Accessed 20 June 2017].

Robbins, SP, Judge, TA, Odendaal, A & Roodt, G. 2009. *Organisational Behaviour: Global and South African perspectives.* 2nd edition. Cape Town: Pearson Education.

Tshudy, T. 2006. An OD map: The essence of organization development in BB Jones and M Brazzel, *The NTL handbook of organizational development and change: Principals practices, and perspectives.* San Francisco: Pfeiffer.

ENDNOTES

1. Church & Waclawski, 1998: 201–202.
2. Church & Waclawski, 1998.
3. Martins, 2016.
4. Martins, 2016.
5. Church & Waclawski, 1998.
6. Rogel, 2015.
7. Church & Waclawski, (1998.
8. Tshudy, 2006.
9. Martins & Coetzee, 2009.
10. Coetzee, 2016.
11. Coetzee, 2016; French & Bell, 1999; Jones & Brazzel, 2006; Martins & Coetzee, 2009.
12. Burke & Litwin, 1992.
13. Coetzee, 2016.

14. Martins & Coetzee, 2009.
15. Martins & Coetzee, 2009.
16. Martins, 2016; Borg & Mastrangelo, 2008.
17. Martins, 1995: 3–5.
18. French & Bell, 1999: 203.
19. Robbins, 2009: 232–233.
20. Cummings & Worley, 2009: 148–149.
21. Horton & Reid, 1991: 185.
22. Ledimo & Martins, 2014.
23. Ledimo & Martins, 2014.

CHAPTER 9

ACTION PLANNING AND LEARNING

by **Nene Molefi**

INTRODUCTION

In the process of organisational diagnosis, gathering data on the core dimension being investigated is half of the picture. Figuring out what to do with that data and how to implement the change you desire most effectively is the other half. Having worked in the field of culture change, leadership and transformation for the last 18 years, my work has been at the coalface of implementation. In the last three years, my consultancy has conducted diagnostic surveys with more than 30 mainly corporate organisations, across many industries and of varying scales, but largely private sector and state-owned enterprises.

We use surveys as a diagnostic tool to identify and address various aspects of the culture and climate of an organisation. The primary focus of these surveys ranges from the extent of employee engagement to the consciousness of leadership on salient aspects of organisational life; diversity and inclusion; values alignment; culture change; and transformation. However, whatever organisational dimension you may be investigating, culture will remain central to the success or failure of any intervention that the survey results demand. Culture, or the way people do things, is often the sticking point in implementation. As so many organisations and leaders are aware, the most compelling action plans can stall at the point of delivery due to stubbornly ingrained patterns of behaviour. These can be embedded in both individuals and entire organisations.

Harvard change leadership and professional adult learning specialists, Kegan and Lahey[1], in their theories on immunity to change, identify the critical difference between technical and adaptive challenges that may be facing an organisation. A technical challenge simply requires the incorporation of new technical skills, whereas an adaptive challenge requires a shift in mindset. In the complex world we live in today and in which business is done, very often adaptive challenges are misdiagnosed as technical challenges. Similarly, sustainable organisational change is not simply about changing short-term behaviours, but it is about changing the mindsets underlying those behaviours.

There are three critical aspects that therefore need to be embedded throughout the action planning process that follows from a diagnostic survey. Firstly, the action has to *mean* something to the actors in the situation. The actors must develop, if not a common understanding, then a common language around the situation, so that they can engage in mutually comprehensible dialogue around it. As illustrated by Viljoen[2], the action planning process has to be *of significance* to the individuals for them to apply their human energy to the task.

However, the most critical dimension of meaning is the emotional buy-in that is required. As organisational change academics and practitioners have been articulating since the 1990s, the "emotional ecology"[3] underlying a challenge needs to not only be taken into consideration, but also needs to form a core part of the action planning process. Finding a way for organisations to discuss the "undiscussables"[4] and work directly with "the emotional life of the organisation"[5] ensures that individuals and teams are directly and personally invested in the outcome of the action planning process.

Secondly, the action planning has to be part of an *action learning* process, as defined by Chris Argyris in the 1970s. This involves an organisation conducting surveys and interviews, organising findings and then, most critically, pausing before action; it needs to take the time to look in the mirror and engage in meaningful feedback sessions that dig deeper into the underlying dynamics at play.

Centralising learning in this process ensures that action plans are not constructed on shaky foundations, but instead emerge through a process where an organisation and its leaders can identify and learn from past mistakes and the psychological dynamics that underpin them. This is very much an iterative process, where the focus is not on an end goal, but instead involves feedback loops and cyclical reflection that allows for the organisation to become a learning organisation on a developmental path.

Finally, an *inclusive approach* is critical to the success of any action planning process, especially for organisations seeking to become an action learning organisation. Inclusion ensures that each individual that makes up the organisation, at whatever level, feels they belong, and is able to bring all of themselves to their work and the tasks at hand, thus maximising the potential for effective action and positive change within an organisation.

Underpinning any inclusive, meaningful and learning process for an organisation looking to change are the relationships that build that organisation. These relationships determine the quality of the work it delivers and the success it strives to achieve. Throughout this chapter, the emphasis is on relationships and communication, as these are the backbone of successful action planning. In her pioneering work on leading change in organisations, particularly on the African continent, Professor Hellicy Ngambi[6] articulates how very often organisations will focus on implementation before their leaders are adequately equipped to deal with change. Leadership's capacity to steer effective action is dependent upon their capacity to build resilient and ethical relationships at and between all levels of their organisation. Ngambi's theory for RARE (Responsible, Accountable, Relevant and Ethical) leadership (2013) is a model of leadership for action and change in the context of diversity, which is of great relevance to the South African context and will thus be explored further in this chapter.

The broad aim of this chapter is to present a practical approach and take a detailed look at the iterative action planning and learning process. This begins with visioning sessions with leadership that establish the tone of the action planning going ahead, followed by survey feedback sessions that serve as a mirror for the organisation. Once a firm foundation of common understanding and ownership has been laid, the action planning and learning process then begins in earnest, through the action planning and learning process moves to the design and planning of interventions, SMART (Specific, Measurable, Attainable, Realistic and Time-bound) action planning, evaluation and follow-up. Action learning is examined in more detail, as well as what it means to be a learning organisation. Detailed case studies are presented and key shining gems and common pitfalls I have witnessed through working closely with organisations in this way are highlighted.

SETTING OUT: SPONSOR, BROKER AND TASK TEAM

The key to the action planning process is in the groundwork of building trust, relationships and understanding before the survey is even administered, and long before any practical action planning takes place. This involves the identification of several individuals and alliances that will help in ensuring that the post-survey intervention is successful.

For any successful partnership, it has to be clear who your main sponsor or "power client" is (normally the CEO or MD, who will put their weight behind the initiative), and who your main "broker client" is (normally the HR director, with whom you will work closely in overseeing the project team). At the outset there needs to have been clarity around why the survey is being conducted, as mentioned in chapter 6, what other surveys have preceded this one, and what the thoughts are around the key challenges facing the organisation. The consultant team then leads the design of the solution in collaboration with the power client and broker client, and usually the senior leadership team.

At the start of the diagnostic process, the consultants will have liaised with the client to establish key individuals that will be overseeing the development of, and communications around, the diagnostic initiative as a whole and the survey process prior to action planning. This is otherwise known as contracting and involves preparing the senior leadership team for the process that is to come[7]. As discussed in chapter 2, and particularly relevant in the case of interventions that focus on culture and climate, this groundwork with the leadership team is critical. It ensures that as consultants we get a sense of the lay of the land prior to a survey engagement, but, more importantly, it gives time and space for the intentions, concerns, complexities and tensions in the leadership team to surface. This allows for the motivation to emerge by experiencing the converse: if there is no change, the organisation's goals and needs will be not met.

Depending on the health of the organisation and the conversations that may already be taking place at this stage, contracting can begin to move the leadership away from a command-and-control form of leadership[8]. This saves leadership from having to expend considerable time continually managing the process and can move them towards an inclusive leadership model which increases the initiative, ownership and engagement from all team members.

In the action planning process itself (see figure 8.1 for a full summary of our model), a representative task team needs to be established to take ownership of the post-survey phase, collaborating on and collectively designing any intervention and actions, thus ensuring ownership of the process across the organisation. If it is a very large organisation, it is important to ensure that every business unit has a small working team that can look at the survey results for their specific unit. The purpose of the working team is now to work on solutions. As mentioned above, leaders might normally feel they need to close themselves off from the rest of the organisation to come up with all the solutions, however employees will know themselves what the most workable solution will be. The job of the representative task team is therefore to both include, and consult with, employees, to determine what they see as the most suitable and sustainable path ahead. While the task team or leadership may not carry all the solutions from this input forward, the action planning process will benefit from the broader context provided during consultations, which will undoubtedly inform the decision-making process.

It is also advisable for the most senior manager in the task team who is seen to be driving the process to be someone from line management, not necessarily someone from HR. In engaging in a culture change process, having someone from line management (for example, the Head of Engineering) actively involved in the task team and trying to come up with solutions gives everybody the impression that this is something that concerns the organisation as a whole. It also confirms that the implementation of action from the survey results is the responsibility of line, with HR or OD as custodians of the process.

Task teams create ownership for whatever dimension of change is being addressed through an organisational diagnosis process. This is partly because there is a group of individuals who are holding each other accountable for the change they wish to see. In addition, task teams have been proven to be particularly effective in having a positive impact on diversity and inclusion in organisations, with the social accountability they generate working as a particularly powerful motivator for changing behaviour.

In a study collating three decades' worth of data on the inclusion of women and minority groups in over 800 companies in the United States of America, it was found that increasing accountability and transparency through the creation of diversity task teams had a dramatic impact on representation[9]. This was done by allowing task teams to set their own targets, design and take actions that could improve representivity, and take responsibility and credit for successes. By asking the task teams themselves to monitor representation at all levels across the organisation, organisations saw an average 9% to 30% increase in the representation of women and minority groups in management over a 5-year period[10]. In addition to promoting accountability, these kinds of task teams engage resistors, as well as increase contact among the diverse individuals within the task team and across departments.

In this way, leadership that values human relationships and connectivity is leadership that can foster responsible behaviour among employees towards each other and all stakeholders, as well as take responsibility for the future of the organisation at large[11]. The task teams help to build a sense of responsibility and accountability, the first two elements in Ngambi's RARE leadership theory, which are used throughout this chapter to highlight the relational aspects required to underpin any process of change for action.

LOOKING IN THE MIRROR: IDENTIFYING PRIORITIES AND A VISION FOR CHANGE

Once the survey has been completed and the results analysed (see chapter 6), as external consultants we will then present these results to the senior leadership team and the task team. These results are the mirror that will reveal what needs to be addressed. We then workshop the results to identify the key themes emerging from the analysis. While there may be a long list of key themes (with one client, 21 emerged!), it is critical to already begin prioritising the focus areas for intervention.

Research into South African organisations in particular has revealed that leadership is seen as inconsistent, driven by the bottom line rather than concern for employees' experiences, with followership reporting high levels of uncertainty and disappointment, taking on a "cope and hope" mentality[12]. Therefore, while there may be a long list of challenges to tackle that may all need attention in time, it is necessary to identify three to four priority areas for the year ahead. This will promote both meaningful engagement from the sponsor/power client, as well as ensuring that they are perceived as having integrity by providing cohesive answers regarding the organisation's priorities.

Having these three to four priority focus areas facilitates strong action planning that can display clear results and be communicated easily and accessibly, thus protecting the integrity of the process for all stakeholders, at all levels. In this way the change is tangible, and visible, and employees will feel heard, have evidence of change, believe in the process and have a sense that if they give input, it will lead to impact.

For this reason, it is critical that the leadership team and the task team have a visioning session to determine a cohesive and meaningful way of taking forward the results and the themes emerging from the results. In this way, the three to four key themes need to be distilled and contained within a vision for change that has a sense of resonance and applicability. This marks the beginning of the action planning process in earnest.

FEEDBACK SESSIONS

In taking the time to complete the surveys and give their opinions, it is vital that all those who participated in the survey have the benefit of seeing the results in an accessible and comprehensible way. The mirror of the survey results thus needs to be reflected back to the organisation as a whole, along with the interpretation of the key themes and the vision for change (into which departmental and employee input will also be sought). This must be done not only electronically and in other organisational communications, but through face-to-face feedback sessions within business units.

The external consultants can give the overall feedback to the Executive Committee, and then also support the heads of each business unit to deliver their own department's results, in person, to their teams. They will present the organisation's overall results, as well as the breakdown of the specific results from within that business unit. This serves as what is often a powerful and uncompromising look in the mirror. In this way, the leadership of each business unit is seen to take ownership of the results, whatever the results might say. By doing this in a visible way, as the leader of the business unit, he or she is saying "I have heard you, I take ownership, and I'm willing to do something (including stand in front of you and face criticism)". The visibility of the internal head of the unit is the most critical thing at this feedback stage.

As discussed in chapter 6, focus groups will have been conducted to test and add depth to the findings from the survey. This is particularly the case with the dimensions in the survey that scored poorly. A smaller sample of the participants will have been asked questions through the focus group around dimensions that generated low scores, and the aim is to find practical examples of when these problems were manifested. For example, if on one of the quantitative survey questions, 60% of respondents felt there was sexism, then the focus group will unpack exactly how this manifests and give concrete examples. Once you have these examples from the focus groups (for example of how racism, sexism or poor performance management manifests in this particular organisation), this information can be incorporated into the feedback sessions. In this way, employees are made aware that their managers and leaders understand the nature of the problems they were pointing out in the survey, and again, that they have been heard.

The purpose of the feedback sessions is therefore to illustrate to all those involved – leadership, managers and employees – that an accurate picture of the organisation was indeed gathered. This is the first step to building a common understanding of the nature and scale of the challenges and opportunities an organisation is facing, and helps to build trust for the process of change ahead. Not attempting to brush negative results under the carpet, but instead taking ownership for them, indicates that leadership has listened and will return to employees not only once, but several times through the process, engaging with them to solicit not only their opinions, but ultimately their buy-in to the process. This is part of the iterative nature of being an action learning organisation, where feedback and engagement flow continuously through any diagnostic process and consequent intervention. In addition, the process of the feedback sessions continues to build and strengthen relationships across the organisation.

A FIRM FOUNDATION FOR ACTION PLANNING

As external consultants, we lead the design of solutions in close partnership with our clients. We take what the survey and focus groups showed us about the organisation from the perspective of the employees, synthesised into the key themes, and draw up likely solutions based on these themes. This ensures that the solution is grounded in the reality of the challenges facing the organisation. These solutions are then taken to senior leadership and the sponsor for further workshopping.

By solution, I do not mean a finite, stand-alone package. Instead, we will generally be proposing a methodology that can structure the way the organisation can initiate change, which they themselves will carry forward into the future. This is done collaboratively so that it is ideally built into, and closely aligned with, the organisation's business planning and operations as a whole.

Prior to initiating any form of action planning, it is critical for the organisation to have moved through the following stages in its process:

1. *Creating a common understanding of the problem*: This relies upon a rigorous analysis of, and engagement with, the survey results, the focus groups and the key themes emerging from them. This is taken to the organisation as a whole through the feedback sessions.
2. *Creating a common language for the road ahead*: Prior to setting out on a new pathway, it is critical that the various key stakeholders actually have a language for how to move ahead.

As identified by Argyris and Kegan & Lahey[13], very often organisations do not even have a language for how to talk about their problems, they are so "undiscussable". Through the visioning phase and feedback sessions, it is critical that a common language and understanding be created, and a way found to talk about the issues at the heart of the challenges facing the organisation. The survey will point to the issues, but a direct means must be found to engage with confidence around core tensions and challenges.

3. *Creating ownership for change:* The foundation for this will have been laid with leadership from the very beginning of the diagnostic process, and will deepen through the various layers of the organisation through the task team, and then management teams within business units. As discussed by Greyvenstein and Cilliers[14], followership will withhold "authorisation" from their leaders if they feel they have been disregarded, and this can inhibit leadership from managing change and transformation effectively. Conversely, as shown by Nishii and Rich[15], in increasing the capacity for employees to take the initiative and ownership of their work, managers benefit from increased efficiencies while also having more engaged workers who make more meaningful contributions. Ownership involves building a sense of responsibility and accountability[16].

4. *Identifying barriers and enablers*: Successful action planning lies in anticipating challenges and identifying supportive elements to develop in the future. In my experience, identifying the barriers can make the difference between success and failure of diagnostic initiatives. I have seen that with many of my clients, if the barriers are identified upfront and discussed, employees are more likely to trust the process and give that critical buy-in. Open acknowledgement of the barriers facing an organisation helps to build accountability, which contributes to building trust and a sense of authenticity. Identifying both the barriers and enablers prior to and during the action planning process helps to maximise the chances of success.

The above can happen at different levels through a combination of visioning workshops with leaders and the task team, the feedback sessions across the organisation, and potentially through an intervention prior to launching the action planning phase.

A post-survey, pre-action planning intervention can be critical to establishing a vision and common language and getting everyone in the organisation on the same page, prior to concrete plans being developed. This creates the common understanding and language needed to navigate the road ahead successfully (as discussed above). This intervention may take the form of one- or two-day workshops (depending on the context and depth of alignment needed), in natural working teams, at a scale to be determined by need and available resources. Generally, the aim is to have the leader of the team in the room, though the priority is to ensure that people feel free to express their honest opinions, and so whether or not leadership is in the room will be decided on between the external consultants and senior leaders on the basis of the context.

ACTION LEARNING: AN INCLUSIVE APPROACH

As discussed in the introduction, one of the most persistent barriers to sustainable action planning that can make organisations and the individuals in them immune to change is not addressing the mindset underlying the action plan[17]. If an organisation is attempting to change, but does not change the mindset underpinning any new action plans, then it has little hope of succeeding. Any action planning process therefore needs to be underpinned by an action learning approach, as conceptualised by Argyris in the 1970s, and expanded upon by the field of organisational diagnosis and development since then.

Argyris[18] argues that most human beings are programmed to resist change due to ingrained patterns of behaviour that have been rewarded since childhood, as attempts to change the status quo are usually met with threat or embarrassment. Very often, the "correct" route to effective action is taken for granted, and this will often focus on the technical aspects of a problem as opposed to incorporating any human aspects. This often results in a mismatch between the intention to change and the actual results. An action learning approach ensures that there is a mechanism in place to not only detect, but also correct, error, through a process of reflection that analyses the assumptions underlying behaviours and actions.

The core of Argyris's action learning theory lies in questioning the assumptions that underpin any actions, through the concept of double-loop learning. Single-loop learning is where "what we get", that is, the results, are analysed on the basis of "what we do", with the action strategies and techniques being assessed at face value. Double-loop learning involves questioning the assumptions, values and beliefs that underpin those action strategies, that is, asking why we do what we do. A key part of this is working with the emotional landscape of a team or organisation where defensive routines and undiscussables are embedded.

In working with clients we therefore work with the "emotional ecology" of an organisation[19]. We create a safe space to explore the undiscussables, identifying barriers to effective action with a range of internal stakeholders. This process ultimately helps release the human energy that is trapped in defensive routines, but that would otherwise be productive. In addition to this emotional dimension, working in the complex social environment of South Africa, the intercultural dimension needs to be considered for any meaningful and inclusive action planning to begin.

Argyris's concept of double-loop learning has been expanded to include action learning in complex intercultural environments such as ours. Bhawuk, Sakuda and Munusamy[20] developed a triple-loop cultural learning model that incorporates the dimension of intercultural sensitivity into the action learning process. In essence, in addition to questioning the underlying assumptions of any actions to better understand the results, an additional reflective loop is added which assesses the host or dominant cultural norms against the additional, multiple, intercultural norms that will be operating in the same space. This not only brings awareness to the complex layering of values and assumptions operating in a working environment, but also ensures that no one perspective dominates, allowing for the formulation of a new, inclusive normative framework that can underpin action planning. A case study to illustrate this comes from our work with a client in the manufacturing sector.

Case study 1: Uncovering unconscious bias in performance management

In this case study, our client was a large manufacturing company. Performance management emerged in the diagnostic survey and focus groups as an issue of contention, with reports of the system being discriminatory and unfair. We worked closely with our broker client, the human resources director, to identify and involve the project team that designed and monitored the performance management system, to get their perspective on the situation. When sitting with the team leader responsible, it is often possible to establish whether there is indeed a problem, or whether employees have the wrong information and the system is in fact fair, in which case the solution is transparent communication on the ratings system.

The feedback in this case was that black employees were consistently being more poorly rated in the performance management system. Working with the performance management team, counting back through a 12-month window and comparing performance reviews by race, it was established that black individuals were consistently scored lower than their white counterparts in the overwhelming majority of cases. This was an indicator that assessment was indeed being influenced by unconscious bias and that an intervention was necessary to counter this bias. Measures needed to be put in place to ensure fairness in performance management. International research has indicated that unconscious bias operates to influence performance ratings negatively on the basis of race and gender, disadvantaging women and black people[21].

In the above situation, had the performance reviews been taken at face value, there may have been the suggestion that the action to be taken was to improve the performance of black employees through mentoring and other support. This would have served to further confirm negative perceptions and bias towards these individuals. Checking the performance management data and questioning the assumptions revealed a more complex picture – one that demonstrated that the human factor can create room for error in a seemingly technical performance, as many international studies have repeatedly shown.

It is often in the intervention phase prior to the active action planning phase that we will draw attention to and provide models for how to work with the emotional and intercultural dimensions of organisational life. This ensures that the most common barriers to effective action are revealed prior to action planning and also that a common language is found for engaging directly with them.

Finally, the third element of our action learning approach is inclusion. Inclusion is our overarching framework for effective action as it ensures that maximum presence and engagement are elicited from each person in an organisation. Whatever the specific challenge may be that the diagnostic process is attempting to overcome, having an inclusive approach multiplies the potential for positive change and effective action in an organisation. Inclusion is the means by which to gain the most value from the diversity within an organisation.

Working to create an inclusive environment involves bringing awareness to patterns of exclusion that have operated in an organisation, whatever these may be – including historical, societal, personality and/or rank-based patterns of who is an insider or an outsider (in relation to the dominant culture within an organisation). After these patterns have been identified, we present various guidelines for how to cultivate an inclusive culture within an organisation as leaders, managers and employees. In this way, an organisation's diversity is turned around to magnify the potential for innovation and adaptability[22]. In the second part of her RARE leadership model, Ngambi[23] argues that relevant leadership seeks to work with group differences and how they affect relationships in the workplace influences the work that is actually done. Relevant leadership also identifies how to respond in an "emotionally intelligent way". This again highlights the importance of engaging with the emotional ecology of an organisation, which will always be influenced by the diversity of its people.

The external consultants will generally work closely with senior leadership and the task team to ensure that they at least have an understanding of diversity, inclusion and inclusive leadership. Where possible, we will work with business units themselves to ensure that the principle of inclusion is incorporated into action planning in the future (see figure 9.1).

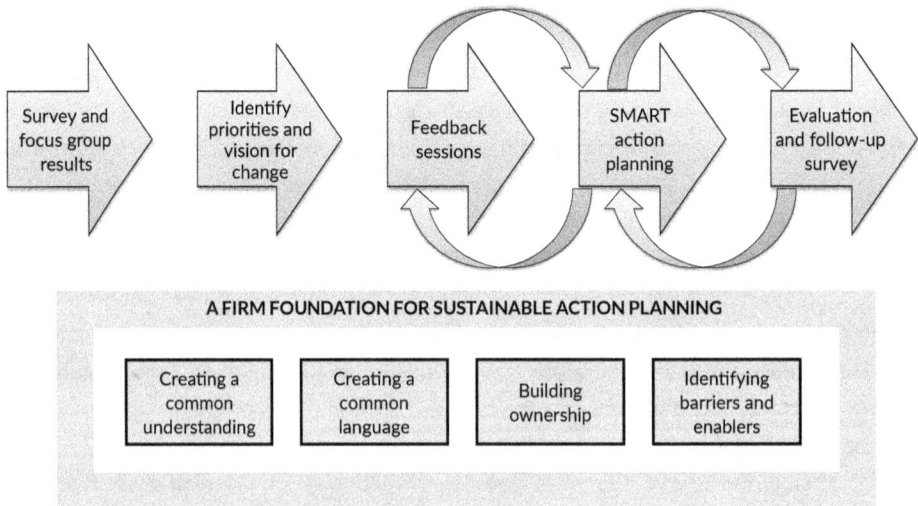

Figure 9.1: Mandate Molefi model for action planning and learning

Figure 9.1 above summarises the action planning and learning process and illustrates the iterative nature of action learning, which ensures inclusivity. Feedback loops between and with leadership, management teams and employees; between the feedback and action planning stages; and between the evaluation and action plans, create a reflexive learning process.

SMART ACTION PLANNING

As you will have noticed, the success of any action planning process relies largely on the preparatory work that has been undertaken before any concrete and practical planning begins. It is critical that the human foundation be laid before the practical work begins, otherwise the implementation phase risks being jeopardised by whatever has previously been swept under the carpet.

Once a solid foundation of understanding has been built across the organisation of what the key challenges are and the inclusive manner in which the organisation aims to tackle them, then the action planning can begin in earnest.

As stressed earlier, to ensure maximum efficiency and buy-in, this will need to take place at departmental level to ensure that the solutions are grounded in the knowledge and experience of the employees who will be taking the actions forward. In addition, the action planning has to be aligned with the planning cycle of the organisation, that is, woven into their normal business planning and operational cycles.

Often organisational diagnoses related to diversity, inclusion and transformation may be relegated to the domain of HR alone, which is where many organisations go wrong. There can be no multiple action planning agendas, with HR having one action plan and the core business another. As demonstrated throughout this chapter, if the technical and human dimensions of action are separated, key insight into and learning on how best to improve performance will be missed.

Owing to the inclusive nature of the diagnostic process to this point, including the survey and feedback process, buy-in to the action planning process should already have been established. Every line manager should feel empowered to take ownership of the process and work with their teams to plan the most effective solutions to the challenge at hand. In the action planning process, it is important to identify what quick wins can be gained to add momentum to the process at both departmental and organisational levels.

We then recommend that action planning take place through every layer of the organisation, starting with the senior leadership, the task team and then every business unit and department. We use the popular SMART (Specific, Measurable, Assignable, Realistic, Time-bound) model to assist with action planning. The action template below (table 9.1) is an example of how to work with four (theoretical) priority focus areas. Each layer of the organisation and head of department will then work through this template, identifying short-, medium- and long-term actions. This action plan will form the instrument for monitoring and evaluation.

Table 9.1: Action planning template

Action Planning Template						
Theme	Description of issue	Resolution or desired action at department level	Targeted positive outcome	Time frame	Responsibility	Enablers
Open communication and teamwork						
Accountability and leading by example						
Individual development						
Equity and empowerment						

The SMART criteria for determining actions demonstrate how specific actions need to be realistic and achievable. In addition, accountability needs to be built in to ensure that there is follow-through. This is established through repeatedly returning to the action plan at regular intervals to monitor progress and ensure continuous engagement, as will be explored in the next section.

Whereas at the feedback stage we take the three or four priority areas from the visioning sessions with senior leadership and the task team to departmental level, in the action planning stage we work from the ground up, trusting the capacity of teams on the ground to know what is best. This involves collating all the departmental action plans and feeding them into a central "dashboard" for executive level. This builds in both ownership and accountability for the action plans at departmental level and the knowledge that there will be follow-up on progress. Part of this process of building accountability can also include ensuring that there is a cost to non-performance in the form of penalties for not doing what has been committed to.

Case study 2: Inclusive task team drives successful SMART action planning

One of our most successful diagnostic interventions around diversity and transformation was with a large organisation in the energy sector. We were able to engage in a multi-year process that saw us conducting a diagnostic survey across the entire organisation, design a large-scale intervention with all staff, and work with an inclusive task team from inception through to action planning, monitoring and evaluation.

As highlighted throughout this article, building strong relationships is critical to the success of any action planning process – both between the consultants and the clients, as well as within the organisation. The success of this diagnostic intervention was due largely to the task team and the accountability the task team encouraged, from the visioning through to the SMART action planning process.

The establishment of the task team and the way it operated in this organisation showed how successful action planning can be if you have the right systemic support. The task team was made up of a range of different internal stakeholders, including leaders, unions and diverse representations of race, gender and departments. The most important thing in task teams is to ensure that everyone on the task team has a role to play, understands this role, has the support of their line manager for being on the task team, and the task team has a sense of momentum in reporting back on successes.

The task team worked closely with the consultants to analyse the survey results and took ownership of the mirror presented to them. While the process of narrowing down priority areas was slow, this was because there was the acknowledgement of the problems the organisation was facing and a desire to deal with them head on. After narrowing down the priorities from 21 to four key areas, the task team was ready to engage line with the vision and action planning.

At this point, the management committees of each department held rigorous SMART action planning meetings, using the templates provided in this chapter. Management teams were supported by consultants to come up with actions in the four priority areas that were actionable, deliverable and owned by individual managers. This then fed into an organisational action planning dashboard at exco level.

The task team met consistently to follow up on the action plans with departments, and there was a clear sense of which line managers were taking the process seriously and which were not. This assisted in driving follow-through on action plans. In working through the action plans in this way, there was increased buy-in and excitement within the task team itself, but also within departments where they felt empowered by working through issues directly themselves. In this way, those on the task team could see the importance and value of their role and were encouraged to continue. The organisation's broader staff, through ongoing communication, could see the same.

In this example, the rigour of the task team filtered down to departmental level. Conversely, when an executive committee is interested in getting feedback on their own performance, this demonstrates the kind of reflexivity and accountability it is asking of its employees, and can ignite ownership and delivery of change. If an organisation can build this kind of two-way feedback mechanism and conversation, it can truly become an organisation that has the capacity to learn and thus grow.

EVALUATION AND FOLLOW-UP

To ensure follow-through on the action planning, teams and departments themselves need to establish how they will monitor progress on actions and provide feedback to employees. These aspects need to be considered particularly at the higher levels, where the communication channels developed through the survey and feedback process must be continued so that employees have a sense of the continuity of the process as a whole and of things happening, as well as important milestones.

We have worked with many organisations that may have an internal leadership team that is very busy with many actions, but in failing to communicate them, they lose the faith of their employees in the process. A critical part of the action planning process and follow-up is a feedback loop to ensure that the whole organisation, especially those who took the survey, have a sense of progress. Part of this may be a commitment to provide communications once a quarter on progress and the issues raised through the diagnostic process.

While the senior leadership team will be overseeing departmental progress as a whole, we encourage departments to develop their own monthly processes to monitor progress. This includes a monthly self-check for managers (see figure 9.2 below), a monthly management team assessment (see figure 9.3 below), the identification of departmental champions to drive the process, and quarterly meetings. Figures 9.2 and 9.3 below provide an example of the kinds of questions to be asked and the common themes that emerge, but these questions and themes will need to be adapted to suit the specific organisational context.

Sample: Monthly self-check for managers

1. What is one **critical challenge** you have experienced over the past month that poses a challenge to transforming culture in your department/organisation?

   ----

2. What is one area where you have experienced **heightened awareness** as a result of the culture change process?

   ----

3. What is the **one example of a positive change** you have seen in your area that will enable transformation going forward?

Figure 9.2: Monthly self-check for managers

Sample: Monthly team assessment

Rate each area: Low — Average — High -5 -4 -3 -2 -1 0 1 2 3 4 5	Current status	Desired future	Gap	Our capacity to address this issue
Open communication and teamwork				
Employee engagement				
Efficiency				
Trust				
Transparency				
Provide a short description of challenges for any areas scoring in the negative:				
Accountability and leading by example				
Effective performance management				
Honesty				
Openness to a range of views				
Respect				
Provide a short description of challenges for any areas scoring in the negative:				
Career development				
Coaching and mentoring				
Succession planning				
Effective training and career pathing				
Continous improvement				
Provide a short description of challenges for any areas scoring in the negative:				
Equity and empowerment				
Fairness				
Visible commitment to transformation				
Inclusive behaviours				
Employee recognition				
Provide a short descriptin of challenges for any areas scoring in the negative:				

Figure 9.3: Monthly team assessment

The monthly team assessment (figure 9.3 above) entails monitoring progress on key outcomes by assessing the gap between current status and desired outcome, along with capacity to achieve this outcome. The departmental champions at all levels are tasked with conducting informal surveys with staff to monitor how they feel things are progressing and to provide anonymous feedback to management. Functional heads also need to have quarterly meetings with staff to ask one question on each of the priority areas, creating an open forum for frank communication with teams.

If used regularly, the above templates (figures 9.2 and 9.3) assist with the sustainability of the process, long after the consultants have exited. It is critical in the field of organisational diagnosis to leave the client with tools that continue the process in the long term. We have worked with organisations that continued to use the tools and frameworks we provided for three to seven years after we exited. The value in this, which needs to be stressed to the senior leadership and power client/sponsor, is that in having that continuity, longer term evaluation, measurement and claiming of success are possible.

In this vein, a follow-up survey the year after the diagnosis and intervention is important. This needs to be exactly the same survey so that a direct comparison can be made and progress accurately assessed. In this later survey, there may well even be a drop in certain dimensions, which can force the client to closely check where problem areas persist (see chapter 6 for examples of comparative surveys). It can be of great value to organisations to return to the same survey repeatedly over a long-term time-frame of many years, and be able to report back to internal and external stakeholders on progress over time.

COMMON PITFALLS IN ACTION PLANNING

In this line of work, you have to accept that you do not have control over the outcome of a diagnosis and intervention. The success or failure of an initiative depends on the willingness and maturity of the leadership and staff to engage with the emotional and intercultural dimensions of the organisation. In this section, I will present some common pitfalls, as well as shining gems, from the last few years.

One major barrier to change is if an organisation has struggled with the same issues for years, and this diagnostic process is one in a line of processes and surveys that have repeatedly failed to have an impact upon, and change, the organisational culture. This leaves the organisation with individuals and even teams who have repeatedly burnt their fingers, who have expressed their views and then experienced either no change or, even worse, been subject to a witch-hunt. This demonstrates failure on the part of leadership to take in feedback and commit at heart level to change.

Similarly, there may be individuals or cohorts in leadership or management teams who have hidden agendas. In this case, action planning and the diagnostic intervention as a whole become based on issues that leadership or management wish to resolve by conducting surveys to identify a problem in a particular business unit or department. This then results in pre-empting the results of the survey and looking for punitive outcomes. When such agendas are hidden within the design, administration and analysis of the survey, not only will we as consultants pick this up, but employees will too, and will disengage from the process.

Finally, a major barrier to success is when there is no commitment to following up, through either evaluating or communicating progress, or both. It is vital that there be communication throughout the action planning and implementation process, so that quick wins and success stories are communicated back to the organisation as a whole. This in turn proves that diagnosis does work, and as an employee and as an organisation, this is valuable. It is also critical to do a post-assessment after conducting the survey, intervention and solution implementation. Without this, there can be no sense of whether any progress has been made, and it also demonstrates a lack of commitment in taking the organisational issues seriously. Employees will sense that "no one cares" (a common perception in South African organisations) and this perpetuates cycles of disengagement.

The truthfulness and authenticity of the leadership team increase the capacity of an organisation to meet these challenges and avoid these pitfalls. This brings us to the final element of Ngambi's model for RARE leadership – that of ethics. Ethical leadership involves being true to yourself and aligning actions to values, thus demonstrating integrity and authenticity. Case studies 2 and 3 demonstrate this principle and represent examples of when action planning has gained momentum across an organisation because of the integrity of the leadership driving the change.

CONCLUSION: BECOMING A LEARNING ORGANISATION

I will end with the case study that, for me, exemplifies a learning organisation, that is, one that will be the most successful in effective action planning and achieving the change it hopes to see. This case study is used here as it beautifully illustrates the core driver of successful action planning: leaders and managers stepping up with integrity to take ownership of the process.

Case study 3: Creating an inclusive culture for women in leadership

We recently worked with a major financial institution in which a core issue emerged around the role of women in the organisation. Whereas at head level there was a sense that the organisation had a "good" culture, the experience of women that emerged through the survey spoke differently. This is a common experience in organisations, where there are no bad intentions and generally employees report that people get along, yet specific, subtle, but nevertheless draining forms of exclusion persist around gender, race and other diversity markers. This speaks to the challenge identified by Kegan and Lahey[24] where an organisation fails to make the adaptive shift in behaviour, whatever apparent buy-in there might be at an intellectual level, for example with regard to gender equity.

In this specific organisation, thankfully, there was a real openness to change but a blindspot around what the problem was and how it could be tackled. As discussed in this chapter, the critical ingredients for successful and sustainable action planning are instilling a sense of ownership of the process at all levels, creating a common understanding and language to engage with the challenges, and building an iterative process between feedback and action, thus creating an action learning trajectory for the organisation.

For this client, which was struggling to create an inclusive environment for women, we proposed a solution after the survey and diagnosis that involved intensive workshops with the first three levels of leadership. These workshops were dialogue sessions in which we built a safe space for frank discussion on key themes that had emerged through the survey, interviews

---

and focus groups. We then engaged in an action planning process through an action learning framework. The outcome of the action planning was specific actions and included where those actions would be housed and who the sponsors would be to ensure that they would be implemented.

What was striking in the case of this client was that the various layers of leadership took full ownership of the process, with sponsors stepping forward, committing to actions and seeing them through. Business unit leaders were held accountable for reporting back on the action plans raised in the dialogue sessions. Six months later there was considerable progress in the representation of women and an improvement in the culture of the organisation towards inclusivity as a whole.

As shown in this chapter, most of the success of action planning is in building a firm foundation throughout the diagnostic process, through a whole range of engagements that build trust, communication and ownership long before any practical planning takes place. Relationships and earnest, accountable leadership are at the heart of this process. While not all clients and leaders will immediately step up to the plate, through building relationships and, more specifically, the *capacity* of different players to relate, organisations build the capacity to learn as they take action.

Inclusive leadership is built upon a continuous cycle of action learning through meaningful and respectful feedback and engagement with the various layers of an organisation. In focusing on action learning as opposed to simply action planning, a cognitive shift is made from needing to change the to-do list of strategies and actions to changing the mindset that has allowed problematic patterns to persist over years of an organisation's life, despite any number of previous action plans and interventions. Making this shift, requires brave and bold leadership and can ensure that individuals and teams feel "directed, aligned, and committed toward shared outcomes for the common good of all, whilst retaining a sense of authenticity and uniqueness"[25]. This ensures that teams and organisations as diverse as those we see in South Africa today can thrive and effectively confront any organisational diagnosis with meaningful and sustainable change.

REFERENCES

Argyris, C. 1993. *Knowledge for action: A guide to overcoming barriers to organisational change.* San Francisco: Jossey-Bass.

Argyris, C & Schön, D. 1974. *Theory in practice: Increasing professional effectiveness.* San Francisco: Jossey-Bass.

Bhawuk, DPS, Sakuda, KH & Munusamy, VP. 2008. Intercultural competence development and triple-loop cultural learning: Towards a theory of intercultural sensitivity, in *Handbook of cultural intelligence: Theory, measurement and applications,* edited by S Ang & LV Dyne. New York: ME Sharpe: 343-355.

Booysen, L. 2014. The development of inclusive leadership practice and processes, in *Diversity at work: The practice of inclusion,* edited by BM Ferdman & BR Deane. San Francisco: Jossey-Bass: 296-329.

Dobbin, F & Kalev, A. 2016. Why diversity programs fail. *Harvard Business Review* July-August: 52-60.

Greyvenstein, H & Cilliers, F. 2012. Followership's experiences of organisational leadership: A systems psychodynamic perspective. *SA Journal of Industrial Psychology* 38(2).

Kegan, R & Lahey, LL. 2009. *Immunity to change: How to overcome it and unlock the potential in yourself and your organisation.* Boston: Harvard Business Press.

Ngambi, H. 2012. *RARE leadership: An effective leadership approach to leading change in organisations.* Randburg: KnowRes.

Ngambi, H. 2013. RARE leadership: An alternative leadership approach for Africa, in *Perspectives on thought leadership for Africa's renewal,* edited by K Kondlo. Pretoria: Africa Institute of South Africa: 110–129.

Nishii, LH & Rich, RE. 2014. Creating inclusive climates in diverse organisations, in *Diversity at work: The practice of inclusion,* edited by BM Ferdman & BR Deane. San Francisco: Jossey-Bass: 330-363.

Viljoen, R. 2015. *Organisational change and development: An African perspective.* Randburg: Knowres.

ENDNOTES

1. Kegan & Lahey, 2009.
2. Viljoen, 2015.
3. Kegan & Lahey, 2009.
4. Argyris, 1993.
5. Kegan & Lahey, 2009.
6. Ngambi, 2012.
7. Nishii & Rich, 2014.
8. Nishii & Rich, 2014.
9. Dobbin & Kalev, 2016.
10. Dobbin & Kalev, 2016.
11. Ngambi, 2012.
12. Greyvenstein & Cilliers, 2012.
13. Argyris, 1993; Kegan & Lahey, 2009.
14. Greyvenstein & Cilliers, 2012.
15. Nishii & Rich, 2014.
16. Ngambi, 2012.
17. Kegan & Lahey, 2009.
18. Argyris, 1993.
19. Kegan & Lahey, 2009.
20. Bhawuk, Sakuda & Munusamy, 2008.
21. Dobbin & Kalev, 2016.
22. Ngambi, 2013.
23. Ngambi, 2012.
24. Kegan & Lahey, 2009.
25. Booysen, 2014.

CHAPTER 10

CONDUCTING MULTICULTURAL RESEARCH INSIGHTS GAINED FROM THEORY AND PRACTICE

by **Dr Rica Viljoen**

Consciously manage the dynamics of multiculturalism in order to develop strengths and synergies from these, including the management of equal opportunities of individuals from different ethnic and gender groups to influence the direction of the organisation.

Jackson, 2004: unknown

INTRODUCTION

In this chapter the, importance of taking multicultural dynamics into account when doing research is considered. Autographic notes are shared from actual research projects in global settings that illustrate the importance of understanding the fine nuances in diverse cultures. To create inclusivity, national cultural dynamics described by Hofstede[1] and spiral dynamic insights as described by Graves, Beck, Laubscher and Viljoen[2] are offered as a way of bridging nationality dynamics by transcending differences in worldviews.

The second part of the chapter deals with grounded theory as a research methodology that can be applied to derive meta-insights, and systemically map dynamics in social systems. Together with systems thinking principles[3], the author uses grounded theory methodology to systemically and narratively describe the data gathered from multiple data sources, such as the Benchmark of Engagement (BeQ), in multicultural research.

In the third part of the chapter the BeQ is presented as a multicultural, sensitive philosophy and tool for describing individual, group and organisational dynamics and its congruence with societal dynamics. Results from various BeQ studies are shared to demonstrate the diversity of national cultures. Stories are shared on what can go wrong in conducting international research. Readers are also asked to reflect on multicultural dynamic insights that have emerged from their own experiences and, to become acutely aware of their own lenses – academically speaking, their ontology and epistemology. The stories shared were purposefully selected to enable the process of pulling down the curtain of one's own mind to make sense of the context in which the research drama actually played out.

CONDUCTING INTERNATIONAL RESEARCH

Conducting international research not only requires the researcher to discard the restricting attitudes and beliefs of the traditional, rigid and hierarchical organisational culture, but also to focus on the vulnerability of social and political conditions, meaning-making of multicultural groupings, and the behaviour of diverse employees. These factors challenge both multicultural researchers and organisational and societal leadership to revisit their practices and processes in a serious way. Due to the fact that there is a great deal of variability in cultural groups it may not only be inaccurate, but, perhaps, directly offensive, to superimpose cultural characteristics onto others without checking one's own assumptions[4]. Conducting a multiculturally sensitive research project or inquiry may assist organisations with better understanding ways in which to create inclusive workplaces that will have a significant positive impact on business indicators such as safe behaviour, productivity, customer centricity and employee engagement[5].

As recently as two decades ago the focus of cultural diversity, and, more specifically, multiculturalism, was concentrated on the following three factors: *Awareness* of one's personal worldviews and the way in which one is the product of cultural conditioning; *knowledge* of the worldviews of culturally different clients; and the *skills* that are necessary for working with culturally different clients[6]. Thoughts evolved exponentially from insights into multicultural dynamics into what LeBaron[7] described as cultural traps. LeBaron[8] referred to five of these traps, namely, the *Automatic Ethnocentricity Trap*, which refers to the belief that the way things are perceived is both natural and normal, the *Taxonomy Trap*, which assumes that it is possible to categorise every kind of cultural information, the *Complexity Trap*, which assumes that cultural complexity and dynamics are so difficult to understand that intercultural effectiveness is impossible, the *Universalism Trap*, which refers to the trap of seeing commonalities only, and thus minimising or failing to notice important cultural differences, and the *Separation Trap*, which refers to the trap of seeing differences and divisions only, and missing what is shared across identity and worldview boundaries. The multicultural survey consultant should be acutely aware of these traps, and must consciously plan to avoid them.

Differences between the individualistic white and collective black cultures pose unique challenges within Africa, and to companies that wish to operate on this continent[9]. This statement does not take the diversity within black cultures into account, however, yet the "context paradox" applies – the possibility that more contexts will be needed to interpret whatever contextual information has already been provided[10]. A theoretical approach that can transcend traditional stereotypes like white and black or other nationality stereotypes, such as Laubscher's[11] human niche theory, can facilitate healing in social systems while simultaneously providing meaningful information about the actual systemic dynamics. The human niche theory prefers to consider similarities and differences in thinking structures rather than other diversity dynamics, and in that way overcomes traditional splits in social systems.

Open systems will continue to exist only through continuous interaction with the environment[12]. Multicultural research should thus consider social environmental dynamics to ensure relevance. Resilient societies are those societies whose members can adapt to new conditions[13]. It becomes important to understand the changes, themes and shifts within the external country context when doing social system inquiries. It should be acknowledged that the external world or context is so diverse that both survey consultants and leaders within organisations should take national dynamics into account in terms of strategy and the way in which organisational efforts are managed, implemented and translated.

The knowledge base that grounds this chapter was synthesised from theory, concepts, research and facts from cross-cultural theory and practices. Further, real-life case studies, stories and discussions were considered. Actual data gathered from research and organisational inquiries were included. Lastly, the personal and professional experiences of the author as a scholar, researcher and organisational development survey consultant were incorporated.

The aim of this chapter is not to carry out a traditional, external analysis (for example, a study of the political, legislative, economic, environmental, social and technological aspects), but rather, through applying multicultural theory such as the human niche theory, to explore the global, African and South African realities that face organisations that operate within these realities and the employees in them. The first part of this chapter underlines the need for multicultural research, and explores global dynamics with the aim of creating an awareness of the impact and implications of the diverse external world on research practices within organisations. The second section deals with a unique integration of grounded theory and systems thinking to describe themes that emerge from rich qualitative and quantitative data during the conducting of multicultural research. In the third section of the chapter, the results of numerous international studies of the Benchmark of Engagement are shared. Further, auto-ethnographic tales[14], are shared of real-life experiences of an ethnographical researcher who conducts research in diverse spaces. These stories highlight not only the importance of being aware of the own ontology and epistemology of the researcher, but warns against any pre-conceived approach towards cultural research. The conclusion is reached that without the consideration of multicultural theory as described in the first section of the chapter, and without the suspension of own mental models and worldviews, a researcher's efforts are seldom successful in various contexts.

PART 1: THE NEED FOR MULTICULTURAL RESEARCH

Increased diversity in the global arena

The forces of globalisation significantly changed the global marketplace in terms of diversity dynamics. Global outsourcing is a strategic alternative for many global companies. The forming and breaking up of trade blocks also impact this diversity. Emerging economies such as Brazil, Russia, China, India and the recent joining of South Africa to the BRICS countries, changed the economic landscape forever. The expansion of organisations in multinational markets, and the vertical integration of supply chain functions across boundaries of countries, force leaders to deal with different social dynamics. Organisations strive to be sustainable in cross-cultural environments where people, social-system dynamics and profits mean different things to different role players. The war against fundamentalism and terrorism showcase cultural clashes between diverse groupings or actors in the international arena. Significant technological enhancements bridge the divide between people from different cultures and different time zones. On the one hand, the implications of the fourth industrial revolution promise a total different future. On the other hand, it illustrates the divide between the developed world and other spaces where the daily question of existence is concerned with survival. Here, pandemics like HIV/AIDS, malaria, Ebola and the

Zika virus are health issues that remain unsolved, and impact the daily life of millions. Migration across borders, as illustrated by the Libyan refugee crisis, requires people to connect with physical, national, social, emotional, intellectual, psychological and spiritual differences.

The need to describe cultural dynamics in an authentic and realistic manner becomes increasingly important to business. An understanding of these dynamics can assist largely in business decision-making inside organisations, in corporate social investments and in dealing with diverse customer bases. Diversity dynamics caused by different national cultures should be consciously acknowledged as organisational researchers and scholars draft their strategies and manage the implementation of these strategies. The complexity of dynamics in multicultural settings further complicate the international business environment, as different worldviews, organising archetypes and thinking structures of different actors in the social system engage together and compete for scarce resources[15].

Describing dynamics in the global arena

As stated in the previous section, it is critical for the multicultural survey consultant to take contextual and cultural dynamics into account. In this part of the chapter, the author discusses various ways to describe these dynamics that impact the over-culture or containing culture of global businesses. Indexes and reports, national cultural theory and questionnaires such as the Benchmark of Engagement (BeQ) that incorporate spiral dynamics as a methodology for describing the multicultural worldview, can be considered as alternative ways of ensuring contextual relevance.

Indexes and reports

Different instruments, reports and indexes may be used to compare companies in respect of specific criteria. The Global Competitiveness Report is a yearly report published by the World Economic Forum to assess the ability of countries to provide high levels of prosperity to their citizens. In turn, a high level of prosperity depends on how productively a country uses its available resources. Therefore, the Global Competitiveness Index published in this report measures the set of institutions, policies and factors that set the sustainable current and medium-term levels of economic prosperity[16]. The Ease of Doing Business Index is an index created by the World Bank. Higher rankings indicate better – usually simpler – regulations for businesses and stronger protection of property rights. Research has shown that improving these regulations has a very positive effect on economic growth. The annual surveys on Economic Freedom in the World and Index of Economic Freedom are two indices that attempt to measure economic freedom. These indices have, in turn, been used in many peer-review studies, which have found that there are several beneficial effects to greater economic freedom. There are certain criticisms of these measurements, for example, property rights that function properly and an efficient rule of law, and not low taxes or a small state, may be important aspects of economic freedom.

Theoretical approaches to describe national culture

Graves and Beck[17] describe sacrificial cultures or collective cultures and expressive cultures where individuals express their viewpoints and are thus individualistic. Triandis, Dunnette and Hough[18] also differentiate between collectivist and individualist cultures. Cox[19] agreed with this differentiation and identified five further areas of behaviour in which a lack of understanding of cultural differences could have a significant impact on the organisation. Hofstede[20] carried out comprehensive research on the cultures of different countries. He (Hofstede) advises that management operating across country boundaries should acquire both knowledge of, and empathy with, the local scene. He also describes the individual versus collectivist aspect of cultures and names five other types of differences between national cultures, namely:

1. The power distance – the degree to which people within a country view inequality among people of that country as normal.
2. Masculine versus feminine – the extent to which a culture is conducive to dominance, assertiveness and the acquisition of possessions as opposed to a culture which is conducive to people, feeling and quality of life. Jung[21] agreed with this view – he described Germany as the white "fatherland" and spoke of dark "Mother Africa".
3. Uncertainty avoidance – the degree to which people in a country prefer structured to unstructured solutions.
4. Long-term versus short-term orientation – long term implies a future orientation, such as savings, as opposed to short term which implies both a past and present perspective such as fulfilling social obligations and showing respect for tradition.
5. Indulgence versus restrained – indulgent societies allow freedom to gratify basic human desires related to enjoying life and having fun, as opposed to restrained societies that are characterised by a perception that gratification should be regulated by social norms.

Viljoen[22] compares other multicultural approaches such as those of Trompenaars[23] and the Globe studies. Disregarding the theoretical approach in which the researcher grounds himself or herself, the collective culture of the relevant country should be taken into account when engaging with a foreign environment or operating in one. Applications available on Apple handsets and iPads, such as CultureLite, provide instant access to these dynamics.

Cultural identity provides a conceptual vehicle for the connection between the individual and the group[24]. Kets de Vries[25] visually summarised the complex topic of culture in the wheel of culture displayed in Figure 10.1 below.

Time
Monochronic/
polychronic
Orientated
toward past/
present/future

Environment
Control/
harmony/good/
evil
Certain/
uncertain/trust/
mistrust

Thinking
Deductive/inductive
Holistic/part orientated

Action orientation
Being orientated/
doing orientated
Internal/external

Power
Egalitarian/hierarchic
Achievement
orientated/ascription
orientated

Emotion
Expressive/inhibited

Relationships
Individualistic/
collectivistic
Universalistic/
particularistic
Competitive/
cooperative

Language
High context/low
context

Space
Private/public

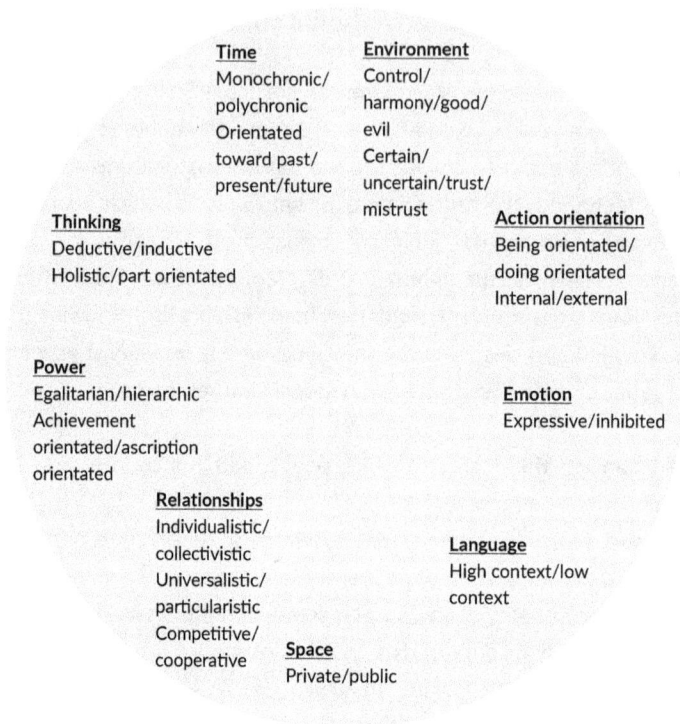

Figure 10.1: The wheel of culture[26]

In Figure 10.1 above, the wheel of culture indicates the areas of culture that Kets de Vries considers when studying multicultural dynamics. Hall[27], meanwhile, differentiates between high-context and low-context cultures. High-context cultures establish social trust first, are relational, reach agreement by general trust and negotiations and are slow and ritualistic. Low-context cultures, on the other hand, do business before relationships follow, value expertise and performance, agree by a specific contract, and keep negotiations as efficient as possible. These aspects must also be considered when conducting research/consulting across cultural boundaries.

Shwartz[28] describes a theoretical model of relations among ten motivational types of values. The Benchmark of Engagement (BeQ) provides an indication of a country's basic values as described by the participants, and can be used as an instrument to describe the diversity of multicultural workforces during a large-scale organisational audit. These values are described in Table 10.1 below.

Table 10.1: Basic values and motivational goals adapted from Schwartz[29]

Basic Value	Central motivational goal
Self-direction	Independent thought and action, choosing, creating and exploring.
Universalism	Understanding, appreciation, tolerance and protection of the welfare of all people and nature.
Benevolence	Preserving and enhancing the welfare of those with whom one is in frequent personal contact.
Conformity/Tradition	Restraint of actions, inclinations and impulses likely to upset or harm others and violate social expectations or norms/respect, commitment and acceptance of the culture or religion provided to an individual.
Security	Safety, harmony and stability of society, relationships and self.
Power	Social status and prestige, control or dominance over people and resources.
Achievement	Personal success through demonstrating competence according to social standards.
Hedonism	Pleasure and sensuous gratification for oneself.
Stimulation	Excitement, novelty and challenge in life.

In Table 10.1, different categories, basic values and motivational goals, which manifest in different countries, are presented. Jung[30] believed that Europe and Africa represented polar opposites – white and masculine versus dark and feminine, but he warned that the East differed markedly from both Europe and Africa. He ascribed this to the differences in philosophy and religion. The differences between Eastern and Western philosophies are depicted in Figure 10.2 below.

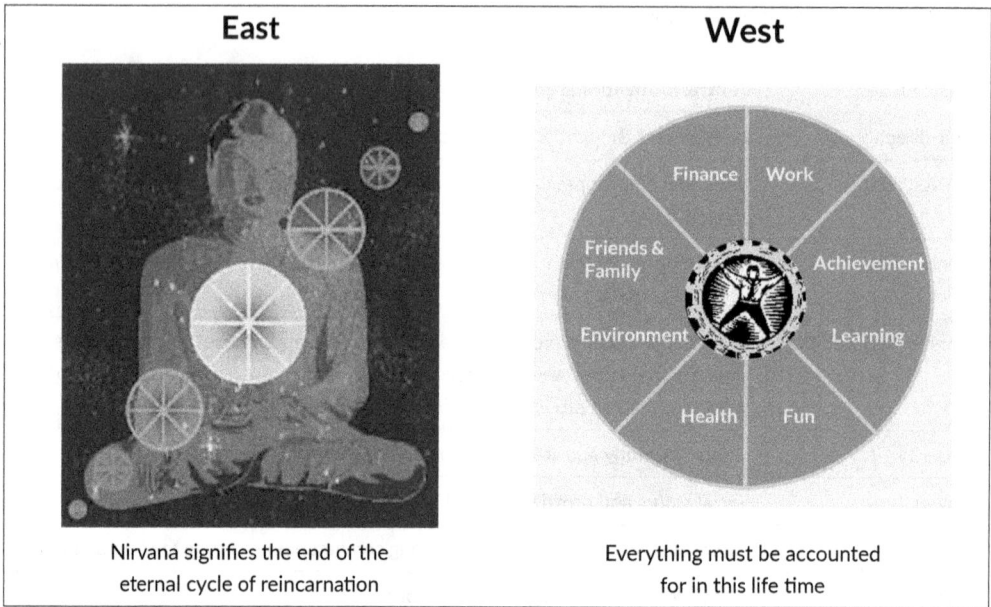

Source: Biblikova and Kotelnikov[31]

Figure 10.2: Eastern versus Western Philosophy

In contrast with the way in which meaning is created in the West and the East (see figure 10.2 above), Viljoen and Laubscher[32] describe the way in which most locals or first nations, as the author prefers to refer to ingenious people from Africa, create meaning. Figure 10.3 shows this philosophical stance graphically.

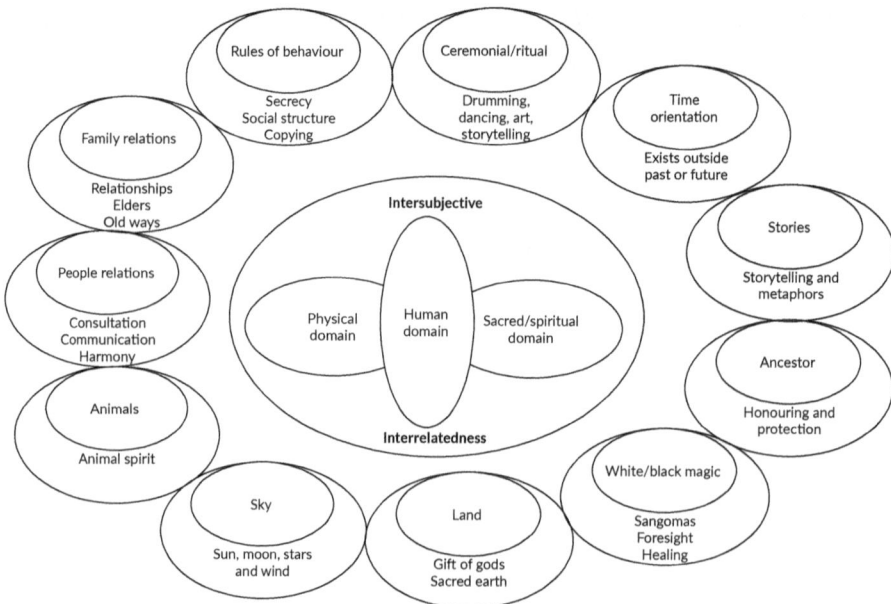

Figure 10.3: Intersubjective interrelatedness of African Purple[33]

When doing research or consulting in a specific country, the multicultural survey consultant should consider the way in which meaning is created, as illustrated in figures 10.2 and 10.3. Specific questions should be incorporated in the actual questionnaire or in the focus groups to ensure that these dynamics are described.

Diversity of worldview

"If we are to achieve a richer culture, rich in contrasting values, we must recognise the whole gamut of human potentialities, and so weave a less arbitrary social fabric, one in which each diverse human gift will find a fitting place."
Margeret Mead[34]

Cultures exist within larger systems which are known as worldviews[35]. Worldviews consist of the following three cultural dimensions, namely, the social and moral, practical and material, and transcendent or spiritual dimensions. According to the online dictionary, dictionary.reference.com, a *worldview* may be defined as "the overall perspective from which one sees and interprets the world" or "a collection of beliefs about life and the universe held by an individual or a group". Cox and Chung[36] agree that cultural differences in perceptions and worldviews may contribute to conflict within the workplace. Further, Viljoen[37] stresses the importance of how different cultural groups with diverse worldviews may have conflicting interpretations of organisational values and engagement dynamics such as respect, trust and support. A survey consultant who aims at describing organisational dynamics in multicultural settings should consider these differences.

Collectively, the worldviews of societies influence the way in which societies behave. Beck and Cohen[38] built on the work of Graves[39], and presented the evolution of societies in the form of a spiral. The phases of the spiral, which are termed vMemes, are summarised in Table 10.2. Beck[40] equates vMemes to psychological DNA, while Laubscher[41] describes these vMemes as human niches and uniquely introduces gifts and side effects of different thinking structures. Seven human niches can be described. These human niches describe the thinking structures, the organising archetypes, and the question of existence of the various groupings. Graves[42] originally characterised the various groupings with a coding structure, which is listed in the second column of Table 10.3 below. During one of his 64 trips to South Africa, while working with South African politicians from 1989 to 1994 on formalising the constitution, Beck[43] introduced colour codes to the various niches to move past nationality in describing thinking structures.

Table 10.2: Human Niches in South Africa[44].

Human Niche	Gravesian code	Gift	Example of side-effect on macro-level	Question of existence	% in South Africa
Beige	AN	Survival	Dysfunctional	How do I survive?	9%
Purple	BO	Relational	Boko Haram	How do we sacrifice for the tribe / our people?	65%
Red	CP	Power	Zimbabwe and Robert Mogabe Mugabe	Who am I if I am not my tribe?	15%
Blue	DQ	Rule following and risk-adverse	Apartheid	How do we sacrifice for the future?	10%
Orange	ER	Achievement and calculated risk	Capitalism in America that collapsed during credit crunch	How can I become successful?	1%
Green	FS	Inclusive and equality	Socialism that goes bankrupt like European states	How do we sacrifice for humanity/the earth?	0.1%
Yellow	GT	Functional and can see all gifts and side-effects	Chaotic	How can you and I survive?	0.001%

In Table 10.2 above, the first column indicates the colour that is used to describe the human niche. In the second column, the original codes that Graves[45] assigned to the specific niche are listed. Each thinking system or niche has a specific gift that is listed in the third column. Every human niche also has side effects – the downside of not considering specific questions of existence. These side effects can be seen in the fourth column. The question of existence of each human niche is listed in the fifth column. It is this over-riding question that impacts life choices, ways in which individuals, groups and geo-political regions organise, and the behaviours that are ultimately valued or disrespected. The last column lists the overall percentages that Laubscher[46] documented. These percentages were determined by a meta-analysis of all the psychological maps (an instrument that describe human niches) that she (Laubscher) administered over a period of almost 40 years in South Africa. Different people from different industries participated in this study, including health care, transport, banking, financial services, retail and mining. Political leaders and union members also completed the instrument. The total number of participants of this study was 2,539,339.

It is important for the multicultural survey consultant to consider the impact of thinking systems or human niches when interpreting survey results, and when it is attempted to describe dynamics of specific organisations. Beck, Laubscher and Viljoen[47] explain that these human niches impact on the way in which societies and the individuals in them organise, decide, communicate and manage. They also describe how individuals and groupings derive meaning, and thus how perceptions are formed. Through understanding the different human niches/thinking systems at play in a multicultural setting, the researcher may gain valuable insight into the systemic dynamics. In the last part of this chapter, various research cases in different countries are presented. The human niche theory was applied in these cases to describe systemic dynamics. The Benchmark of Engagement (BeQ), as described by Viljoen[48], reflects human niche distributions in large social systems. This instrument was developed as an outcome of the author's doctoral study on sustainability in which universal prerequisites for inclusivity were conceptualised. For example, all humans want to be respected, however respect has a different meaning in different contexts. Results from different BeQ studies in different countries are presented in the third part of this chapter.

Beck and Cohen[49] and Viljoen and Laubscher[50] state that in most of Africa, emerging and undeveloped economies had suffered the consequences of European colonialism, and had yet to experience the agrarian movement. Africa is still filled with superstition, magical practices and clan and tribal conflicts. It is characterised by periods of social implosion and lawlessness. Doing research in Africa, and other emerging and undeveloped economies, requires researchers to emerge themselves in the thinking structure of the world in which they find themselves. YELLOW is a thinking structure that stands separately, and sees the gifts and side effects of all the other human niches. Multicultural researchers should thus design their research strategy from YELLOW. This implies that the researcher must be acutely aware of the systemic dynamics, and far from trying to heal or fix these dynamics, describe both the gifts and the unintended consequences of the culture under study.

Viljoen and Laubscher[51] describe the challenge for Africa as how, on the one hand, PURPLE people can compete internationally in BLUE and ORANGE ways, but how, on the other hand, PURPLE wisdom and soulfulness can be remembered in the rest of the world. Viljoen[52] stresses that the international leadership challenge is how BLUE and ORANGE leadership in organisations can enable their PURPLE and RED majority employee group to feel included and consulted so that BLUE standard operating processes can be executed.

Harrison[53] studied the reasons why certain African companies that had escaped third-world conditions, namely, excessive authoritarian structures and stagnant economies, had survived. He found that countries that were prospering were characterised by the emergence of a Puritan-Confucian-Islamic type of work ethic, the existence of the values associated with individual initiative, a stable society in terms of law and order, and respect for personal rights and property – thus awakening BLUE/ORANGE. Viljoen and Laubscher[54] support these findings, and explain the impact of the British education system (BLUE) on PURPLE culture.

CONCLUSION

There are salient differences between the social, economic, legal and historical contexts of different countries, which impact on employment practices, localisation and other legislation, influencing the valuing of diversity. These differences also have a major implication on organisational culture, climate and ways in which organisational values are interpreted. Multicultural survey consultants should be acutely aware of their own worldviews and assumptions, as well as those of the social system that they study.

It is not the intention of this chapter to explore the differences between the cultures of indigenous countries. The intent is rather to leave the reader with a sense of the tremendous diversity presented by cross-border operations. Furthermore, an attempt was made to create the awareness that no system should ever be viewed from the perspective of the mental model of the leader or the survey consultant, but instead through inquiry and the sharing with an individual within the context of his or her climate, group, organisation and/or societies. Lastly, the author urges the reader to acknowledge that workers from different nationalities will always manifest diverse mental models that will be influenced by national cultural dynamics, and that this will directly influence the way in which they operate within a system.

PART 2: GROUNDED THEORY AND SYSTEMS THEORY INTEGRATED – A POSITIONING

A journey begins before the travellers depart. So, too, our Grounded Theory adventure begins as we seek information about what a grounded journey entails and what to expect along the way.

Charmaz, 2006: 1

Introduction and background

In this part of the chapter, Grounded Theory is introduced as a research methodology that can deal with the challenges of the rich data provided by multicultural research in diverse settings. The methodology of Grounded Theory was originally developed by two sociologists, namely Glaser[55] and Strauss[56]. Strauss[57], who was influenced by Thomas, Hughes and Blumer [58], contributed to the methodology by highlighting the need for field research to develop a discipline as the basis for social action, and to acknowledge the complexity and variability of both phenomena, as well as that of human action. He stressed the belief that individuals were actors who assumed roles in response to problems, and that they acted from a basis of meaning. Strauss[59] also emphasised the importance of an awareness of the interrelationship between conditions, actions and consequences. Glaser[60] identified the need for comparison of data to identify, develop and relate concepts.

In systems thinking processes, as described by Ackoff[61], the causality between factors that impact the system under study, and the containing system or over-culture, as Viljoen[62] describes it, are considered. The over-culture describes the behavioural dynamics in the containing system of the organisation that is studied. Grounded theory methodology and systems thinking methods can be integrated on various levels – from the philosophical to the methodological level.

Philosophical stance

Charmaz[63] took the view that it is not possible to discover either data or theories. Rather, grounded theories are constructed through both present and past involvement as well as through interaction with people, perspectives and research practices. Grounded theory is thus constructivistic and/ or interprevistic in nature. This ontological stance ensures that grounded theory is a relevant and applicable way of describing multicultural dynamics. A post-modernistic stance allows for creative ways of dealing with rich data.

Methodology

Grounded theory can be adapted as a methodology or method. This means that a survey consultant can structure a research project in a constructivistic/interprevistic manner, or merely apply the methods of grounded theory to construct a framework or meta-insights – thus only applying the coding and analysis methods to make sense of emerging themes in the data.

Traditionally grounded theory belongs in the Path of Integral Research, as described by Lessem and Schieffer[64] who refer to grounded theory as a method of theorising. If applied in its traditional manner, it is linked to critical rationalism. However, by only using grounded theory methods at different phases of the research/consulting project, and integrating other ways of analysing data such as systems thinking methods, not only can meta-insights be derived, but the leverage point in systems can be identified. This allows scientist practitioners to translate scholarly research into organisational interventions that can optimise systemic dynamics.

If grounded theory coding is used as a data-analysis method, and the data-gathering phase can be enriched by data gathered from phenomenology, life history, oral history, auto-ethnography, narrative inquiry or even co-operative inquiry, the philosophical stance shifts and becomes more post-modernistic and phenomenological. Schurinck[65] explains that even quantitative data can be used in grounded theory. As grounded theory is typically conducted when there is a lack of literature or theory for describing a phenomenon under study, the author argues that an emergent stance is adopted to deal with the ethnographical dynamics of multicultural environments.

Viljoen[66] uniquely applies design thinking principles during grounded theory research 1 as a data analysis method to describe the current reality and the ideal future. Thus a more pragmatic path of research is followed. Traditional grounded theory can develop into Engaged Theory, which is a methodological framework that strives to make sense of a social complexity[67]. It steers away from detailed empirical analysis about things, people and processes to a way in which those people, things and processes can be framed differently.

---

1   This method is used to conduct data analysis of multi-method research projects such as the Benchmark of Engagement.

In contrast to the typical grounded theory, Engaged Theory is reflexive in several ways[68]; it acknowledges that every step of the research project already entails making theoretical presuppositions. Engaged Theory has multiple levels of theoretical abstraction, and makes a clear distinction between theory and method. Thus, social theory is an argument about a social phenomenon. In this instance a break is made with the dominant philosophy of classical grounded theory, and a movement towards a post-classical sensibility becomes visible.

Grounded theory contextualised

Grounded theory can be described as follows: "think systematically about data and relate them in very complex ways"[69]. It is here where the author believes that design thinking methodologies, as described by Ackoff[70], can play an important role. A more inductive way with a coding method in a grounded theory manner can generate themes, and apply them in a more theoretical approach that is deductive.

The outcome of grounded theory is a framework or meta-insights about a phenomenon or the dynamics in a social setting. Causal diagrams of design thinking can be applied to contextualise a framework like this. It is thus a valuable methodology to construct theory if topics, contexts or cultures are under-explored.

Glaser[71] stated that the aim of grounded theory is to discover the theory which is implicit in the data. Charmaz[72] added that labels should be attached to data segments to depict what every segment is about. Data are compared to emerging theory. If there is a difference between the emerging theory and the literature, then efforts are to be made to extend the theory. Levels of abstraction are built directly from the data and additional data are gathered to confirm and refine emerging analytical categories[73].

To enable them to be consistent with the views of Blumer[74] in respect of sensitising concepts, multicultural survey consultants who conduct grounded theory often commence their studies with a certain research interest and a set of general concepts, which sensitise them to ask a specific kind of question.

The use of literature in grounded theory

Kelle[75] stresses the importance of the integration of existing knowledge with new empirical observations during any scientific discovery process. He explains that researchers must draw on existing theoretical knowledge to interpret, describe and explain empirical data. It is, however, important that "this style of inquiry should be supplemented by strategies of further corroboration of the empirically contentful categories and propositions developed in the on-going course of theory building"[76]. Grounded Theory is used in the BeQ to derive meta-insights of the specific cultural dynamics that manifest in the specific environment. Each BeQ inquiry is viewed as a new research project. The latest literature is considered aligned with the organisational leadership philosophy and the specific industry dynamics. The practice of suspending literature until themes emerge is congruent with ethnographical ontology and epistemology.

Strauss and Corbin[77] describe grounded theory as "theory that was derived from data, systematically gathered and analysed through the research process. In this method, data collection, analysis, and eventual theory stand in close relationship to one another". Charmaz[78] states that grounded theory "consists of systemic, yet flexible guidelines for collecting and analysing qualitative data to construct theories grounded in the data themselves".

Owing to the fact that grounded theories are drawn from data, it is likely that these theories will offer insight, lead to enhanced understanding, and shed light on potential action. Sandelowski[79] identified creativity as an essential characteristic of a grounded theory researcher. Patton[80] was of a similar view, and stated that both critical and creative thinking are needed as "qualitative evaluation... (is) both the science and the art of analysis".

"The grounded theory researcher should read for ideas, and conceptually connect these to the developing theory in order to enhance theoretical sensitivity"[81]. As it is important to allow themes to emerge from the data, literature is often kept aside until much later in the triangulation process. Only after themes that emerged from data have been described, is literature consulted. A deliberate effort is made to find evidence for the findings in theory. If it is lacking, new theory is written. In Africa, as in other emerging economies, traditional wisdom and even languages are manifested in oral format (for example Bambara, spoken in Mali, which is not a written language). Ways of introducing traditional wisdom, stories and ethnographical realities need to be founded, as most theory is created through the traditional, western thinking school[82]. Grounded theory is a methodology that can assist greatly in allowing untold stories to be told and unheard voices to be documented, especially so in survey research.

Data Gathering

Grounded theory typically begins with both a research situation and data[83]. Themes that emerge from data are coded. Data can be gathered through interviews, focus groups, case studies, solicited data and personal journals. Categories and properties are identified from notes. Viljoen-Terblanche[84] argues that narratives such as auto-ethnographies, life histories and confessional tales[85] can also serve as data-gathering methods for grounded theory studies. In multicultural settings, storytelling can be used with rich outcomes as a data-gathering method. Schurink[86] explains that even quantitative data can be incorporated in a grounded theory inquiry. This allows the multicultural survey consultant to compare or incorporate the findings from both qualitative and quantitative data to describe dynamics in diverse settings.

The BeQ, as described by Viljoen[87], studies the human energy in a social system by describing dynamics on individual, group, organisational and societal levels. Viljoen[88] incorporates multi-method data-gathering ways in the BeQ. Interviews with an ethnographical nature, focus groups, world café methodology, stories, journals and observations, together with field notes, form part of this process. Only later is the voice of theory consulted to see whether if the themes that emerge from data are is supported by literature. If not, new theory is developed. If the literature is richer than the emerging themes from the data, then insights gained from the data-gathering phase are strengthened by theoretical understanding. The credibility of a study is largely enhanced if results that were achieved through various multi-method data gathering and themes from literature are is comparable. If the theory accurately describes the data that emerged, it is viewed as triangulated.

Data Analysis

The process of naming or labeling concepts, categories and properties is known as *coding*. Open coding refers to conceptualising on the first level of abstraction. This coding is often done in the margin of field notes, but it can also be done electronically. The survey consultant can go back and forth comparing data and coding themes. A different collaboration, namely, between Strauss and Corbin[89], describes an axial coding process for the development of grounded theory.

Axial coding is commenced by looking at interrelationships. The question is asked: What impacts on what? It is here that causal diagrams of design thinking are very handy, as it is in this phase that the author applies design thinking methods to describe multicultural settings. During axial coding the researcher attempts to identify the types of phenomena, contexts and causal and intervening conditions and consequences that are relevant to the domain that is under study. Axial coding may be viewed as having evolved from the work of Strauss and Glaser[90]. A further development is the integration of design thinking methods to deal with causalities in the framework creation phase of the research. In Figure 10.4 below a typical qualitative process flow can be seen. Systems thinking principles are included in Figure 10.4.

Selective coding is typically done after a core variable has been identified, and delimits the study[92]. Theoretical coding interweaves theoretical understandings into emerging themes. Viljoen-Terblanche[93] uniquely integrates systems thinking methods during the data analysis phase of a grounded theory research process. As can be seen in figure 10.4, themes are allowed to emerge from data before literature are reviewed in an attempt to pre-empt initial assumptions on behalf of the survey consultant.

Glaser[94] warned against the preconception of interview guides and ruled for data gathering and collection during the application of grounded theory. He advised against the forcing of interview data into preconceived categories. Therefore, the question: "What is happening here?" was borne in mind in two respects during the interviews and focus groups, namely; "What are the basic social processes?" and "What are the basic social psychological processes?" It is this positioning of grounded theory that lends itself to dealing with multicultural dynamics – research where researchers should be acutely aware of their own ontologies and epistemologies to describe ethnographical phenomena in a truthful and authentic manner.

To enable researchers to come to a true understanding of the perspective from which answers are provided and stories are told, they must reflect on issues such as the angle from which the point of view was given and the different meanings attributed to the process by the different participants[95].

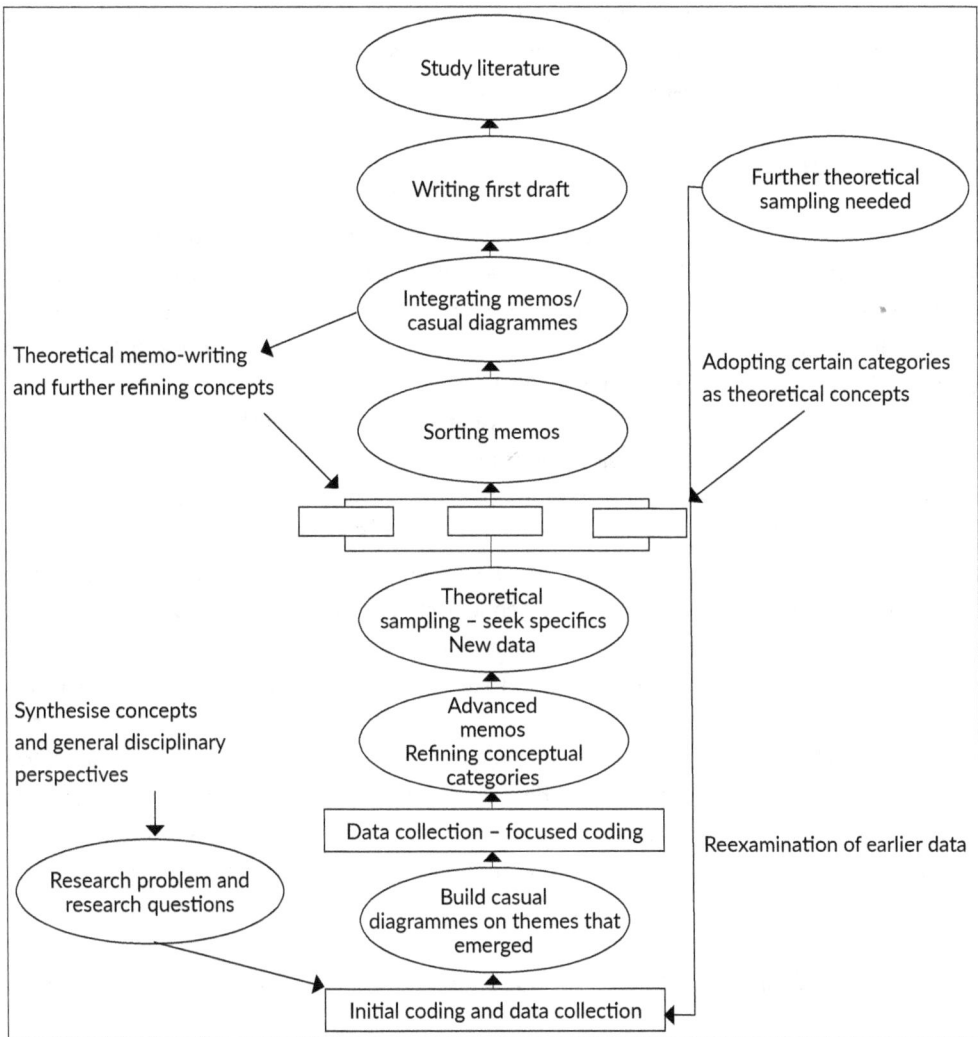

Figure 10.4: *Qualitative process flow to construct grounded theory through design thinking principles. Adapted from Charmaz by Viljoen-Terblanche*[91]

Shortcomings of grounded theory

Today, different forms of grounded theory can be found in literature, and these are applied with success in both academic and other writings[96]. Yet Lofland and Lofland[97] accuse grounded theory studies of building analysis on haphazard and skimpy data, while Creswell[98] is of the view that grounded theory is based upon a limited number of interviews (20 to 30 interviews), and argued that in a major study more data sources are needed. These shortcomings can be addressed by ensuring that strategies that ensure quality of data are in place. These strategies are described in the paragraph below.

It is not possible to divorce the view of the researcher totally from the research, however by declaring the ontology and epistemology of the researcher and ensuring that quality data is ensured, the risk of subjectivism can be overcome.

Ensuring quality data

Thorne[99] states that in terms of conducting research, different disciplines comply with different standards. Charmaz[100] identified credibility, originality, resonance and usefulness as criteria for solid grounded theory studies, and compiled a comprehensive list of questions that can be asked to test the standard of the research. Glaser and Strauss[101] tested for relevance in terms of the concept's fit, relevance, workability and modifiability.

Ellis[102] highlights the fact that language is not transparent, and that there is no universal standard of truth. She argues that all validity is contextually interpretive and dependent on the understanding of the research about the observation[103]. A way then, to redefine validity, is to consider if all stakeholder views are reflected in the text. Further, ontological and educational authenticity concerns itself with whether there is raised awareness in the research participants. On the other hand, catalytic and tactical authenticity studies whether actions by participants and researchers were focused on prompt social and political action when desired. The multicultural survey consultant should be very aware of how to deal with considerations about validity in diverse settings.

Viljoen-Terblanche[104] also underlines the importance of triangulation from data gathered from multiple sources and the in-face validity in dealing in multicultural settings. Viljoen[105] stresses that everyone who participates in organisational research projects or inquiries must receive feedback. Not only are the results validated by testing the initial findings with research participants, but employees also feel that their opinions are listened to and that they are consulted. This can serve as an organisational development intervention. In multicultural settings, it is even more important to discuss research findings with participants as sensitive cultural nuances can be explored and even understood.

CONCLUSION

The purpose of grounded theory is to generate explanatory theory that allows for better insight and understanding of social and psychological phenomena. Grounded theory offers an interpretive portrayal of the world in question, and not an exact portrayal of this world[106]. By applying systems thinking methods, a systemic diagram can serve as the framework or meta-insights for a grounded theory research project or inquiry. Grounded theory is used as methodology to tell the story of humans and the systems in which they function. Some of the findings in conducting this methodology are described below, both quantitatively and qualitatively, by means of ethnographical tales.

PART 3: INTERNATIONAL COMPARISONS

The Benchmark of Engagement philosophy was applied in 45 countries to describe I-engage dynamics, total engagement scores and multicultural dynamics. For this comparison, organisational dynamics were excluded. Internationally, more than 75,000 people participated in the study. The following criteria were applied when selecting the countries to be included here:

1. More than 2,000 people per country participated in the study in the quantitative part of the study.
2. In-depth interviews were done with at least 100 people in the country.
3. The results were triangulated and the participants confirmed the results.
4. The sample group included not only employees of a local organisation, but also members of the society in which the organisation was functioning.
5. Data was considered for inclusion here only if the sessions were facilitated by external researchers, and with the help of trained translators.

The BeQ is divided into four sections. The I-engage section describes individual dynamics in the system. This scale has a Cronbach Alpha of 0.78, which is deemed reliable by Nunnaly[107]. One of the subscales, namely respect, has a Cronbach's Alpha of 0.9. The multicultural dynamics are only an indication of the dynamics in the system, however these dynamics were confirmed with participants of the study, which ensured face validity. The human niche indicator describes thinking systems accurately with a 95% certainty.

The We-engage describes dynamics on the group domain, while the Org-engage studies the organisational gestalt - how things manifest in the collective. The Society-engage integrates the powerful theory of human niches as described by Viljoen and Laubscher[108] and, based on the work of Graves and Beck[109]. In this section, the over-culture of an organisation is described as the contextual dynamics the largely impact the actors in that system. For this chapter only the I-engage and the Society-engage factors are considered. This is done for comparison purposes.

In all the studies grounded theory methodology was selected to construct an understanding of the social dynamics that were at play. The criteria to ensure a quality grounded theory study as described in Part 2 of this chapter were applied, and the researchers ensured that the findings were transferable, modifiable, relevant, authentic and fit. Triangulation took place by comparing quantitative results with the qualitative themes that emerged from the data, and ultimately with literature.

As the whole argument of this chapter is that one should not underestimate the contextual dynamics, and as the results in Table 10.3 already deal with inferential statistics, only descriptive statistics were applied here to showcase the different country dynamics, rather than to reach generic averages. Viljoen[110] reminds us that the intent of the study should be considered in deeming it either quantitative or qualitative, and not the actual research methods applied. In this case the data analysis was inductive, exploratory and descriptive.

Table 10.3: BeQ results for Africa[a]

	West Africa			Central Africa			North Africa			East Africa			Southern Africa					Average
	Ghana	Nigeria	Mali	DRC	São Tomé	Cameroon	Egypt	Morocco	Algeria	Tanzania	Kenya	Zambia	South Africa	Zimbabwe	Namibia	Botswana	Swaziland	Average
Self Direction	31	89	32	28	27	32	46	31	33	28	29	25	57	79	35	23	14	38
Universalism	83	64	89	68	69	80	72	82	79	86	88	84	76	77	88	81	80	79
Benevolence	96	63	89	88	88	96	80	94	92	97	91	89	64	79	92	80	78	86
Tradition	89	82	92	83	85	90	79	88	82	90	89	92	73	80	81	83	83	85
Security	83	62	86	88	86	82	79	79	76	84	81	87	74	71	79	81	82	80
Power	89	91	95	87	87	82	79	81	79	86	88	85	77	89	71	82	93	85
Conformity	92	62	93	65	68	79	75	73	68	90	91	90	73	88	82	89	91	81
Achievement	46	79	39	31	32	33	46	39	42	36	39	32	59	45	29	31	29	40
Hedonism	42	69	36	24	24	32	36	37	41	33	40	34	58	12	25	24	16	34
Stimulation	36	70	21	18	16	19	37	22	36	36	26	27	53	26	22	21	9	29
Collectivistic	78	42	54	51	51	69	49	70	66	79	76	77	75	68	76	84	71	67
Uncertainty avoidance	76	59	69	73	61	70	59	71	60	89	86	88	59	33	76	66	55	68
Long term focus	43	48	35	38	39	42	32	46	39	39	23	21	55	23	34	31	12	35
Indulgence	28	42	14	19	20	26	36	29	28	17	23	21	43	18	38	21	8	25
Masculine	35	79	71	69	67	39	94	71	79	42	39	34	69	77	59	71	91	64
I-engage	71	79	63	64	63	64	71	65	69	60	62	67	75	69	71	68	59	67
Engagement	70	65	61	60	58	63	62	61	65	68	65	68	67	72	71	73	57	65

	West Africa			Central Africa			North Africa			East Africa			Southern Africa					
	Ghana	Nigeria	Mali	DRC	São Tomé	Cameroon	Egypt	Morocco	Algeria	Tanzania	Kenya	Zambia	South Africa	Zimbabwe	Namibia	Botswana	Swaziland	Africa
BEIGE	12	9	32	17	31	24	16	18	15	16	18	14	9	23	21	13	27	19
PURPLE	72	36	52	51	51	69	47	69	65	79	74	76	65	63	69	75	71	64
RED	8	48	14	32	17	7	35	12	19	5	6	9	15	9	3	3	2	14
BLUE	5	6	2	0	0	0	2	1	1	0	2	1	10	5	7	9	0	3
ORANGE	2	1	0	0	1	0	0	0	0	0	0	0	1	0	0	0	0	0
GREEN	1	0	0	0	0	0	0	0	0	0	0	0	0	0	0	0	0	0
YELLOW	0	0	0	0	0	0	0	0	0	0	0	0	0	0	0	0	0	0
TURQUOISE	0	0	0	0	0	0	0	0	0	0	0	0	0	0	0	0	0	0

Table 10.3: BeQ results for the rest of the world[b]

	Australia	Philippines	Hong Kong	North America	Canada	Brazil	Peru	Venezuela	Finland	Croatia	Netherlands	Russia	Spain
						South America							
Self Direction	66	21	44	76	89	32	21	19	77	55	79	65	66
Universalism	56	72	69	71	81	49	82	44	79	45	78	71	63
Benevolence	71	68	71	70	73	55	81	58	56	31	71	61	72
Tradition	61	83	85	61	64	59	91	51	57	43	49	71	77
Security	76	81	79	67	71	43	90	43	67	93	65	69	77
Power	45	80	89	44	53	57	92	35	31	56	36	72	36
Conformity	81	83	86	68	78	58	87	49	81	61	69	71	68
Achievement	65	32	45	76	77	44	23	21	78	79	92	71	57
Hedonism	65	42	67	89	81	38	18	49	51	61	67	73	81
Stimulation	66	42	61	67	61	43	23	29	41	42	81	61	71
Collectivistic	87	75	77	57	53	35	70	45	88	54	56	74	73
Uncertainty avoidance	79	33	45	59	67	44	89	23	69	33	51	72	41
Long term focus	80	35	36	75	79	23	12	9	82	16	76	55	34
Indulgence	61	36	51	72	65	39	31	33	74	66	86	49	81
Masculine	42	27	33	85	89	86	12	79	84	78	84	74	36
I-engage	70	59	63	79	82	61	56	50	82	79	88	67	71
Engagement	71	68	66	72	71	62	67	49	75	73	71	70	61

	Australia	Philippines	Hong Kong	North America	Canada	Brazil	Peru	Venezuela	Finland	Croatia	Netherlands	Russia	Spain
BEIGE	2	19	8	1	1	17	19	13	1	7	0	13	34
PURPLE	15	75	68	11	8	33	69	45	8	23	0	39	17
RED	6	6	11	9	12	48	11	42	3	35	13	12	39
BLUE	66	0	9	39	37	2	1	0	23	31	25	35	1
ORANGE	5	0	4	31	32	0	0	0	5	4	29	1	39
GREEN	6	0	0	7	8	0	0	0	57	0	31	0	1
YELLOW	0	0	0	2	2	0	0	0	2	0	1	0	0
TURQUOISE	0	0	0	0	0	0	0	0	1	0	1	0	0

It is clear from the international cultural dynamics comparisons in Table 10.3 that the expressive systems as described by the human niche theory or individualistic cultures as described by Graves[111] have higher scores on self-direction, achievement, hedonism, stimulation and indulgence than sacrificial or collective systems. On the other hand, collective systems constantly measured higher levels of universalism, benevolence, tradition, security, power and conformity.

Long-term focus only occurs within BLUE and ORANGE thinking systems, while PURPLE and BLUE highly avoid uncertainty. In contrast, RED and ORANGE systems have low uncertainty avoidance scores. BLUE and ORANGE are largely underrepresented in Africa, and there are almost no GREEN or YELLOW systems at play in this continent. What should, however, be emphasised, is the high prevalence of BEIGE in Africa. Some international texts suggest that BEIGE is extinct, but it is clear from this research that the percentage of BEIGE in human niches is grossly underestimated. As Viljoen[112] explains, if poverty is solved the manifestation of BEIGE can be radically decreased, however there will always be a larger component of BEIGE in emerging economies than traditionally anticipated. Recent statistics on refugees indicated that 1 out of 113 people on earth is displaced[113]. This provides evidence for the claim of the large percentage of BEIGE in this continent.

The I-engage quotient/score determines the measure to which an individual feels respected, regarded, has resilience and will take personal responsibility for his or her own actions. Viljoen[114] found that the I-engage score correlates significantly with emotional intelligence, and ultimately describes the capacity of the individual to engage and apply his or her human energy at the organisation. From table 10.1 it seems as if countries with collectivistic cultures have significantly lower I-engage scores, whereas countries with more individualistic cultures have higher I-engage quotients.

The overall engagement score, as described by the BeQ, measures the human energy in the system to perform and correlates directly with business results – the higher the human energy to perform, the better the business indicators[115]. To a degree it is meaningless to compare the level of engagement of different countries with each other, because in the end leadership largely creates the culture that impacts on performance[116]. However, as an indicator, it can provide an overall sense of how the country compares to other countries in terms of human energy in the system to perform. Ultimately, it may be helpful to understand the human challenges that leaders are up to when managing in different countries.

A day in the life of a multicultural survey consultant

In this section, auto-ethnographic tales as described by Sparkes[117] are shared. The stories were constructed from field notes during numerous BeQ studies. The purpose of this section is to create awareness of the challenges and pitfalls of conducting multicultural research, and of how easy meaning-making happens from the perspective of the survey consultant. Simultaneously, this part of the chapter highlights the tremendous learning and exposure that can be gained by doing multicultural research.

The case of collective leadership

The author once visited the Geita gold mine, which is situated close to Lake Victoria in Tanzania, to do a culture research study. Typically, such a research process would start with an initial interview with the general manager of the mine. In this case, it was Peter Turner with whom the researcher attempted to conduct an in-depth interview. Since the interview would be of an ethnographical nature, she started with a very generic question. This was somewhere in the lines of: "And how are things going according to your thinking?" Without blinking his eyes, Peter responded with: "You go and have a look into the eyes of my security guard at the gate, and you come and tell me."

The unusual honour of being crowned as a chief in that region of Tanzania was later bestowed on Peter.

At about the same time, in another area of Tanzania, there was a large function for the expatriate general manager who was retiring. On the night of the function, 126 supervisors worked together to steal the untraceable gold powder from the gold room. All the supervisors were imprisoned by the police. No one explained what occurred. Two days later an instruction from high up in parliament instructed the organisation to either reinstitute all the supervisors, or lose their license to operate in the country. The supervisors were back at work within a week. During this time, the author was conducting research there. Very interested in why no one sold out the culprit, she I asked around to find out what had happened. The message from the system was clear: "If the cat is away, the mice will play." The people felt disregarded. They had not been treated with dignity. The collective decided to remind the expatriates that they were guests in the country, and were after all not in control.

Theoretical explanation

The Tanzanian system had a human niche distribution of 96% PURPLE, 2% RED and 2% BLUE. PURPLE people are relational. Peter Turner was seen as respectful. He greeted everyone every time he saw them. He also knew all the employees by name. He even knew something about their families. His human niche was GREEN. The GREEN inclusive worldview is quite congruent with PURPLE thinking structures, hence he was deeply valued by his staff.

In the second case, the PURPLE employees collectively asserted their power to show that they were in control. Disregarding threats of sentencing and dismissal, they stood by each other in executing the shared plan. The gold never surfaced.

The case of an instruction going wrong

The manager of an international research project added a picture of sheriff with a gun to a document that asked for progress feedback. The picture was accompanied with a slogan "give feedback or else". In the South African context, the business leaders responded instantly with feedback, yet the mail led to eight complaints from the Australian operations to the CEO of the organisation; they felt insulted by the threat made by the project manager. The Ghanaian operation simply did not respond to the request. On asking why not, they responded that they experienced disrespect, and would not respond to such a mail.

Theoretical explanation

The human niche distribution for the South African operations of this mining house was strong individualistic ORANGE. For the collective BLUE Australian and collective PURPLE Ghanaian operations, the impact of the mail was insulting and disrespectful. In the BLUE case, a complaint was made to the higher level in the BLUE hierarchy. In the PURPLE case, the collective decided not to respond, nor to share their feelings. From a Hofstede perspective, the South Africans were direct and masculine and the Australians and Ghanaians feminine. In Australia there is mate-ship. In Ghana, the baboon has spoken.[2]

Getting the humour wrong

An extensive research study was done in Tanzania to deal with the cultural integration of contractors and the mine company. The temporary employees were happy to join the full-time service of the mother company, and the employees of the mother company were also very satisfied that their brothers would receive similar benefits. The study did not incorporate multicultural theory or dynamics. An industrial theatre intervention (26 theatre plays) was facilitated to enhance the organisational dynamics. Although a sense of energy was soon felt, the expatriates became very uncomfortable, as it seemed that only the voice of the employees were heard, and not that of management. An effort was made to improve the situation by using humour, but no one laughed when expected. The entire transformational effort was diluted when the general manager left three months after the intervention; he joined a competitor mining house together with eight of the twelve top managers. New management could not deal with the energy that was unleashed lower down in the system by the interventions, which this manifested in industrial relation actions and dissatisfaction. The mine almost became unmanageable, and the author decided never to offer or facilitate industrial theatre interventions again. Little did she know that later, a similar approach that was followed in Ghana, and that was strongly influenced by spiral dynamics, would be viewed as the highlight of her professional career. In Ghana industrial theatre was used again, but this time multicultural theory was considered. The successful transformation of Damang Gold mine in Ghana is documented in the book Inclusive *Organisational Transformation: Human Niches for Africa*. Almost 10 years after the industrial theatre intervention, the locals still refer to the cantata (a local term for a drama) as life-changing.

---

2   The collective is called the Baboon in Ghana (Viljoen, 2014).

Theoretical explanation

When doing multicultural research, it is critical to incorporate the theories described in the first part of this chapter and to be aware of the fine nuances in the way in which social systems make sense of the world around them. In this case, the integrated dynamics of the Tanzanian psyche were not understood. The consultants were left with generic results on which the industrial theatre was constructed; what was meant to be humorous was not seen to be funny at all. The delicate power dynamics between expatriates and locals were misinterpreted (interpreted from a South African perspective) and the theatre eroded the goodwill of the expatriates. The human niche theory could have assisted greatly in understanding the systemic dynamics. In any organisational inquiry process, it is critical to gain the buy-in and support of the management team. In this case, the team left the organisation soon after the interventions with devastating consequences. The new management team could not deal with the energy in the system. Further, the real transformational potential of a well-researched industrial theatre intervention did not manifest, as some of the multicultural dynamics were not described accurately and therefore did not have the optimal impact. The mine struggled to rebalance for the next six years.

Measuring incorrectly

Early in the year 2000, the author of this chapter participated in an international research project with one of the world's largest gold producers. She was still a junior researcher, and a framework of a famous professor was used to determine behaviour-based safety dynamics. The model described how employees felt in terms of respect, support, trust and other climate dynamics. The author was sent as multicultural survey consultant to three mines in Mali. A paper-based questionnaire was administered. It was hard going. The top management team spoke French, and were communistic and fundamentalist Moslem. The local language was Bambara. This is an oral symbolic language that cannot be written. The consultant team had to work with translators who sometimes had to translate from English to French and then to Bambara. The author had to learn the hard way that the construction of French sentences is different to that of English sentences, and that her translator needed her to begin with the second part of the sentences. Typically in her work she used silence in the middle of sentences for effect – a practice that confused the translators.

Mali was then the third poorest country in the world, thus the researcher very soon learned to appreciate their culture. It was her task to give feedback on the findings and to do joint action planning on how to enhance organisational dynamics. The first few days were fruitless; disregarding all her attempts, the groups that she worked with were non-responsive. Soon it became clear that the employees were so collectivistic that during the tea circle after work the group would decide what their collective view would be, and that view would dictate the agenda for the next day. She decided to gate-crash a tea circle, however she was denied the opportunity to join since only males were allowed. The author then began to give homework on the first day for the next day, which enabled her to work with the collective view in the class.

The author soon was called Djenebe Traore, which means that she was viewed as a princess who brought help. To be considered part of the royal family escalated her social standing. That meant that if she paid someone a compliment on, for example, having a nice watch, he had to give it to her or else would seem to be rude. The impact of this on ethics in an organisation is clear.

Working closely with her Malian colleagues, it became quite clear that they had come to wrong conclusions in our research. Statistically, it seemed as if the employees did not trust management, however during the feedback sessions it became very clear that they did indeed trust management – they were simply so fundamentalist that they would never say that they trusted any man. They put their trust in Allah. All efforts of the research team were null and void as they did not consider the multicultural interpretations of an aspect such as trust.

On leaving Mali, the head of the union thanked the author for the value added to their business by saying: "Djenebe, for a woman you spoke sense."

In follow-up work, the author allowed her junior male researcher to do the talking. It was from the same region where years later she spoke to an organising member of Boko Haram who passionately argued that they would not like their daughters to be exposed to American television and schooling systems. The way in which they resolved this issue (by abducting the girls) made more sense to them than my worldview.

Theoretical explanation

This case was first described in the Ashgate book, *Inclusive Organisational Change*[118]. The research methodology did not consider multicultural dynamics; an instrument that was used in banking in South Africa was used in mining in Mali. Our research approach did not describe the social or cultural dynamics, nor did it consider multicultural theory as described in the first part of this chapter. Many dollars were lost as the results did not have face validity. The cost implication for organisations was worse than the actual money spent on the research project. If the employees did not trust management, this attempt would have done more damage than good. The choice of a research team must be influenced by the gender dynamics in a country and the impact of social structures in organisations must not be underestimated. This case created an immense awareness in the author to always consider over-culture and multicultural dynamics when doing research in diverse settings.

The mystery of non-responsive focus groups

The first time that I conducted the BeQ study in two different mines in Australia, all the groups were very non-responsive. The study comprised of a quantitative section in the form of questions that measured on a five-point Likert scale, and a qualitative section that dealt with ended questions. Here descriptive responses were required. In total 32 sessions were conducted where data was gathered in the first year of study, however not one of the open-end questions was answered, and not even a single response was captured.

The BeQ methodology also incorporated feedback sessions in the form of joint action planning sessions. The group was first asked whether the findings made sense to them (to confirm face validity), and then to plan how they could improve the dynamics in their sphere of influence. The human niche theory was incorporated to describe national cultural dynamics. After the initial stage, where there was almost no interaction from the groups, and without being armed with content analysis of the descriptive part, the author again expected the groups to be reserved during the feedback sessions. To her surprise, a warm and enthusiastic conversation followed the initial quantitative feedback. The breakthrough came when sharing the multicultural dynamics, and the sessions turned out to be fulfilling and meaningful.

Theoretical explanation

The psyche of the Australian research participants was largely BLUE. They felt that they understood their reality better than South Africans, and found it very patronising that a person from another country could come and tell them where to improve. However, their culture could also be described as feminine[119]. They shy away from conflict, and therefore would rather be quiet than disagree in public. The feminine side in their psyche is quite accommodating. As the research described these aspects of their culture accurately, they did not feel judged or criticised; they rather felt understood and respected. They thoroughly enjoyed seeing the implications of the way in which they did business. In years to come long essays were written in the open question section and the work there was valuable – both from a research and from a cultural perspective.

BLUE is an efficient and reliable thinking niche that considers long-term implications on the collective. It is risk adverse. In BLUE systems, Viljoen[120] explains, all goes well if you do what the collective wants. It is a polite, decent thinking system where issues that are threatening are not discussed in open forums, and the best foot is put forward to strangers. The realisation that the researchers suspended their own thinking to truly emerge themselves in the way in which Australians organise and create meaning, led to inclusion of the research team into the midst of the Australians. It transcended both the researchers and them. The face validity of the BeQ instrument, as well as the acknowledgement that nations are different, resulted in a long-standing and satisfying working relationship between the Australian mines and the researchers.

Everything is not always how it seems

Sometimes multicultural survey consultants try too hard. Initially, when working in Ghana, concept cards were used as a way of stimulating conversation. The participants were asked to choose a phrase card that best described how they felt, but this did not yield the rich data that was anticipated. Only on understanding that Ghanaians are largely PURPLE and therefore skilled at using metaphors and stories, was the data-gathering technique was adapted to be more relational and appreciative, and was conducted in the form of storytelling. The insights gained from this study impacted positively and permanently on the researcher's life.

Another example of everything not always being how it seems was experienced in Hong Kong. On face value Hong Kong employees appear to be BLUE and ORANGE. They have a long-term vision, are integrated in the most recent technology, wear the most famous brand-name clothes, handbags and shoes, and are permanently on the world-wide web. Doing extensive BeQ studies in this space confirmed, however, that most members the sample group were PURPLE. Rituals are in the order of the day, ancestor worship is happening daily, elders are deeply respected, and the face of seniors is publicly saved. In understanding the real underlying belief in a system, not only did the employees feel understood and listened to when feedback was provided, but management of organisations were provided with valuable information on how to deal with people dynamics in their companies.

Lost in translation

The BeQ was translated from English into Afrikaans, Sotho, Xhosa and Zulu. The language departments of local universities were used for this purpose, but it became very clear that not everyone that spoke Sotho, Xhosa or Zulu could read their academic versions. Further, most participants asked us to translate the questions into Afrikaans or English. Not all the languages described the constructs in the same way. The BeQ was also translated into French, Spanish and Mandarin, however European Spanish is not the same as Peruvian Spanish. It is advisable that a local person assist with translation into written form, as the value of a local language specialist to assist in the translation of a questionnaire cannot be underestimated.

During a session in Ghana one of the translators was also a union member, but the research team was unaware of this. During the data-gathering phase, the passion in the voice of the translator and the questions discussed were not congruent, so that the researcher asked the head of department to also translate for her. It became clear that the union member was trying to influence the results. Moving forward, the researcher always chose a neutral employee upfront, and from the start involved him or her in the research design, trained them in the research methodology, and ensured that all the constructs were well understood and that no additional personal reflections were shared during translation.

A few years ago, the author dealt with a difficult cultural integration in Peru. On introducing her to the various focus groups, everyone giggled. Her translator, George, just shook his head when she asked him why they reacted in that way. Three weeks later, on completion of the last session, George told her that her name had an alternative meaning, not to be mentioned here, in that environment. On consecutive trips to Peru, the author introduced herself as Ricky. Even a person's name may be a stumbling block in getting entry into a research setting.

Africa is not for sissies

Doing research in Africa is often not for the faint-hearted. Some of the Ghanaian mines are situated just above the equator. In summer the temperature reaches 48 degrees Celsius and humidity levels measure 98%. This is malaria world. Doing research in such a setting requires the researcher to be available at shift changes, which are often early in the morning and very late at night. Mali, Nigeria and the DRC have similar weather conditions. During one such a session under African skies, with just a damaged grass roof between them and a massive African storm in Mali, the author's co-researcher continuously pushed her around. The author was totally invested in the group dynamics, and became slightly irritated with her colleague. She did not realise that the minute she stood still spiders dropped from the roof. Her co-researcher was gently moving her out of the way of the approaching spiders.

In PURPLE cultures, it is important to first ask the permission from the local chief or elders in the village before one physically starts with the work. In that way, the social structure supports the research efforts. In these cultures, it is considered rude not to eat what is served. The author ended up reluctantly eating snakes, spiders, raw fish and guinea pigs. It is important for ethnographical researchers to emerge themselves in the culture that they study, and to request support for the research from the local chiefs or elders in the social system.

Malaria mosquitos are most active during the early morning and at dawn. It is also the time of the day when most shifts change. The author once asked a 32-year old Ghanaian if he ever had malaria. He burst out in uncontrollable laughter. Later he explained that he probably had malaria the same number of times that she had flu. She had made a wrong assumption based on her own living truth and sounded quite foolish. She ended up by getting malaria three times.

When cultures collide

Weber and Camerer[121] stressed the importance of cultural integration during mergers and acquisitions, while Aon Hewitt[122] identified cultural integration issues as the second most important direct driver of why efforts to join systems and/or organisations fail. In the South African context, Barclays started to disinvest in the African market in 2015 due to conflicting risk profiles of the United Kingdom and those of the African continent. Gold Fields disinvested in South Africa during 2012 as the country was viewed as a high-risk labour environment. A clear understanding of multicultural dynamics upfront, before a company extends its footprint into a new operating environment, should not only inform the due diligence process, but can provide valuable information to leadership on how to optimise dynamics in the multicultural environment.

The magic of mother Africa

Emerging oneself as multicultural survey consultant in emerging economical settings or PURPLE-environments is a life-changing experience. The ethnographical insights gained, lessons from the elders on how they survived over decades, and how to operate when there are hardly any resources or options available, are truly insightful. A lot of goodwill can be gained by learning how to communicate a bit in the local language. Suspending own assumptions are critical to allow oneself to see and experience what is actually happening in another cultural setting. In exposing oneself to African wisdom, the beauty of PURPLE (as described by Laubscher, Viljoen and Laubscher[123]), namely soulfulness, belonging and relatedness are experienced – a sense of being that will follow the author for the rest of her life.

The multicultural researcher

Cross, Bazon, Dennis and Isaacs[124] conceptualise cultural competence on a continuum that moves from cultural destructiveness to cultural incapacity, to cultural blindness, to cultural pre-competence, to cultural competence and ultimately cultural proficiency. The cross-cultural researcher should ideally display high levels of cultural competence. Dolan and Kawamura[125] describe habits that can be acquired to develop cross-cultural mind sets. These habits include the acceptance of ambiguity, the acceptance of differences, security in one's own culture, suspension of judgement and the desire to learn from others, interest in people, communication skills, a spirit of curiosity and creativity, emotional intelligence, a sense of humour and an interest in context and process. The multicultural survey consultants should also develop these habits to be an effective researcher. Other skills that consultants should develop are discussed in Chapter 1.

CONCLUSION

In this chapter the author presented various theoretical approaches to describe multicultural dynamics. Grounded Theory, integrated with systems thinking, is positioned as research methodology that adequately deals with the dynamics and complexity of doing multicultural research. Systems thinking methodology is uniquely integrated to visually describe systems dynamics in multicultural settings. The BeQ and narrative stories are used as data-gathering methods to provide rich data of not only individual, but also cultural dynamics in social systems. The chapter concludes with a comparison of findings form different multicultural environments where the BeQ was used extensively to describe systemic dynamics. The author hopes that this chapter leaves the reader with not only an awareness of the gifts that conducting ethnographical research provides, but also stimulates interest in conducting multicultural research in more than a quantitative way.

REFERENCES

Ackoff RL. 2003. Iconoclastic management authority, advocates a "systemic" approach to innovation. Strategy & Leadership. 31(3): 19-26.

Aon Hewitt. 2013. *Cultural Integration and why it fails*. Available on: http://www.gethppy.com/employee-engagement/why-most-cultural-integrations-in-ma-fail [Accessed on 13/08/2016].

Beck, D. 2013. *The Master Code. Spiral Dynamics Integral Accreditation*. Course notes. Santa Barbara: Adizes Business School.

Beck, DE & Cohen, CC. 1996. *Spiral dynamics: mastering values, leadership, and change*. Cambridge:Blackwell.

Blumer, KP. 1969. *Symbolic interactionism: perspective & method*. Englewood Cliffs, New Jersey: Prentice Hall.

Biblikova, A & Kotelnikov, V. 2002. *Managing cross cultural differences. Ten-3 Business Ecoach*. Available online at: http://ventures.powweb.com/business_guide/crosscuttings/crosscultural_differences.html [Accessed on 07/03/16].

Breuer, J & Freud, S. 1955. Studies in hysteria. In *The standard edition of the complete psychological works of Sigmund Freud*, 2. Edited by J Strachey. London: Hogarth Press: 1-307.

Capek, ME & Mead, M. 2006. *Effective philanthropy organizational success through deep diversity and gender equality.* California: MIT Press: 1-3.

Charmaz, K. 2006. *Constructing Grounded Theory: A Practical Guide through Qualitative Analysis.* 1st edition. London: Sage Publications Ltd.

Chemers, MM, Oskamp, S & Costanzo, MA. (eds). 1995. *Diversity in organizations: new perspectives for a changing workplace.* California: Sage Publications.

Chung, WVL. 1997. *Ethnicity and organizational diversity.* London: University Press of America.

Corbin, J. 1991. Anselm Strauss: an intellectual biography, in *Social organization and social process: essays in honor of Anselm Strauss,* edited by DR Maines. New York: Aldine de Gruyter: 7-44.

Creswell, J. 1994. *Research design: qualitative & quantitative approaches.* Thousand Oaks, CA: Sage.

Cross, L, Bazron, BJ, Dennis, KWD & Isaacs, MR. 1989. *Towards a cultural competent system of care.* Available online at https://www.ncjrs.gov/App/publications/abstract.aspx?ID=124939 [Accessed on 13//05/2016].

Corbin, J & Strauss, A. 1990. Grounded Theory Research: Procedures, Canoncs and Evaluative Criteria. *Zeitschrift fur Soziologie,* 19(7): 418-427.

Cox, T. 2002. Taking diversity to the next level. *Executive Excellence,* 19:19.

Dolan, SL & Kawamura, KM. 2015. *Cross Cultural Competence, A Field Guide for Developing Global Leaders and Managers.* Bingley: Emerald Group.

Ellis, C. 2004. *The ethnographical I.* Walnut Creek: CAL AltaMira Press

Freud, S. 1964. *Jokes and their relationship to the unconscious,* New York: Norton.

Glaser, B. 1992. *Basics of grounded theory analysis.* Mill Valley, CA: Sociology Press.

Glaser, BG. 1998. *Doing grounded theory: issues and discussions.* Sociology Press: 254.

Glaser, B & Strauss, A. 1967. *The discovery research.* New York: Aldine de Gruyter

Graves, C. 1974. Human nature prepares for a momentous leap. *The Futurist,* April: 72-87.

Global Competitiveness Report. 2004. *World Economic Forum* http://www.weforum.org/en/initiatives/gcp/Global%20Competitiveness%20Report/index.htm [Accessed on 07/07/14].

Goulding, C. 2002. *Grounded theory: a practical guide for management, business and market researchers,* London: Sage Publications Ltd.

Hall, E. 1983. *The dance of life: The other dimension of time.* New York: Doubleday.

Harrison, NE. 2000. *Constructing sustainable development.* Albany: SUNY Press.

Hofstede, G. 1984. *Culture's consequences: international differences in work-related values.* Beverly Hills: Sage.

Hofstede, G. 1991. *Cultures and organizations: software of the mind.* New York: McGraw-Hill.

Hofstede, G. 1996. *Images of Europe: past, present and future,* edited by P. Joynt & M. Warner: 147-165.

Holcomb-McCoy, CC & Meyers, JE. 1999. Multicultural competencies and counselor training: a national survey. *Journal of Counseling and Development,* 77: 294-300.

Hughes, JL. 1956. Expressed personality needs as predictors of sales success. *Personnel psychology,* 9: 347-357.

Jackson, T. 2004. *Cross-cultural theory and methods: management and change in Africa.* London: Routledge.

James, P. 2006. *Globalism, Nationalism, Tribalism: Bringing Theory Back In,* London: Sage Publications.

Jung, CG. 1954. On the Nature of the Psyche. 1988 edition, in H Read, et al. (eds.). *The Collected Works of CG. Jung* (vol. 8). Princeton: Princeton University Press (original work published 1948).

Kelle, U. 1995. *Theories as heuristic tools in qualitative research, in openness in research: the tension between self and other,* edited by I Maso, PA Atkinson, S Delamont & JC Verhoeven. Assen: Van Gorcum: 33-50.

Kets De Vries MFR. 2001. *The leadership mystique.* London: Prentice Hall.

Laubscher, LI. 2013. *Human Niches: Spiral Dynamics for Africa.* Available at http://www.mandalaconsulting.co.za/Documents/Thesis%20 %20Loraine%20Laubscher.pdf [Accessed on 15/08/2016].

LeBarOn, M. 2005. *Bridging cultural conflicts: a new approach for a changing world.* San Francisco:Jossey-Bass.

Lessem, R & Schieffer, A. 2010. *Integral Research and Innovation: Transforming Enterprise and Society.* Farnham: Gower Ashgate.

Lessem, R & Schieffer, A. 2015. *Integral Polity*. Farnham: Gower Ashgate.

Lofland J & Lofland LH. 1984. *Analyzing social settings: a guide to qualitative observation and analysis*. 2nd edition. Belmont, CA: Wadsworth.

Nienaber, H & Martins, N. 2015. *Employee Engagement in South Africa*. Randburg: Knowledge Resources.

Nunnally, JC. 1978. Assessment of Reliability. In: *Psychometric Theory*. 2nd edition. New York: McGraw-Hill.

Patton, MQ. 2001. *Qualitative Research & Evaluation Methods*. 3rd edition. London: Sage Publications, Inc.

Sandelowski, M. 1995. Aesthetics of qualitative research. *Image*, 27: 205-209.

Schurink, WJ. 2004a. *Lecture Two: Qualitative Research and its Utilization in Management Studies. Qualitative Research: Introducing Key Features of An Interpretive Approach To Social Science Research*, University of Johannesburg, 19 January 2005. Waterkloof Glen, Pretoria.

Schutte, PC. 2004. *Employee satisfaction and customer service: a literature perspective*. Johannesburg: IGH. Unpublished.

Schwartz, P. 2003. The racism of diversity. *Capitalism Magazine*, 12(15). http://www.capmag.com/article. asp?ID=3399 [Accessed on 07/03/15].

Senge, PM. 2003. Creating desired futures in a global economy: reflections. The SOL. *Journal on Knowledge, Learning and Change*. Cambridge: The Society for Organizational Learning.

Sparkes, AC. 2000. Autoethnography and narratives of self: reflections on criteria in action. *Sociology of Sport Journal*, 17: 21-41.

Sparkes, AC. 2007. Embodiment, academics, and the audit culture: a story seeking consideration. *Qualitative Research*, 7(24): 521-50.

Strauss, A & Corbin, J. 1998. *Basics of Qualitative Research : Techniques and Procedures for Developing Grounded Theory*, {SAGE Publications}. Available at: http://www.amazon.ca/exec/obidos/redirect?tag=citeulike09-20&path=ASIN/0803959400 [Accessed September 12, 2013].

Strauss, A. 1990. *Creating sociological awareness*. New Brunswick: Transaction Publishing.

Strauss, A. 1987. *Qualitative analysis for social scientists*. Cambridge, England: Cambridge University Press.

Sumner, T & Shum, SB. 1998. From documents to discourse: shifting conceptions of scholarly publishing, in *Human Factors in Computing Systems*. Los Angeles: ACM Press. 4: 18-23.

Thomas, RR. 1996. *Redefining diversity*. New York: American Management Association.

Thorne, S. 2000. *Data analysis in qualitative research*. Vancouver: School of Nursing, University of British Columbia.

Triandis, HC, Dunnette, M & Hough, L. (eds). 1994. *Handbook of industrial and organizational psychology*. 4. Palo Alto: Consulting Psychologists Press.

UNHCR. 2016. *United Nations Refugee Agency*. Available online at http://www.unhcr.org/news/latest/2016/6/5763b65a4/global-forced-displacement-hits-record-high.html [Accessed on 13 January 2017].

Viljoen, RC. 2012. Africa is not for sissies. *Da Vinci Institute for Innovation and Technology Newsletter.* December. Modderfontein.

Viljoen, RC. 2014. *Inclusive Organisational Transformation: An African Approach*. Farnham: Gower Ashgate.

Viljoen, RC. 2015a. *Organisational Change and Development: an African perspective*. Randburg: Knowledge Resources.

Viljoen, RC. 2015b. Engagement in diverse workspaces: An African and international application, in *Employee Engagement in South Africa*, edited by H Nienaber & N Martins. Randburg: Knowledge Resources.

Viljoen, RC & Laubscher, LI. 2015a. Spiral dynamics integral, in Lessem, R, Schieffer, A (eds.). (2015) *Integral Polity*. Farnham: Gower Ashgate.

Viljoen, RC & Laubscher, LI. 2015. African spirituality. Insights from the cradle of mankind. In Spiller, C & Wolfgramm, R (eds.). *Indigenous spiritualties at work: Transforming the spirit of business enterprise*. Charlotte: Information Age Publishing.

Viljoen-Terblanche, RC. 2008. *Sustainable organisational transformation through Inclusivity.* www://uir.unisa. ac.za/bitstream/handle/10500/726/?sequence=2. [Accessed on 31 July 2013].

Trompenaars, F. 1994. *Riding the waves of culture: understanding diversity in global business.* Burr Ridge: Irwin.

Weber, RA & Camerer, CF. 2013. *Cultural Conflict and Merger Failure: An Experimental Approach.* Available online at https://people.hss.caltech.edu/~camerer/mgtsci03.pdf [Accessed on 13/06/2016].

ENDNOTES

1. Hofstede, 1984.
2. Graves, 1974; Beck, 2013; Laubscher, 2013 and Viljoen, 2014, 2015a.
3. Ackoff, 2003.
4. LeBaron, 2005.
5. Viljoen, 2015b.
6. Holcomb-McCoy & Meyers, 1999.
7. LeBaron, 2005.
8. LeBaron, 2005.
9. Viljoen-Terblanche, 2008.
10. Sumner & Shum, 1998.
11. Laubscher, 2013.
12. Senge, 2005.
13. Viljoen-Terblanche, 2008.
14. Sparkes, 2007.
15. Viljoen & Laubscher, 2015b.
16. Global Competitiveness Report, 2014.
17. Graves, 1974 & Beck, 2013.
18. Triandis, Dunnette & Hough, 1994.
19. Cox, 2002.
20. Hofstede, 1984, 1991 and 1996.
21. Jung, 1953.
22. Viljoen, 2016.
23. Trompenaars, 1994.
24. Chemers, Oskamp & Costanzo, 1995.
25. Kets de Vries, 2001.
26. De Vries, 2001.
27. Hall, 1983.
28. Shwartz, 2012.
29. Schwartz, 2003.
30. Jung, 1953.
31. Biblikova & Kotelnikov, 2002.
32. Viljoen & Laubscher, 2015b.
33. Viljoen & Laubscher, 2015b.
34. Mead, 1901-1978.
35. LeBaron, 2005.
36. Cox, 2002; Chung, 1997.
37. Viljoen, 2014.
38. Cohen, 1996.
39. Graves, 1974.
40. Beck, 2013.
41. Laubscher, 2013.
42. Graves, 1974.
43. Beck, 2013.
44. Laubscher & Viljoen, 2014.
45. Graves, 1974.
46. Laubscher, 2013.
47. Beck, 2013; Laubscher, 2013; Viljoen, 2015a.
48. Viljoen, 2016.
49. Beck & Cohen, 1996.
50. Viljoen & Laubscher, 2015b.
51. Viljoen & Laubscher, 2015b.
52. Viljoen, 2015a.
53. Harrison, 1990.
54. Viljoen & Laubscher, 2015a.
55. Glaser, 1988, 1992.
56. Strauss, 1987.
57. Strauss, 1987.
58. Thomas, 1966; Hughes, 1965 and Blumer, 1969.
59. Strauss, 1987.
60. Glaser, 1988, 1992.
61. Ackoff, 2003.
62. Viljoen, 2015a.
63. Charmaz, 2006: 10.
64. Lessem & Schieffer, 2010.
65. Schurinck, 2012.
66. Viljoen, 2012.
67. James, 2006.
68. James, 2006.
69. Corbin & Strauss, 1990: 99.
70. Ackoff, 2003.
71. Glaser, 1992.
72. Charmaz, 2006.
73. Charmaz, 2006.
74. Blumer, 1969.
75. Kelle, 2005.
76. Kelle, 2005: 15.
77. Strauss & Corbin, 1998: 12.

78. Charmaz, 2006: 2.
79. Sandelowski, 1995.
80. Patton, 1990: 434.
81. Goulding 2002: 71.
82. Lessem & Schieffer, 2010; Viljoen, 2014; Booysens, 2015.
83. Viljoen-Terblanche, 2008.
84. Viljoen-Terblanche, 2008.
85. Sparkes, 2000.
86. Schurink, 2004.
87. Viljoen, 2016.
88. Viljoen, 2015a.
89. Strauss, 1990; Corbin, 1991.
90. Strauss & Corbin, 1998.
91. Charmaz, 2006; Viljoen-Terblanche, 2008.
92. Glaser, 1988.
93. Viljoen-Terblanche, 2008.
94. Glaser, 1998.
95. Charmaz, 2006.
96. Charmaz, 2006.
97. Lofland & Lofland, 1984.
98. Creswell, 1994.
99. Thorne, 2000.
100. Charmaz, 2006: 182.
101. Glaser & Strauss, 1967, Glaser, 1978; Glaser, 1998.
102. Ellis, 2004: 123.
103. Breuer & Freud, 1955.
104. Viljoen-Terblanche, 2008.
105. Viljoen, 2015b.
106. Charmaz, 2006.
107. Nunnaly, 1978.
108. Viljoen & Laubscher, 2015a.
109. Graves, 1974; Beck, 2013.
110. Viljoen, 2015a.
111. Graves, 1974.
112. Viljoen, 2015a.
113. United Nations Refugee Agency, 2016.
114. Viljoen, 2015a.
115. Viljoen, 2015a.
116. Schutte, 2004; Viljoen-Terblanche, 2008; Viljoen, 2015a.
117. Sparkes, 2007.
118. Viljoen, 2014a.
119. Hofstede, 1996.
120. Viljoen, 2014.
121. Weber & Camerer, 2003.
122. Hewitt, 2011.
123. Laubscher, 2013; Viljoen & Laubscher, 2015a.
124. Cross, Bazon, Dennis & Isaacs, 1989.
125. Dolan & Kawamura, 2015: 125.

CHAPTER 11

THE ORGANISATIONAL AND PSYCHOLOGICAL IMPACT OF ORGANISATIONAL DIAGNOSIS

by **Claude-Hélène Mayer & Aden-Paul Flotman**

INTRODUCTION

This chapter provides insights into the organisational and psychological impact of organisational diagnosis. Firstly, it refers to the significance of organisational diagnosis, its nature and role, and its influence as an intervention. In the next section, the psychological impact of organisational diagnosis is described, taking the organisational participants, the consultant-employee relationship, and the organisational system into account. In this context, the chapter deals with themes of risk and change and their management with regard to organisational diagnosis. Furthermore, it refers to the consultant as a diagnostic tool in organisational diagnosis and the concepts of transference and counter-transference from a psychoanalytical perspective. Finally, some guiding questions for diagnostic reflection are provided for practitioners in the field and a few concluding remarks are made.

Organisations are expected to survive and thrive in an environment which is increasingly characterised by competition, uncertainty, turbulence and change[1]. Change is normal, inevitable and even necessary. In this ambiguous and ambivalent environment, organisations should have the inherent capability, responsiveness and resilience to adapt to new situations in an almost effortless and seamless fashion. Early on, organisational analysts and consultants[2] emphasised the importance of understanding organisations as living systems before attempting to intervene in them, hence the importance of conducting a proper, comprehensive organisational diagnostic intervention. Any form of assumption, judgement and desire regarding the functioning of the organisation needs to be suspended until a comprehensive analysis (by collecting historical, factual and interpretive data) has been conducted.

A turbulent business context compels organisations not only to be responsive, but also to engage in the most appropriate actions at the most opportune time. Organisations, therefore, have to take up the challenge of conducting speedy and regular organisational diagnostic interventions. However, this process is often fraught with risk, challenges and unintended consequences. The psychological impact of organisational diagnosis as an intervention is subsequently explored, but first, the significance of organisational diagnosis, the nature of organisations, and the purposive nature of diagnosis are discussed.

THE SIGNIFICANCE OF ORGANISATIONAL DIAGNOSIS

Organisational diagnosis has always been and still remains a critical issue in organisational development in general and in change management in particular. Effective diagnosis is dependent on the assumptions of the survey consultant regarding the nature and dynamics of an organisation. Next, the significance of organisational diagnosis pertaining to the nature of organisations, its role and organisational diagnosis as a purposive intervention are explored.

The nature of organisations

Our philosophical and theoretical assumptions about what constitutes organisations as well as our understanding of the purpose of the intervention often determine the rest of the diagnostic process. According to Morgan[3], researchers and survey consultants often fail to appreciate the rich diversity and multidimensionality of organisations, and consequently the temptation is to focus on one perspective, reality or lens through which the organisation is viewed. Organisations are then approached as static instead of dynamic realities. Theories and organisational models are useful tools (also see chapters 1 and 3) in the hands of survey consultants, because it facilitates their understanding and the action that should be taken within this organisational reality[4]. However, in the simplification of the organisational reality, the survey consultant could end up with a one-sided view or an inaccurate picture of the organisation. Hence the saying, "If you have only a hammer in your toolbox, all problems will look like nails".

Some organisational consultants have been propagating a more systemic, psychological and psychodynamic view of organisational reality with an emphasis on the psychological and emotional nature of organisations[5]. Levinson cited in Van Tonder[6] draws attention to the emotional and psychological nature of modern-day organisations by suggesting the following:

1. Organisations mirror family structures and develop out-groups (who will be alienated) and in-groups (characterised by narcissistic tendencies).
2. Organisations follow leaders, and despite differences in leadership styles over time, the founding father's philosophies and practices often remain in the DNA of the organisation.
3. Organisations will always experience change. As a result of an attachment to objects, people and practices, change is experienced as a "loss" to be mourned in the interest of healthy adaptive practices.

The emotional nature of organisational life often results in heightened levels of shame, fear, anxiety, envy and greed. The denial of this component of organisational life could lead to inaccurate diagnoses and the failure of organisational development interventions. The presence of emotion or affect at the core of organisations needs to be acknowledged, especially during the diagnostic phase. Next the role of diagnosis and its purposive nature are explored.

The role of effective diagnosis

Organisational diagnosis has been approached and conceptualised from a number of perspectives. Beer and Spector[7], for example, stress the balance between what is functional and what could be regarded as dysfunctional when defining organisational diagnosis as a "process that helps an organization to highlight its capabilities and change the non-functional aspects of its culture and behavior paths as the basis for ... effectiveness and continuous improvement".

Other scholars like Beckhard[8] regard diagnosis as an intervention that results in the provision of information about predefined elements of the organisation. However, organisational diagnosis is generally regarded as one technique for the improvement of organisational performance[9], and the most suitable intervention for the future development of an organisation[10]. In addition, it should be a "whole-system evaluation" process[11].

In this chapter the authors define organisational diagnosis as a recursive process characterised by immersion, collaborative sense-making and interaction between client system and practitioner, aimed at understanding the current functioning of the organisational system and possible determinants of this distinctive way of functioning through the collection of valid, pertinent, manifest and latent data.

Purposive diagnosis: Organisational diagnosis as intervention

Organisational diagnosis is not the flavour of the month; it is an intervention aimed at a specific purpose (see chapter 1). It is initiated with top management's admission that there is a problem to be solved, an expectation to be fulfilled, or a need to be addressed[12]. Generally, from an organisational development perspective, organisational diagnosis is embarked upon in the interest of *improving organisational effectiveness*. It then involves the assessment or diagnosis of the organisation's current level of functioning in order to design appropriate change interventions. From a *change management* perspective, Janićijević[13] contends that diagnosis should essentially address the shortcomings of the organisation. Therefore, the purpose of the intervention would be aimed at answering the following questions: Why should the organisation change? What should the content of change include? In other words, what should be changed in the organisation? It also provides stakeholders with useful information for *general decision-making*. According to Smith[14] this includes:

> "...feedback to organizational members have a critical role in assessing employee's attitudes, training needs, diagnosing organizational situations, and motivating organization members so that they constitute an important research tool in developing and maintaining effective organizations."

Through the diagnostic process the consultant enters into the organisational system, which will have an inevitable psychological impact on employees and the organisation as a system. Next, the psychological impact of this entry is explored.

THE PSYCHOLOGICAL IMPACT OF ORGANISATIONAL DIAGNOSIS ON EMPLOYEES

Organisational interventions, such as diagnosis, can be extremely daunting, disruptive and threatening to the emotional life of the employee and the organisation, as well as to the existing power relationships in the workplace. Organisational analysts working from a psychodynamic perspective claim that entering the client system is a psychodynamic activity with unconscious elements operating inside and between consultants and the client system[15]. Organisational analysts such as Diamond[16] propose that:

> "...without the concept of unconscious processes, consultants work at a manifest and superficial level of structure and strategy without understanding the psychological meaning of these perpetuated structures and strategies and thereby without a lens for interpreting irrational and dysfunctional practices."

Organisational diagnosis is therefore an active and psychological process through which the consultant interacts and collects data from various areas in the client system. This data collection process could take the form of interviews, focus groups, surveys, or observation. A solid, trusting working relationship with the client system is imperative to effective diagnosis. Various dynamics of this relationship are subsequently explored.

Impact on the employee-consultant relationship

It is important for consultants to be aware of and attempt to suspend their preconceived ideas, methodologies and inferences about the client system. As analysts we all have our favourite tools, interventions and approaches to diagnosis. The client system can detect if consultants have already reached a conclusion regarding the functioning of their system, which this could have an adverse effect on the consultant-client system relationship. An effective working relationship with the client system is critical during every phase of the diagnostic process. Poor relationships could result in inaccurate and irrelevant information, and perhaps even the deliberate fabrication of information (sabotage).

When entering a client system, one enters into a "psychological contract" with employees. A good relationship is built on clarifying the purpose of the intervention and exploring mutual expectations. Cummings and Worley[17] provide a series of questions that could form the core of the diagnostic contract and relationship with the client:

1. Who am I?
2. Why am I here and what am I doing?
3. Who do I work for?
4. What do I want from you and why?
5. How will I protect your confidentiality?
6. Who will have access to the data?
7. What is in it for you?
8. Can I be trusted?

These questions need to be satisfactorily answered by the consultant because they will influence the psychological and emotional disposition of the client system. Failure to do this would inevitably result in growing insecurity and uncertainty, fear and anxieties, and crippling distrust between the consultant and employees. Burnes and Cooke[18] suggest that an honest and trusting relationship with the client system would ensure that the primary objectives of diagnosis are achieved, namely:

1. To obtain data about the health and current functioning of the organisation.
2. To galvanise positive energy emanating from the belief that change is possible.
3. To nurture collaborative relationships to sustain the change effort.

It is, therefore, evident that organisational analysts and other practitioners can easily be influenced and manipulated in the modern-day organisational crucible of ever-changing needs, increased expectations and assumptions, instant gratification and an insatiable need for organisational action. These practices and multiple relationships leave consultants open to collusion with the client system[19]. We can, therefore, conclude that organisational survey consultants need to be cognisant of the following:

1. Effective knowledge and understanding of the organisation requires the consultant to "immerse" herself/himself into the client system (experience from the inside).
2. Practitioners must be aware of how they are emotionally and psychologically "received" and "used" by various dimensions of the client system[20].
3. The conscious and unconscious investment employees and the rest of the organisational system have made in terms of relationships (and relatedness) with the organisation and its leadership[21] – they are, therefore, prepared to fight to maintain the status quo.
4. Organisational interventions often involve feelings of pain in the form of uncertainty, the dislodging of attachments to procedures, structures and routines, and subsequent feelings of loss as a result of this change.
5. We need to attend to the emotional component of change by being aware of potential defensive reactions (a form of resistance/sabotage) to change by allowing employees to mourn this loss and provide effective (good enough) containment during this period of emotional disruption[22].
6. Consultants must be able to distinguish between their personal defensive inclinations (what is going on in my guts) and repressive processes on the one hand, and the internal object relations of the client on the other.
7. Consultants must also be aware of issues of transference and counter-transference which could make them vulnerable and render their work ineffective (this phenomenon is further explored in section 11.4.1).
8. Consulting for large organisational systems could place consultants in an extremely powerful position, thus they need to be aware of their own narcissistic tendencies when working in and with such a system.

9. It is advisable for organisational consultants to identify a second party to help them to regularly process their personal internal object relations.

10. Since consultants often assume that they can conduct any kind of consultation, irrespective of their skill-set, it is recommended that they reflect on and are aware of their applicable skills to ensure an optimal consultation. Relevant skills would include, intra-personal, inter-personal, diagnostic and relationship-building skills.

Next, the impact of the diagnostic process on the organisational system as a whole is discussed.

The impact of organisational diagnostics on the organisational system

Organisational diagnosis – as we have described it before – is a process which supports an organisational system to enhance its capacity to assess and change dysfunctional aspects to improve organisational development, effectiveness and learning[23]. It is seen as a valuable technique for creating and sustaining a competitive advantage[24] by having the organisation's health diagnosed[25]. The survey consultant therefore views the organisation as an entire system operating on a micro, meso and macro level.

Gallagher[26] has developed an organisational diagnosis approach which includes six primary elements of the system, namely:

1. *Vision* (goals, primary task, core, values, etc).
2. *People* (competence and commitment for the job and teamwork, type of people, satisfaction with the job and the organisation).
3. *Dynamics* (managing change and stability, trust and climate).
4. *Structures and processes* (adequate and appropriate resources for the task, eg technology, architecture, spaces, etc. for effective information flow, problem-solving, planning, conflict, etc. teams to carry out needed tasks, effective linkages and cooperation between subsystems).
5. *Leadership* (ability to think and manage strategically, stay in touch and enable the environment, to set direction and enable movement).
6. *Environment* (forces and trends external to the organisation that impact on the organisation (society or larger organisational system of which the organisation is part).

The application of such an organisational diagnosis process is not without risk, and the required skills and abilities to deal with it on different system levels are described in the following section.

Risks and dealing with risks

Organisational diagnosis usually brings about different reactions and challenges on various levels of the organisation, which might even be perceived as risks. It requires a serious consideration of different levels of the environment (societal levels), the organisation (structure, culture, elements, etc. and the organisational participants over a significant period of time[27].

Diagnosis usually brings risks to an organisation, particularly when the organisation is characterised by simplistic and superficial approaches, uses individual blame to excuse mismanagement, blames mismanagement on bureaucracy, or views itself as a space where only the fittest can survive[28]. In such a case organisational diagnosis can become an increased risk for the organisation. Organisations that explore new markets and investment possibilities usually require a greater tolerance for risk and failure than organisations that do not explore as much[29]. Particularly for organisations which are based on a strict bureaucracy, risk-taking becomes a problem. Their organisational cultures are often averse to risk and error, which means that they usually resist new and different ideas. They rate control higher than action and loyalty higher than innovation, and provide a small number of managers with authority[30]. Organisational diagnostics can also contribute to a heightened awareness of organisational culture, structures and processes, and then help to find interventions to handle change. In such a case risks decrease and organisations stabilise. An example would be Eskom whose organisational culture has been described as a barrier to knowledge sharing[31], yet it has to remain agile and competitive within a very competitive and turbulent global market.

At the same time, the process of organisational diagnosis can impact on the micro level of organisational dynamics by helping the management of the organisation to accept that challenges exist within the organisation[32]. This openness on the level of the organisational participants can lead to the identification of problems and challenges on the surface of the organisation, which might lead to the search for underlying systemic problems through the use of diagnostic data and collection techniques[33]. However, this in-depth search might lead to anxieties or the perception of threat and risk within the organisation, as explained below.

Change as a threat to current organisational dynamics

It has been pointed out that organisational diagnosis is particularly important with regard to organisational development and change within an organisation[34]. Cobb[35] emphasises four areas (ie environment, culture, structure and process) with regard to the macroanalysis and diagnostics to successfully implement change within organisations. Accordingly, organisational diagnosis responds to three questions, namely "Why?" (the causes of change), "How?" (process of change) and "What?" (content of change) should change within organisations?[36] Organisational diagnosis primarily responds to questions 1 and 3 for the purpose of changing the organisation and improving it in terms of actions towards an improved organisational functioning[37]. However, change in organisations takes place only when the organisational system is ready for complex changes on all organisational system levels[38]. According to Cummings and Worley[39], change management processes in organisations involve social (people) and technological (technology, tools, techniques and supporting functions such as leadership and strategy) components. Therefore, the foci regarding change should mainly be on the aspects of culture, structure and systems within organisational change management processes. Most sources of problems and conflicts are found in these areas of the organisation, according to Saeed and Wang[40]. These authors highlight the fact that organisational diagnosis should take socio-ecological sustainability into consideration when managing future-oriented change in organisations.

It has been emphasised that organisational diagnostics often lead to failure in organisational change management due to the fact that certain aspects are neglected, the wrong unit of analysis is chosen[41], or that survey consultants focus on the one-best-way approach which does not exist[42].

Here, an applicable example would be the use of the Myers Briggs Type Indicator (MBTI), quality groups, adventure-based teaming activities, and more recently, coaching and mentoring programmes. The unregulated nature of the current market often allows practitioners to engage in these activities without the necessary accredited training and qualifications.

Organisational change becomes a problem when it is experienced as personal loss and associated with processes of grief and mourning, which lead to defensiveness, denial, anger, disorganisation, re-organisation and the search for the lost object[43]. In such an event, changes are usually not effectively implemented. Before change can happen functionally and appropriately, the feelings of organisational participants need to be acknowledged, uncertainties need to be accepted, and consciousness and awareness should be created regarding the personal involvement in the processes. If these unconscious and latent motivations of human behaviour are not addressed in change management processes, they will lead to a failure in the change management process[44]. Furthermore, particularly anxieties – which organisational participants cannot deal with adequately – lead to problems in change management processes, since any form of change within the organisation implies an interruption of the anxiety-containing system within an organisation and leads to the release of anxiety into the system[45]. Within this context, the Marikana (South Africa) incident comes to mind, where striking mineworkers had lost their lives at the hands of the South African security forces. The impression was created that it was an anxiety-provoking situation for police, because "a militant group stormed toward the police firing shots and wielding dangerous weapons"[46]. When consciousness is enhanced around these anxiety-provoking dynamics, organisational diagnosis and change can lead to changes in status quo, power and power relations, changes in leadership, self-examination and the preservation of leadership within the organisation. According to Gilpin-Jackson and Marshak[47], self-examination of leaders with regard to their feelings – such as fear, anger, shame and guilt – might become one of the most challenging aspects in organisational diagnosis, development and the consultancy process. Consequently, all of these fields of anticipated changes can lead to an increase in anxieties and their release into the system.

THE CONSULTANT AS DIAGNOSTIC TOOL FROM A PSYCHOANALYTICAL PERSPECTIVE

As discussed previously, organisational diagnosis impacts on organisational and systemic levels, and is impacted by them on the micro, meso and macro levels. In addition consultants and the consultant-client relationship have to be taken into account in organisational diagnosis[48]. Consultants function as diagnostic tools in organisational analysis, diagnostics and processes; they contribute through their subjective experiences, feelings and reflections to organisational diagnosis[49].

Particularly from the viewpoint of psychoanalytically oriented survey consultants, the consultant needs to be seen as a diagnostic instrument in the organisational context who has to cope with a complex and challenging environment in which he/she has to function[50]. In this context, the organisational consultant needs to take his/her own subjective experiences within the organisation into account while listening to the organisational stories and the subjective experiences of the organisational participants and, by paying attention to recurring organisational patterns, integrate them into interpreting organisational texts[51]. Although psychoanalytical consultants pay attention to organisational dynamics, the task environment, social structure, work groups and so on, they usually tend to focus even more on the underlying, unconscious meanings, stories, assumptions, and collective anxieties which occur in organisations and their participants. By focusing on unconscious patterns within organisations, conflicts, fantasies, suppressed feelings and other defence mechanisms might occur which are closely related to structures of authority and power, roles and relationships, anxieties and fears, strategies for adaptation and performance, and organisational design development[52]. To access these unconscious processes and understand and interpret unconscious organisational aspects, the consultant can use the concepts of transference (as based on Levinson:1972a) and counter-transference as essential conceptual frameworks of organisational diagnosis. For example, as practitioners we may be asking our stakeholders about very difficult things during the diagnostic process that evoke negative thoughts and emotions. We then may be central in re-experiencing those emotions, almost as if we are the personification of them. When we experience such strong and "out of character" emotions, transference and counter-transference could be at play. These concepts support the understanding of the subjective meanings of individual and collective experiences, as well as actions within organisations. It is assumed that if organisational participants become aware of these dynamics, this awareness could help to provide alternative possibilities of behaviour[53].

Hunt[54] points out that there are three basic assumptions that need to be taken into account with regard to the relationship between the consultant/researcher and the client/researched:

1. Unconscious processes take place which are often outside the conscious awareness.
2. Unconscious meanings are linked to everyday life. These meanings are connected to a complex web of significances which often have their roots in childhood experiences. Childhood experiences and images are transferred onto present-day objects and influence and structure present-day relationships in either positive or negative ways.
3. Psychoanalysis is seen as the theory of intra-psychic conflict and refers to the fact that conscious and unconscious thoughts and emotions run counter to each other and create conflict within individuals, who then carry these contradictory aspects into organisations.

Based on these three assumptions, the survey consultant needs to focus on the intra-psychological conflicts which are expressed in conflicting or contradictory approaches to relationships, experiences, performance or roles and tasks. The consultant has to pay attention to these contradictions in his/her relationship with organisational participants and their relationship with the consultant. She/he must interpret the transference taking place within the relationships and/

or the attachment displayed within different actors and elements of the organisational system and her/himself[55].

Transference and counter-transference in individuals and groups in organisations

Transference is defined as the displacement of feelings through behavioural patterns, experienced with significant figures during childhood, onto a person in a current relationship[56]. Diamond and Allcorn[57] highlight the fact that transference occurs mainly unconsciously, therefore it is not in the awareness of the individual. In addition, transference is triggered by familiar experiences, assumptions and archaic feelings which are rooted in previous attachments[58]. Depending on that relationship or early life experiences, the person may form either a positive or negative transference. For example, if someone had difficulties with their parents, or some other influential person such as a teacher in their earlier life time, they transfer (without being consciously aware of it) these feelings. If a father, for instance, was a very authoritarian person, which the individual found it difficult to be on the receiving end of, the individual might transfer those difficult feelings onto those that the individual perceives to be in a position of power. On the other hand, if the individual, for instance, had a kind and supportive mother, it is possible that the transference of feelings would be a positive transference onto the people perceived as kind and supportive[59]. In organisations, structural hierarchies and concepts of authority and power often provide a context for re-occurrences of (re)experienced object relations and for transference and counter-transference dynamics[60]. People who have had painful experiences might find it difficult to trust others and might be challenging to work with, or a client who is anxious about rejection would try to seek your approval at all times[61], and the survey consultant needs to be aware of these underlying currencies.

Counter-transference works as transference and is defined in a narrower way. Counter-transference is a specific reaction to the clients' transference, meaning that the consultant's own unconscious and partly conscious transference to the client is reflected. It arises from the consultant's feelings, attitudes and thoughts about the client's transference onto the consultant, and aspects stemming from the consultant's life that are displaced onto the client. All of these aspects belong to the concept of counter-transference and influence the consultant's diagnostic understanding of the client and the surrounding organisational system. When the consultant finds him/herself feeling and/or acting outside of his/her normal pattern of behaviour towards a client or client group, it may be a clue that the consultant is experiencing a counter transference. It might take a session or two with the client to see a pattern in their behaviour that requires a specific response from the consultant[62].

In organisational diagnostics, consultants pay attention to concepts of transference and counter-transference, nuances of unconscious dynamics, shared thoughts, experiences, feelings, actions and their underlying roots and meanings. Consultants can gain a deeper, multidimensional understanding of the workplace through creating this awareness of transference and counter-transference which co-exist. To be able to decode the underlying unconscious dynamics, the consultant needs to understand the artefacts, events and experiences that are unconsciously significant to organisational participants and can use him-/herself as a tool to diagnose the organisation. In such a case the consultant becomes the instrument of observation, i.e. of data collection, thereby "revealing the subjective and inter-subjective world of work"[63]. Consequently, the consultant needs to be trained to distinguish the organisational dynamics from the unconscious individual as well as group transferences, which are likely to "end up transferring historical experiences onto the groups and divisions that surround them within the organizational milieu"[64]. Group Relations conferences offer opportunities to learn about group, organisational and social dynamics; the exercise of authority and power; and the relationship of organisations to their social, political and economic environments. The SIOPSA Interest Group in Systems Psychodynamics of Organisations (IGSPO) also provides training conferences on an annual basis. This workshop is designed for practitioners in Industrial Psychology, Organisational Development and Human Resources Management and Development, who are interested in diagnosing, learning about, making sense of, and consulting to organisational behaviour manifesting above and below the surface of consciousness. Often transference and counter-transference dynamics are evoked by a consultant's presence, which, at the same time, reveals psychologically defensive reactions, fears and anxieties. Usually the clients' reactions to these dynamics are familiar responses that have been used since childhood and are described as "psychological regression"[65].

Psychoanalysis, transference and counter-transference as a basis for creating change in organisations

It has been pointed out that the use of psychoanalysis in work, organisations and organisational diagnosis contributes considerably to our understanding of organisations and how they function by taking into account the unconscious[66]. Therefore, the concepts of transference and counter-transference can guide consultants in different fields of intervention and provide a new or different perspective on management, organisations and organisational participants[67]. It has been emphasised that consultants differ in terms of receiving projections, managing transference, and dealing with triggers, characteristics and systemic valence. They might experience counter-transference on different cognitive and emotional levels, and distinguish between personal and group emotions, explore projections and manage transference in various ways[68].

The understanding and use of the concepts of transference and counter-transference can support the creation of change within the organisational diagnostic processes if the consultant keeps an observing and self-reflective stance, which she/he then makes accessible for reflection and examination together with the client. The state of "not knowing", open-mindedness and reflection[69] might lead to reduced narcissistic distractions, self-centeredness and anxieties within the organisation. However, it has been pointed out that psychologically grounded approaches in organisational consultation need trained consultants and an appropriate handling of the analysis of clients, non-systemic interventions, and collusion[70].

Because the consultant provides containment of the client's anxieties and other emotions as described by Bion[71], the client might become more trusting and experience regression on a more conscious level. The containment of emotions by the consultant can provide the client with the ability to engage in deeper reflection and learning, which, in turn, might lead to change. Diamond and Allcorn[72] suggest the use of positive transference dynamics to establish alliances with organisational participants. Consultants should also contain and hold the alliances within their capacity as consultants and become part of the organisational dynamics, while at the same time, keeping an exterior view of the dynamics within the organisation. Clients display an increased openness, trust and reflection on communication when consultants gather data in an objective, fair and non-judgemental way. However, it must be taken into account that, in the context of psychoanalytic organisational consultancy, organisational diagnostics is highly complex and time consuming. If based on a detailed on-site diagnosis of the organisation within the systemic context which requires change, it can provide continued learning and immersion.

GUIDELINES FOR DIAGNOSTIC REFLECTIONS

In the light of the discussion above, it is obvious that organisational consultants and analysts need to reflect and prepare for entry into the client system. The following series of questions could assist with this preparation:

1. Consultants have their own preconceived ideas about the general functioning of organisations. How would you attempt to raise your personal consciousness by the *suspension* of your assumptions, judgments, and desires?
2. How would you work with the challenge of *seduction* when tempted to work with only one perspective/reality, thereby ignoring the rich multidimensionality of the organisation?
3. How would you go about building a *healthy working relationship* with different aspects of the client system?
4. How would you become aware of and work with your *own attachments* (tools, people, objects, experiences, etc.) as a consultant during the diagnostic process?
5. What do your *anxieties and discomfort* tell you about what is happening in the client system?
6. How would you manage the modern-day expectation of instant solutions, successes and *gratification*, especially when this comes from the executive team?
7. Given your history, personality and profile, how could you be *"used" emotionally and psychologically* by the client system?
8. How would you work with the *organisational realities of pain and loss*?
9. How would you raise your personal consciousness around issues of *transference and counter-transference*?

Having addressed these reflective questions for oneself, the organisational consultant and analyst should be better prepared to deal with the conscious and unconscious elements of organisational life. Consciousness will be enhanced when reflection becomes the norm, rather than the exception;

personal authorisation happens through continuous training and development, and by keeping the entire system in mind when working with the client system.

CONCLUDING REMARKS

This chapter provided insight into the psychological impact of organisational diagnosis, and pointed out that organisational diagnosis is a complex field of work and consultancy. It has been shown that organisational diagnosis involves not only the application of quantitative diagnostics and the application of questionnaires within organisations, but also a deeply-rooted awareness, mindfulness and strong connection with the conscious and unconscious involvement of the (role of the) consultant in the system. The survey consultant uses various tools in organisational diagnostics, and should guard against him-/herself becoming an ineffective and inappropriately applied tool in the process of change, risk management and organisational development. The consultant will remain effective through continuous professional development and by striving to be objective, non-judgemental and reflexive.

This chapter tried to create an awareness with regard to organisational and psychological impacts in the context of organisational diagnosis. Practical reflections are provided at the end of the chapter. This is only the beginning of creating an awareness among survey consultants, however, who might need to read further literature on the self as an instrument or tool, and on the systemic interrelationships involved in organisational diagnostics and development.

REFERENCES

Amado, G. 2009. Potential space: The threatened source of individual and collective creativity. *Socio-Analysis* 11, 16–35.

Argyris, C. 1970. *Intervention theory and method: A behavioral science view*. Reading, MA: Addisson-Wesley.

Arnaud, G. 2012. The contribution of psychoanalysis to organization studies and management: an overview. *Organization Studies*, 22(9): 1121-1135.

Baum, HS. 1994. Transference in organizational research. *Administration & Society*, 26(2): 135–57.

Beckhard, A. 1969. *Organisational learning*. Reading, MA: Addison-Wesley.

Beer, M. & Spector, B. 1993. Organizational Diagnosis: its role in Organizational Learning. *Journal of Counseling & Development* 71(6): 642–650.

Bion, WR. 1959. *Experiences in groups*. New York: Basic Books.

Blackman, D. O'Flynn, J & Ugyel, L. 2013. *A Diagnostic Tool for Assessing Organisational Readiness for Complex Change*. Paper presented to the Australian and New Zealand Academy of Management conference, Hobart, 4–6 December 2013.

Burnes, B. & Cooke, B. 2012. Review article: The past, present and future of organization development: Taking the long view. *Human Relation* 65(11): 1395-1429.

Burnes, B. & Jackson, P. 2011. Success and Failure in Organizational Change: An Exploration of the Role of Values. *Journal of Change Management* 11(2): 133–62.

Burton, RM. & Obel, B. 2004. *Strategic organizational diagnosis and design. The dynamics of fit*. 3rd edition. New York: Springer Science and Media.

Cilliers, F. Rothmann, S. & Struwig, WH. 2004. Transference and counter-transference in systems psychodynamic group process consultation: the consultant's experience. *SA Journal of Industrial Psychology*, 30(1): 72-81.

Cobb, AT. 1986. Political Diagnosis: Applications in Organizational Development. *Academy of Management Review* 11: 482–496.

Cummings, TG & Worley, CG. 2009. *Organization Development & Change.* 9th edition. Mason: South Western Center of Learning.

Cummings, TG & Worley, CG. 2015. *Organization Development & Change.* 10th edition. Mason: South Western Center of Learning.

Czander, WM. 1997. *The psychodynamics of work and organizations.* New York: Guilford.

Diamond, M. 2003. Organizational Immersion and Diagnosis: the work of Harry Levinson. *Organisational and Social Dynamics* 3(1): 1–18.

Diamond, M & Allcorn, S. 2003. The cornerstone of psychoanalytic organizational analysis: psychological reality, transference and counter-transference in the workplace. *Human Relations* 56(4): 491–514.

Dimitrov, PL. 2008. *Organisational Psychodynamics: Ten introductory lectures for students, managers and consultants.* http://www. orgdyne.com/

Driver, M. 2003. Nothing clinical, just business? Reflections on psychoanalytically grounded organizational diagnosis and intervention. *Human relations* 56(1): 39–59.

Fordyce, JK & Weil, R. 1983. Methods for finding out what is going on in *Organisational Development. Theory, Practice and Research* edited by W French, C-H Bell & R Zawacki. Plan, TX: Business Publications.

Gabriel, Y. 1993. Organisational nostalgia: reflections on "The Golden Age", in *Emotion in organisations,* edited by S Fineman. London: Sage.

Gallagher, R. 2006. *Organizational Diagnosis: six primary elements of the system.* http://static1.1.sqspcdn.com/static/f/1002566/24323703/1391538434570/orgdiog+model+.pdf?token=XziKGDtwjdmaXrGHCiSoTNyiSNA%3D

Gardner, W.L. & Schermerhorn, J.R. 2008. Unleashing individual potential performance gains through positive organisational behaviour and authentic leadership. *Organisational Dynamics* 33(3): 270–281.

Gilpin-Jackson, Y. 2015. Transformative learning during dialogic OD, in *Dialogic organization development: The theory and practice of transformational change,* edited by GR Bushe & RJ Marshak. Oakland, CA: Berrett-Koehler Publishers: 245–267.

Hayes, J. 2002. *The Theory and Practice of Change Management.* New York: Palgrave.

Harrison, MI & Shiron, A. 1999. *Organizational diagnosis and assessment. Bridging theory and practice.* Thousand Oaks: Sage.

Hunt, J.C. 1989. *Psychoanalytic aspects of fieldwork.* London: Sage.

James, K & Huffington, C. 2004. What is the emotional cost of distributed leadership? in *Working Below the Surface: The emotional life of contemporary organizations,* edited by C Huffington, D Armstrong, W Halton, L Hoyle & J Pooley. London: Karnac.

Janićijević, N. 2010. Business processes in organisational diagnosis. *Management* 15(2): 85–106.

Jin, K G & Drozdenko, RG. 2010. Relationships among perceived organizational core values, corporate social responsibility, ethics, and organizational performance outcomes: An empirical study of information technology professionals. *Journal of Business Ethics* 92: 341–359.

Jones, G. 2004. *Organizational Theory, Design and Change.* New York: Addison Wesley.

Kets de Vries, MFR & Miller, D. 1991. Leadership styles and organisational cultures : The shaping of neurotic organisations, in *Organisations on the couch: Clinical perspectives on organizational behaviour and change,* edited by MFR Kets de Vries & Associates. San Francisco: Jossey-Bass.

Kume, V & Leskaj, E. 2015. Beyond Organizational Diagnosis, comparisons between Albania and Kosovo case of Tax Directorate. *Administration and Public Management* 24/2015.

Lee, D & Brower, RS. 2006. Pushing the Envelope on Organizational Effectiveness: Combining an Old Framework and a Sharp Tool. *Public Performance & Management Review* 30: 155–178.

Levinson, H. 1972a. *Organizational diagnosis*. Cambridge, MA: Harvard University Press.

Levinson, H. 1972b. Easing the pain of personal loss. *Harvard Business Review* 50(5): 80–88.

Levinson, H. 1994. Why the behemoths fell: Psychological roots of corporate failure. *American Psychologist* 49(5): 428–436.

Linklater, J & Kellner, K. 2008. Don't just do something ... stand there: using action learning to help organisations work with anxiety. *Action learning: Research and Practice* 5(2): 167–172.

Manzini. AO. 1988. *Organizational Diagnosis: A Practical Approach to Company Problem Solving and Growth*. New York: American Management Association.

Marshak, RJ. 2016. Anxiety and change in contemporary organization development. *OD Practitioner* (4681): 11–19.

McCormick, DW & White, J. 2000. Using oneself as an instrument for organizational diagnosis. *Organization Development Journal* 18(3): 49–61.

McMahon, G. 2017. *What do tranference and counter transference mean?* Retreived January 31, 2017 from http://www.cognitivebehaviouralcoachingworks.com

Mersky, RR. 2008. Lost in transition: The use of role objects in today's postmodern organisations. *Organisational and Social Dynamics* 8(1): 97–112.

Mitonga-Monga, J, Flotman, AP & Cilliers, F. 2016. Workplace ethics, culture and work engagement: The mediating effect of ethical leadership in a developing world context. *Journal of Psychology in Africa* 26(4): 326–333.

Moore, BE & Fine, BD. 1990. *Psychoanalytic terms and concepts*. London: The American Psychoanalytic Association and Yale University Press New Haven.

Morgan, G. 1990. *Images of organisation*. Beverly Hills, CA: Sage.

Mullins, LJ. 2013. *Management and organizational behaviour*. Harlow: Prentice Hall.

Neves, P. 2009. Readiness for Change: Contributions for Employee's Level of Individual Change and Turnover Intentions. *Journal of Change Management*, 9(2): 215-31.

Pettigrew, A. 1987. Introduction: researching strategic change, in *The Management of Strategic Change*, edited by A Pettigrew. London: Basil Blackwell.

Popovici, V-I. 2013. Organization – Organizational diagnosis – organizational performance – essential elements in development of a nation. *Advances in Fiscal, Political and Law Science*. Proceedings of the 2nd International Conference on Economics, Political and Law Science (EPLS'13), Brasov, Romania, June 1-3, 2013, WSEAS Press, 151-156. http://www.wseas.us/e-library/conferences/2013/Brasov/EPLS/EPLS-00.pdf

Postma, TJB & Kok, RAW. 1998. *Organisational diagnosis in practice*. (Online) available at http//som.eldoc.ub.rug.nl/FILES/reports/1995-1999/themeB/1998/98B11/98b11.pdf, accessed on September 5 2016.

Saeed, BB & Wang, W. 2014. Sustainability Embedded Organizational Diagnostic Model. *Modern Economy* 5: 424–431.

Sievers, B & Beumer, U. 2005. *Organisational role analysis and consultation: The organisation as inner object*. London: Karnac.

Smith, FJ. 2003. *Organisational surveys: The diagnosis and betterment of organisations through their members*. London: LEA.

Stegerean, R, Gavrea, C & Marin, A. 2010. Application of diagnostic model: An empirical study. *Journal Studia Universitatis Babes-Bolyai Negotia*. Babes-Balyai University, Faculty of Business.

Stein, HF & Allcorn, S. 2013. Good enough leadership: A model of leadership. *Organisational & Social Dynamics* 14(2): 342–366.

Stupart, R. (16 August 2012). "The Night Before Lonmin's Explanation". *African Scene*. Retrieved 11 August 2016.

Van Tonder, CL. 2014. *Organisational change: Theory and practice*. Pretoria: Van Schaik.

ENDNOTES

1. Gardner & Schermerhorn, 2008; Jin & Drozdenko, 2010; Mitonga-Monga, Flotman & Cilliers, 2016.
2. Bion, 1959; Levinson, 1972a; Mullins, 2013; Sievers & Beumer, 2005.
3. Morgan, 1990.
4. Hayes, 2002; Janićijević, 2010; Jones, 2004.
5. Czander, 1997; Kets de Vries & Miller, 1991; Gabriel, 1993.
6. Levinson, 1994 cited in Van Tonder, 2014: 31.
7. Beer & Spector, 1993: 72.
8. Beckhard, 1969.
9. Kume & Leskaj, 2015.
10. Stegerean et al., 2010.
11. Postma & Kok, 1998.
12. Kume & Leskaj, 2015.
13. Janićijević, 2010
14. Smith, 2003: 12.
15. Amado, 2009; James & Huffington, 2004; Mersky, 2008.
16. Diamond, 2003: 8.
17. Cummings & Worley, 2015.
18. Burnes and Cooke, 2012.
19. Mersky, 2008.
20. Diamond & Allcorn, 2003; Levinson, 1972b.
21. Diamond, 2003.
22. Stein & Allcorn, 2013.
23. Argyris, 1970; Beer & Spector, 1993.
24. Lee & Brower, 2006.
25. Saeed & Wang, 2014.
26. Gallagher, 2006.
27. Popovici, 2013.
28. Popovici, 2013.
29. Burton & Obel, 2004.
30. Harrison & Shirom, 1999.
31. Maharaj, 2005.
32. Argyris, 1970.
33. Fordyce & Weil, 1983.
34. Janićijević, 2010.
35. Cobb, 1996.
36. Pettigrew, 1987.
37. Janićijević, 2010.
38. Blackman, O'Flynn & Ugyel, 2013.
39. Cummings & Worley, 2009.
40. Saeed & Wang, 2014.
41. Neves, 2009.
42. Burnes & Jackson, 2011.
43. Levinson, 1972b.
44. Levinson, 1972a.
45. Linklater & Kellner, 2008.
46. Stupart, 2012.
47. Gilpin-Jackson, 2015; Marshak, 2016.
48. Levinson, 1972a.
49. McCormick & White, 2000.
50. Driver, 2003.
51. Diamond & Allcorn, 2003.
52. Diamond & Allcorn, 2003.
53. Dimitrov, 2008.
54. Hunt, 1989.
55. Baum, 1994.
56. Moore & Fine, 1990.
57. Diamond & Allcorn, 2003.
58. Diamond & Allcorn, 2003.
59. McMahon, 2017.
60. Diamond & Allcorn, 2003.
61. McMahon, 2017.
62. Mc Mahon, 2017.
63. Diamond & Allcorn, 2003: 66.
64. Diamond & Allcorn, 2003: 69.
65. Diamond & Allcorn, 2003: 70.
66. Arnaud 2012.
67. Arnaud, 2012.
68. Cilliers, Rothmann & Struwig, 2004.
69. Diamond, 2003.
70. Driver, 2003.
71. Bion, 1959.
72. Diamond & Allcorn, 2003.

CHAPTER 12

ETHICAL AND PRIVACY CONSIDERATIONS FOR RESEARCH

by **Adéle da Veiga**

INTRODUCTION

Organisations have a moral responsibility to ensure that they conduct research with integrity and in an ethical manner. This means that the rights and privacy of employees or other participants in the research must be protected and research results should be accurate and truthfully reported without manipulation, falsification or cheating, using a sound and scientific approach.

There are volumes of personal data available to organisations that can be utilised for research purposes, such as the information customers provide for credit checks, home loan applications, loyalty cards, or online purchases using an organisation's website such as online shopping at Woolworths or Pick n Pay. From an employee's perspective, organisations have data that are collected as part of the recruitment process in the form of a curricula vitae, psychometric test data, demographic information which is used for broad-based black economic empowerment (BBBEE) reporting purposes, salary information, performance evaluation information, trade union membership details, medical aid claims, sick leave days taken, monitoring information of access to internet websites, entry and access times of access cards, and so on. Existing data are used in everyday business by organisations to understand the as-is environment, trends and to implement strategies for interventions to meet organisational strategies and objectives. For example, staff turnover figures can be analysed with the objective to improve retention strategies, or the demographic traits of people buying certain consumer goods over the internet can be analysed for targeted marketing initiatives.

Organisations also conduct opinion and attitude surveys to derive additional data for a specific purpose, for example organisational culture, organisational climate, employee or customer satisfaction surveys. Demographical information of respondents is collected as part of this process to identify areas of concern and to focus and prioritise interventions. For example, an area of concern identified in an organisational culture survey might be trust. If the data are segmented based on the demographical information, it is possible to identify if employees in a certain department, job level or age group are perhaps more negative than the rest of the employees in order to implement actions plans tailored for that specific group.

Organisations that use or collect employee or customer data and, specifically, personal information as part of their research, should pay attention to ethical and privacy considerations. They should take care to comply with the necessary ethics code of conduct, industry and organisational policies and also regulatory requirements. If the ethical or privacy rights of research participants are violated, it could result in a violation of human rights, fines and even prosecution.

This chapter aims to provide consultants (research practitioners) with an overview of ethical and privacy considerations in the context of the South African environment. To achieve this, the concept of ethics from a corporate governance perspective and then relevant ethical values that must be embedded in research activities will be examined. Protecting the privacy of research participants is one of the ethical values that are discussed. Specific emphasis is placed on privacy in this chapter in the light of the regulatory requirements that apply to privacy, and to aid organisations to understand the practical measures that must be implemented to achieve privacy through the protection of personal information.

If organisations process any personal information, for example of employees or customers, then the POPIA, 2013 (POPIA) applies. The objective of this Act is to put measures in place to protect the privacy of South African citizens. Organisations are required to comply with the conditions of the Act. The conditions of the POPIA relate to ethical values in the processing of personal information. It makes good business sense to implement privacy principles as part of the research process to protect the participants, and to ensure that the data are only used for the intended purposes. In this chapter, the objectives of the POPIA and how it defines "personal information" and "processing" to understand the relevance to research projects are discussed. Each of the conditions in the POPIA is discussed and illustrated in terms of how it relates to organisational research where personal information are collected or processed.

The chapter concludes with a checklist of ethical and privacy requirements developed specifically for organisational research projects. The conditions of the POPIA are integrated in the checklist to aid organisations with compliance measures. The checklist can be used by consultants during each phase of the research project to identify what ethical and privacy tasks to undertake.

Organisations have to review each research project and identify the ethical and privacy implications to ensure that the project is conducted with integrity and in line with required policies and regulations. The scope of this chapter focusses on research in the social, human resources and industrial psychology context. It is therefore important that the information in this chapter should be used as a reference and that organisations should identify any additional industry, organisational and regulatory related ethical and privacy requirements that are applicable to each research project.

OVERVIEW OF ETHICS

The King IV Code of Governance for South Africa[1] defines ethics as, "considering what is good and right for the self and the other, and can be expressed in terms of the golden rule, namely, to treat others as you would like to be treated yourself. In the context of organisations, ethics refers to ethical values applied to decision-making, conduct, and the relationship between the organisation, its stakeholders and the broader society".

Research projects within an organisation should not only be to the benefit of the organisation and its strategic objectives, but should also consider what is good for the employees and other stakeholders who participate. The King report[2] outlines that the board of directors should ensure that organisations have a code of conduct as well as ethics-related policies that are implemented.

The code of conduct should be integrated in all the processes of the organisation, including research projects.

Various ethical codes for research have been established since the violation of human rights in experiments conducted by Nazis during the Second World War[3]. For example, the Code of Human Research Ethics of the British Psychological Society (BPS)[4], the Ethical Principles of Psychologists and Code of Conduct of the American Psychological Association (APA)[5], and The European Code of Conduct for Research Integrity[6] by the European Science Foundation.

There are various professional bodies in South Africa that have similar ethical codes that can provide guidance to researchers or consultants (referred to as consultants for the remainder of the chapter). The South African Board for People Practices (SABPP) has core ethical values that human resource practitioners should uphold[7], as well as a code of conduct[8]. Similarly, the Health Professions Council of South Africa has an Ethical Rules of Conduct (HPCSA)[9], while members of the Information Systems Audit and Control Association (ISACA)[10] for audit professionals in information technology have to conform to their Code of Professional Ethics. Furthermore, the Human Sciences Research Council (HSRC) published a Code of Research Ethics[11], which gives guidelines for research projects in their domain and serves as a sound guideline for organisations engaged in research.

Consultants are accountable for ensuring that they uphold ethical research values as outlined in ethical codes of conduct in their domain, organisational policies, and relevant local and international legislation. These should be considered in all phases of the research project, from the planning stage up to the report writing and action planning.

GUIDELINES TO CONDUCT ETHICAL RESEARCH

Conducting research though integrity

Integrity is a universal value that must be embedded in research projects. It should be embedded in all research projects when using a questionnaire, survey, interview, psychometric test or any other assessment instrument. The Singapore Statement on Research Integrity[12] is a good reference for research integrity principles, and can be found at www.singaporestatement.org. It comprises four integrity principles for research, namely:

1. "Honesty in all aspects of research;
2. Accountability in the conduct of research;
3. Professional courtesy and fairness in working with others; and
4. Good stewardship of research on behalf of others".

These four principles can be unpacked further to contextualise them for organisational research, as outlined in table 12.1.

Table 12.1: Singapore Statement on Research Integrity (2010) and contextualisation thereof (Compiled by A. Da Veiga)

Singapore statement on research integrity	Contextualisation for organisation research
Honesty in all aspects of research (Singapore statement:2010)	The principle of honesty must be applied in all phases and activities of the research project, for example, honesty in conveying the research objectives to the participants and how their data will be used and with whom it will be shared, honesty when analysing and reporting the data, and honesty when using citations in the research publications.
Accountability in the conduct of research (Singapore statement:2010)	Consultants are not only accountable to ensure that the research project objectives are met, but also to the participants, their research team members and the institution or organisations funding the research.
Professional courtesy and fairness in working with others (Singapore statement:2010)	Various stakeholders are involved in the research process such as funding organisations, research ethics committees, research team members, participants on an individual basis or in the context of an organisation or community, statisticians, consultants, and so on. Stakeholders must be treated in a professional manner and clear roles and responsibilities should be defined. A fair selection process should be used when identifying respondents for the sample.
Good stewardship of research on behalf of others (Singapore statement:2010)	Research projects should be managed and activities supervised and monitored to ensure that objectives are met, deadlines are achieved and that the rights of all stakeholders are protected.

Ethical values in research

There are various ethical values that must be embedded in the research or audit process. The key ethical values pertaining to research projects, as summarised and explained by the author, are listed below:

Accountability
The consultant is accountable to manage the research project in a responsible manner. Therefore, decisions must be taken while considering ethical values such as the ones listed below[13].

Autonomy
The rights of research participants should be respected and their decisions to participate or not to participate through informed consent[14].

Best interest
Consultants should put the interest of the participants above their own interest of the research project[15].

Benevolence

Protecting all stakeholders in the research and conducting research with possible benefits while reducing harm to participants and the environment[16].

Community

All research activities should be carried out to benefit the community and should be in line with codes of conduct and regulatory requirements, for example the Occupational Health and Safety Act 85 of 1993[17].

Compassion

There should be compassion for research participants, especially if vulnerable groups participate, for example people with disabilities or children, to ensure that their individual and social needs are respected.[18]

Confidentiality

All personal information of participants collected through research should be kept confidential, as agreed with the participants in the informed consent agreement, unless disclosure is required through regulatory requirements. Personal information of participants should not be shared with third parties to whom consent was not obtained from the research participant. Where possible, participants should respond in an anonymous manner or a pseudonym should be used[19].

Excellence

Research activities should be conducted in a professional manner using objectivity, and research practitioners should be competent, having the necessary experience and skills[20].

Honesty

All research activities should be conducted with honesty by disclosing accurate and timely information to participants and stakeholders, and applying the research methodology and analysis methods correctly[21].

Human rights

The human rights of all research participants and stakeholders should be considered throughout the research process[22]. An example is voluntary inclusion, which was added to the Human Rights Charter of 1948[23].

Impartiality and independence

Consultants should declare conflicts of interest, for example, if they have interests in the entity that funds the research[24].

Integrity

Responsible research should be conducted in line with the values of honesty, quality, ownership, accountability and fairness[25].

Justice
Consultants should treat all individuals and groups with sensitivity and fairness, irrespective of their demographical traits. If rewards or compensation are offered, they should be provided to all participants in a fair manner[26].

Objectivity and independence
Consultants should conduct all research activities with objectivity in line with their professional codes of conduct, organisational policies and regulatory requirements[27]. The organisational committee that reviews and approves the research project should be independent. Any monitoring or auditing activities should be conducted by independent roles or parties to identify any irregularities.

Privacy
The privacy requirements for personal information as outlined in laws such as the Protection of Personal Information Act 4 of 2013 (POPIA) must be conformed with at all times. The personal information of research participants should be protected through security controls and processes, and only be used for the agreed purposes with the research participant[28].

Respect
The dignity of each research participant and all stakeholders should be respected, therefore informed consent should be obtained from participants[29].

Tolerance
The values, beliefs and perceptions of research participants should be respected[30]. Where interviews or focus groups are used to collect data, it is important to tolerate the various perceptions of the research participants and not to influence them in any way.

Transparency
Research participants should be informed of all the risks, expectations, aims and implications of the research[31]. Research results should be communicated to the relevant stakeholders in line with the consent that the research participants agreed to[32].

Truthfulness
Consultants should conduct all research activities in an honest way, and give truthful and accurate information and feedback to respondents and relevant stakeholders[33].

Table 12.2 below gives practical examples of how each of the ethical values can be embedded in research.

Table 12.2: Examples of ethical values in practice (Compiled by A. Da Veiga)

Value	Examples of ethical values for organisational research projects
Accountability	An explicit research mandate from the sponsor outlining the terms of the research[34].
Autonomy	Signed informed consent forms from all participants and approval letters from gatekeepers. For example, Department of Education approval is required if research is conducted in schools or an approval letter from the Chief Executive Officer (CEO) or relevant manager that research can be conducted in an organisation. Parents must sign the informed consent forms where children are involved as research participants.
Best interest/ well-being	Briefing participants about the research aims through a meeting, e-mail or informed consent agreement.
Benevolence	Conducting a risk assessment of the research project by considering the type of information that is collected, how it is collected, who the research participants are, and what research methods are applied to ensure the benefit outweighs the risks.
Community	Identifying research problems in the community as well as strategies to integrate the research contributions in the community.
Compassion	If vulnerable groups are used, for example disabled people, compassion can be illustrated by ensuring that facilities used for focus group sessions make provision for disabled people, such as having wheel chair access and restrooms.
Confidentiality	Hard copy data should be stored in a secure room or cabinet. Electronic data should be stored on a device that is password protected or encrypted, depending on the sensitivity of the data. Where sensitive data files are e-mailed, they should also be password protected or encrypted.
Excellence and competency	Using a valid and reliable questionnaire to contribute to the scientific value of the research. It is also important to ensure that the instrument is valid and reliable for the specific population (considering whether invariance testing of the questionnaire was conducted for the specific population).
Honesty	Reporting valid and accurate data in the research reports.
Human rights	Fair selection of research participants representing all biographical groups.
Impartiality and independence	The research team should declare any conflicts of interest, and research activities (eg financial resources) should be audited by an independent team.
Integrity	Ethical values should be embedded in the research process. To apply it consistently, research ethics policies and codes of conduct should be implemented in organisations.
Justice	Recognition of copyright where existing questionnaires are used, approval to use from the developers and fair compensation.
Objectivity	Making research conclusions based on data and facts.
Privacy	Protecting private information through de-identification techniques or not collecting sensitive personal information.

Value	Examples of ethical values for organisational research projects
Respect	The participants are free to decide if they want to participate and free to withdraw at any time.
Tolerance	Documenting all views and perceptions in focus group sessions and giving each participant an equal opportunity to raise their views.
Transparency	Information reporting of research findings to relevant stakeholders and not hiding any important information.
Truthfulness	Acknowledgement of collaborators and citations for references in the research report.

PRIVACY REGULATORY REQUIREMENTS IN SOUTH AFRICA

The individual's right to privacy, as outlined in the Constitution of the Republic of South Africa (1996) and effected through regulation such as the POPIA of 2013, should be considered in each phase of the research project. Ensuring the privacy of research participants is a critical component of research. The processing of personal information or data is regulated in over 100 countries[35]. In South Africa, the POPIA of 2013[36] regulates the processing of personal information as required by the Constitution of the Republic of South Africa (1996), which provides everyone with the right to privacy. This right relates to, "protection against the unlawful collection, retention, dissemination and use of personal information; with the objective of promoting the protection of personal information"[37].

The POPIA is applicable to research projects where personal information about a research participant is processed as part of the research project. This personal information not only relates to the participant's name, surname, age, gender, race, contact information and residential information, but also includes information pertaining to their well-being, opinions, views and preferences, which are often collected as part of research in social sciences.

The definition of personal information in the POPIA is as follows:

"...**personal information**" means information relating to an identifiable, living, natural person, and where it is applicable, an identifiable, existing juristic person, including, but not limited to—

1. information relating to the race, gender, sex, pregnancy, marital status, national, ethnic or social origin, colour, sexual orientation, age, physical or mental health, well-being, disability, religion, conscience, belief, culture, language and birth of the person;
2. information relating to the education or the medical, financial, criminal or employment history of the person;
3. any identifying number, symbol, e-mail address, physical address, telephone number, location information, online identifier or other particular assignment to the person;
4. the biometric information of the person;
5. the personal opinions, views or preferences of the person;

6. correspondence sent by the person that is implicitly or explicitly of a private or confidential nature or further correspondence that would reveal the contents of the original correspondence;
7. the views or opinions of another individual about the person; and
8. the name of the person if it appears with other personal information relating to the person or if the disclosure of the name itself would reveal information about the person;"[38].

If any of the above personal information fields are processed as part of the research project, the POPIA applies. In many research projects, personal information are not collected, are anonymised, or pseudonyms are used to protect the privacy of the research participants. However, individuals can in some instances still be identified if two or more fields of personal information are combined. For instance, if survey data is segmented on age groups across departments, it might be possible to identify an individual if there is only one employee in a certain age group in a specific department. Care should then be taken when reporting the results, such as not reporting on demographical areas where there are less than five respondents[39].

Juristic information refers to information about an organisation, partnership, trust or another type of legal entity, such as the organisation's name, address, names of directors, e-mail and contact information, tax and VAT numbers and so on. If a survey is conducted whereby data is collected from various organisations, then the organisational information should be processed under the same conditions as when personal information of individuals are processed. Thus, the ethical values and privacy considerations would also apply to juristic information that are part of research projects.

It is the consultant's responsibility to establish the risk of personal information exposure, and to implement the necessary controls to mitigate it to preserve confidentiality, and to uphold the right to privacy. Risk in research projects is discussed later in this chapter..

Privacy rights of research participants

Research participants have privacy rights from a regulatory and ethical perspective. If personal information of participants (individuals or legal entities) is processed, they have rights as outlined in the POPIA. A summary of these rights are discussed below in the context of research projects, however the POPIA should be consulted for more in-depth information.

1. The research participant should be notified by the organisation conducting the research that his/her/its personal information are being collected[40].
2. If there has been unauthorised access to the personal information, then the research participant should be informed[41].
3. Research participants have the right to enquire from the organisation conducting the research if it holds any personal information about them. The process to follow to request the information should be recorded in the organisation's Promotion of Access to Information Act, 2000 (PAIA) manual[42].

4. Research participants can also request, where necessary, the correction, destruction or deletion of their personal information following certain procedures of section 24 of POPIA[43].
5. Research participants can object to the processing of their information, which relates to the concept of voluntary participation[44].
6. Research participants have the right not to have their personal information, that were collected as part of the research, used for direct marketing by means of unsolicited electronic communications, except if certain conditions of section 69 apply[45].
7. Automated processing alone cannot be used to make decisions about research participants that affect them, for example how they will receive benefits or compensation related to the research[46].
8. Research participants can submit a complaint to the Information Regulator or institute civil proceedings if they feel that their personal information were not protected or were interfered with[47]. If an organisation is found guilty of an offence against the POPIA, it can result in penalties such as a fine or imprisonment up to ten years, as well as administrative fines not exceeding R10 million[48].

POPIA conditions and research

The POPIA has eight conditions and a number of additional requirements. The next paragraphs explain how these conditions are interpreted, applied and described in the context of organisational research projects.

It is important to note that the POPIA does not apply where personal information has been de-identified to an extent where it cannot be re-identified again[49]. However, the ethical principles of research always apply to research projects, such as voluntary participation, and care should be taken that research respondents cannot be identified when their demographical information are combined and when data are segmented for analysis and reporting purposes.

Accountability (POPIA:2013, section 8)

Accountability refers to the research entity and what measures it should implement to ensure compliance with the POPIA. This means that governance controls should be in place such as research policies and ethics codes of conduct, processes for approval of research and obtaining of consent, defined roles and responsibilities of relevant research committees and stakeholders, adequate supervision and monitoring procedures for research projects.

Processing limitation (POPIA:2013, 9 to 12)

Processing limitation includes four requirements:

1. *Lawfulness of processing (POPIA:2013, section 9)*
    All processing must be conducted in a lawful manner whereby the research participant's privacy is not contravened. Processing refers to a number of operations that can be conducted

using personal information, "the collection, receipt, recording, organisation, collation, storage, updating or modification, retrieval, alteration, consultation or use; dissemination by means of transmission, distribution or making available in any other form; or merging, linking, as well as restriction, degradation, erasure or destruction of information"[50]. If personal information of research participants is processed using any of the above operations, it should be done in a lawful manner considering the other privacy conditions and ethical values. This does not only apply to electronic data, but to all records that could include personal information such as, "writing on any material; information produced, recorded or stored by means of any tape-recorder, computer equipment, whether hardware or software or both, or other device, and any material subsequently derived from information so produced, recorded or stored; label, marking or other writing that identifies or describes anything of which it forms part, or to which it is attached by any means; book, map, plan, graph or drawing"[51].

2. *Minimality (POPIA:2013, section 10)*

    The information collected about research participants should only relate to those fields that are necessary to conduct the research. Thus, excessive biographical information should not be collected. The more data one collects, the more responsibility one has to protect them, especially if the data are sensitive personal information such as a respondent's health, disability or criminal information.

3. *Consent, justification and objection (POPIA:2013, section 11)*

    This condition relates directly to informed consent, which was listed in table 12.2 as an ethical value. Research involving humans cannot be conducted if the research participant did not consent to it, unless is it required for the "performance of a public law duty by a public body"[52]. The organisation conducting the research should make sure that it has evidence of the consent. As such, it is important to obtain a signature for hard copy questionnaires from the research participant confirming that he or she or it is willing to take part in the research. For electronic surveys, participants can confirm participation by selecting a "Yes" or "No" option for consent. In order for a research participant to make an informed decision, the following should be communicated to them in an information document, informed consent agreement, or on the first page of an electronic survey:

    -   The objective of the research.
    -   The organisation's name that is conducting the research and/or the sponsor.
    -   Why the research participant has been selected to participate.
    -   What the benefits/negative consequences are for the research participant to take part.
    -   What the benefits are of the study for the participants, the community or broader society.
    -   That all personal information will be dealt with in a confidential manner.
    -   That the privacy of the participant will be ensured.
    -   That data will either be anonymised, pseudonyms or de-identification will be used.
    -   What measures will be implemented to protect the research participant's data (For example, will hard copy questionnaires be physically secured in a room and will voice recordings be saved in a secure database or file server with access control? For how long will the data be stored and will they be destroyed after the purpose has been achieved

for which they were originally collected? Many ethical committees of universities propose a five-year period after which data should be destroyed. In addition, one should also consider who will have access to the data, for example only the consultant and statisticians.)

- That a research participant participates voluntarily.
- That a research participant can withdraw at any time.
- Whether the research participants will receive any compensation or incentives.
- Where the research results will be published and/or how they will be communicated to research participants.
- Who approved the research project, for example the organisation's research integrity committee, risk committee or a professional body.
- A list of categories of third parties with whom the research data might be shared.

The Declaration of Helsinki[53], which focuses on ethics in medical research also addresses consent and explains that consent should consist of three aspects. The first is to ensure that the organisation gives adequate information to the research participant about the research project in terms of the risks and potential benefits. The second is to confirm if the research participant understands the requirements and, in some cases, one might need to make use of an interpreter. Thirdly, the research participant should decide whether he or she or it is willing to participate in the research project. If the research participant decides to participate, their signature should be obtained as proof of consent[54].

Where electronic surveys are used, one can consider including a tick box with an "agree" button for research participants to click in order to proceed. It must, however, be ensured that individuals cannot consent and complete electronic surveys on behalf of someone else. This can be achieved by implementing information security control such as passwords or cookies.

4. *Collection directly from the data subject (POPIA:2013, section 12)*
   Research data about a research participant should be collected directly from the person, unless the information can be collected from a public record such as a public database, magazine, newspaper, telephone directory or website.

Purpose specification (POPIA:2013 sections 13 and 14)

Purpose specification relates to two conditions, namely collection for a specific purpose and the retention of the data.

1. *Collection for a specific purpose (POPIA:2013, section 13)*
   The research participant's data must be collected for an explicitly defined purpose, which should have been defined as part of the research project objectives and communicated to the research participant in order to give informed consent.
2. *Retention (POPIA:2013, Section 14)*
   The personal information collected as part of a research project can only be retained for the period necessary to meet the objective, or the purpose for which it was collected, or for the period required by policy or regulatory requirements. However, if the personal information

has been de-identified and appropriate information security controls have been implemented to protect it, it can be retained for longer periods for historical, statistical or organisational research purposes.

Further processing (POPIA:2013, section 15)

Personal information collected as part of the research project should only be used for the purposes of the research project. It is unethical to use it for other purposes or to share or sell it to third parties for other purposes such as marketing.

If the organisation would like to use the personal information collected as part of the research project for other purposes, they should first obtain the consent of the research participants, unless it is required as part of a requirement of a law.

Information quality (POPIA:2013, section 16)

It should be ensured that the personal information collected is accurate and complete in order to derive valid and reliable research findings. If electronic surveys are used one can, for instance, use drop-down answer boxes for certain answers. It is also possible to validate that numbers are not entered in text fields and that text is not entered in number fields. The data can be scanned for duplicate entries, which could occur if respondents stand a chance to win a prize for participating and completed more than one questionnaire to increase their chances.

Openness (POPIA:2013, sections 17 and 18)

1   *Documentation (POPIA:2013, section 17)*
    Openness refers to the documentation that must be maintained in terms of the POPIA to specify the process to request access to personal information fields processed by organisations. This might be applicable in cases where an organisation conducts customer satisfaction surveys whereby personal information of customers are collected for the research.
2   *Notification to data subject when collecting personal information (POPIA:2013, section 18)*
    This section in POPIA outlines what information the organisation should give to its employees or customers when collecting their personal information for research purposes. Refer to the section about processing limitation for the information that should be communicated for informed consent purposes.

Security safeguards (POPIA:2013, sections 19 to 22)

1   *Security measures on integrity and confidentiality of personal information (POPIA:2013, section 19)*
    Security measures should be implemented to ensure the integrity and confidentiality of personal information processed as part of research projects to prevent loss, damage or unauthorised disclosure of the personal information. It is advisable to consult the Information Security Department or Information Technology Department to establish if the necessary security controls are in place where data are collected, stored, shared, transferred and retained using information technology systems.

2   *Information processed by an operator or person acting under authority (POPIA:2013, section 20)*
     Third parties (referred to as an operator in the POPIA) are often contracted to assist with research projects such as survey distribution, data capturing and analysis. It is critical to ensure that the third parties implement the necessary confidentiality and privacy controls to protect personal information of research participants.

3   *Security measures regarding information processed by an operator (POPIA:2013, section 21)*
     The POPIA requires that organisations should ensure that there is a written contract in place between them and third parties who process personal information on behalf of the organisation for purposes of a research project. In such a contract, the organisation will specify the required ethical and privacy-related measures that the third party must comply with such as not to disclose the information to unauthorised parties and not to use them for other purposes.

4   *Notification of security compromises (POPIA:2013, section 22)*
     The research participants should be notified if their personal information has been accessed or acquired by an unauthorised person or party. The POPIA has specific requirements that must be followed to notify individuals of security compromise, such as e-mailing the respondents or publishing it in the news media. It also contains a number of aspects that must be included in the notification, such as an explanation of the possible consequences and what the organisation will be doing to address the security compromise.

Data subject participation (POPIA:2013, sections 23 to 25)

1   *Access to personal information (POPIA:2013, section 23)*
     Section 23 in POPIA provides more information about the right of a research participant to request from an organisation if and what personal information they have about him or her or it. This request should be processed free of charge and in a reasonable time period. The categories of third parties with whom personal information was shared can also be requested. For more information refer to section 23, as well as the Promotion of Access to Information Act, 2000 (PAIA).

2   *Correction of personal information (POPIA:2013, section 24)*
     Correction of personal information refers to the right of the research participant to request the organisation to correct or delete his or her or its personal information that was processed as part of the research project. This includes the personal information that third parties might have processed on behalf of the organisation.

3   *Manner of access (POPIA:2013, section 25)*
     The manner of access section in the POPIA refers to the Promotion of Access to Information Act, which specifies the process for request to personal information.

Vulnerable participants (POPIA:2013, sections 26 to 33)

The POPIA distinguishes between personal information and "sensitive personal information". This applies to information of children under the age of 18, religious or philosophical beliefs of people, information about a person's race or ethnic origin, trade union membership, political persuasion, health or sex life, criminal behaviour or biometric information. Sensitive personal information could often relate to vulnerable participants in research. Vulnerable communities could also relate to research participants whose first language is not the same as the language used in the research questionnaire or interviews.

In cases where the above personal information are collected, the organisation should ensure that:

1. personal information are de-identified so that individuals cannot be re-identified;
2. through the reporting of the research data, it should not be possible to identify the identity of an individual, for example if there is only one person of a specific racial group in a department and the data are reported on a department level per racial group;
3. consent has been obtained from the research participant to voluntarily participate in the research;
4. parents consented for children under the age of 18;
5. if research is conducted in a school, the Department of Education's consent has been obtained;
6. if health information are collected, the approval from the Department of Health might be required as well as other necessary gatekeeper approval; and
7. if the language of the questionnaire or interview is different to the language of the research participant, the informed consent form has been translated and that an interpreter is available for focus groups or interviews to assist with discussions and questions.

Rights of data subjects regarding direct marketing by means of unsolicited electronic communications, directories and automated decision making (POPIA:2013, section 69)

This requirement of the POPIA aims to protect South African citizens from unsolicited electronic communications. From a research perspective, it is important that bulk e-mails should not be sent out to customers to complete surveys as this could be seen as unsolicited electronic communication, especially if the individual is not an existing customer of an organisation. The POPIA makes provision for the use of e-mails if consent has been obtained and they are sent to existing customers. Existing customers should have the option to opt out for future communications. Should a bulk e-mail approach be used to target potential customers, the POPIA requires that the potential customer be contacted only once with the option to opt-in for future communications. This also applies to survey emails.

Transborder information flows (POPIA:2013, section 72)

This section of the POPIA deals with the transferring of personal information of citizens of South Africa to a foreign country. This might be applicable in cases where multinational organisations conduct research whereby personal information of employees or customers is shared with an office or third party in another country. In such an instance, it is again important to inform them that their personal information will be sent to another country, and to obtain consent from the research participant, unless the data is de-identified or other provisions apply such as contractual requirements. It should also be ensured that the third party implements the necessary ethical and privacy requirements to protect the respondent's personal information.

UNDERSTANDING RISK IN RESEARCH

The risk profile of each research project is different. The organisation should aim to achieve a balance between the potential risk to the research participants and the community and the potential benefit[55]. In all instances, it is important to obtain informed consent from the research participants, even if the potential to harm is low. For organisations to establish the inherent risk of their research projects, they need to consider a number of aspects in terms of the research participants, the type of data collected and the methods used to collect the data. It is an important to ensure that all stakeholders are aware of the likelihood of harm and the measures that should be implemented to mitigate or minimise risk as far as possible.

One can establish the inherent risk of the research project by considering the following aspects:

1. **Humans versus no humans:** Determine if data are collected in the public domain or directly from research participants. If personal information are collected directly from research participants, the risk is higher and additional measures should be implemented to minimise potential harm, such as informed consent and confidentiality measures. The risk is lower if the personal information are obtained in the public domain, such as from a telephone directory, or if the individual willingly placed their personal information in the public domain.
2. **Personal information versus de-identified or anonymous data:** Establish if personal information will be collected or not at all. The risk is low if no personal or demographic information are collected that can be used to identify an individual. If personal information are de-identified or anonymised, the risk is also lower.
3. **Sensitive versus non-sensitive personal information:** Where sensitive personal information (religious or philosophical beliefs of people, information about a person's race or ethnic origin, trade union membership, political persuasion, health or sex life, criminal behaviour) are collected, the risk of potential harm could be higher and controls should be implemented to minimise any possible harm, stress or inconvenience to research participants.
4. **Research methods:** The research methods could include quantitative and qualitative research. A project where experiments are conducted on animals or people are of a higher risk than anonymous surveys. Where the risk of harm to the research team or participants is high, controls should be implemented to minimise negative consequences, discomfort, inconvenience and harm.
5. **Research topic:** If the research topic is controversial, it could result in a higher risk, for example criminal studies or HIV research.
6. **Vulnerable versus non-vulnerable groups:** If vulnerable groups are part of the research participants, such as children or disabled people, then additional measures should be implemented to protect them.

7. **Trans-border data flows:** When personal information of South African citizens are sent outside of South Africa for the purpose of the research project, the risk is higher than when the personal information are processed in South Africa.

Figure 12.1 portrays four risk categories ranging from a low to a high risk. It is the responsibility of the organisation to establish the risk related to the research project in order to ensure that adequate controls are implemented to mitigate or minimise the risk. These risk categories are related to those used by some universities in assessing the risk profile of academic research projects[56]. The potential to harm does not necessarily only relate to the research participants, but could also affect the safety of the consultant, the reputation of the organisation, or result in compliance issues if the necessary regulatory aspects are not adhered to.

It is advised that research teams should not commence with research activities until they have established the research project risks and identified how they will mitigate or minimise them. The sponsor should also be aware of the risks in order to approve the project, and similarly the research participants should be made aware of potential harm in order to give informed consent prior to the engagement with the research project.

Category 2 – MEDIUM TO LOW RISK	Category 4 – HIGH RISK
Humans involved De-identified personal information/ anonymous data Non-sensitive personal information Surveys, interviews, focus groups Uncontroversial topic Minimal harm	Humans involved directly Personal information collected Sensitive personal information Surveys, interviews, focus groups, experiments, observations, etc. Vulnerable group (e.g. HIV patients) Controversial and sensitive topic Trans-border data flows High likelihood of harm
Category 1 – LOW RISK	Category 3 – MEDIUM RISK
No/indirect humans involved De-identified personal information/ anonymous data Information collected in public domain Data analysis using existing data Uncontroversial topic Low to no harm	Humans involved directly Personal information collected Sensitive personal information Surveys, interviews, focus groups, experiments, observations, etc. Vulnerable group (e.g. children) Likely harm

Figure 12.1: Research project risk categories (based on the Unisa standard operating procedure for research ethics risk assessment, Unisa SOP:2015)

The four risk categories are as following:

"Category 1 – Low risk" refers to research projects where there is no potential of harm or a very low potential. It is expected that the risk that the research participants would face would not exceed that of everyday circumstances, for example, summarising employee performance data to define a training and succession plan for the organisation.

"Category 2 – Medium to low risk" relates to research projects where there is minimal harm in the form of inconvenience, stress or any other discomfort. These projects would typically relate to opinion surveys like an organisational culture survey, however no personal identifiable information are collected in the process. If personal information are collected, it is de-identified or anonymised.

"Category 3 – Medium risk" includes research projects where there is a potential of inconvenience or discomfort or harm. In this case participants can experience harm in the form of physical harm, stress or a negative impact on their self-esteem[57]. However, if controls are implemented, the risk can be reduced or eliminated. In these types of research projects humans are directly involved, for example, through observation. The data collected are of a sensitive nature and individuals could potentially be identified. Not all the aspects listed under this category might apply, but if two or more apply, category 3 might be applicable.

"Category 4 – High risk" refers to research projects where the likelihood of risk is high. Humans are involved directly and sensitive personal information are collected. It could also relate to vulnerable groups or controversial research topics. In some instances, personal information could also be sent outside of South Africa. Not all the aspects listed under this category might apply, but if two or more apply, category 4 might be applicable.

GUIDELINES FOR ETHICAL RESEARCH WHERE THE PRIVACY OF RESEARCH PARTICIPANTS IS PROTECTED

The ethics values and privacy considerations discussed thus far in this chapter provides research practitioners with guidance to conduct research with integrity. Table 12.2 summarises the various concepts. The objective is to provide researchers with a comprehensive and practical checklist of the ethical and privacy aspects to consider in organisational research projects. A Yes-No scale can be used to assess whether the aspects are in place. The checklist is not exhaustive, but should be customised to an organisation's industry, code of ethics and applicable regulatory requirements. It can then be used as input for approval of research projects.

Table 12.2: Ethical and privacy checklist for research projects (Compiled by A. Da Veiga)

Ethical and privacy checklist for research projects	Yes / No
Accountability The organisation has a research policy in place. The organisation/industry has an ethics code of conduct. The necessary industry, government, etc. approval was obtained. Ethical and privacy measures were considered. The organisation's research ethics policy requirements were complied with.	
Best interest /well-being An information session for research participants about the research project was conducted or relevant communication (e.g. e-mail) was sent to them. Where research relates to a controversial research topic, measures have been implemented to minimise or mitigate potential harm to the research team and research participants.	
Benevolence (links to risk) A risk assessment has been conducted to identify potential harm. Adequate mitigation strategies have been defined for medium-risk and high-risk projects.	
Community It has been established how the research project will address a problem in the community (e.g. organisation) and how the benefits of the project will be integrated into the community.	
Compassion If vulnerable groups are used as part of the research participants, measures have been implemented to accommodate them (e.g. access for disabled people, assistance for people who cannot use a computer).	
Confidentiality The information document explains to participants that their information will be kept confidential. Confidentiality is ensured for all research participants. Confidentiality is ensured for hard copy data of research participants. Confidentiality is ensured for data of research participants in electronic format (including voice recordings). The confidentiality of research participants is protected in research publications and reporting.	
Excellence and competency The research team has the necessary skills and experience to conduct the project.	
Honesty and truthfulness All risks and benefits were communicated to research participants. Credit was given to all stakeholders and funding organisations. All sources were referenced and cited. All authors of the research report were given credit in publications. Data analysis was conducted using reliable and valid statistical methods. Research results were communicated to the stakeholders and research participants. All data were reported accurately.	

Ethical and privacy checklist for research projects	Yes / No
Validity and reliability Research instruments are valid and reliable. Registered psychometrists and psychologists perform registered psychometric tests.	
Human rights Respondents are included in the sample using a correct and scientific sampling method. Each respondent will have a fair opportunity to be included in the sample. Respondents have the right to withdraw at any time. Respondents have a choice to participate, thus voluntary participation is used. All respondents are treated with respect and in a professional manner at all times.	
Impartiality and independence All conflicts of interest have been declared for all stakeholders. Monitoring and supervision activities are incorporated in the project and are conducted by an independent team.	
Integrity The research ethics policy is applied consistently for all phases of the research project.	
Justice Copyright of diagnostic instruments have been recognised.	
Objectivity All findings and recommendations are based on facts.	
Privacy If personal information of research participants was collected, it has been de-identified so that individuals cannot be re-identified. If anonymous surveys or interviews are used, analysis and reporting will not expose the identity of individual research participants. The information document explains to research participants how the privacy of their information will be protected. **Vulnerable groups** If research is conducted in a different language than that of the research participant, it will be ensured that the informed consent and information document is translated and that an interpreter is present in discussions to answer questions. **Sensitive personal information** The information document specifically informs the research respondents that sensitive personal information will be collected and for what purposes. Sensitive personal information are de-identified so that it cannot be re-identified or a pseudonym is used. If sensitive personal information are collected, measures have been implemented to reduce the likelihood of harm to research participants. **Lawfulness** All processing of data is conducted in a lawful manner not infringing on the research participant's privacy rights.	

Ethical and privacy checklist for research projects	Yes / No
Minimality Only relevant personal information pertaining to the research objectives is collected.	
Consent and autonomy Consent has been obtained from relevant gatekeepers such as the project sponsor, funding organisations, professional bodies, government parastatals, etc. An information document has been drafted for research participants explaining the research objectives, purpose, risks, benefits, who is conducting the research, confidentiality, privacy, compensation, feedback, publications, withdrawal, security measures of personal data (anonymisation/de-identification, password protection, etc.), cross-border transfers, third-party involvement, timeframes, compensations, project approval and any other relevant project information. The informed consent form has been signed by all research participants. Evidence of consent can be retrieved where consent was obtained in electronic format.	
Collection directly from research participant Where data could not be collected in the public domain, they have been collected directly from the research participant.	
Purpose specification The purpose for the collection of personal information is clearly discussed in the information document given to research participants.	
Retention The retention period of research data has been defined in line with organisational policy, industry requirements and relevant laws. The method of destruction of data in hard copy and electronic format has been defined.	
Further processing The research data will not be used for any other purpose than that agreed with the research participants and in line with the research project objectives.	
Information quality Measures have been implemented to ensure the data quality, such as the removal of duplicate entries and input validation.	
Documentation The organisation's PAIA manual includes what information research participants can request and what process they should follow to do so.	

Ethical and privacy checklist for research projects	Yes / No
Security measures Back-ups of research data will be made. Passwords are used on computers and electronic devices where research data is stored. Access is controlled to files and databases where data are stored. Sensitive data files are encrypted (password protected) when e-mailed. The Information Technology Department has implemented the necessary technical controls to protect the organisation's network and applications such as firewalls and antivirus software. **Third parties (operators)** Contracts are in place with all third parties who work on the research project or who process any data of the research participants. Third-party contracts stipulate that: - privacy and security measures must be in place to protect research participant data; - third parties are prohibited from using research participant data for any purpose other than that agreed with the research participant; and - third parties are prohibited from sharing research participant data with any unauthorised parties. **Notification of security compromises** There is a process in place that can be followed to notify research participants if their personal information has been accessed or acquired by an unauthorised person. **Trans-border flows** Research participants are informed if their personal information are sent outside of South Africa. Research participants' consent has been obtained to send their information outside of South Africa. It is ensured that the necessary privacy and security controls are in place for the processing of the personal information outside of South Africa. **Direct marketing** Research participants are only invited to participate in surveys if they are existing customers or employees and have opted in for such communications. Research participants are only contacted once using bulk mail to participate in surveys marketed to them if they opted in for such communications.	
Respect The research participants have the right to withdraw at any time.	
Tolerance Research participants have a fair opportunity to give their opinions and views.	

CONCLUSION

In this chapter, the ethical and privacy considerations that research practitioners should follow when conducting research were discussed. Consultants should be aware of the ethical codes, industry standards and regulatory requirements that apply to research projects so as to protect the research participants, themselves and the organisation.

In this chapter, the concept of ethics and the relevant ethical values that must be embedded in research activities were also discussed. Practical examples of the ethical values were provided to aid organisations to embed them in research projects. The concept of privacy was discussed in more detail, focussing on the requirements of the POPIA and how the conditions apply to research projects.

Attention was given to aspects that must be considered to establish the risk profile of a research project in order to ensure that necessary controls are implemented to minimise or mitigate the identified risks. The ethical values and privacy considerations are summarised in an ethics and privacy checklist for organisations. This checklist provides a summary of important ethical and privacy principles that must be considered for research projects. It can further aid organisations to compile a customised ethics and privacy checklist for their environment, to establish if they considered the ethical requirements as well as the applicable privacy regulatory requirements for the processing of personal information of research participants.

REFERENCES

Acts Online. 2013. Protection of Personal Information Act (POPIA), 2013, (Act No. 4 of 2013). Retrieved January 26, 2017 from https://www.acts.co.za/protection-of-personal-information-act-2013/notice_no__912_of_2013 [Accessed 6 July 2017].

All European Academics (ALLEA). 2017. The European Code of Conduct for Research Integrity. Retrieve from http://ec.europa.eu/research/participants/data/ref/h2020/other/hi/h2020-ethics_code-of-conduct_en.pdf [Accessed 6 July 2017].

American Psyciological Association (APA). 2010. *Ethical Principles of Psychologists and Code of Conduct*. Retrieved January 26, 2017, from https://www.apa.org/ethics/code/principles.pdf

Babie, E. 2004. *The practice of social research*. 10th edition. Belmont, CA: Thomson Wadsworth.

British Psychology Society (BPS). 2010. *Code of Human Research Ethics*. The British Psychological Society 2010. Retrieved January, 26, 2017, from http://www.bps.org.uk/sites/default/files/documents/code_of_human_research_ethics.pdf

Bryman, A. 2012. *Social research methods*. 4th edition. Oxford: Oxford University Press.

Flick, U. 2006. *An introduction to qualitative research*. 3rd edition. London: Sage Publications: 44-46.

General Ethical Guidelines for the Health Professions Council of South Africa (HPCSA). 2008a. *Annexure 12, Ethical and Professional Rules of the Health Professions Council of South Africa as Promulgated in Government Gazette R717/2006*. Retrieved January, 26, 2017, from http://www.hpcsa.co.za/conduct/Ethics

Human Sciences Research Council (HSRC). *Code of Research Ethics*. (n.d.). Retrieved January, 26, 2017, from http://www.hsrc.ac.za/en/about/research-ethics/code-of-research-ethics

Information Systems Audit and Control Association (ISACA). (n.d). *Code of Professional Ethics*. Retrieved August, 2, 2016, from http://www.isaca.org/certification/code-of-professional-ethics/pages/default.aspx

Institute of the Directors of South Africa (IoDSA). 2016. *King IV Report on Corporate Governance for South Africa*. Retrieved January, 26, from https://c.ymcdn.com/sites/iodsa.site-ym.com/resource/collection/684B68A7-B768-465C-8214-E3A007F15A5A/IoDSA_King_IV_Report_-_WebVersion.pdf

Institute of the Directors of South Africa (IoDSA). 2009. *King III Report on Corporate Governance for South Africa*. Retrieved January, 26, 2017, from http://www.library.up.ac.za/law/docs/king111report.pdf

Kruger, M, Ndebele, R & Horn L. 2014. *Research Ethics in Africa: A Resource for Research Ethics Committees.* Stellenbosch, SA: African Sun Media.

Martins, EC. 2010. *Identifying organisational and behaviour factors that influence knowledge retention.* Unpublished D Lit et Phil thesis. Pretoria: University of South Africa.

Miller, RL & Brewer JD. 2003. *The A-Z of Social Research.* London: Sage Publications: 96-99.

Mitchell, ML & Jolley JM.2007. *Research design explained.* 6th edition. London: Thomson Wadsworth: 35-36.

Ndebele, P, Mwaluko, G, Kruger M, Ouwe O, Oukem-Boyer M & Zimba M. 2014. *History of Research Ethics Review in Africa in Research in Africa,* edited by M. Kruger, P. Ndebele & L Horn. Stellenbosch, SA: Sun Press.

Acts Online. 2013. *Promotion of Access to Information Act, 2000 (Act No. 2 of 2000).* Retrieved August, 8, 2016, from https://www.acts.co.za/promotion-of-access-to-information-act-2000/index.html

SA Board for People Practitioners (SABPP). (2017a). *The Code of Conduct.* Retrieved February, 2, 2017, from http://sabpp.co.za/wp-content/uploads/2016/12/SABPP_CODE_OF_CONDUCT.pdf

SA Board for People Practitioners (SABPP). (2017b). *The Code of Ethics for HR Consultants.* Retrieved February, 2, 2017, from http://sabpp.co.za/wp-content/uploads/2016/12/Code_of_Ethics_for_HR_Consul.pdf

South African Government. 1996. *The Constitution of the Republic of South Africa.* Retrieved from http://www.gov.za/documents/constitution/constitution-republic-south-africa-1996-1 [Accessed 16 August 2016].

Science Connect. 2011. The European Code of Conduct for Research Integrity. Retrieve from http://www.esf.org/fileadmin/Public_documents/Publications/Code_Conduct_ResearchIntegrity.pdf [Accessed 8 August 2016].

Steneck, N, Mayer, T & Anderson M. The Singapore Statement on Research Integrity. 2nd and 3rd World Conference on Research Integrity. 2010. from www.singaporestatement.org [Accessed 8 August 2016].

The Singapore Statement on Research Integrity. 2010. from www.singaporestatement.org [Accessed 8 August 2016].

Unisa. 2007. Unisa Code of Ethics and Conduct. Unpublished internal document. Unisa.

Unisa. 2015. Unisa Guidelines for Ethics Review. Unpublished internal document. Unisa.

Unisa. 2015. Unisa Standard Operating Procedure for Research Ethics Risk Assessment. Unpublished internal document. Unisa.

ENDNOTES

1. The King IV Code of Governance for South Africa, 2016: 8.
2. The King Reports, 2009.
3. Flick, 2006.
4. BPS, 2010.
5. APA, 2010.
6. The European Code of Conduct for Research Integrity, 2011.
7. SABPP, 2017a.
8. SABPP, 2017b.
9. HPCSA, 2008.
10. ISACA, 2016.
11. HSRC, 2017.
12. The Singapore Statement on Research Integrity, 2010.
13. Unisa Code of Ethics and Conduct, 2007.
14. Mitchell & Jolley, 2007: 35; HSRC, 2017; HPCSA, 2008.
15. HPCSA, 2008.
16. Miller & Brewer, 2003:99; Unisa Code of Ethics and Conduct, 2007.
17. Flick, 2006: 45; HPCSA, 2008.

18. HPCSA, 2008.
19. Miller & Brewer, 2003: 97; POPIA, 2013; HSRC, 2017.
20. Unisa Code of Ethics and Conduct, 2007; ISACA, 2016; HPCSA, 2008; HSRC, 2017; SABPP, 2017A
21. Miller & Brewerton, 2003:89; Singapore Statement, 2010.
22. HPCSA, 2008.
23. Ndebele, Mwaluko, Kruger, Ouwe, Oukem-Boyer & Zimba, 2014.
24. The European Code of Conduct for Research Integrity, 2011.
25. Singapore statement, 2010; HPCSA, 2008; Unisa, 2007; SABPP, 2017A.
26. HSRC, 2017; HPCSA, 2008.
27. Babie, 2004: 76; The European Code of Conduct for Research Integrity, 2011; ISACA, 2016.
28. Miller & Brewer, 2003: 97; Unisa Code of Ethics and Conduct, 2007; ISACA, 2016.
29. Unisa Code of Ethics and Conduct, 2007; HSRC, 2017; HPCSA, 2008; SABPP, 2017A.
30. HPCSA, 2008.
31. Mitchell & Jolley, 2007: 36; HSRC, 2017.
32. ISACA, 2016.
33. Babie, 2004: 69.
34. HSRC, 2017.
35. Greenleave, 2010.
36. POPIA, 2013.
37. POPIA, 2013.
38. POPIA, 2013: 14.
39. Martins, 2010: 286.
40. POPIA, 2013, section 18.
41. POPIA, 2013, section 22.
42. POPIA, 2013, section 23.
43. POPIA, 2013, section 24.
44. POPIA, 2013, section 11.
45. POPIA, 2013, section 69.
46. POPIA, 2013, section 71.
47. POPIA, 2013 section 74, 99.
48. POPIA, 2013, sections 107, 109.
49. POPIA, 2013, section 6
50. POPIA, 2013:14.
51. POPIA, 2013:14
52. POPIA, 2013, section 11.
53. Kruger, Ndebele & Horn, 2014.
54. Kruger, Ndebele & Horn, 2014.
55. Babie, 2004: 64.
56. Unisa SOP, 2015.
57. Bryman, 2012: 135.

CHAPTER 13

A FEW CONCLUSIONS

by **Nico Martins**

INTRODUCTION

The twelve preceding chapters have provided a comprehensive overview of the phases of organisational diagnoses in the South African context and the international research the authors have consulted in the field. In this chapter the focus is on the most important learning points, a brief introduction to interventions followed by a survey effort and the changing role of the survey consultant.

IMPORTANT LEARNING POINTS

After reading the preceding chapters, you have probably come to the same conclusion as many other practitioners and students in the field of organisational surveys, namely that a survey is not an easy option for solving a problem or organisational problems. That being said, it is important to keep in mind that to propose interventions to an organisation without a scientific investigation is similar to a medical doctor prescribing a medical procedure without a proper consultation. A medical consultation is defined as "a procedure whereby, on request by one physician, another physician reviews a patient's medical history, examines the patient, and makes recommendations as to care and treatment. The medical consultant often is a specialist with expertise in a particular field of medicine"[1]. It is thus important for any survey consultant to adhere to all the important criteria of conducting an organisational survey.

In our opinion, you need to bear in the mind the following important points when conducting an organisational survey:

1. Is there a justification for conducting the survey? The survey consultant needs to be professional enough to distinguish between a flavour-of-the-month decision and a real organisational need. The question is if the organisational survey will provide the information the organisation needs.
2. Does the client understand that a survey is part of a diagnosis process and not only a single step? If the client is not aware of this it is your role as survey consultant to explain the diagnosis process in detail. The overview in exhibit 1.1, in chapter 1 of a detailed organisational diagnosis action plan can provide more clarity.
3. Many organisations labour under the misconception that a few interviews or a questionnaire with a few questions constitute a scientific survey. As the survey expert you need to clarify the survey methodology (qualitative/quantitative or mixed method).

4. Many survey consultants conduct surveys without a clear and well-defined diagnostic model. The authors of this book propose that a diagnostic model or models should be used when conducting organisational diagnoses.

5. An important step in any organisational diagnosis is to identify all the stakeholder groups and to engage them in the survey process. This not only ensures that no groups are neglected, but also covers diversity and multi-cultural aspects, and helps to detect and manage pockets of resistance.

6. As highlighted in chapter 3, only valid and reliable assessment instruments must be used. If that is not possible a scientific process must be followed to develop and test the reliability and validity of newly developed instruments. The consequences of not using valid and reliable instruments are that recommendations may be incorrect and the interventions may not have the desired effect. This is usually the case when organisations contact a survey consultant to investigate why their previous survey interventions have not led to any positive changes.

7. The selection of the survey methodology or the combination of survey methodologies is an important decision to take in the South African environment. As discussed in chapter 4, the survey methodology can either enhance the credibility of your survey or lead to distrust in the process.

8. In addition, it is important to conduct focus groups and interviews to support the survey results, if needed. As discussed in chapter 5, planning and conducting interviews and focus groups in a multi-cultural environment need to be done scientifically but with an understanding of the demographic cultures and the organisational environment.

9. The analysis of the data is an art which, in many instances, requires the assistance of a statistician. The purpose of the data analysis is always to provide an easily understandable picture of the results to the organisation to urge it to take the necessary action.

10. In many instances it is important to verify the survey results by means of focus groups or interviews, especially if there are trust problems in the organisation and if the survey needs confirmatory data to confirm the statistical results.

11. One of the most neglected steps in the survey process is the action planning process. It is of vital importance that the survey consultant should plan the survey process in such a manner that the organisation feels inclined to follow the survey with the proposed interventions.

12. Local organisations need to compare their results with international survey results to provide a benchmark. This is especially important if members of senior management are international appointments or would like to compare the South African results to international trends.

13. An important aspect to keep in mind when conducting a survey is its psychological impact. Survey consultants and organisational development consultants often forget that the moment they embark on a survey it has an impact on employees in the organisation.

14. The ethical and privacy considerations for surveys were highlighted in chapter 12. The importance of these considerations cannot be emphasised enough. A survey consultant can use this aspect to a competitive advantage if it is managed effectively.

INTERVENTIONS

In chapter 9 the action planning process was discussed. In this chapter, the author gives a brief overview of some typical interventions survey consultants can propose. According to Geldenhuys[2], an intervention is a sequence of planned activities with the purpose of enabling the client to function more efficiently and effectively. The classic action research model, portrayed below in figure 13.1, focuses on planned change as a cyclical process.

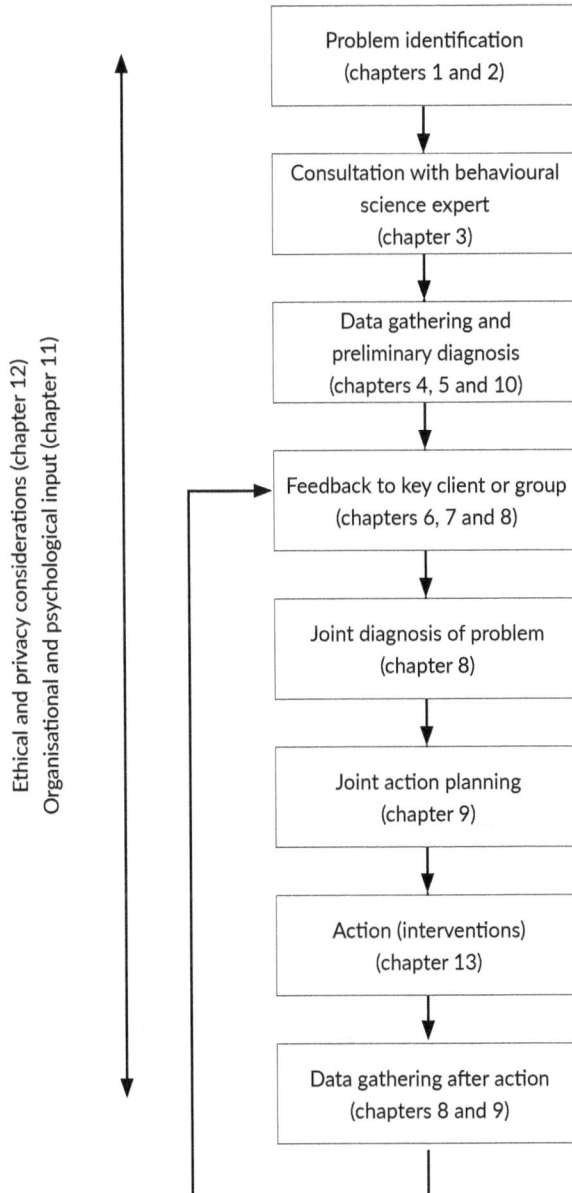

Figure 13.1: Action research model (adapted from Cummings & Worley[3])

As can been seen from figure 13.1, all aspects of the model, except the intervention phase, have been addressed in the preceding chapters. According to Cummings and Worley[4], the following criteria are important in determining if interventions are effective:

1. The information on which the interventions are based should be valid and based on an accurate diagnosis of the organisation. It should therefore fulfill the identified needs of the organisation. Effective interventions provide members with the opportunity to make free and informed choices and gain their commitment in the planned changes.
2. Interventions should have a scientific basis, meaning that there should be valid knowledge that the chosen interventions will lead to the undertaken outcomes. This emphasises the importance of setting up a monitoring plan.
3. Effective interventions should enhance the organisation's capacity to manage change. After an intervention, the members involved should be empowered to better implement change activities themselves. The involvement and engagement of the affected members throughout the organisational development process are thus of paramount importance.

Four main categories of interventions are used by practitioners when they propose interventions for organisations, namely human process interventions, techno-structural interventions, human resource interventions and strategic change interventions. Geldenhuys[5] summarises the interventions in these four main categories (see table 13.1 below).

Table 13.1: Four categories of operational development (OD) intervention used in organisational change

Category	Focus	Application
Human process interventions	The focus is on individual, interpersonal and group behaviour in organisations, and how individuals meet their objectives and accomplish the tasks assigned to them.	Interventions concerning the individual: • Diagnostic instruments such as the Myers-Briggs Type Indicator (MBTI) and assessment centres • Executive coaching • Career management and development Interventions concerning interpersonal relations and group dynamics: • Process consultation. The aim is to help members develop skills and to understand and be able to identify group and interpersonal problems themselves. • Third-party intervention. This helps to resolve conflict that may develop from substantive or interpersonal issues by using methods such as problem solving, conciliation and bargaining. • Teambuilding. The OD practitioner helps workgroups become more effective in the accomplishment of tasks.

Category	Focus	Application
Human process interventions (continued)		Intervention concerning a system-wide process: • Organisation confrontation meeting. This is used when management needs to organise resources for immediate problem solving. They identify problems, set targets and work on problems. • Intergroup relations. This refers to interaction between departments and groups in the organisation. OD practitioners use the intergroup conflict model to enable the two groups to become aware of and understand the cause of conflict, and then use an appropriate method to solve the problem.
Techno-structural interventions	The focus is on the structure (division of labour and hierarchy) and technology (task methods and job design).	Techno-structural interventions concerning restructuring of the organisation: • Structural design. This refers to division of labour away from the traditional organisational overall work to a more integrative and flexible process. • Downsizing. This refers to decreasing the size of the organisation through redesign, outsourcing and employee layoffs. • Reengineering. This refers to radical redesign of the organisation's core work process. Techno-structural interventions concerning employees in decision making: • Parallel structure. These structures (union-management) operate together with formal organisation and offer members alternative settings to handle problems and come to solutions. • Total quality management. Organisational members want to improve the quality as part of their normal operation at work. • High-involvement organisations. A high level of employee involvement is promoted when changes take place in structure, human resource management (HRM) practices and work design. Techno-structural interventions concerning engineering, motivational and sociotechnical approaches to work design: • Job enrichment. This creates jobs where employees experience high levels of autonomy and performance feedback. • Self-management teams. Self-management work teams are set up to solve problems, implement solutions and take responsibility for the outcomes.

Category	Focus	Application
Techno-structural interventions (continued)		Kormanik (2005) also includes the following as methods of techno-structural intervention: organisational structure and systems, space and psychical settings, organisational process redesign, change management, job enrichment and design, knowledge management, organisational learning and competency-based management.
Human resource interventions	The focus is on the integration and incorporation of employees in the organisation. The notion here is to integrate employees in the organisation in an acceptable manner and to develop the potential and talent of employees.	HRM interventions concerning performance: • Goal setting. Meetings periodically take place between managers and subordinates to plan work, and to review and achieve goals. Management by objectives is used. • Performance appraisal. This provides feedback about goal setting and reward systems. • Reward system. This is a process to improve employee satisfaction and performance by using innovative pay, promotion and benefits approaches. HRM interventions concerning talent management and development: • Coaching and mentoring. This involves a one-on-one process that focuses on personal learning between the OD practitioner and the client. • Management and leadership development. This focuses on competencies needed to lead the organisation into the future by using action learning, simulations and case studies. • Career planning and development. This focuses on the retention of valuable staff and the improvement of their quality of work life. HRM interventions concerning supporting members in the organisation: • Managing workforce diversity. This implies making organisations more accommodating to diversity regarding lifestyle preferences, cultural values and other differences. • Employee stress and wellness. This intervention makes use of employee assistance programmes (EAPs) and stress management programmes.
Strategic change interventions	The focus is on the internal functioning of the organisation, and links to the larger environment that changes and transforms at a rapid pace.	Strategic change interventions concerning the organisation's internal operations and environment: • Organisational redesign. This focuses on elements such as structure, work design and HRM practices to align them to the organisation's strategy. • Integrated strategic change. This helps with how planned change can add value to the organisation's strategy. • Culture change. This helps members pull in the same direction to form a strong organisation culture

Category	Focus	Application
Strategic change interventions (continued)		Strategic change interventions concerning continuous organisational change: • Dynamic strategising. This helps with the building of a strategic system that can adapt to the changing process. • Self-designing organisations. This helps to show how to solve existing problems. • Learning organisations. This focuses on the capability of the organisation and the development of new knowledge to increase the performance of the organisation. • Built-to-change organisations. This helps with the continuous change process to make it more efficient for the organisation. Strategic change interventions concerning how organisations collaborate with one another: • Mergers. This helps two or more organisations form a new identity when they merge. • Alliances. These helps two or more organisations form a joint ground for sharing resources. • Networks. This helps two or more organisations solve problems together and perform the task by addressing current network problems.

It is important to note that the interventions are focused on the individual, the team and the organisation. It requires knowledge and skills in all the mentioned categories and applications to implement or facilitate interventions. An individual survey consultant or a small team of consultants usually do not have all the knowledge and skills to implement interventions. They can solve this problem by liaising with other consultants who specialise in the required interventions and so become active learners. As discussed in chapter 8 longitudinal studies (more than one survey) can add value to organisational diagnosis as it can quantify shifts in the underlying beliefs and assumptions of employees and ultimately the organisational culture. In this it can help survey consultants, OD practitioners, HR practitioners and line management to believe in the value of interventions and follow-up surveys.

THE FUTURE ROLE OF THE SURVEY CONSULTANT

After reading the previous chapters, you should have a good understanding of the complexities survey consultants face today. In the late 1990s, Church and Waclawski[6] noted the complexities involved in designing, conducting and analysing surveys and action planning. It should come as no surprise then that the role of the survey consultant is constantly expanding. Other complexities survey consultants have to deal with, include intercultural demands in a multi-racial country, the organisational and psychological impact of diagnoses, and the ethical and privacy considerations for research.

In the past organisations were satisfied with a paper questionnaire or an e-mail questionnaire. Nowadays, the development of specific survey software programs, internet online survey platforms, and surveys on smartphones and Facebook have changed and keep changing the survey landscape. The various generational cohorts also pose different challenges to survey consultants. Younger generations are more inclined to use Facebook and smartphone surveys than typical Baby Boomers who are more used to paper and electronic surveys. The use of sophisticated quantitative software packages such as Atlas.ti has added to this new survey world. Organisations have begun to understand the value of mixed method survey designs and increasingly requests that their surveys should include both. Not only have software packages become more sophisticated, clients are also more educated about the value of surveys and the implementation of action planning. Many organisations today use surveys for strategic purposes, change management and the tracking of interventions (longitudinal studies), to mention a few. Church and Waclawski had already noted in 1998 that for survey consultants to be effective and to survive in the competitive survey marketplace, they also need to be change agents. Consider all the changes in the 18 year, since then. In figure 13.2 the future role of the survey consultant is portrayed.

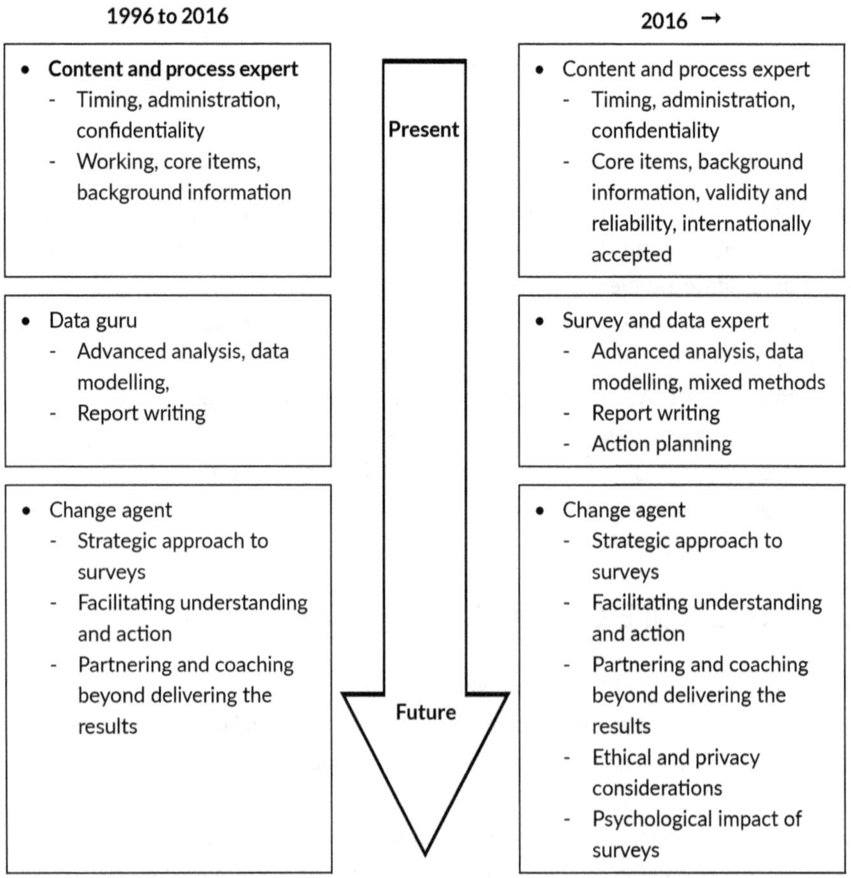

1996 to 2016

2016 →

• **Content and process expert**
  - Timing, administration, confidentiality
  - Working, core items, background information
	• Content and process expert
	  - Timing, administration, confidentiality
	  - Core items, background information, validity and reliability, internationally accepted

• Data guru
  - Advanced analysis, data modelling,
  - Report writing
	• Survey and data expert
	  - Advanced analysis, data modelling, mixed methods
	  - Report writing
	  - Action planning

• Change agent
  - Strategic approach to surveys
  - Facilitating understanding and action
  - Partnering and coaching beyond delivering the results
	• Change agent
	  - Strategic approach to surveys
	  - Facilitating understanding and action
	  - Partnering and coaching beyond delivering the results
	  - Ethical and privacy considerations
	  - Psychological impact of surveys

Present

Future

Figure 13.2: Future role of the survey consultant (adapted from Church & Waclawski[7])

It is clear from figure 13.2 that the successful survey consultant needs to be skilled in more than one area. The new role of survey consultants can be summarised as follows:

Content and process experts

Future survey consultants will only be effective in a country such as South Africa if they have been trained as survey consultants (degree in psychology, industrial psychology or management psychology), and also understand the technical aspects of surveys. In addition, they must be able to operate in different cultural contexts and facilitate different language, cultural and generational groups[8]. Their assessment instruments need to be valid and reliable, and should be tested for invariance across different biographical groups[9].

Survey and data experts

The ever-changing multimedia landscape has created new opportunities as well as challenges for survey consultants. Survey consultants need to be able to use more than one survey methodology to conduct surveys as organisations typically request a combination of an online electronic survey, a paper-and-pencil survey and a smartphone survey. Lately a number of organisations have been using social media such as Facebook for surveys. The use of multi-survey methods can influence aspects such as the cost of the survey, ethical considerations, privacy and the support of multimedia specialists. In South Africa there is also the dilemma that certain population segments cannot access computers or their specific applications. Therefore, non-electronic surveys will still be necessary in the future[10]. Research by Al-Omiri[11] in Saudi Arabia, highlights the advantages of using e-mails for surveys of people working in multinational corporations. However, he noted that the issue of a respondent's first language must be considered in all methods of data collection from an international population.

Apart from the analysis of data by means of descriptive and inferential statistics, clients are also interested in the practical value of survey results. Clients are increasingly interested in practical models or diagnostic models, as discussed in chapters 1 and 6. Clients want to understand the potential value of proposed interventions which focus on specific survey dimensions. These recommendations are only possible if regression analysis and structural equation modelling analysis are conducted to indicate cause-and-effect relationships.

Organisations are also becoming increasingly interested in understanding their survey results and require mixed methods when conducting surveys. Survey consultants thus need to be able to conduct surveys (quantitative) and focus groups and interviews (qualitative), and integrate the results.

As discussed in chapter 9, the added value for organisations are the action planning process. It is vital that a survey consultant should have the skills to act as a facilitator for the action planning process to urge the company to implement interventions. Olivier[12] sees the intervention process as one of the most important steps in the facilitation process. Despite the numbers of surveys that they are involved in, it appears that companies do not always put enough effort or time into planning the change[13]. Borg and Mastrangelo[14] reiterate the importance of action after a diagnosis: "The ES (employee satisfaction) literature usually strongly recommends conducting an ES only if it leads to actions." The planning component of action planning is thus a crucial step in bringing about desired change. Part of the process of action planning needs to be an evaluation of the actions planned. This can be done either by means of a follow-up survey or by using feedback from an appointed task team[15].

Change agents

Change agents can be described as those individuals who campaign to promote changes, act as facilitators of the planned change process, and enable and empower employees to adapt to and accept the changes[16]. In the fast-changing South African work environment, employee representatives or union representatives are often regarded by their colleagues as change agents[17]. Survey consultants need to be able to act as change agents on a strategic level. Church and Waclawski[18] summarise the role as "a strategic mindset and accompanying toolkit for designing, implementing and using surveys to create lasting change. The new roles are very exiting but also pose challenges to the current and new generations of survey consultants".

Given the importance of survey data it is vital for survey consultants to understand and apply the ethical and privacy considerations of their professional bodies or country for research and surveys. If they do not, they may find themselves out of work or, more seriously, in court.

Not many survey consultants or organisations give consideration to the organisational and psychological impact of organisational diagnoses. It has been shown that organisational diagnoses involve the application of quantitative diagnostics and the application of questionnaires in organisations, as well as a deeply rooted awareness, mindfulness and strong connection with the conscious and unconscious involvement of the role of the survey consultant in the system. The survey consultant needs to be trained to distinguish the organisational dynamics from the unconscious individual as well as group transferences.

The role of the survey consultant is dynamic and constantly changing. In future, the challenges for the survey consultant will be to keep up to date with technology changes (changes in the electronic media) and survey methodology, and act as facilitator.

CONCLUDING REMARKS

The authors hope that the combination of classic survey methodology as well as emerging survey methodology in the South African context will be of value to the South African and African survey consultant. As we have noted in the book, a number of techniques have been tested over and over again. However, with the changing work environment new techniques are constantly being tested and applied. We wish you luck with your future survey experiences.

REFERENCES

Al-Omiri, M. 2004. A preliminary study of electronic surveys as a means to enhance management accounting research. *Management Research News* 30(7):510–524.

Borg, I, & Mastrangelo, PM. 2009. *Employee surveys in management: theories, tools and practical applications.* Toronto: Hogrefe.

Cummings, TG & Worley, CG. 2015. *Organizational development and change.* 10th edition. Mason, OH: South Western Center of Learning.

Church, AH & Waclawski, J. 1998. *Designing and using organizational surveys: A seven-step process.* San Francisco: Jossy Bass.

Geldenhuys, D. 2016. Designing intervention, in *Fundamentals of organisational development,* edited by N Martins & D Geldenhuys. Cape Town: Juta.

Kormanik, MB. 2005. *White males in transition: developing the experiences of a stalled career.* Unpublished doctoral dissertation, The George Washington University, Washington, DC.

Lunenburg, FC. 2010. Managing change: the role of the change agent. *International Journal of Management, Business and Administration* 13(1):1–6.

Martins, N. 2014. Factorial invariance of the South African culture instrument. *Problems and Perspectives* 12(4) special issue:242–252

Martins, N & Close, D. 2016. The role of generational groups in South African organizations, in *Generational differences in work values and ethics,* edited by M Sharabi. New York: Nova Publishers.

Mosby's Medical Dictionary, 8th edition. 2009. Retrieved 5 December 2016 from http://medical-dictionary.thefreedictionary.com/medical+consultation.

Olivier, B. 2016. Facilitation skills, in *Fundamentals of organisational development,* edited by N Martins & D Geldenhuys. Cape Town: Juta.

Perkins, GH. 2004. Will libraries' web-based survey methods replace existing non-electronic methods? *Information Technology and Libraries* 23(3):123–126.

Van Niekerk, M & Martins, N. 2016. Testing for measurement invariance for employee engagement across different demographic groups in South Africa. *Journal of Contemporary Management* 14:24-59.

Van der Linde-de Klerk, M, Martins, N & De Beer, M. 2014. The development of a change agent identification framework for South African change agents. *South African Journal of Labour Relations* 38(1):93–115.

Waclawski, J & Church, AH. 2002. *Organizational development: a data-driven approach to organizational change.* Boston, MA: Jossey-Bass.

ENDNOTES

1. Mosby's Medical Dictionary, 2009.
2. Geldenhuys, 2016.
3. Cummings & Worley, 2015.
4. Cummings & Worley, 2015.
5. Geldenhuys, 2016.
6. Church & Waclawski, 1998.
7. Church & Waclawski, 1998.
8. Martins & Close, 2016.
9. Martins, 2014; Van Niekerk & Martins, 2016.
10. Perkins, 2004.
11. Al-Omiri, 2004.
12. Olivier, 2016.
13. Church & Waclawski, 1998.
14. Borg & Mastrangelo, 2009: 389.
15. Martins, 2016.
16. Lunenburg, 2010.
17. Van der Linde-de Klerk, Martins & De Beer, 2014.
18. Church & Waclawski, 1998: 275.

Index

A

accountability, 164, 206, 209, 214–215, 217, 275–277, 279, 282, 291
accredited training, necessary, 264
accuracy, 41, 74, 100, 107–108, 176–179
action learning, 128, 204, 208, 210–212, 219, 220, 271, 304
action planning, 11, 20, 58, 146, 184, 203–216, 218–220, 247, 275, 300–301, 305–306–308
action planning and learning, 205, 207, 209, 211–213, 215, 217, 219, 221
action plans, 12, 192–193, 203–204, 210, 212–215, 220, 273
  detailed organisational diagnosis, 1, 11, 14, 16, 299
action research process, 5
action strategies, 210
action technologies, 138
action template, 213
advanced analysis, 306
aesthetics of qualitative research, 254
African cultures, 22
African languages, 68
African perspective, 81, 141, 221, 254
African workplace culture, 5
age generation categories, 96
age groups, 6, 198–199, 273, 281
analysis
  building, 239
  comprehensive, 45, 257
  descriptive, 115
  detailed, 162, 182–183, 200
  document, 45–46, 76–77
  efficient, 72
  external, 225
  in-depth, 151
  preliminary, 11, 19
  qualitative, 145, 159–160, 188, 253
  quantitative, 170
  regression, 158, 185, 198–199, 307
  stakeholder, 28–29
analysis methods, 235, 277
analysis process, 135
  practical, 160
  thematic content, 160
analysts, 260, 268
anonymisation, 293
anonymise data, 135
anonymity, 59, 75, 85, 92–93, 95
anonymised focus groups, 141
anonymous data, 288–289
anxieties, 117, 186, 258, 261, 263–265, 267–268, 271

applied sampling, 109
approaches, 4–5, 32, 35–36, 39–42, 45, 71–72, 74, 113–115, 118, 124, 126, 165, 171, 174, 260
  business-focused, 10
  contradictory, 265
  conversational, 74
  diagnostic, 42, 174
  flexible, 41
  goal, 63
  mixed-method, 162, 165
  multicultural, 227
  pre-conceived, 225
  qualitative, 7, 41–43, 72
  scientific, 273
  sociological, 115
  systematic, 8, 36, 188
  theoretical, 224, 227, 236, 252
  traditional, 63
approval, 5, 69, 169, 266, 279, 282, 287, 290–291
area sampling, 88
assessing organisational readiness, 269
assessment, 40, 42, 46, 70, 176, 178, 211, 259, 270
  change agent identification, 81
  organisation's health, 26
  psychological, 79–80
assessment frameworks, 62–63, 80, 150
assessment instruments, 39, 46, 54–56, 79, 275, 300, 307
assessment tools, 39
awareness of legal consequences, 161, 164
awareness of legal responsibility, 163

B

Balanced Scorecard, 62–63
balancing expectations, 186
barriers, 209–212, 218, 220, 263
basic methodology, 80
benchmark, 12, 54, 149, 155–156, 183, 186, 200, 223, 225–226, 228, 233, 235, 241, 300
benchmark results, 51–53, 155–157, 198
benchmark surveys, 182, 200
benefits, 7, 9, 14, 72, 88–89, 159, 190, 206–207, 246, 274, 277, 279, 282–284, 288, 291, 293
benefits and limitations, 7–8, 72, 78, 103
BeQ, 54, 223, 226, 228, 233, 236–237, 241– 243, 244, 248–249, 250, 252
bias, 8, 41, 44, 70–71, 73, 75, 78, 125, 141, 175, 188, 211
biographical, 70, 100, 105, 150, 192, 198–199
BLUE and ORANGE thinking systems, 244
boundaries, 27, 102, 117, 122, 225, 228
broad-based black economic empowerment (BBBEE), 273